THE
SORROWS
OF EMPIRE

THE
SORROWS
OF EMPIRE

Militarism, Secrecy, and the End of the Republic

CHALMERS JOHNSON

METROPOLITAN BOOKS

HENRY HOLT AND COMPANY

NEW YORK

Metropolitan Books
Henry Holt and Company, LLC
Publishers since 1866
115 West 18th Street
New York, New York 10011

Metropolitan Books™ is a registered
trademark of Henry Holt and Company, LLC.

Library of Congress Cataloging-in-Publication Data
Johnson, Chalmers A.
The sorrows of empire : militarism, secrecy, and the end of the Republic / Chalmers
Johnson—1st ed.
p. cm.
Includes index.
ISBN 0-8050-7004-4
1. Militarism—United States.   2. Military-industrial complex—United States.   3. United
States—Military policy.   4. United States—Foreign relations—2001–   5. United
States—Politics and government—2001–   6. Civil-military relations—United States.
7. Imperialism.   8. Intervention (International law).   9. Official secrets—United States.
I. Title.
UA23.J5697 2004
355.02'13'0973—dc22   2003056214

First Edition 2004
Designed by Fritz Metsch
Maps and graph by James Sinclair
Printed in the United States of America
5   7   9   10   8   6   4

CONTENTS

THE
SORROWS
OF EMPIRE

PROLOGUE:

THE UNVEILING OF THE

AMERICAN EMPIRE

Our nation is the greatest force for good in history.
PRESIDENT GEORGE W. BUSH,
Crawford, Texas, August 31, 2002

A s distinct from other peoples on this earth, most Americans do not
recognize—or do not want to recognize—that the United States
dominates the world through its military power. Due to government
secrecy, they are often ignorant of the fact that their government garrisons the globe. They do not realize that a vast network of American military bases on every continent except Antarctica actually constitutes a
new form of empire.

Our country deploys well over half a million soldiers, spies, technicians, teachers, dependents, and civilian contractors in other nations and
just under a dozen carrier task forces in all the oceans and seas of the
world. We operate numerous secret bases outside our territory to monitor what the people of the world, including our own citizens, are saying,
faxing, or e-mailing to one another. Our globe-girding military and intelligence installations bring profits to civilian industries, which design
and manufacture weapons for the armed forces or undertake contract
services to build and maintain our far-flung outposts. One task of such
contractors is to keep uniformed members of the imperium housed
in comfortable quarters, well fed, amused, and supplied with enjoyable,

affordable vacation facilities. Whole sectors of the American economy have come to rely on the military for sales. On the eve of our second war on Iraq, for example, the Defense Department ordered 273,000 bottles of Native Tan sunblock (SPF 15), almost triple its 1999 order and undoubtedly a boon to the supplier, Control Supply Company of Tulsa, Oklahoma, and its subcontractor, Sun Fun Products of Daytona Beach, Florida.[1]

The new American empire has been a long time in the making. Its roots go back to the early nineteenth century, when the United States declared all of Latin America its sphere of influence and busily enlarged its own territory at the expense of the indigenous people of North America, as well as British, French, and Spanish colonialists, and neighboring Mexico. Much like their contemporaries in Australia, Algeria, and tsarist Russia, Americans devoted much energy to displacing the original inhabitants of the North American continent and turning over their lands to new settlers. Then, at the edge of the twentieth century, a group of self-conscious imperialists in the government—much like a similar group of conservatives who a century later would seek to implement their own expansive agendas under cover of the "war on terrorism"—used the Spanish-American War to seed military bases in Central America, various islands in the Caribbean, Hawaii, Guam, and the Philippines.

With the Second World War, our nation emerged as the richest and most powerful on earth and a self-designated successor to the British Empire. But as enthusiastic as some of our wartime leaders, particularly President Franklin D. Roosevelt, were for the task, the American people were not. They demanded that the country demobilize its armies and turn the nation's attention to full employment and domestic development. Peace did not last long, however. The Cold War and a growing conviction that vital interests, even national survival, demanded the "containment" of the Soviet Union helped turn an informal empire begun during World War II into hundreds of installations around the world for the largest military we ever maintained in peacetime.

During the almost fifty years of superpower standoff, the United States denied that its activities constituted a form of imperialism. Ours were just reactions to the menace of the "evil empire" of the USSR and its satellites. Only slowly did we Americans become aware that the role of the military was growing in our country and that the executive branch—the "imperial presidency"—was eroding the democratic underpinnings of our constitutional republic. But even at the time of the Vietnam War and the abuses of power known as Watergate, this awareness never gained sufficient traction to reverse a Cold War–driven transfer of power from the representatives of the people to the Pentagon and the various intelligence agencies, especially the Central Intelligence Agency.

By the time the Soviet Union collapsed in 1991, and with it the rationale for American containment policies, our leaders had become so accustomed to dominance over half the globe that the thought of giving it up was inconceivable. Many Americans simply concluded that they had "won" the Cold War and so deserved the imperial fruits of victory. A number of ideologists began to argue that the United States was, in fact, a "good empire" and should act accordingly in a world with only one dominant power. To demobilize and turn our resources to peaceful ends would, they argued, constitute the old-fashioned sin of "isolationism."

In the first post–Cold War decade, we mounted many actions to perpetuate and extend our global power, including wars and "humanitarian" interventions in Panama, the Persian Gulf, Somalia, Haiti, Bosnia, Colombia, and Serbia, while maintaining unchanged our Cold War deployments in East Asia and the Pacific. In the eyes of its own people, the United States remained at worst an informal empire. After all, it had no colonies and its massive military forces were deployed around the world only to maintain "stability," or guarantee "mutual security," or promote a liberal world order based on free elections and American-style "open markets."

Americans like to say that the world changed as a result of the September 11, 2001, terrorist attacks on the World Trade Center and the Pentagon. It would be more accurate to say that the attacks produced a dangerous change in the thinking of some of our leaders, who began to see our republic as a genuine empire, a new Rome, the greatest colossus in history, no longer bound by international law, the concerns of allies, or any constraints on its use of military force. The American people were still largely in the dark about why they had been attacked or why their

State Department began warning them against tourism in an ever-growing list of foreign countries. ("Why do they hate us?" was a common plaint heard on talk shows, and the most common answer was "jealousy.") But a growing number finally began to grasp what most non-Americans already knew and had experienced over the previous half century—namely, that the United States was something other than what it professed to be, that it was, in fact, a military juggernaut intent on world domination.

Americans may still prefer to use euphemisms like "lone superpower," but since 9/11, our country has undergone a transformation from republic to empire that may well prove irreversible. It suddenly became "un-American" to question the Bush administration's "war on terrorism," let alone a war on Iraq, or on the whole "axis of evil," or even on the sixty or so countries that the president and his secretary of defense announced contained al-Qaeda cells and so were open targets for unilateral American intervention. The media allowed themselves to be manipulated into using sanitized expressions like "collateral damage," "regime change," "illegal combatants," and "preventive war" as if these somehow explained and justified what the Pentagon was doing. At the same time, the government was making strenuous efforts to prevent the new International Criminal Court from ever having the option of considering war crimes charges against American officials.

This book is a guide to the American empire as it begins openly to spread its imperial wings. Its reach is global: as of September 2001, the Department of Defense acknowledged at least 725 American military bases existed outside the United States. Actually, there are many more, since some bases exist under leaseholds, informal agreements, or disguises of various kinds. And more have been created since the announcement was made. The landscape of this military empire is as unfamiliar and fantastic to most Americans today as Tibet or Timbuktu were to nineteenth-century Europeans. Among its recent additions are the al-Udeid air base in the desert of Qatar, where several thousand American military men and women live in air-conditioned tents, and the al-Masirah Island naval air station in the Gulf of Oman, where the only diversion is "wadi ball," a cross between volleyball and football. It includes expensive, permanent garrisons built between 1999 and 2001 in such unlikely places as Kosovo, Kyrgyzstan, and Uzbekistan. America's modern empire of bases also has its entertainment and getaway spots, much like those north Indian hill towns the administrators of the British Raj used for rest and recreation in the summer heat. The modern equivalents of Darjeeling, Kalimpong, and Srinagar are the armed forces' ski and vacation center at Garmisch in the Bavarian Alps, its resort hotel in downtown Tokyo, and the 234 military golf courses it operates worldwide, not to mention the seventy-one Learjets, thirteen Gulfstream IIIs, and seventeen Cessna Citation luxury jets used to fly admirals and generals to such spots. At a cost of $50 million apiece, each Gulfstream accommodates twelve passengers plus two pilots, one flight engineer, a communications systems operator, and a flight attendant.

Like empires of old, ours has its proconsuls, in this case high-ranking military officers who enforce extraterritorial "status of forces agreements" on host governments to ensure that American troops are not held responsible for crimes they commit against local residents. Our militarized empire is a physical reality with a distinct way of life but it is also a network of economic and political interests tied in a thousand different ways to American corporations, universities, and communities but kept separate from what passes for everyday life back in what has only recently come to be known as "the homeland." And yet even that sense of separation is disappearing—for the changing nature of the empire is changing our society as well.

For example, slowly but surely the Department of Defense is obscuring and displacing the Department of State as the primary agency for making and administering foreign policy. We now station innumerably more uniformed military officers than civilian diplomats, aid workers, or environmental specialists in foreign countries—a point not lost on the lands to which they are assigned. Our garrisons send a daily message that the United States prefers to deal with other nations through the use or threat of force rather than negotiations, commerce, or cultural interaction and through military-to-military, not civilian-to-civilian, relations. This point was made clear in a speech at the military academy at West Point on June 1, 2002, when President George W. Bush argued that the

United States must be prepared to wage a "war on terror" against as many as sixty countries. "We must take that battle to the enemy, disrupt his plans and confront the worst threats before they emerge." Americans must be "ready for preemptive action when necessary to defend our liberty and to defend our lives. . . . In the world we have entered, the only path to safety is the path of action. And this nation will act."

As historian Arthur Schlesinger Jr., adviser to President John F. Kennedy, observed on the first anniversary of the 9/11 attacks, "One of the astonishing events of recent months is the presentation of preventive war as a legitimate and moral instrument of U.S. foreign policy. . . . During the Cold War, advocates of preventive war were dismissed as a crowd of loonies. . . . The policy of containment plus deterrence won the Cold War. After the collapse of the Soviet Union, everyone thanked heaven that the preventive-war loonies had never got into power in any major country. Today, alas, they appear to be in power in the United States."[2] He was referring specifically to the first Bush administration's secretary of defense, Dick Cheney—now, of course, vice president—the second Bush administration's secretary of defense, Donald Rumsfeld, and their cronies in the Pentagon. The last time civilian and uniformed militarists even approximated the domination of American political life we see today was when Secretary of Defense Robert McNamara was dictating policy toward Vietnam.

Like most other Americans who are not actively involved with the armed forces, I paid very little attention to our empire of military bases until February 1996, when I made my first visit to our de facto American military colony of Okinawa, a small Japanese island that we have continuously occupied since 1945. My last encounter with the military had ended forty years earlier—when, in the summer of 1955, I left active duty as a naval officer in the western Pacific. In 1996, in the wake of the rape of a twelve-year-old Okinawan girl by two American marines and a sailor, I was invited by the island's governor, Masahide Ota, to speak about the problem of our bases. I visited Kin village—almost totally swallowed by the marines' massive Camp Hansen, where the abduction and rape had occurred—and interviewed local officials. I came away deeply disturbed both by Okinawan hostility and by the fact that no serious American strategy could explain the deployment of thirty-eight separate bases on the choicest 20 percent of the island.

It was apparent from the numerous beaches, golf courses, and other recreational facilities reserved for the use of our military and the duplication involved in separate air force, navy, and Marine Corps airfields that the bases had simply sprouted willy-nilly with the advent of the Cold War. No consideration had been given to equitable land use or the lives of the 1.3 million Okinawans. The military's situation in Okinawa struck me as similar to that of Soviet troops in East Germany after the Berlin Wall came down. In both cases the troops preferred to stay on because the pleasures of life as a legionnaire in an imperial garrison far outstripped those of life back in the "homeland."

The troops and their families were happy with their clubs, apartments, gyms, swimming pools, and shopping malls (known in military argot as "base exchanges") and undoubtedly preferred Okinawa to being stuck in small stateside towns like Oceanside, California, adjacent to the Marine Corps base at Camp Pendleton. If nothing else, the penalty for a rape conviction in California is considerably more onerous than for servicemen convicted of the same felony in Okinawa by the Japanese. Under terms of the Status of Forces Agreement the United States imposed on Japan in 1953, the Japanese are even required to provide special meals for those few American servicemen turned over to Japanese authorities and actually imprisoned. On average there were 2,800 calories in the meals served to Japanese prisoners but 4,000 in those served to the twelve Americans jailed at the end of 2001.[3]

After visiting Okinawa, I began to research, and write about, the history of our military there—from the final bloody battle of World War II against the Japanese army to the attempts of senior U.S. officers and Department of Defense officials to trivialize the rape of September 4, 1995.[4] My perspective was that of an academic. I had spent my life as a university professor studying the politics and economics of Japan and China, not as an analyst of America's global military hegemony. As was true of many Japanese not resident in Okinawa, I tended to see the island's situation as unique and at worst a sad case of Pentagon complacency and neglect. The solution seemed self-evident: close some of the unneeded bases, return substantial ground forces to American territory, lessen the burdens imposed on the Okinawan people, and so begin to reverse some of the hatred of the United States evident everywhere on the island. I thought that if the Pentagon imposed real priorities, it might even be able to preserve some of its facilities there, like Kadena Air Force Base, that might prove useful in a post–Cold War world. Otherwise, it seemed to me that sooner or later the Okinawans would revolt and throw us out, as the Filipinos had done in 1992 and the South Koreans threatened to do in 2003—just as the East Berliners had done to the Soviet Union in 1989.

Only slowly did I come to understand that Okinawa was typical, not unique. The conditions there—expropriation of the island's most valuable land for bases, extraterritorial status for American troops who committed crimes against local civilians, bars and brothels crowding around the main gates of bases, endless accidents, noise, sexual violence, drunk-driving crashes, drug use, and environmental pollution—are replicated anywhere there are American garrisons. Compared with the numerous bases on the Japanese mainland, the more than one hundred installations in South Korea, and the huge deployments in Germany, Britain, Italy, the Balkans, the Persian Gulf, Latin America, and elsewhere, Okinawa is not unusual except in the number of bases given the size of the island. America's military proconsuls being publicity-averse, the American press seldom visits, or reports on, its empire of bases. I had been given a glimpse into an aspect of contemporary American life that most Americans never see.

In light of these experiences, in the late 1990s I devoted myself to writing a book about American foreign policy, which I entitled *Blowback*, using the CIA's term for the unanticipated consequences of unacknowledged actions in other people's countries. My intention was to warn my fellow Americans about the conduct of our foreign policy over the previous half century, focusing particularly on the decade after the demise of the Soviet Union and on the evolving political situation in East Asia. The book appeared in the early spring of 2000. In it I argued that many aspects of what the American government had done abroad virtually invited retaliatory attacks from nations and peoples who had been victimized. The blowback from the second half of the twentieth century has only just begun. In a sense, blowback is simply another way of saying that a nation reaps what it sows. Although individual Americans usually know what they have sown, they rarely have the same knowledge at a national level, since so much of what the managers of our empire have done has been kept secret.

Although I became interested in our overseas bases when I visited Okinawa, I had already gained some insight into the organization of American imperialism and its secret operations. From 1967 to 1973, I served as a consultant to the Office of National Estimates of the Central Intelligence Agency.[5] I had been asked to join a panel of about twenty international relations specialists from outside the agency to read drafts of national intelligence estimates and offer nonbureaucratic critiques of them. Intelligence estimates are formal analyses and conclusions compiled from raw intelligence data that the CIA director is charged with coordinating with the other intelligence agencies and then delivering to the president and his advisers. These estimates, which do not indicate the sources of the intelligence under consideration, are written in an inoffensive bureaucratic prose intended to smooth over differences of interpretation between, say, the State Department's intelligence bureau and the Defense Intelligence Agency. I was invited to become a consultant by Richard Helms, the director, who only a few years later would be convicted of lying under oath to Congress for testifying that the agency had nothing to do with the overthrow of President Salvador Allende of Chile. Thus began my introduction to the secret world.

In 1967, I was best known as an academic specialist on China. The agency was interested in my opinions on several major issues of the time—the war in Vietnam, the Sino-Soviet split, and the internal Maoist purge of the Communist Party known as the Cultural Revolution, as well as insurgency and counterinsurgency, what the Chinese called People's War, a subject that then preoccupied Washington. The meetings with us outside consultants were held twice a year in former director Allen Dulles's home on the property of Camp Peary, then a "secret" CIA training base in Virginia.

Although I had been given a very high security clearance, I soon found that I did not have to worry about inadvertently disclosing national secrets. The best reason to keep the national intelligence estimates secret, I once told my wife, was their utter banality. Perhaps they were so highly classified because it would have been embarrassing to have it known that such conventional journalism passed for strategic thought in the Oval Office. The meetings were convivial and stimulating, but only rarely did national estimates wander from the standard militarist wisdom of the Vietnam War era. (On the other hand, CIA analysts who knew Vietnam well privately applauded Daniel Ellsberg's release of "The Pentagon Papers," because they were convinced that the war could not be won.)

There was one perk associated with being a consultant to the Office of National Estimates that I greatly treasured: the library in Dulles's home, filled with the latest CIA reports on subjects not on the agenda, back copies of old intelligence estimates, and classified journals devoted to the tradecraft of spying, was open all night. Those who did not spend the evening playing poker or telling one another tales of Cold War derring-do were welcome to sit in the library and browse through the collected documents for as long as they could stay awake. I recall spending most of one night reading in fascinating detail how the Russians had sprung their spy George Blake from Wormwood Scrubs Prison in London.

In the course of this enlightening nocturnal activity, I slowly realized that, at the CIA, the tail wagged the dog, that America's real business was covert activities, not intelligence collecting and analysis. During World War II, William J. Donovan founded the Office of Strategic Services, the CIA's predecessor. Only later did I learn that "an internal CIA history of Donovan's imprint on the Agency says he saw intelligence analysis as a convenient cover for subversive operations abroad. This subterfuge proved useful down the years."[6] So much for the valuable contributions of my consultancy, an experience that cured me of any tendency to think that the government keeps secrets as a matter of national security. Agencies classify things in order to protect themselves from congressional scrutiny or from political or bureaucratic rivals elsewhere within the government. True secrets need not be classified. They are simply closely held by prudent leaders. Interestingly enough, in September 2002, as the Bush administration was daily terrifying the world with statements about Saddam Hussein's clandestine weapons and the need for a preventive invasion of Iraq, the CIA revealed that there was no national intelligence estimate on Iraq and that it had not thought to prepare one for over two years.[7]

Part and parcel of the growth of militarism in the United States, the CIA has evolved into the president's private army to be used for secret projects he personally wants carried out (as, for example, in Nicaragua and Afghanistan during the 1980s). One begins to understand why John F. Kennedy was such an avid fan of Ian Fleming's James Bond tales. In 1961, Kennedy listed *From Russia with Love* as one of his favorite books. No doubt he envied Dr. No and the head of SMERSH, both of whom had private, semimilitary forces at their disposal to do whatever they wanted. Kennedy found his first in the CIA, until it humiliated him in the failed Bay of Pigs operation in Cuba, and then in the army's Green Berets.

Today the CIA is just one of several secret commando units maintained by our government. In the Afghan war of 2001, the CIA's semimilitary operatives worked so closely with army Special Operations troops (Green Berets, Delta Force commandos, etc.) that it became impossible to distinguish them. The United States has proudly admitted that its first casualty in the Afghan invasion was a CIA operative. During August 2002, Defense Secretary Donald Rumsfeld revealed plans to expand Special Operations forces within the military and merge them with the CIA's Special Activities Division (its covert operatives). Although it seems unlikely that the numerous private armies of our government can ever fully overcome interservice and bureaucratic rivalries, their story is an integral part of the growth of American militarism and the secrecy that accompanies it.[8]

The present book, *The Sorrows of Empire*, follows from my earlier book *Blowback*. In that book I assumed that the American government still functioned more or less as it had during the Cold War, and I stressed the potential for conflict in East Asia. But I did not focus on the extent of militarism in America or on the vast empire of military bases that had sprung up more or less undetected and that is today a geopolitical fact of life. In the wake of September 11, 2001, it no longer seems necessary to issue warnings; instead a diagnosis, even an autopsy, may be more appropriate. In my opinion, the growth of militarism, official secrecy, and a belief that the United States is no longer bound, as the Declaration of Independence so famously puts it, by "a decent respect for the opinions of mankind" is probably irreversible. A revolution would be required to bring the Pentagon back under democratic control, or to abolish the Central Intelligence Agency, or even to contemplate enforcing article 1, section 9, clause 7 of the Constitution: "No money shall be drawn from the Treasury, but in Consequence of Appropriations made by Law; and a regular Statement and Account of the Receipts and Expenditures of all public Money shall be published from time to time."

This article is the one that empowers Congress and makes the United States a democracy. It guarantees that the people's representatives will know what the state apparatus is actually doing and it authorizes full disclosure of these activities. It has not been applied to the Department of Defense or the Central Intelligence Agency since their creation. Instead there has been a permanent policy of "don't ask, don't tell." The White House has always kept the intelligence agencies' budgets secret, and deceptions in the defense budget date back to the Manhattan Project of World War II and the secret decisions to build atomic bombs and use them against the Japanese. In 1997, then Senator Robert Torricelli (D-New Jersey) proposed an amendment to the 1998 Defense Authorization bill requiring that Congress disclose aggregate intelligence expenditures. He lost, but he was able to point out that the intelligence agencies spend more than the combined gross national products of North Korea, Libya, Iran, and Iraq—and they do so in the name of the American people but without any advice or supervision from them.

The subject matter of this book is American militarism, its physical presence in the world, the growth of the "special forces" as a private army of the president, and the secrecy that allows ever more militarized and secret institutions to live and thrive. This is not an optimistic report. As the great sociologist of the modern state, Max Weber, concluded, "Every bureaucracy seeks to increase the superiority of the professionally informed by keeping their knowledge and intentions secret. Bureaucratic administration always tends to be an administration of 'secret sessions': in so far as it can, it hides its knowledge and action from criticism. . . .

The concept of the 'official secret' is the specific invention of the bureaucracy, and nothing is so fanatically defended by the bureaucracy as this attitude. . . . In facing a parliament the bureaucracy, out of a sure power instinct, fights every attempt of the parliament to gain knowledge by means of its own experts or interest groups. . . . Bureaucracy naturally welcomes a poorly informed and hence a powerless parliament—at least in so far as ignorance somehow agrees with the bureaucracy's interests."[9]

Weber could have been describing America's government today. In the war against Afghanistan the only information available to the public and its representatives came from the Department of Defense. The military has become expert at managing the news. Following the attacks of September 11, government at every level began to restrict information available to the public, including charges it was bringing against people it had picked up in Afghanistan and elsewhere and was holding incommunicado in a Pentagon prison in Cuba. Our newspapers began to read like official gazettes, television news simply gave up and followed the orders of its corporate owners, and the two political parties competed with each other in being obsequious to the White House.

As militarism, the arrogance of power, and the euphemisms required to justify imperialism inevitably conflict with America's democratic structure of government and distort its culture and basic values, I fear that we will lose our country. If I overstate the threat, I am sure to be forgiven because future generations will be so glad I was wrong. The danger I foresee is that the United States is embarked on a path not unlike that of the former Soviet Union during the 1980s. The USSR collapsed for three basic reasons—internal economic contradictions driven by ideological rigidity, imperial overstretch, and an inability to reform. Because the United States is far wealthier, it may take longer for similar afflictions to do their work. But the similarities are obvious and it is nowhere written that the United States, in its guise as an empire dominating the world, must go on forever.

1

IMPERIALISMS, OLD AND NEW

What was the name of that river which Julius Caesar crossed? Was it not
called the Rubicon? Yesterday, Mr. Bush may have crossed the very same
river.

ROBERT FISK,
Middle East correspondent for the London *Independent,*
reporting from the United Nations, September 13, 2002

American leaders now like to compare themselves to imperial Romans,
even though they do not know much Roman history. The main lesson for the United States ought to be how the Roman Republic evolved
into an empire, in the process destroying its system of elections for its
two consuls (its chief executives), rendering the Roman senate impotent,
ending forever the occasional popular assemblies and legislative comitia
that were at the heart of republican life, and ushering in permanent military dictatorship.

Much like the United States today, the Roman Republic had slowly
acquired an empire through military conquest. By the first century BC, it
dominated all of Gaul, most of Iberia, the coast of North Africa, Greece,
the Balkans, and parts of Asia Minor. As the Canadian essayist Manuel
Miles observes, "There is no historical law prohibiting a republic from
possessing an empire. There is a trend toward autocratic takeovers of
imperial republics, however, especially after they reach a certain stage of
growth. Even now this process is underway in the USA—the President,
like the first Roman emperors, decides when and where to wage war, and
his Senate rubber stamps and extorts the funding for his imperial adventures, just as the original came to do in the time of Caesar and Octavian."[1]

The Roman senate, much like Congress, worked well enough for two centuries. But by the first century BC, the size of the empire and the armies its maintenance required overwhelmed the capacities of the senate and the consuls. In 49 BC, Julius Caesar violated Roman law by bringing his army across the small stream called the Rubicon in northern Italy and plunged the country into civil war among the imperators, the generals of Rome's large armies. After the Battle of Actium in 31 BC, Octavian emerged as the most powerful of the generals and assumed dictatorial powers in order to end the military civil wars. In 27 BC, the senate passed most of its power on to him, giving him the name of Augustus. As the first emperor, he reigned from 27 BC to AD 14. Within a few decades, the Roman senate had grown to over a thousand members, while being reduced to little more than a club of the old aristocratic and military families. Rome ruled all of the known world except for China, but in the process Roman democracy was supplanted by dictatorship, and eventually the Romans were overwhelmed by the world of enemies they had created. To the very end Roman armies pretended to speak for "the senate and the Roman people" and paraded under banners emblazoned with the Latin initials SPQR (*Senatus Populusque Romanus*). But the days when the senate mattered were long past; empire had become an end in itself.

As the Roman republic was disintegrating, not all of its citizens quietly acquiesced in the loss of their democratic rights. In Shakespeare's famous version of the politics of those days, one citizen, Cassius, asks Brutus, "Upon what meat doth this our Caesar feed that he is grown so great?" In a sense this book is an attempt to answer that question in the context of an American imperium. To start, consider just one proposition on which today's imperialists—poisoned by false pride and self-glorifying assumptions—have fattened. I am referring to the dangerously misleading conclusion that the United States caused the Soviet Union's collapse and therefore "won" the Cold War. The mind-set that produced this conclusion offers clues to how the United States, like ancient Rome, embarked on the path toward militarism and empire.

Among American triumphalists, devoted fans of Ronald Reagan, and old star-wars enthusiasts, there is a myth that President Reagan's sponsorship of what he called the strategic defense initiative (SDI)—a never-completed, never-deployable, largely space-based defense against intercontinental ballistic missiles—set off a competition with the USSR over defense spending that ultimately caused the latter's downfall. The triumphalists allege that even though Reagan's star-wars proposals never came within light-years of working, they forced the USSR into an arms race that broke its back economically. Reagan's "evil empire" speech, his support of anti-Soviet guerrillas in Afghanistan, and his illegal support of "counterrevolutionaries" (contras) against the elected government of Nicaragua—so this argument goes—created a climate in which SDI was decisive. Thus, despite an almost unbroken record of mistaken assessments and misplaced advice about the strength and problems of the USSR during its final decade, Robert Gates, George H. W. Bush's CIA director, still concludes in his memoir, "In my view, it was the broad resurgence of the West—symbolized by SDI—that convinced even some of the conservative members of the Soviet leadership that major internal changes were needed in the USSR. That decision, once made, set the stage for the dramatic events inside the Soviet Union of the next several years."[2]

Yet according to Anatoly Dobrynin, the long-serving Soviet ambassador to Washington, as early as February 1986 Russian president Mikhail Gorbachev had concluded that "the United States is counting on our readiness to build the same kind of costly system [as SDI], hoping meanwhile that they will win this race using their technological superiority. But our scientists tell me that if we want to destroy or neutralize the American SDI system, we only would have to spend 10 percent of what the Americans plan to spend."[3] Among Gorbachev's scientific advisers, none was more important than Andrei Sakharov, who participated in the creation of the Soviet Union's hydrogen bomb and later became a brave critic of his country's human rights record and the winner of the 1975 Nobel Peace Prize.

On December 23, 1986, Gorbachev ordered Sakharov and his wife, Yelena Bonner, released from internal exile in the city of Gorky, where they had been sent by the Politburo for criticizing the Soviet invasion of

Afghanistan. The freeing of Sakharov was one of Gorbachev's earliest and most important acts of glasnost, or "openness," which ultimately led to the unraveling of the Soviet system, but he also wanted Sakharov's advice on SDI. Given in secret meetings in Moscow in February 1987, Sakharov's analysis was unequivocal: "An SDI system would never be militarily effective against a well-armed opponent; rather, it would be a kind of 'Maginot line in space'—expensive and vulnerable to counter-measures. It would not serve as a population defense, or as a shield behind which a first strike could be launched, because it could be easily defeated. Possibly SDI proponents in the United States were counting on an accelerated arms race to ruin the Soviet economy, but if so they were mistaken, for the development of counter-measures would not be expensive."[4]

Rather than hiking investments in new weaponry, the Soviets actually were in the process of cutting back. In the mid-1980s, revised CIA estimates of Soviet spending on weapons procurement indicated that the actual rate of increase had been a measly 1.3 percent a year, not the 4 to 5 percent the CIA had previously reported to the president, and that Russian appropriations for offensive strategic weapons had actually declined by 40 percent. Such estimates were ideologically unacceptable to Secretary of Defense Caspar Weinberger, who sent them back to the CIA. There Director Gates "ordered SOVA [the CIA's Office of Soviet Analysis] to send Weinberger a memo focusing on Soviet economic strengths."[5]

In fact, U.S. intelligence agencies did not see the crisis of the Soviet Union coming and never gave our political leaders an accurate assessment of the initiatives undertaken by Mikhail Gorbachev. On August 19, 1991, the USSR finally succumbed to a domestic coup d'état thanks to an internal process of delegitimization that Gorbachev himself had initiated. The United States had little or nothing to do with it.

While Gorbachev was attempting internal perestroika (economic restructuring) and glasnost (the end of secrecy and the release of political prisoners), the defining event that made clear to the world how far the process of reform had gone occurred on the night of November 9, 1989. The Berlin Wall fell. Here again, the crucial acts were not American but West German. In his scholarly dissection (commissioned by the German

Bundestag) of what he calls "one of the biggest paternity disputes ever," Hans-Hermann Hertle explains: "Following a secret agreement with Bonn, they [the Hungarians] opened the border to Austria for GDR [German Democratic Republic, i.e., East German] citizens on 10 September [1989]. In return, the Federal Republic gave Hungary credit in the amount of DM 500 million and promised to make up losses that Hungary might suffer from retaliatory measures by the GDR. Tens of thousands of East Germans traveled to the Federal Republic via Austria in the days and weeks that followed. The GDR experienced its largest wave of departures since the construction of the Berlin Wall in 1961. This mass exodus demonstrated the weakness of the SED [Socialist Unity Party of Germany, i.e., the Communist Party] leadership on this issue and undermined the regime's authority in an unprecedented manner."[6]

It is a commonplace in the teaching of international relations that empires do not give up their dominions voluntarily. The USSR was a rare exception to this generalization. Inspired by Gorbachev's idealism and a desire to become members of the "common European house" and to gain international recognition as a "normal" state, some reformers in the Soviet elite believed that rapprochement with Western European countries could help Russia resume its stalled process of modernization. As the Russian historian Vladislav Zubok has observed, "At certain points, . . . Soviet political ties to France and West Germany became more important and perhaps warmer on a personal level than relations with some members of the Warsaw Pact."[7] Much like the Hungarian Communist Party chief Imre Nagy in the 1956 anti-Soviet uprising in Budapest and Czech Communist Party first secretary Alexander Dubcek in the 1968 Prague revolt, Gorbachev had turned against the imperial-revolutionary conception of the Soviet Union inherited from Stalin. He willingly gave up the Soviet empire in Eastern Europe as the price for reinvigorating the Soviet Union's economic system.

The American leadership did not have either the information or the imagination to grasp what was happening. Totally mesmerized by academic "realist" thought, it missed one of the grandest developments of modern history and drew almost totally wrong conclusions from it. At one point after the Berlin Wall had come down, the U.S. ambassador to the Soviet Union actually suggested that the Soviets might have to intervene militarily in Eastern Europe to preserve the region's "stability."[8]

After some hesitation the American government and military decided that, although the Cold War in Europe had indeed ended, they would not allow the equally virulent cold wars in East Asia and Latin America to come to an end.[9] Instead of the Soviet Union, the "menace" of China, Fidel Castro, drug lords, "instability," and more recently, terrorism, weapons of mass destruction, and the "axis of evil"—Iran, Iraq, and North Korea—would have to do as new enemies. In the meantime, the United States did its best to shore up old Cold War structures and alliances, even without the Soviet threat, expanding the NATO alliance into Eastern Europe and using it to attack Serbia, a former Communist country. The Pentagon, in turn, demanded that military spending be maintained at essentially Cold War levels and sought a new, longer-term rationale for its global activities.

Slow as Washington was to catch on to what was happening in the Soviet Union—as late as March 1989 senior figures on the National Security Council were warning against "overestimating Soviet weakness" and the dangers of "Gorbymania"—the leadership moved with remarkable speed to ensure that the collapse would not affect the Pentagon's budget or our "strategic position" on the globe we had garrisoned in the name of anti-Communism. Bare moments after the Berlin Wall went down and even as the Soviet Union was unraveling, Pentagon chief Dick Cheney urged increased military spending. Describing the new defense budget in January 1990, Michael R. Gordon, military correspondent of the *New York Times,* reported that "in Cheney's view, which is shared by President [George H. W.] Bush, the United States will continue to need a large Navy [and interventionist forces generally] to deal with brushfire conflicts and threats to American interests in places like Latin America and Asia." Two months later, when the White House unveiled a new National Security Strategy before Congress, it described the Third World as a likely focus of conflict: "In a new era, we foresee that our military power will remain an essential underpinning of the global balance, but less prominently and in different ways. We see that the more likely demands for the use of our military forces may not involve the Soviet Union and may be in the Third World, where new capabilities and approaches may be required."[10] It should be noted that the Pentagon and the White House presented these military plans well before Iraq's incursion into Kuwait and the ensuing crisis that resulted in the Persian Gulf War of 1991.

The National Security Strategy of 1990 also foresaw the country's needing "to reinforce our units forward deployed or to project power into areas where we have no permanent presence," particularly in the Middle East, because of "the free world's reliance on energy supplies from this pivotal region." The United States would also need to be prepared for "low-intensity conflict" involving "lower-order threats like terrorism, subversion, insurgency, and drug trafficking [that] are menacing the United States, its citizenry, and its interests in new ways. . . . Low-intensity conflict involves the struggle of competing principles and ideologies below the level of conventional war." Our military forces, it continued, "must be capable of dealing effectively with the full range of threats, including insurgency and terrorism." Through such self-fulfilling prophecies, the military establishment sought to confront the end of the Cold War by embarking on a grandiose new project to police the world.

At the same time, American ideologists managed to convince the public that the demise of the Soviet Union was evidence of a great American victory. This triumphalism, in turn, generated a subtle shift in the stance the United States had maintained throughout the Cold War. The United States no longer portrayed itself as a defensive power, seeking only to ensure its security and that of allied nations in the face of potential Soviet or Communist aggression. Without a superpower enemy, the first hints of the openly—proudly—imperial role it would take on in the new century emerged, as the Pentagon, rather than declaring victory and demobilizing, began to test the waters in a variety of new capacities, some of which would be expanded and some discarded in the years to come.

The United States now assumed, slowly and by degrees, responsibilities for humanitarian intervention, the spread of American-style "market democracy" via globalization, open warfare against Latin American drug cartels and indigenous political reform movements, the quarantining of "rogue states," leadership of an endless "war on terrorism," and finally "preventive" intervention against any potentially unfriendly power any-where that threatened to possess the kinds of weapons of mass destruc-tion the United States first developed and still wished to monopolize. Within a decade of the end of the Cold War in Europe, the United States's position in the world underwent a fundamental transformation. In the view of William A. Galston, deputy assistant to President Bill Clinton for domestic policy from 1993 to 1995, "Rather than continuing to serve as first among equals in the postwar international system, the United States would act as a law unto itself, creating new rules of international engage-ment without agreement by other nations."[11] The United States no longer seemed to care how many enemies it made.

The period between the fall of the Berlin Wall and the first anniversary of the 9/11 attacks in the United States encompasses thirteen years and three presidents. From 1989 to 2002, there was a revolution in America's relations with the rest of the world. At the beginning of that period, the conduct of foreign policy was still largely a civilian operation, carried out by men and women steeped in diplomacy, accustomed to defend-ing American actions in terms of international law, and based on long-standing alliances with other democratic nations. There had always been a military component to the traditional conduct of foreign policy, and men from a military background often played prominent roles as civ-ilian statesmen. From time to time militarists went well beyond what the public expected of them—as in the secret support for and illegal financing of right-wing armies in Central America during the Reagan administration. But, in general, a balance was maintained in favor of con-stitutional restraints on the armed forces and their use. By 2002, all this had changed. The United States no longer had a "foreign policy." Instead it had a military empire.

With the end of the Cold War the huge Eurasian territory between the Balkans and Pakistan, formerly off-limits as the sphere of influence of the Soviet Union, opened up for imperial expansion. America quickly deployed military forces into this critical region and prepared to fight wars with regimes that stood in the way. During this period of little more than a decade, a vast complex of interests, commitments, and projects was woven together until a new political culture paralleling civil society came into existence. This complex, which I am calling an empire, has a definite—even defining—physical geography, much of it acquired during World War II and the Cold War but not recognized for what it was because the rationale of containing the Soviet Union disguised it. It consists of permanent naval bases, military airfields, army garrisons, espionage listening posts, and strategic enclaves on every continent of the globe.

Of course, military bases or colonies have been common features of imperial regimes since ancient times, but in the past they were always there to secure or defend conquered territories and to exploit them economically. The United States began like a traditional empire. We occupied and colonized the North American continent and established military outposts, called forts—Fort Apache, Fort Leavenworth, Sutter's Fort, Fort Sam Houston, Fort Laramie, Fort Osage—from coast to coast. But in more modern times, unlike many other empires, we did not annex territories at all. Instead we took (or sometimes merely leased) exclusive military zones within territories, creating not an empire of colonies but an empire of bases. These bases, linked through a chain of command and supervised by the Pentagon without any significant civilian oversight, were tied into our developing military-industrial complex and deeply affected the surrounding indigenous cultures, almost invariably for the worse. They have helped turn us into a new kind of military empire—a consumerist Sparta, a warrior culture that flaunts the air-conditioned housing, movie theaters, supermarkets, golf courses, and swimming pools of its legionnaires. Another crucial characteristic that distinguishes the American empire from empires of the past is that the bases are not needed to fight wars but are instead pure manifestations of militarism and imperialism.

The distinction between the military and militarism is crucial. By *military* I mean all the activities, qualities, and institutions required by a nation to fight a war in its defense. A military should be concerned with ensuring national independence, a sine qua non for the maintenance of personal freedom. But having a military by no means has to lead to *militarism,* the phenomenon by which a nation's armed services come to put their institutional preservation ahead of achieving national security or even a commitment to the integrity of the governmental structure of which they are a part. As the great historian of militarism Alfred Vagts comments, "The standing army in peacetime is the greatest of all militaristic institutions."[12] Moreover, when a military is transformed into an institution of militarism, it naturally begins to displace all other institutions within a government devoted to conducting relations with other nations. One sign of the advent of militarism is the assumption by a nation's armed forces of numerous tasks that should be reserved for civilians.

Overseas bases, of which the Defense Department acknowledges some 725, come within the scope of the peacetime standing army and constitute a permanent claim on the nation's resources while being almost invariably inadequate for actually fighting a war. The great enclaves of bases, such as those in Okinawa or Germany, have not been involved in combat since World War II and are not really intended to contribute to war-fighting capabilities. They are the headquarters for our proconsuls, visible manifestations of our imperial reach. During the second Iraq war, for example, the United States did not use its Persian Gulf and Central Asian bases except to launch bombers against Iraqi cities—an activity more akin to a training exercise, given American air superiority, than to anything that might be called combat. Virtually all of the actual fighting forces came from the "homeland"—the Third Infantry Division from Fort Stewart, Georgia; the Fourth Infantry Division from Fort Hood, Texas; the First Marine Division from Camp Pendleton, California; and the 101st Airborne Division from Fort Campbell, Kentucky. The bases in Qatar, Saudi Arabia, Bahrain, the United Arab Emirates, Oman, and elsewhere served primarily as high-ranking officers' watering spots and comfortable sites for their remote-control command posts. The American network of bases is a sign not of military preparedness but of militarism, the inescapable companion of imperialism.

A major problem for that network is financing. Most empires of the past paid for themselves or at least attempted to do so. The Spanish, Dutch, and British Empires all enriched their homelands through colonial exploitation. Not so the empire of bases. Militarized and unilateral, it tends to subvert commerce and globalization because it weakens international law and the norms of reciprocity on which trade depends. It thereby adds enormously to the indirect economic burdens of our imperium, a subject to which I shall return later in this book. Occasionally, our empire of bases makes money because, like the gangsters of the 1930s who forced the people and businesses under their sway to pay protection money, the United States pressures foreign governments to pay for its imperial projects. During the first Iraq war, the United States extracted $13 billion from the Japanese and later boasted that it had even made a small net profit from the conflict. But the more open and assertive we become in our claims to dominate the world, the less appealing the old "mutual security" schemes become for other rich but militarily impotent countries. A contraction of trade, capital transfers, and direct subsidies will undermine the U.S. empire of bases much faster than was the case for the older, self-financing empires.

Life in our empire is in certain ways reminiscent of the British Raj, with its military rituals, racism, rivalries, snobbery, and class structure. Once on their bases, America's modern proconsuls and their sous-warriors never have to mix with either "natives" or American civilians. Just as they did for young nineteenth-century Englishmen and Frenchmen, these military city-states teach American youths arrogance and racism, instilling in them the basic ingredients of racial superiority. The base amenities include ever-expanding military equivalents of Disneyland and Club Med reserved for the exclusive use of active-duty men and women, together with housing, athletic facilities, churches, and schools provided at no cost or at low fixed prices. These installations form a more or less secret global network many parts of which once may have had temporary strategic uses but have long since evolved into permanent outposts. All of this has come about informally and, at least as far as the broad public is concerned, unintentionally. If empire is mentioned at all, it is in terms of American soldiers liberating Afghan women from Islamic fundamentalists, or helping victims of a natural disaster in the Philippines, or protecting Bosnians, Kosovars, or Iraqi Kurds (but not Rwandans, Turkish Kurds, or Palestinians) from campaigns of "ethnic cleansing."

Whatever the original reason the United States entered a country and set up a base, it remains there for imperial reasons—regional and global hegemony, denial of the territory to rivals, providing access for American companies, maintenance of "stability" or "credibility" as a military force, and simple inertia. For some people our bases validate the American way of life and our "victory" in the Cold War. Whether the United States can afford to be everywhere forever is not considered an appropriate subject for national discussion; nor is it, in the propagandistic atmosphere that has enveloped the country in the new millennium, appropriate to dwell on what empires cost or how they end.

The new empire is not just a physical entity. It is also a cherished object of analysis and adulation by a new army of self-designated "strategic thinkers" working in modern patriotic monasteries called think tanks. It is the focus of interest groups both old and new—such as those concerned with the supply and price of oil and those who profit from constructing and maintaining military garrisons in unlikely places. There are so many interests other than those of the military officials who live off the empire that its existence is distinctly overdetermined—so much so that it is hard to imagine the United States ever voluntarily getting out of the empire business. In addition to its military and their families, the empire supports the military-industrial complex, university research and development centers, petroleum refiners and distributors, innumerable foreign officer corps whom it has trained, manufacturers of sport utility vehicles and small-arms ammunition, multinational corporations and the cheap labor they use to make their products, investment banks, hedge funds and speculators of all varieties, and advocates of "globalization," meaning theorists who want to force all nations to open themselves up to American exploitation and American-style capitalism. The empire's values and institutions include military machismo, sexual orthodoxy, socialized medicine for the chosen few, cradle-to-grave security, low pay, stressful family relationships (including the murder of spouses), political conservatism, and an endless harping on behaving like a warrior even though many of the wars fought in the last decade or more have borne less resemblance to traditional physical combat than to arcade computer games.

Among the thousands of pages of propaganda distributed by the Pentagon to celebrate its victory over the Taliban in Afghanistan was a story about a female air force captain sitting at a command post in Pakistan monitoring an unmanned Predator drone over Afghanistan. Suddenly, she spotted a group of Afghan men milling around a Toyota SUV and concluded they were "terrorists." She ordered in a navy plane armed with a conventional bomb to which a device had been attached that, via a satellite-based global positioning system and inertial guidance, was programmed to hit within thirty to forty-five feet of its target. As the navy pilot dropped his bomb, she could not help crying out to the unsuspecting figures on her computer screen, "Run. Get out of the way! You are going to be killed!" A few seconds later they were indeed dead. Perhaps this story was distributed to demonstrate the innate humanity of our new breed of warriors even though they may fight from hundreds of miles away or from 35,000 feet in stealth bombers. But M. Franklin Rose, a specialist on robotics working for the army, does not think such twinges of empathy will last very long: "So many of these young soldiers grew up on video games and computers, they grew up trusting machines."[13]

Death as antiseptic as in any video game is now de rigueur in the operations of our high-tech armed forces—and is commonly unrestrained by international or domestic law of any kind. For example, on November 4, 2002, the government acknowledged that it had initiated a strike in Yemen similar to the one described above in Afghanistan. A Predator unmanned surveillance aircraft, in this case monitored by CIA operatives based at a French military facility in Djibouti and at CIA headquarters in Virginia, fired a missile that destroyed an SUV said to contain a senior al-Qaeda terrorist.[14] Not only was the vehicle so completely vaporized that this claim cannot be verified but the nature of the strike itself—coming after the Yemeni government reportedly refused to act on information passed to it by the CIA—must give pause to other governments. Why could a Hellfire missile released from a remote-controlled drone not destroy reputed terrorists in the Philippines, in Singapore, or in Germany, whatever a local government might think or wish?

During the post–Cold War period, a new set of managers took the helm of the military establishment. They were more interested than their predecessors in warfare employing weapons launched from great heights, or from over the horizon, or from outer space. They were determined to avoid casualties among their own ranks, both to make service in the volunteer armed forces more attractive and to not alarm the citizens who supply the manpower and pay for the military's activities and lifestyle. This mode of warfare continues the World War II practice of bombing residential areas and cannot avoid, despite the touting of "precision" weaponry, the indiscriminate killing of nonbelligerents and innocent bystanders. There is nothing new about this. The Romans killed or enslaved their captives, plundered and destroyed their enemies' cities, and slaughtered entire populations without distinguishing between combatants and noncombatants. Twentieth-century "total war," associated above all with air power, was known in medieval times as "Roman war." In general, writes Sven Lindquist in his history of bombing, "the laws of war protect enemies of the same race, class, and culture. The laws of war leave the foreign and the alien without protection."[15] Hiroshima and Nagasaki exemplify the latter. The novel aspect today is our hypocrisy about our "precision-guided" munitions. American propaganda resolutely ignores the carnage our high-tech military imposes on civilian populations, declaring that our intentions are by definition good and that such killings and maimings are merely "collateral damage." Such obfuscation is intrinsic to the world of imperialism and its handmaiden, militarism.

Imperialism is hard to define but easily recognized. In the words of the early-twentieth-century English political economist John Hobson, imperialists are "parasites upon patriotism."[16] They are the people who anticipate "profitable businesses and lucrative employment" in the course of creating and exploiting an empire. They hold military and civilian posts in the imperial power, trade with the dominated peoples on structurally favorable terms, manufacture weapons and munitions for wars and police actions, and provide and manage capital for investment in the colonies, semicolonies, and satellites that imperialism creates.

The simplest definition of imperialism is the domination and exploitation of weaker states by stronger ones. Numerous sorrows follow from this ancient and easily observable phenomenon. Imperialism is, for example, the root cause of one of the worst maladies inflicted by Western

civilization on the rest of the world—namely, racism. As David Abernethy, an authority on European imperialism, observes, "It was but a
short mental leap for people superior in power to infer that they were
superior in intellect, morality, and civilization as well. The superiority
complex served as a rationalization for colonial rule and, by reducing
qualms over the rightness of dominating other people, was empowering
in its own right."[17]

According to a long tradition of writing about imperialism, if dominion by a stronger state does not include the weaker state's "colonization,"
then it is not imperialism. Some writers have employed the term *hegemony* as a substitute for imperialism without colonies, and in the post–
World War II era of superpowers, hegemonism became coterminous
with the idea of Eastern and Western "camps." Always complicating matters has been a long-standing American urge to find euphemisms for
imperialism that soften and disguise the U.S. version of it, at least from
other Americans. Theodore Roosevelt, for example, professed to be not
an imperialist but an "expansionist." Arguing for the annexation of the
Philippines, he said, "There is not an imperialist in the country. . . .
Expansion? Yes. . . . Expansion has been the law of our national growth."[18]

Abernethy is typical in insisting that in a real empire a stronger state
must advance a *formal* claim over a weaker one. "Colonialism," Abernethy writes, "is the set of formal policies, informal practices, and ideologies employed by a metropole to retain control of a colony and to benefit
from control. Colonialism is the consolidation of empire, the effort to
extend and deepen governance claims made in an earlier period of
empire building."[19]

Of course, European imperialism was indeed intimately linked to
colonies and committed to fostering emigration to its possessions on a
truly stupendous scale. Millions of Europeans migrated to the communities created by imperialism in North and South America, Australia, New
Zealand, and South Africa. In turn, millions of Africans were transported
as slaves to American and Caribbean colonies. As the Europeans expanded
globally, their political leaders and colonial administrators paid millions
of Chinese and Indians to emigrate or tricked them into emigrating—

sometimes as indentured servants—to European and American colonies and territories in Southeast Asia, the Indian Ocean, the Caribbean, Africa, and the United States.

European nations also systematically used their colonies as dumping grounds for their criminals and political dissidents in conscious attempts to forestall domestic revolution. Governments imposed sentences of "transportation" in order to get rid of those they thought might become radicals or revolutionaries. After the 1848 workers' uprising in Paris, the French government paid more than fifteen thousand Parisians to move to colonial Algeria. The British commonly transported Irish and other radicals to prison colonies in North America and, after the American Revolution, Australia. Against this background, Abernethy naturally argues that the very concept of imperialism makes no sense once colonialism and colonialists are removed from the picture.

But this is a historically circumscribed view. As time passed, emigration and colonialism became less frequent accompaniments of imperialism. Today imperialism manifests itself in several different and evolving forms and no particular institution—except for militarism—defines the larger phenomenon. Imperialism and militarism are inseparable—both aim at extending domination; "where the one," in Vagts's terms, "looks primarily for more territory, the other covets more men and more money."[20] Certainly, there are several kinds of imperialism that do not involve the attempt to create colonies. The characteristic institution of so-called neocolonialism is the multinational corporation covertly supported by an imperialist power. This form of imperialism reduces the political costs and liabilities of colonialism by maintaining a facade of nominal political independence in the exploited country. As the Cuban revolutionary Che Guevara observed, neocolonialism "is the most redoubtable form of imperialism—most redoubtable because of the disguises and deceits that it involves, and the long experience that the imperialist powers have in this type of confrontation."[21]

The multinational corporation partly replicates one of the earliest institutions of imperialism, the chartered company. In such classically mercantilist organizations, the imperialist country authorized a private company to exploit and sometimes govern a foreign territory on a monopoly basis and then split the profits between government officials and private investors. The best known of these were the English East India Company, formed in 1600; the Dutch East India Company, created in 1602; the French East India Company in 1664; and the Hudson's Bay Company in 1670. The chartered company and the modern multinational corporation differ primarily in that the former never pretended to believe in free trade whereas multinational corporations use "free trade" as their mantra.

Neither formal colonialism nor the neocolonialism of the chartered company or multinational corporation exhausts the institutional possibilities of imperialism. For example, neocolonial domination need not be economic. It can be based on a kind of international protection racket—mutual defense treaties, military advisory groups, and military forces stationed in foreign countries to "defend" against often poorly defined, overblown, or nonexistent threats. This arrangement produces "satellites"—ostensibly independent nations whose foreign relations and military preparedness revolve around an imperialist power. Such was the case during the Cold War with the East European satellites of the former Soviet Union and the East Asian satellites of the United States, which at one time included Taiwan, the Philippines, South Vietnam, and Thailand but now are more or less reduced to Japan and South Korea.

The self-governing dominion of the British Empire has been a variant of the satellite. Canada, Australia, and New Zealand have been distinguished from other British crown colonies entirely along racial lines: unlike those not given dominion status, they are populated primarily by white European emigrants. Still another variant is the client state, a dependency of an imperialist power whose resources, strategic location, or influence may sometimes offer it the leeway to dictate policy to the dominant power while still relying on it for extensive support. Examples would include Israel vis-à-vis the United States, China and Vietnam vis-à-vis the USSR before the Sino-Soviet split, and North Korea between 1960 and 1990, when it could play China and the Soviet Union against each other.

During the Cold War, the United States and the Soviet Union each claimed to be opposed to old-style European imperialism and thus not to

be imperialist powers. Long before World War II, however, both countries had built empires—the United States in Latin America and the
Pacific, the Russians in the Caucasus and Central Asia—and both acquired
new territories in the course of fighting that war. Each, however, had to
disguise its long-standing imperialist practices as something far more
benign, and each, in the Cold War years, developed a set of elaborate
myths about the threat of the other side and the need to maintain "forward deployed" military forces constantly ready to repel a "first strike."
The world's two most powerful nations agreed on at least one thing—
that their military presences were required on all the continents of the
world in order to forestall a superpower war.

The foreign military bases of both superpowers became the characteristic institutions of a new form of imperialism. Both countries enthusiastically adopted the idea that they were in mortal danger from each other,
even though they had been allies during World War II. The Cold War, and
particularly the standoff in Central Europe, had conveniently defined the
purpose of the approximately 1,700 U.S. military installations in about
one hundred countries that existed during that period.[22] The forces on
these bases were all engaged in a grand project to "contain Soviet expansionism," just as the Soviet Union's forces were said to be thwarting
"American aggression."[23] In 1989, while the Soviet Union started giving
its satellites their freedom and then fell apart in the course of glasnost—
of trying to explain how it had acquired them in the first place—the
United States was still engaged in the brutal repression of rebellions or
rebellious regimes in the small countries of Central America in the name
of preventing a Soviet takeover in the New World.

The military paranoia of the Cold War promoted massive military-
industrial complexes in both the United States and the USSR and helped
maintain high levels of employment through "military Keynesianism"—
that is, substantial governmental expenditures on munitions and war
preparedness. The Cold War also promoted employment in the armed
forces themselves, in huge espionage and clandestine service apparatuses,
and in scientific and strategic research institutes in universities that came
to serve the war machine. Both countries wasted resources at home,

[of 1962], we faced a generally status quo, risk-averse adversary." These are words that could not have been uttered in the White House prior to the fall of the Berlin Wall in 1989.

Both sides used the alleged menace of the other—in the case of the United States in East Asia, the "threat" of Communist China—to justify their occupation and exploitation of foreign territories. The United States applied the same kind of reasoning in Latin America, defining the democratically elected government in Guatemala in 1954, the revolutionary government of Cuba in 1959, and the Sandinista government in Nicaragua in 1979 as Communist threats. This excuse served as a cover for an ever-lengthening series of American interventions and coups against Latin American governments deemed unfriendly to American interests. From the CIA's overthrow of the Jacobo Arbenz government in Guatemala and its catastrophic Bay of Pigs invasion of Cuba, it was only a short step to the "falling dominoes" of Southeast Asia and the ruinous intervention in Vietnam.

The initial effect of the Cold War was to justify the grip of both superpowers on numerous territories each had defended or liberated during World War II—the Soviets primarily in Central Europe, the Americans in England, the North Atlantic, Western Germany, Italy, Japan, and South Korea. In 1953, for example, the U. S. government secretly forced part of the indigenous population of Greenland, an island about three times the size of Texas and a Danish colony since 1721, to move—it gave them four days' notice and threatened to bulldoze their houses—to make way for a vast expansion of Thule Air Force Base, a strategic expanse of some 234,022 acres disguised since World War II as a "weather station." In fact, throughout the Cold War, the Greenland base was a refueling spot for bombers scheduled to fly routes into the Soviet Union in the event World War III broke out. (Today, it is considered a critical location for the Bush administration's ballistic missile defense scheme.[25]) After more than fifty years, the air force shows no signs of leaving despite continuous protests by the Inuit of Greenland and numerous lawsuits filed in the Danish Supreme Court.

Once the military has acquired a base, it is extremely reluctant to give it up. Instead, new uses are found for it. The American presence on Okinawa, for example, was first justified by the need to mount an invasion of the main Japanese islands (made unnecessary by the atomic bombs and Japan's surrender), then as a secure enclave for fighting the war in Korea, next as a forward base for deploying force against China, then as a B-52 bomber base and staging area for the Vietnam War, a training area for jungle warfare, and most recently a home base for troops and aircraft that might be used elsewhere in Asia or the Middle East. As Patrick Lloyd Hatcher, a historian and retired U.S. Army colonel, writes, "Foreign real estate has the same attraction for American defense planners that Nimitz-class aircraft carriers do for admirals and B-2 stealth bombers and heavy Abrams tanks do for generals. . . . They can never have enough."[26] In short, the imperialism of the superpowers during the Cold War centered on the deployment of military forces in other people's countries. It took the specific form of the establishment of foreign military bases and the fostering of docile satellites in each superpower's sphere of influence.

America's foreign military enclaves, though structurally, legally, and conceptually different from colonies, are themselves something like micro-colonies in that they are completely beyond the jurisdiction of the occupied nation. The United States virtually always negotiates a "status of forces agreement" (SOFA) with the ostensibly independent "host" nation, a modern legacy of the nineteenth-century imperialist practice in China of "extraterritoriality"—the "right" of a foreigner charged with a crime to be turned over for trial to his own diplomatic representatives in accordance with his national law, not to a Chinese court in accordance with Chinese law. Extracted from the Chinese at gun point, the practice arose because foreigners claimed that Chinese law was barbaric and "white men" should not be forced to submit to it. Chinese law was indeed concerned more with the social consequences of crime than with establishing the individual guilt or innocence of criminals, particularly those who were uninvited guests in China. Following the Anglo-Chinese Opium War of 1839–42, the United States was the first nation to demand "extrality" for its citizens. All the other European nations then demanded the same rights as the Americans. Except for the Germans, who lost their Chinese colonies in World War I, Americans and Europeans lived an "extraterritorial" life until the Japanese ended it in 1941 and Chiang Kai-shek's Kuomintang stopped it in 1943 in "free China."

Rachel Cornwell and Andrew Wells, two authorities on status of forces agreements, conclude, "Most SOFAs are written so that national courts cannot exercise legal jurisdiction over U.S. military personnel who commit crimes against local people, except in special cases where the U.S. military authorities agree to transfer jurisdiction."[27] Since service members are also exempt from normal passport and immigration controls, the military often has the option of simply flying an accused rapist or murderer out of the country before local authorities can bring him to trial, a contrivance to which commanding officers of Pacific bases have often resorted. At the time of the terrorist attacks on New York and Washington in September 2001, the United States had publicly acknowledged SOFAs with ninety-three countries, though some SOFAs are so embarrassing to the host nation that they are kept secret, particularly in the Islamic world.[28] Thus their true number is not publicly known.

U.S. overseas military bases are under the control not of some colonial office or ministry of foreign affairs but of the Department of Defense, the Central Intelligence Agency, the National Security Agency, the Defense Intelligence Agency, and a plethora of other official, if sometimes secret, organs of state. These agencies build, staff, and supervise the bases— fenced and defended sites on foreign soil, often constructed to mimic life at home. Since not all overseas members of the military have families or want their families to accompany them, except in Muslim countries these bases normally attract impressive arrays of bars and brothels, and the criminal elements that operate them, near their main gates. The presence of these bases unavoidably usurps, distorts, or subverts whatever institutions of democratic government may exist within the host society.

Stationing several thousand eighteen-to-twenty-four-year-old American youths in cultures that are foreign to them and about which they are utterly ignorant is a recipe for the endless series of "incidents" that plague nations that have accepted bases. American ambassadors quickly learn the protocol for visiting the host foreign office to apologize for the behavior of our troops. Even in closely allied countries where English is spoken, local residents get very tired of sexual assaults and drunken driving by foreigners. During World War II, the British satirized our troops as "over-paid, over-sexed, and over here." Nothing has changed.

Before setting out on a tour of these bases and a look at how they grew and spread, we need briefly to consider contemporary militarist thought in the United States and its origins. The bases support the military and are its sphere of influence, but it is the military itself and its growth during and following the Cold War that have caused the definitive transformation of these bases from staging areas for various armed conflicts into permanent garrisons for policing an empire.

At the time that Caesar was camped in Ravenna and thinking of advancing south across the Rubicon in direct violation of the Roman senate's orders, something occurred that seemed to force his hand. According to the historian and biographer Suetonius, shepherds and soldiers were lured to the riverbank by the sound of pipers. Among them were some trumpeters. One of them, for reasons that are obscure, sounded the advance. The troops took this as their cue to move aggressively to the other side of the river. Caesar is said to have remarked, "Let us go where the omens of the gods and the crimes of our enemies summon us. The die is now cast." Similarly, it would seem, post–Cold War American militarists have cast the die and the American people have blindly marched across their own Rubicon to become an empire with global pretensions.[29]

2

THE ROOTS OF AMERICAN
MILITARISM

Overgrown military establishments are under any form of government inauspicious to liberty, and are to be regarded as particularly hostile to Republican liberty.

PRESIDENT GEORGE WASHINGTON,
Farewell Address, September 17, 1796

This conjunction of an immense military establishment and a large arms industry is new in the American experience. . . . In the councils of government, we must guard against the acquisition of unwarranted influence, whether sought or unsought, by the military-industrial complex. The potential for the disastrous rise of misplaced power exists and will persist. We must never let the weight of this combination endanger our liberties or democratic processes. We should take nothing for granted.

PRESIDENT DWIGHT D. EISENHOWER,
Farewell Address, January 17, 1961

In the United States, the first militarist tendencies appeared at the end of the nineteenth century. Before and during the Spanish-American War of 1898, the press was manipulated to whip up a popular war fever, while atrocities and war crimes committed by American forces in the Philippines were hidden from public view. As a consequence of the war the United States acquired its first colonial possessions and created its first military general staff. American "jingoism" of that period—popular sentiment of boastful, aggressive chauvinism—took its cue from similar tendencies in imperial England. Even the term *jingoism* derived from the refrain of a patriotic British music-hall song of 1878, taken up by those who supported sending a British fleet into Turkish waters to counter the advances of Russia.

On the night of February 15, 1898, in Havana harbor, part of the Spanish colony of Cuba, a mysterious explosion destroyed and sank the American battleship USS *Maine*. The blast killed 262 of its 374 crew members. The *Maine* had arrived in Havana three weeks earlier as part of a "friendly" mission to rescue Americans caught up in an ongoing Cuban insurrection against Spanish rule. Its unspoken missions, however, were to practice "gunboat diplomacy" against Spain on behalf of the Cuban rebels and to enforce the Monroe Doctrine by warning other European powers like Germany not to take advantage of the unstable situation.

Two official navy investigations concluded that an external blast, probably caused by a mine, had ignited one of the battleship's powder magazines, though Spain maintained that it had nothing to do with the sinking of the *Maine*. Later analysts, including Admiral Hyman Rickover, have suggested that spontaneous combustion in a coal bunker may have been the cause of what was likely an accidental explosion.[1] Though the navy raised and subsequently scuttled the *Maine* in 1911, what happened to it in 1898 remains a puzzle to this day.

But there was no puzzle about the reaction to the news back in the United States. Assistant Secretary of the Navy Theodore Roosevelt instantly declared the sinking to be "an act of dirty [Spanish] treachery." The French ambassador to Washington advised his government that a "sort of bellicose fury has seized the American nation."[2] William Randolph Hearst's *New York Journal* published drawings illustrating how Spanish saboteurs had attached a mine to the *Maine* and detonated it from the shore. Hearst then sent the artist Frederic Remington to Cuba to report on the Cuban revolt against Spanish oppression. "There is no war," Remington wrote to his boss. "Request to be recalled." In a famous reply, Hearst cabled, "Please remain. You furnish the pictures, I'll furnish the war."[3] And so they both did. Thanks to Hearst's journalism and that of Joseph Pulitzer in his *New York World,* the country erupted in righteous anger and patriotic fervor. On April 25, 1898, Congress declared war on Spain.

On May 1, Admiral George Dewey's Asiatic Squadron, forced to leave the British colony of Hong Kong because of the declaration of war, attacked the Spanish fleet at Manila Bay and won an easy victory. With Filipino nationalist help, the Americans occupied Manila and began to think about what to do with the rest of the Philippine Islands. President William McKinley declared that the Philippines "came to us as a gift from the gods," even though he acknowledged that he did not know precisely where they were.[4]

During the summer of 1898, Theodore Roosevelt left the government and set out for Cuba with his own personal regiment. Made up of cowboys, Native Americans, and polo-playing members of the Harvard class of 1880, Roosevelt's Rocky Mountain Riders (known to the press as the Rough Riders) would be decimated by malaria and dysentery on the island, but their skirmishes with the Spaniards at San Juan Hill, east of Santiago, would also get their leader nominated for a congressional Medal of Honor and propel him into the highest elected political office.

Peace was restored by the Treaty of Paris, signed on December 10, 1898, a treaty that launched the United States into a hitherto unimaginable role as an explicitly imperialist power in the Caribbean and the Pacific. The treaty gave Cuba its independence, but the Platt Amendment passed by the U.S. Congress in 1901 actually made the island a satellite of the United States, while establishing an American naval base at Guantánamo Bay on Cuba's south coast. Senator Orville Platt of Connecticut had attached an amendment to the Army Appropriations Bill, specifying the conditions under which the United States would intervene in Cuban domestic affairs. His amendment demanded that Cuba not sign any treaties that could impair its sovereignty or contract any debts that could not be repaid by normal revenues. In addition, Cuba was forced to grant the United States special privileges to intervene at any time to preserve Cuban independence or to support a government "adequate for the protection of life, property, and individual liberty." The marines would land to exercise these self-proclaimed rights in 1906, 1912, 1917, and 1920.

In 1901, the United States forced Cuba to incorporate the Platt Amendment into its own constitution, where it remained until 1934— including an article that allowed the United States a base at Guantánamo until both sides should "agree" to its return, a stipulation the American government insisted upon on the grounds that the base was crucial to the defense of the Panama Canal. The Platt Amendment was a tremendous humiliation to all Cubans, but its acceptance was the only way they could avoid a permanent military occupation.

Even though the Canal Zone is no longer an American possession, Guantánamo Bay remains a military colony, now used as a detention camp for people seized in the U.S.-Afghan war of 2001–02 and the Iraq war of 2003. (Because Guantánamo is outside the United States, these prisoners are said to be beyond the protection of American laws, and because the Bush administration has dubbed them "unlawful combatants," a term found nowhere in international law, it is argued that they are also not subject to the Geneva Conventions on the treatment of prisoners of war. On October 9, 2002, the U.S. government dismissed the commandant at Guantánamo, Brigadier General Rick Baccus, for being "too soft" on the inmates.)[5] The United States did not directly annex Cuba in 1898, only because of its pretensions to being an anti-imperialist nation, its desire to avoid assuming Cuba's $400 million debt as well as Cuba's large Afro-American population, and Florida's fears that, as a part of the country, the island might compete in agriculture and tourism.

The Paris treaty also transferred the Spanish territories of Puerto Rico and Guam to American sovereignty, where they remain to this day.* Most important, in exchange for a mere $20 million payment to Spain, the treaty awarded to the United States the entire Philippine archipelago—3,141 islands located off the coast of China and Vietnam, some 7,952 miles from Los Angeles but less than 2,000 miles from Tokyo. The payment, however modest, was important to America's leaders, proof that they were not, as some critics charged, engaged in a "land grab" similar to those of the other new imperialist powers of the time—Germany, Russia,

---

*During the period 1894–98, the United States also stage-managed a coup d'état against Queen Lili'oukalani of Hawaii and annexed her islands, and in 1903, Theodore Roosevelt, by then president, fomented a revolution in the isthmus of Panama in order to separate it from Colombia and acquire the territory needed for the Panama Canal, a strategic centerpiece of imperial planning. A century later, such techniques had become a standard part of the American repertoire, only now executed under the rubric of CIA and Pentagon–administered "covert actions."

Italy, Belgium, and Japan—not to mention the old imperialists, Britain, France, Spain, and the Netherlands.

The Filipinos themselves proved less than eager to be "benevolently assimilated," as President McKinley put it, and under the leadership of a nationalist patriot, Emilio Aguinaldo, who had aided Admiral Dewey in wresting control of Manila from the Spaniards, they revolted against their new American overlords. Although American troops captured Aguinaldo in 1901 and forced him to swear loyalty to the United States, the fighting went on until 1903. Whereas the Spanish-American War (Cubans call it the Spanish-Cuban-American War) cost only 385 American deaths in combat, some 4,234 American military personnel died while putting down the Filipino rebels. The army, many of its officers having gained their experience in the Indian wars, proceeded to slaughter at least 200,000 Filipinos out of a population of less than eight million. During World War II, in a second vain attempt to escape imperialist rule with the help of a rival imperialist power, Aguinaldo collaborated with the Japanese conquerors of the islands.

Exercising what the historian Stuart Creighton Miller calls its "exaggerated sense of innocence," the United States portrayed its brutal colonization of the Filipinos as divinely ordained, racially inevitable, and economically indispensable.[6] These ideas had a powerful impact on the Japanese, who were attempting both to lead an anti-Western Asian renaissance and to join the imperialists in exploiting the weaker nations of East Asia. Their emulation of other "advanced" nations in taking the imperialist route would lead ultimately to war with the United States.

One prominent American imperialist of the time, Senator Albert Beveridge of Indiana, was fond of proclaiming, "The Philippines are ours forever . . . and just beyond the Philippines are China's illimitable markets. . . . The Pacific ocean is ours." A constant theme in the congressional debate over annexation of the Philippines was that they were the "stepping-stones to China." Beveridge believed it America's duty to bring Christianity and civilization to "savage and senile peoples," never mind that most Filipinos had been Catholics for centuries.[7] Even opponents of annexation like Senator "Pitchfork Ben" Tillman of South Carolina argued that it was absurd to talk about teaching self-government to people "racially unfit to govern themselves."[8] At the time Tillman made his comment, the most powerful political force in the United States was New York's Tammany Hall, not exactly a model of enlightened self-government. President McKinley called the Filipinos his "little brown brothers," while the troops in the field sang a ditty with the line "They may be brothers of McKinley, but they sure as hell are not brothers of mine." Such attitudes, high and low, contributed, ironically enough, to an emerging Japanese sense of racial superiority and a growing belief in their divinely ordained "manifest destiny" to liberate Asia from Western influence.

The Spanish-American War not only inaugurated an era of American imperialism but also set the United States on the path toward militarism. In traditional American political thought, large standing armies had been viewed as both unnecessary, since the United States was determined to avoid foreign wars, and a threat to liberty, because military discipline and military values were seen as incompatible with the openness of civilian life.[9] In his famous Farewell Address of September 17, 1796, George Washington told his fellow Americans, "The great rule of conduct for us in regard to foreign nations is—in extending our commercial relations— to have with them as little political connection as possible."[10] To twenty-first-century ears, this pronouncement seems highly idealistic and, if perhaps appropriate to a new and powerless nation, certainly not feasible for the world's only "superpower." Washington's name is still sacrosanct in the United States, but the content of his advice is routinely dismissed as "isolationism."

Nonetheless, Washington had something quite specific in mind. He feared that the United States might develop a state apparatus, comparable to those of the autocratic states of Europe, that could displace the constitutional order. This would inevitably involve a growth in federal taxes to pay for the armies and bureaucracies of the state, a shift in political power from the constituent states of the union to the federal government, and a shift within the federal government from the preeminence of the Congress to that of the president, resulting in what we have come to call the "imperial presidency." The surest route to these unwanted outcomes, in Washington's mind, was foreign wars. As James Madison, the primary author of the Constitution, wrote: "Of all enemies to public liberty, war is, perhaps, the most to be dreaded, because it comprises and develops the germ of every other. War is the parent of armies; from these proceed debts and taxes; and armies, and debts, and taxes are the known instruments for bringing the many under the domination of the few."[11] The Declaration of Independence accused the English king of having "affected to render the Military independent of and superior to the Civil Power," and the First Continental Congress condemned the use of the army to enforce the collection of taxes. These attitudes lasted about a century. With the Spanish-American War, the government began to build a military machine—and to tolerate the accompanying militarism—that by the end of the twentieth century had come to seem invincible.

During the summer of 1898, in Tampa, Florida, where American military forces had gathered for the assault on Santiago, Cuba, no single military or political authority had been in charge. Waste, confusion, and disease were rampant. Theodore Roosevelt had, in fact, exploited this disorganization to raise the Rough Riders. In 1899, President William McKinley appointed Elihu Root secretary of war, and Root, in 1903, made a signal contribution to American militarism by creating a "general staff" of senior military officers directly under him to plan and coordinate future wars. In testimony before Congress and in his annual reports as secretary of war, Root occasionally mentioned the confusion at Tampa in 1898 as evidence of the need for such an organization. But his real purpose was much broader. He argued that "the almost phenomenal success that has attended . . . German (Prussian) arms during the last thirty years is due in large degree to the corps of highly trained general staff officers which the German army possesses." He concluded: "The common experience of mankind is that the things which those general staffs do have to be done in every well-managed and well-directed army, and they have to be done by a body of men especially assigned to them. We should have such a body of men selected and organized in our own way and in accordance with our own system to do those essential things."[12]

On February 14, 1903, following Root's advice, Congress passed legislation that created the predecessor to today's Joint Chiefs of Staff. Root could hardly have imagined that his modest contribution to military efficiency would result a century later in thousands of military officers toiling away in the Pentagon on issues of weapons, strategic planning, force structure, and, in military jargon, C4ISR (command, control, communications, computers, intelligence, surveillance, and reconnaissance). Back in 1903, a week after setting up the general staff, Root established a complementary institution of militarism, the Army War College, first located in Washington, DC, and later moved to Carlisle, Pennsylvania. In his speech at the laying of the cornerstone for the original college, Root insisted, "It is not strange that on the shore of the beautiful Potomac, in a land devoted to peace, there should arise a structure devoted to increasing the efficiency of an army for wars. The world is growing more pacific; war is condemned more widely as the years go on. . . . Nevertheless, selfishness, greed, jealousy, a willingness to become great through injustice, have not disappeared, and only by slow steps is man making progress. So long as greed and jealousy exist among men, so long the nation must be prepared to defend its rights."[13] In addition, as part of his modernization effort, Root brought federal standards and methods to the semi-independent state militias and renamed them the National Guard.

Perhaps Root was right that, having achieved the industrial foundations of military might, the United States needed to pay attention to the global balance of power and modify its institutions accordingly. But there is no doubt about what we lost in doing so. Washington's warnings about the dangers of a large, permanent military establishment to American liberty would be ever more worshiped and less heeded over time, while the government came to bear an ever-vaguer resemblance to the political system outlined in the Constitution of 1787.

In 1912, Woodrow Wilson, then governor of New Jersey, former president of Princeton University, distinguished political scientist, and author of *Congressional Government,* one of the few genuine classics on the American political system, was elected president on the Democratic ticket. He had benefited greatly from the split in the Republican Party caused by former President Theodore Roosevelt's attempt to return to politics. As the leader of the first Democratic administration in twenty years, Wilson single-mindedly set out to reform the corruption and inequities associated with America's Gilded Age. He cut tariffs, imposed an income tax under the Sixteenth Amendment, created the Federal

Reserve system to perform central bank functions, enacted a federal child labor law, levied the first estate tax, and inaugurated numerous other changes that moved political power in the United States irreversibly toward Washington and the presidency.

But it was in foreign policy where, for better or worse, he made the greatest innovations. Wilson began with the Mexican revolution that broke out in 1910. He could not resist interfering and backing one faction over another. This was, of course, nothing new for an American government that already had Caribbean colonies and semicolonies. It was the way he justified these acts that distinguished him from the turn-of-the-century Republican imperialists and that ultimately made him the patron saint of the "crusades" that would characterize foreign policy from intervention in the First World War through the 2003 invasion of Iraq. Woodrow Wilson was an idealist and a Christian missionary in foreign policy. He was always more concerned to do good than to be effective.

The child of a chaplain in the Confederate army, Wilson was an elder of the Presbyterian Church and a daily reader of the Bible. As one of his biographers, Arthur S. Link, observes, "He never thought about public matters, as well as private ones, without first trying to decide what faith and Christian love commanded in the circumstances."[14] Born in Virginia, Wilson was also a racist and a prude. Because of America's republican form of government, its security behind the two oceans, and what he saw as the innate virtues of its people, Wilson strongly believed in the exceptionalism of the United States and its destiny to bring about the "ultimate peace of the world." He did not see America's external activities in terms of realist perspectives or a need to sustain a global balance of power. He believed instead that peace depended on the spread of democracy and that the United States had an obligation to extend its principles and democratic practices throughout the world.[15]

Before he was finished in Mexico, he had ordered the navy to occupy Veracruz in April 1914; provoked Francisco "Pancho" Villa's raid of March 9, 1916, on Columbus, New Mexico; and dispatched General John J. Pershing on an unsuccessful punitive expedition deep into Mexican territory to capture Villa. Wilson publicly regarded himself as Mexico's tutor on its form of government, a role that soured Mexican-American relations for decades. A war with Mexico was barely averted, but this heavy-handed meddling in the affairs of a neighbor disguised by a cloud of high-flown rhetoric about liberal, constitutional, and North American ideals did not go unnoticed. Japan repeatedly used the precedent, along with its own rhetoric of "liberation" from Western imperialism, to justify armed interventions in Manchuria and revolutionary China, which were on Japan's doorstep. The United States had no cogent response—except ultimately to go to war with Japan over behavior the latter had learned from the United States.

With the outbreak of the First World War in Europe, Wilson followed George Washington's advice and remained neutral. His position was extremely popular with the public, and in 1916 he was reelected on the campaign slogan "He Kept Us out of War." From the outbreak of war former President Theodore Roosevelt and Elihu Root, by then a senator, had proved outspoken critics of Wilson's insistence on neutrality. However, Wilson, when he finally did lead the country to war in 1917, turned out to be—as his Mexican adventures indicated—far more than a classic imperialist in the 1898 mold. He was, in fact, precisely the kind of president George Washington had warned against. Roosevelt and his colleagues advocated an American imperialism, modeled on British precedents, that sought power and glory for their own sakes through military conquest and colonial exploitation. Wilson, on the other hand, provided an idealistic grounding for American imperialism, what in our own time would become a "global mission" to "democratize" the world. More than any other figure, he provided the intellectual foundations for an interventionist foreign policy, expressed in humanitarian and democratic rhetoric. Wilson remains the godfather of those contemporary ideologists who justify American imperial power in terms of exporting democracy.

Popular attitudes toward Germany slowly changed, reflecting the public's underlying pro-British sentiments and the effectiveness of Anglo-American propaganda that Germany's submarine warfare against English shipping was "uncivilized." The issue came to a head on May 7, 1915, when a German submarine torpedoed the British Cunard Lines passenger ship *Lusitania* off the Irish coast. Some 128 Americans, along with several hundred citizens of other countries, lost their lives. The Germans maintained that the ship was carrying Canadian soldiers, which was not technically true (the men had not yet been inducted into the Canadian army) and that the *Lusitania*'s captain had deliberately failed to zigzag as prescribed by British Admiralty regulations. The German kaiser suggested that the captain had thus invited the sinking of his own vessel to inflame American opinion against Germany. The British were carrying out an equally effective blockade of German ports, but their practice was to stop offending ships and remove the passengers and crew before sinking them. The German U-boat, on the other hand, had given the *Lusitania* no warning. Wilson's antiwar and anti-imperialist secretary of state, William Jennings Bryan, was inclined to be conciliatory toward Germany in order to avoid war. On June 9, 1915, however, Bryan resigned and Wilson replaced him with Robert Lansing, a professional diplomat and advocate of entering the war on the Anglo-French-Russian side.

Wilson and Lansing continued to negotiate with Germany for almost two years, trying to obtain a pledge that passenger ships would not be attacked. Instead, on January 31, 1917, Germany declared a policy of unlimited submarine warfare against all ships calling at British ports, neutral as well as belligerent. On February 3, Wilson broke diplomatic relations with Germany. He was also irritated by evidence that German agents were secretly offering to aid Mexican revolutionaries against the United States. In a war message to Congress on April 2, 1917, Woodrow Wilson declared German aggression a threat not simply to the United States but to humanity itself. Germany, he said, was waging "warfare against mankind. It is a war against all nations." Not satisfied that the defeat of Germany was sufficient justification for American participation, he added a new, more ambitious war aim: "The world must be made safe for democracy." America, he explained, must fight "for the rights and liberties of small nations, for a universal dominion of right by such a concert of free peoples as shall bring peace and safety to all nations and make the world itself at last free." According to Wilson, these were purposes "we have always carried nearest to our hearts."[16] He asked for a declaration of war and got it four days later. In the year and a half still remaining in the war, some 130,274 American soldiers lost their lives on the Western Front.

On January 8, 1918, in a speech to Congress, Wilson unveiled his famous Fourteen Points, through which he intended to achieve a peace of reconciliation. The first of these points called for "open covenants openly arrived at," but at the peace conference itself Wilson discovered that Britain, France, and Japan, all allies in the war, had negotiated a series of secret treaties among themselves transferring parts of China to Japan in return for Japanese recognition of European spheres of influence in Asia. Wilson accepted Japan's control over a part of China in order to keep Japan in his proposed League of Nations, little realizing that the Chinese revolution was already well advanced and had begun to achieve a popular following. The Bolshevik Revolution of 1917 had inspired many Chinese and the peoples of European and American colonies in East Asia to study Marxism and Leninism and to seek the help of Soviet Russia in setting up local Communist parties. Nothing recommended Bolshevism more than the vociferous fear it seemed to elicit throughout the capitalist world.

When Wilson, however, turned down a Japanese request for an article in the Treaty of Versailles recognizing the principle of racial equality, the Japanese stiffened their positions and determined to obtain everything they could from a peace treaty. But perhaps most disruptive of future peace was the discovery by the colonized peoples of the British, French, Dutch, and American empires that the most famous of Wilson's Fourteen Points—"self-determination for all peoples"—applied only to the defeated Austro-Hungarian and Ottoman empires, and even there only to white people. Self-determination was not being offered to the peoples of British India, or French Indochina, or the Netherlands East Indies, or the Philippines. On board Wilson's ship bound for Europe, Secretary of State Lansing had written in his diary, "The more I think about the president's declaration of the right of self-determination the more convinced I am that it is bound to be the basis of impossible demands on the peace conference—what misery it will cause."[17] Much of the rest of the twentieth century would be devoted to efforts by colonized peoples to achieve, through rebellion, urban insurrection, and guerrilla warfare, what Wilson had denied them in the treaty ending World War I.

These tragedies of hubris and naïveté ended in personal tragedy for Wilson. On his arrival in Paris for the peace negotiations, he had declared, "We have just concluded the war to end all wars." The League of Nations that he intended to create would, he believed, prevent future wars by acting against aggressors. But on November 19, 1919, and again on March 19, 1920, the U.S. Senate, led by Henry Cabot Lodge, declined to ratify the Treaty of Versailles as an encroachment on American sovereignty, and the United States itself never became a member of the League of Nations. Even Secretary of State Lansing had opposed the treaty, and Wilson, now semiparalyzed by a stroke, asked for his resignation. The Republicans returned to power in November 1920, and the new president, Warren G. Harding, quickly concluded a separate peace with Germany. At the end of 1920, Wilson was finally awarded the Nobel Peace Prize, but it was—even more than usual—a meaningless gesture. Marshal Ferdinand Foch of France, supreme commander of all Allied forces at war's end, remarked of "Wilson's" peace at Versailles, "This is not a peace treaty, it's a twenty years armistice."[18] Foch did not live to see how precisely his prediction would be fulfilled.

With Woodrow Wilson, the intellectual foundations of American imperialism were set in place. Theodore Roosevelt and Elihu Root had represented a European-derived, militaristic vision of imperialism backed by nothing more substantial than the notion that the manifest destiny of the United States was to govern racially inferior Latin Americans and East Asians. Wilson laid over that his own hyperidealistic, sentimental, and ahistorical idea that what should be sought was a world democracy based on the American example and led by the United States. It was a political project no less ambitious and no less passionately held than the vision of world Communism launched at almost the same time by the leaders of the Bolshevik Revolution. As international-relations critic William Pfaff puts it, "[The United States was] still in the intellectual thrall of the megalomaniacal and self-righteous clergyman-president who gave to the American nation the blasphemous conviction that it, like he himself, had been created by God 'to show the way to the nations of the world how they shall walk in the paths of liberty.'"[19]

If World War I generated the ideological basis for American imperialism, World War II unleashed its growing militarism. It was then, as retired Marine Colonel James Donovan has written, that the "American martial spirit grew to prominence."[20] The wars with Germany and Japan were popular, the public and the members of the armed forces knew why they were fighting, and there was comparatively little dissent over war aims. Even so, the government carefully managed the news to sustain a warlike mood. No photos of dead American soldiers were allowed to be printed in newspapers or magazines until 1943, and the Pentagon gave journalists extensive guidance on how to report the war.[21]

World War II saw the nation's highest military participation ratio (MPR)—that is, percentage of people under arms—of any of America's wars. With some 16,353,700 men and women out of a total population of 133.5 million serving in the armed forces, World War II produced an MPR of 12.2 percent. Only the MPR of the Confederate side in the Civil War was higher, at 13.1 percent, but the overall ratio for both sides in the Civil War was 11.1 percent. The lowest MPRs, both 0.4 percent, were in the Mexican (1846–48) and Spanish-American Wars, followed by the Persian Gulf War of 1991 at 1.1 percent.[22] (This latter figure is, however, unreliable since a significant portion of the forces "under arms" at the time of the Gulf War were not engaged in combat or even located in the gulf region but were manning the United States's many garrisons and ships around the world.)

World War II produced a nation of veterans, proud of what they had achieved, respectful but not totally trusting of their military leaders, and almost uniformly supportive of the use of the atomic bombs that had brought the war to a rapid close. President Franklin Roosevelt played the role of supreme commander as no other president before or since. He once sent a memo to Secretary of State Cordell Hull saying, "Please try to address me as Commander-in-Chief, not as president."[23] Congress did not impose a Joint Committee to Conduct the War on Roosevelt, as it had on President Lincoln during the Civil War, and military institutions like the Joint Chiefs of Staff were still informal and unsupervised organizations created by and entirely responsible to the executive branch. As Colonel Donovan has observed, "With an agreed policy of unlimited war, Congress was also satisfied to abdicate its responsibilities of controlling the military establishment. . . . Some military leaders believed civilian control of the military was a relic of the past, with no place in the future."[24]

The most illustrious of World War II's American militarists, General Douglas MacArthur, challenged the constitutional authority of President Harry Truman during the Korean War, writing that it was "a new and heretofore unknown and dangerous concept that the members of our armed forces owe primary allegiance or loyalty to those who temporarily exercise the authority of the Executive Branch of the Government rather than to the country and its Constitution which they are sworn to defend. No proposition could be more dangerous."[25] On April 11, 1951, Truman charged MacArthur with insubordination, relieved him of his command, and forced him to retire. Truman's action was probably the last classic assertion of the constitutional principle that the president and the civilians appointed by him control the military. During the presidencies of John F. Kennedy and Bill Clinton, in particular, the high command would often be publicly restive about the qualities of the commander in chief and come close to crossing the line of constitutional legality without actually doing so. As we shall see, during the Kennedy administration the Joint Chiefs of Staff proposed that the military secretly carry out terrorist incidents in the United States and use them as a pretext for war with Castro's Cuba, and President Clinton was never able to regain full authority over the high command after the firestorm at the beginning of his administration over gays in the military.

After World War II, high-ranking military officers, including Generals Marshall and Eisenhower, moved into key positions in the civilian hierarchy of political power in a way unprecedented since the Civil War. George C. Marshall, the wartime chief of staff, became the country's first secretary of state from a military background. (There have been only two others since: General Alexander Haig in the Reagan administration and General Colin Powell in the second Bush administration.) Paradoxically, General Marshall left his name on what is probably the country's single greatest foreign policy failure, the 1946 Marshall Mission to China, which attempted to mediate between the Communists and the Nationalists in the Chinese civil war, and its single greatest success, the 1947 Marshall Plan, which helped rebuild postwar Europe economically.

But World War II, although a popular war, did not create American militarism, and had the Cold War not ensued it is reasonable to assume that traditional American opposition to standing armies and foreign wars would have forcefully reasserted itself. If there has been a growing trend toward militarism, there also remains a vein of deep suspicion of armies. The military almost totally demobilized in the years immediately after 1945 even though the draft remained in place until 1973, when an all-volunteer military came into being following almost a decade of protests against the war in Vietnam. On a pragmatic level, the public has proved ambivalent about wars because of the casualties they produce. And World War II produced the second-largest number of casualties of all America's wars.

The Civil War, by far the bloodiest war in our history, had profoundly affected popular attitudes and generated a deep resistance on the part of the American people to sending their sons and daughters into battle. The number of combat deaths for both sides in the Civil War was 184,594, considerably less than the 292,131 American deaths in World War II. However, when one adds in the 373,458 Civil War deaths from other causes—disease, privation, and accidents, including deaths among prisoners of war—the Civil War total becomes 558,052 wartime deaths. The figures for World War II, with 115,185 deaths from other causes, total 407,316.[26]

World War II was not as bloody as the Civil War, except in one important measure, that of intensity of combat, which is well conveyed by the ratio of those killed in action *per month*.* The Civil War lasted forty-eight months and saw 3,846 killed per month, whereas World War II lasted forty-four months (for the United States) with 6,639 killed per month. It was this intensity of combat that Americans remember from World War

---

*Men and women killed in action on both sides in the Civil War amounted to 4.8 percent of those in the armed forces, whereas it was 1.8 percent during World War II. The number of dead from all causes in the Civil War was 14.4 percent but only 2.5 percent for World War II. The number of casualties, both killed and injured, in the Civil War was 25.1 percent of those in uniform but only 6.6 percent for World War II.

II. It made them skeptical about future wars, particularly those in which there was no immediate threat to the United States or in which the United States had not been attacked. The legacy of World War II for the development of militarism was thus ambiguous. More Americans participated in the war effort more enthusiastically than in any other conflict, seemingly breaking the hold of traditional doubt about the value of war making. On the other hand, the country swiftly demobilized after the war and people returned to their normal peacetime pursuits.

In the years immediately following World War II, the great military production machine briefly came to a halt, people were laid off, and factories were mothballed. Some aircraft manufacturers tried their hands at making aluminum canoes and mobile homes; others simply went out of business. With the onset of the Cold War, however, and the rise of a professional military class, many of the norms characteristic of wartime were reinstated, and the armaments industry went into full production. Between 1950 and 2003, the United States experienced four periods of intense military mobilization accompanied by huge spurts in weapons purchases (see graph).

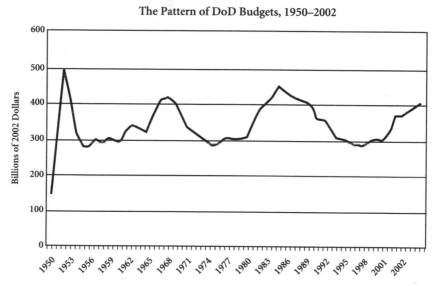

The Pattern of DoD Budgets, 1950–2002

Source: Michael E. O'Hanlon, "Limiting the Growth of the U.S. Defense Budget," Brookings Institution *Policy Brief,* no. 95 (March 2002). Used with permission.

The first and most significant peak in weapons purchases occurred during the Korean War (1950–53), even though only a fraction of it went for armaments to fight that war. Most of the money went into nuclear weapons development and the stocking of the massive Cold War garrisons then being built in Britain, Germany, Italy, Japan, and South Korea. Defense spending rose from about $150 billion in 1950, measured in 2002 purchasing power, to just under $500 billion in 1953. The second buildup financed the Vietnam War. Defense spending in 1968 was over $400 billion in 2002 dollars. The third boom was Ronald Reagan's splurge, including huge investments in weapons systems like the B-2 stealth bomber and in high-tech research and development for his strategic defense initiative, funds that were largely hidden in the Pentagon's "black budget." Spending hit around $450 billion in 1989. The second Bush administration launched the latest binge in new weaponry, fueled in part by public reaction to the 9/11 attacks. On March 14, 2002, the House of Representatives passed a military budget of $393.8 billion, the largest increase in defense outlays in almost twenty years.[27]

But no less significant is what happened to the military budget between the peaks. At no moment from 1955 to 2002 did defense spending decline to pre–Cold War, much less pre–World War II, levels. Instead, the years from 1955 to 1965, 1974 to 1980, and 1995 to 2000 established the Cold War norm or baseline of military spending in the age of militarism. Real defense spending during those years averaged $281 billion per year in 2002 dollars. Defense spending even in the Clinton years, after the collapse of the Soviet Union, averaged $278 billion, almost exactly the Cold War norm. The frequent Republican charge that Clinton cut military spending is untrue. In the wake of the Reagan defense buildup, which had so ruined public finances that the United States became the world's largest debtor nation, he simply allowed military spending to return to what had become its normal level.

From the Korean War to the first years of the twenty-first century, the institutionalization of these huge defense expenditures fundamentally altered the political economy of the United States. Defense spending at staggering levels became a normal feature of "civilian" life and all members of Congress, regardless of their political orientations, tried to attract defense contracts to their districts. Regions such as Southern California became dependent on defense expenditures, and recessions involving layoffs during the "normal" years of defense spending have been a standard feature of California's economy. In September 2002 it was estimated that the Pentagon funneled nearly a quarter of its research and development funds to companies in California, which employed by far the largest number of defense workers in any state. Moreover, this figure is undoubtedly low because many Southern California firms, like Northrop Grumman in Century City, TRW in Redondo Beach, Lockheed Martin in Palmdale, and Raytheon in El Segundo, are engaged in secret military programs whose budgets are also secret.[28]

Americans are by now used to hearing their political leaders say or do anything to promote local military spending. For example, both of Washington State's Democratic senators, Patty Murray and Maria Cantwell, as well as a Republican senator from Alaska, Ted Stevens, voted to include in the fiscal year 2003 defense budget some $30 billion to be spent over a decade to lease Boeing 767 aircraft and modify them to serve as aerial tankers for refueling combat aircraft in flight, a project not even listed by the air force in its top sixty priorities or among its procurement plans for the next six years. The bill also provided for the air force's paying to refit the planes for civilian use and deliver them back to Boeing after the leases were up. "It is in our national interest . . . to keep our only commercial aircraft manufacturer healthy in tough times," Murray commented.[29] Boeing, of course, builds the planes at factories in Washington State. In 2000, Stevens, an influential member of the Senate Appropriations Committee and its Defense Appropriations Subcommittee, received a $10,000 donation to his personal reelection campaign and $1,000 for his political action committee from Boeing; in 2001, it gave him an additional $3,000. Dennis Hastert, the Speaker of the House of Representatives, so liked the provisions in the bill that he tacked on funds for the leasing of four new Boeing 737 airliners for congressional junkets. Such obvious indifference to how taxpayers' monies are spent, bordering on corruption, no longer attracts notice. It has become a standard feature of politics.

The military-industrial complex has also become a rich source of places to "retire" for high-ranking military officers, just as many executives of defense contractors receive appointments as high-ranking officials in the Pentagon. This "circulation of elites" tends to undercut attempts at congressional oversight of either the Defense Department or defense contractors. The result is an almost total loss of accountability for public money spent on military projects of any sort. As *Insight* magazine journalist Kelly O'Meara has noted, in May 2001 the deputy inspector general at the Pentagon "admitted that $4.4 trillion in adjustments to the Pentagon's books had to be cooked to compile . . . required financial statements and that $1.1 trillion . . . was simply gone and no one can be sure of when, where or to whom the money went."[30] This amount is larger than the $855 billion in income taxes paid by Americans in fiscal 1999. The fact that no one seems to care is also evidence of militarism.

The onset of militarism is commonly marked by three broad indicators. The first is the emergence of a professional military class and the subsequent glorification of its ideals. Professionalism became an issue during the Korean War (1950–53). The goal of professionalism is to produce soldiers who will fight solely and simply because they have been ordered to do so and not because they necessarily identify with, or have any interest in, the political goals of a war. In World War II, the United States fought against two enemies, Nazi Germany and militarist Japan, that, with the aid of government propaganda, could be portrayed as genuinely evil.[31]

The United States did its best to depict the North Koreans, and particularly the Communist Chinese, who entered the war in late 1950, as "yellow hordes" and "blue ants," but as James Michener's novel *The Bridges at Toko-Ri* (1953) so well described, the public was much less emotionally involved than it had been during World War II. With public support slackening, the military high command turned to inculcating martial values into the troops, making that the most vital goal of all military instruction, superseding even training in the use of weapons. These values were to include loyalty, esprit de corps, tradition, male bonding, discipline, and action—generally speaking, a John Wayne view of the world. And inasmuch as conscripts constituted most of the still citizen army in those years, there was much work to do. Combat veterans of World War II tended to denigrate Wayne for his Hollywood-style machismo displayed in films like *Fighting Seabees* (1944). William Manchester, the biographer of General Douglas MacArthur and himself a veteran of the war in the Pacific, recalled how, shortly after the Battle of Okinawa, wounded soldiers and marines booed Wayne, who did not serve in the military, off a stage at the Aiea Heights Naval Hospital in Hawaii when he walked out in a Texas hat, bandanna, checkered shirt, two pistols, chaps, boots, and spurs.[32]

The kind of professionalism the military leadership had in mind was never actually achieved during the Korean War or, for that matter, the Vietnam War primarily because the men asked to do the fighting were mostly conscripts. The inequities of conscription, combined with high levels of casualties among those unable to evade the draft, destroyed much of the pride in being a member of the armed forces. Officers understood this and devoted themselves to furthering their own careers—getting their "tickets punched," as the phrase went. During the Vietnam years in particular, the military began to employ increasingly rapid cycles of rotation in and out of the war zone to prevent disaffection and even mutiny. Korea and Vietnam did not come close to producing the casualty levels of World War II, but because our soldiers were still fundamentally civilians and did not understand the purposes of these wars, they and their families often became disillusioned or even deeply alienated.

The Korean War had a military participation ratio of 3.8 percent, Vietnam 4.3 percent. There were 33,651 American deaths in Korea, and 47,369 in Vietnam. Nonbattle deaths for the Korean War are unknown; they number 10,799 for Vietnam. Some 2.7 million Americans served in Vietnam, of whom 304,000 were wounded in action and over 75,000 were permanently disabled by their injuries. As of Memorial Day 1996, there were 58,202 names of the dead engraved on the Vietnam War Memorial in Washington, DC. Approximately 1,300 men are still listed as missing in action.[33] Both wars were intensely unpopular, and the presidency was won three times by promises to bring them to an end—Eisenhower in the Korean era, and Johnson and Nixon in the Vietnam years (though both men proceeded to expand the war once elected).

When it became apparent during Vietnam that the military draft was being administered in an inequitable manner—university students were

exempted while the weight of forced military service fell disproportion-
ately on minorities and those with insufficient means to avoid it—the
government chose to abolish the draft rather than apply it equitably. Ever
since, service in the armed forces has been entirely voluntary and has
become a route of social mobility for those to whom other channels of
advancement are often blocked, much as was the case in the former
Imperial Japanese Army during the 1930s, where city dwellers were commonly deferred from conscription "for health reasons" and the military
was seen as a way out of the impoverished countryside. In the U.S. Army
in 1997, 41 percent of enlisted personnel were nonwhite (a subject to
which I shall return).

In addition to ending the draft and so turning the military into a
strictly "professional" force, Vietnam contributed to the advance of militarism, counterintuitively, exactly because the United States lost the war.
This defeat, deeply disillusioning to America's leadership elites, set off a
never-concluded debate about the "lessons" to be learned from it.[34] For a
newly ascendant far right, Vietnam became a just war that the left wing
had not had the will or courage to win. Whether they truly believed this
or not, rightist political leaders came to some quite specific conclusions.
As Christian Appy observes, "For Reagan and Bush [then Reagan's vice
president], the central lesson of Vietnam was not that foreign policy had
to be more democratic, but the opposite: it had to become ever more the
province of national security managers who operated without the close
scrutiny of the media, the oversight of Congress, or accountability to
an involved public."[35] The result has been the emergence of a coterie of
professional militarists who classify everything they do as secret and
who have been appointed to senior positions throughout the executive
branch.

Not all of these militarists wear uniforms. The historian Alfred Vagts
defines "civilian militarism" as the "interference and intervention of civilian leaders in fields left to the professionals by habit and tradition." Its
effects are often anything but benign. In general, civilian militarism leads
"to an intensification of the horrors of warfare. [In World War II, for
example,] civilians not only . . . anticipated war more eagerly than the
professionals, but played a principal part in making combat, when it

came, more absolute, more terrible than was the current military wont or habit."[36] Civilians are driven more by ideology than professionals, and when working with the military, they often feel the need to display a warrior's culture, which they take to mean iron-fisted ruthlessness, since they are innocent of genuine combat. This effect was particularly marked in the second Iraq war of 2003, when many ideologically committed civilians staffing the Department of Defense, without the experience of military service, no less of warfare, dictated strategies, force levels, and war aims to the generals and admirals. Older, experienced senior officers denigrated them as "chicken hawks."[37] This prominent role for civilian militarists was an unintended consequence of the Vietnam War.

During Vietnam, the Joint Chiefs of Staff (JCS) often opposed the decisions of President Lyndon Johnson. They wanted a wider war than the president did, even at the risk of a nuclear war with China. As a historian of the JCS, H. R. McMaster, explains: "The president and [Secretary of Defense Robert] McNamara shifted responsibility for real planning away from the JCS to ad hoc committees composed principally of civilian analysts and attorneys, whose main goal was to obtain a consensus consistent with the president's pursuit of the middle ground between disengagement and war. . . . As American involvement in the war escalated, Johnson's vulnerability to disaffected senior military officers increased because he was purposely deceiving the Congress and the public about the nature of the American military effort in Vietnam."[38]

The old and well-institutionalized American division of labor between elected officials and military professionals who advised elected officials and then executed their policies was dismantled, never to be recreated. During the Reagan administration, an ever-burgeoning array of amateur strategists and star-wars enthusiasts came to occupy the White House and sought to place their allies in positions of authority in the Pentagon. The result was the development of a kind of military opportunism at the heart of government, with military men paying court to the pet schemes of inexperienced politicians and preparing for lucrative postretirement positions in the arms industry or military think tanks. Top military leaders began to say what they thought their political superiors wanted to hear, while covertly protecting the interests of their individual services or of their minifiefdoms within those services.[39] The military establishment increasingly became a gigantic cartel, operated to benefit the four principal services—the army, navy, Marine Corps, and air force—much the way the Organization of the Petroleum Exporting Countries (OPEC) functions to maintain the profits of each of its members. Shares of the defense budget for each service have not varied by more than 2 percent over the past twenty-five years, during which time the Soviet Union collapsed and the United States fought quite varied wars in Panama, Kuwait, Haiti, Somalia, Bosnia, Kosovo, Afghanistan, and Iraq. Military needs did not dictate this stability.

During the 1990s and in the opening years of the twenty-first century, lobbyists and representatives of groups wanting to face off against nations like China that might pose future challenges to American hegemony took charge of virtually all politicomilitary policy.[40] They often sought to purge the government of experts who stood in their way, and the influence of the State Department notably withered. For example, Kurt M. Campbell, former deputy assistant secretary of defense for East Asian and Pacific affairs in the Clinton administration, notes approvingly that China policy has increasingly been taken over by a new "'strategic class'—that collection of academics, commentators and policymakers whose ideas help define the national interest." He says that this new crop of military experts, of which he is a charter civilian member, is likely not to know much about China but instead to have "a background in strategic studies or international relations" and to be particularly watchful "for signs of China's capacity for menace."[41] These are the attitudes not of prudent foreign policy thinkers but of militarists.

The second political hallmark of militarism is the preponderance of military officers or representatives of the arms industry in high government positions. During 2001, the administration of George W. Bush filled many of the chief American diplomatic posts with military men or militarists, including Secretary of State General Colin Powell, a former chairman of the Joint Chiefs of Staff, and the deputy secretary of state, Richard Armitage, who was undersecretary of defense in the Reagan administration. At the Pentagon, President Bush appointed Peter B. Teets, the former president and chief operating officer of Lockheed Martin Corporation, as undersecretary of the air force; former brigadier general and Enron Corporation executive Thomas E. White as secretary of the army (he resigned in April 2003); Gordon England, a vice president of General Dynamics, as secretary of the navy; and James Roche, an executive with Northrop Grumman and a retired brigadier general, as secretary of the air force.[42] It should be noted that Lockheed Martin is the world's largest arms manufacturer, selling $17.93 billion worth of military hardware in 1999. On October 26, 2001, the Pentagon awarded Lockheed Martin a $200 billion contract, the largest military contract in our history, to build the F-35 "joint-strike fighter," an aircraft that conceivably could have been useful during the Cold War but is irrelevant to the probable military problems of the twenty-first century.

Richard Gardner, a former ambassador to Spain and Italy, estimates that, by a ratio of at least sixteen to one, the United States spends more on preparing for war than on trying to prevent it.[43] During the 1990s, the United States was notoriously delinquent in paying its dues to the United Nations and at least $490 million in arrears to various multilateral development banks. By comparison, in the wake of the terrorist attacks of September 11, the United States was well on its way to annual defense budgets exceeding $400 billion.

The third hallmark of militarism is a devotion to policies in which military preparedness becomes the highest priority of the state. In his inaugural address, President George W. Bush said, "We will build our defenses beyond challenge, lest weakness invite challenge. We will confront weapons of mass destruction, so that a new century is spared new horrors." But no nation has the capacity to challenge the United States militarily. Even as the new president spoke, the Stockholm International Peace Research Institute was compiling the 2001 edition of its authoritative SIPRI Yearbook. It shows that global military spending rose to $798 billion in 2000, an increase of 3.1 percent from the previous year. The United States accounted for 37 percent of that amount, by far the largest proportion. It was also the world's largest arms salesman, responsible for 47 percent of all munitions transfers between 1996 and 2000. The country was thus already well prepared for war when the younger Bush came into office. Since his administration is devoted to further enlarging

America's military capabilities—a sign of militarism rather than of military preparedness—it has had to invent new threats in order to convince people that more is needed. In many ways, the terrorist attacks of 9/11 came as manna from heaven to an administration determined to ramp up military budgets.

At the beginning of the twenty-first century, the United States's nuclear arsenal comprised 5,400 multiple-megaton warheads atop intercontinental ballistic missiles based on land and at sea; an additional 1,750 nuclear bombs and cruise missiles ready to be launched from B-2 and B-52 bombers; and a further 1,670 nuclear weapons classified as "tactical." Not fully deployed but available are an additional 10,000 or so nuclear warheads stored in bunkers around the United States.[44] One would think this might be more than enough preparedness to deter the three puny nations the president identified in early 2002 as the country's major potential adversaries—two of which, Iran and North Korea, had been trying unsuccessfully to achieve somewhat friendlier relations with the United States. The staggering overkill in our nuclear arsenal—its ability to destroy the planet several times over—and the lack of any rational connection between nuclear means and nuclear ends is further evidence of the rise to power of a militarist mind-set.

No single war or occurrence caused American militarism. Rather, it sprang from the varied experiences of American citizens in the armed forces, ideas about war as they evolved from one war to the next, and the growth of a huge armaments industry. As the international relations theorist Ronald Steel put it at the height of the Vietnam War: "We believe we have a responsibility to defend nations everywhere against communism. This is not an imperial ambition, but it has led our country to use imperial methods—establishment of military garrisons around the globe, granting of subsidies to client governments and politicians, application of economic sanctions and even military force against recalcitrant states, and employment of a veritable army of colonial administrators working through such organizations as the State Department, the Agency for International Development, the United States Information Agency, and the Central Intelligence Agency. Having grown accustomed to our empire and having found it pleasing, we have come to take its institutions and its assumptions for granted. Indeed, this is the mark of a convinced imperial power: its advocates never question the virtues of empire, although they may dispute the way in which it is administered, and they do not for a moment doubt that it is in the best interests of those over whom it rules."[45]

The habitual use of imperial methods over the space of forty years became addictive. It ultimately transformed the defense establishment into a militarist establishment and vastly enlarged the size and scope of the role played by military forces in the political and economic life of the nation.

3

TOWARD THE NEW ROME

It's the same old dream—world domination.
IAN FLEMING,
Doctor No (1958)

In the American political tradition, "empire" has normally been a term of opprobrium. President Ronald Reagan famously used it to demonize the Soviet Union, which he labeled an "evil empire." Since the end of the Cold War, and particularly since the attacks of September 2001, however, the idea of empire has gained traction here. As Andrew Bacevich, a professor of international relations, describes the change, "In all of American public life there is [now] hardly a single prominent figure who finds fault with the notion of the United States remaining the world's sole military superpower until the end of time."[1] Not since the jingoists of the Spanish-American War have so many Americans openly called for abandoning even a semblance of constitutional and democratic foreign policy and endorsed imperialism. Now, as then, the imperialists divide into two groups—those who advocate unconstrained, unilateral American domination of the world (couched sometimes in terms of following in the footsteps of the British Empire) and those who call for an imperialism devoted to "humanitarian" objectives.

Typical of the former is the widely read *Washington Post* columnist Charles Krauthammer. After the terrorist attacks of 2001, he celebrated the "success" of the American bombing campaign in Afghanistan with an article entitled "Victory Changes Everything." "The elementary truth," he wrote, "that seems to elude the experts again and again—Gulf war,

Afghan war, next war—is that power is its own reward. Victory changes everything, psychology above all. The psychology in the region [Central Asia] is now one of fear and deep respect for American power. Now is the time to use it to deter, defeat, or destroy the other regimes in the area that are host to radical Islamic terrorism."[2] But even six months before the president declared "war on terrorism," Krauthammer asserted: "America is no mere international citizen. It is the dominant power in the world, more dominant than any since Rome. Accordingly, America is in a position to re-shape norms, alter expectations and create new realities. How? By unapologetic and implacable demonstrations of will."[3]

Many among the commentator class agree with Krauthammer. Robert D. Kaplan believes that the United States must not only take on the role of successor to the British Empire but that we must be devious and secretive about it. "Covert means are more discreet and cheaper than declared war and large-scale mobilization. . . . There will be less and less time for democratic consulation, whether with Congress or with the U.N."[4] Walter Russell Mead of the Council on Foreign Relations, who thinks that the United States is "the gyroscope of world order," is fearful that the American public, if left to its own preferences in a post–Cold War world, would demobilize as it has done in the past and return the country to its time-honored constitutional norms and restraints on executive power. To prevent that from occurring, Mead advocates open imperialism to fill the void left by the Cold War.[5]

Few of these writers like to dwell on what, concretely, the United States has done in the past and will have to continue to do to maintain its empire. From the moment we turned Japan and South Korea into political satellites in the late 1940s, the United States has paid off client regimes, either directly or through rigged trade, to keep them docile and loyal. We have taught state terrorism to thousands of Latin American military and police officials at the army's School of the Americas at Fort Benning, Georgia. We have utilized the Central Intelligence Agency and the International Monetary Fund to bring about "regime changes" via coups, assassinations, or economic destabilizations and have bombed or invaded countries that have openly broken with or opposed our hegemony. The civilian costs of these Cold War operations were high. To take

just one example, the militarists whom the United States assisted in coming to power in Indonesia in 1965 slaughtered at least half a million of
their people, claiming they were supporters of the Communist Party. Our
embassy supplied the Indonesian army with lists of people it thought
should be executed.[6]

In Latin America, the United States implemented a policy that was the
mirror image of the former USSR's "Brezhnev Doctrine," which called for
Soviet military forces to intervene against any socialist country that tried
to opt out of the Soviet bloc, as Czechoslovakia did in 1968. On December 20, 1989, George H. W. Bush sent 26,000 troops, including U.S. Navy
SEALs, Army Rangers, and the Eighty-second Airborne Division, into
Panama to depose the local leader, Manuel Noriega, a former ally and
CIA "asset" who had ceased to follow Washington's orders. In the course
of bombing Panama City, the American military killed 3,000 to 4,000
Panamanian civilians. (No one knows for sure exactly how many and no
one in the United States has ever cared to find out.) Eyewitnesses and several independent humanitarian groups reported widespread atrocities,
including the murder of unarmed civilians, the shoveling of their bodies
into mass graves, and the burning to the ground of the old workers' bar-
rio of El Chorrillo. It was evidently Bush's intent to decimate the Panamanian army, the main force backing Noriega, and to ensure that even
after sovereignty over the Panama Canal was returned to Panama, that
country would remain within the American orbit. The cover story for
"Operation Just Cause" was that Noriega dealt in recreational drugs
bound for the American market.

This demonstration of power occurred only a few weeks after the fall
of the Berlin Wall. Gorbachev had already renounced the Brezhnev Doctrine in a speech the year before at the United Nations. When, on Christ-
mas Eve 1989, Jack F. Matlock, the ambassador to Moscow, met with
Deputy Foreign Minister I. P. Aboimov to sound him out about Soviet
intentions in Eastern Europe, Aboimov told him, "We stand against
any interference in the domestic affairs of other states and we intend to
pursue this line firmly and without deviations. Thus, the American side
may consider that 'the Brezhnev Doctrine' is now theirs as our gift."[7]

Actions like the invasion of Panama are intrinsic to imperialist behavior.

When the historical record is considered, American foreign policy over the past half century may not prove to be particularly exceptional or evil, but the gap between what the government has been doing and the explanations it has given to the public continues to widen. Our imperialists like to assert that they are merely bringing a measure of "stability" to the world. For them, dirty hands belong to older empires, not to our own and—if they see us as following in British footsteps—not to our predecessor's either. Max Boot, a former editor at the *Wall Street Journal*, for example, believes, "We are an attractive empire. . . . Afghanistan and other troubled lands today cry out for the sort of enlightened foreign administration once provided by self-confident Englishmen in jodhpurs and pith helmets."[8] It is unclear whether Boot is indifferent to the ruthless and bloody repression that stood behind the British Empire or has simply never heard of events like the 1919 Amritsar Massacre, in which the British army slaughtered Punjabis until it ran out of ammunition; or the use of the Andaman Islands as a camp for political prisoners, complete with torture and forced labor; or the bombing and machine-gunning of, and the occasional use of poison gas against, rebellious Iraqis after Britain seized Mesopotamia from Turkey following World War I; or the decision to partition India, which led to the wholesale slaughter of Hindus and Muslims and to a bloody fifty-year-old war over Kashmir. If this was enlightened foreign administration, one hesitates to imagine what unenlightened imperialism might have looked like.

The intellectual heritage of America's neoconservative triumphalists is a complex amalgam of the military imperialism of Theodore Roosevelt and the idealistic imperialism of Woodrow Wilson. Most neocons have their roots on the left, not on the right. A number of them came out of the Trotskyist movement of the 1930s and 1940s. During the first thirty years of the Cold War, they adopted an anticommunist liberalism, which during the Reagan administration led them to embrace militarism and right-wing imperialism. These neocon defense intellectuals espouse preventive war, modeled on Israel's 1981 raid on Iraq's Osirak nuclear reactor, but they are simultaneously enthusiasts for the forcible spread of democracy, or at least so they claim in their propaganda. One of their apologists, Max Boot, calls neocon foreign policy "hard Wilsonianism."[9]

Their crowning achievement thus far was the 2003 war against Iraq, which the United States devastated in a one-sided military assault and then occupied. As the historian Paul Kennedy observes, Iraq had Western-style democracy thrust upon it through "an odd combination of Wilsonian idealism and Reaganite muscularity."[10]

Another group of American ideologues might be called humanitarian imperialists. They are globalist liberals, direct descendants of Woodrow Wilson. They believe in "making the world safe for democracy" and in the idea, endorsed by former President Bill Clinton, that the United States has history on its side. (Thus, just before his 1998 trip to Beijing, Clinton chastised China, the world's oldest continuously extant civilization, for languishing on "the wrong side of history.") These soft imperialists prefer to use the term *imperialism* with a prettifying modifier—they advocate "postmodern imperialism," "imperialism lite," "neoimperialism," "liberal imperialism," and above all the "right of humanitarian intervention."[11] As genuine Wilsonians, they advocate, for example, self-determination for people such as the Palestinians, whereas the neocons have a record of indifference to their plight.

Sebastian Mallaby, an editorial writer and columnist for the *Washington Post*, is a typical exponent of such liberal imperialism. "The rich world increasingly realizes that its interests are threatened by chaos," he writes, "and that it lacks the tools to fix the problem."[12] To deal with the danger of "failed states," he thinks "an imperial America" should fill the global gap. "The question is not whether the United States will seek to fill the void created by the demise of European empires but whether it will acknowledge that this is what it is doing." At no point does he mention that European (as well as American and Japanese) imperialism was a root cause of today's failed states in what used to be called the Third World. Mallaby proposes, among other things, that the United States create a new American-dominated "international" organization modeled after the International Monetary Fund and the World Bank to "fill the security void that empires left."

The complex issue at the heart of liberal imperialism is "humanitarian intervention." (The neocon triumphalists, generally speaking, are uninterested in anything with the adjective *humanitarian* attached to it.) The idea behind the term is: a powerful nation may violate another nation's sovereignty and even forcibly displace its administration in order to stop or prevent gross violations of human rights, ethnic cleansings, genocide, state terrorism, the operations of "death squads," or large-scale military reprisals against civilians. The International Commission on Intervention and State Sovereignty, cochaired by a former foreign minister of Australia, refers to such actions as "the responsibility to protect" and offers detailed conditions that, in its view, must be met for such intrusions ever to be justified.[13] These include that serious and irreparable harm to human beings is actually occurring or is imminent, that the use of military force is a last resort, that the military force employed is appropriate in scale, and that there are reasonable prospects for success.

Since the early 1990s, the United States has claimed such humanitarian motivations in a series of armed intrusions in Somalia, Haiti, Bosnia, and Kosovo. Humanitarian intervention was not originally raised as a factor in our invasion of Afghanistan. After we got there, however, the Bush administration claimed that one of our concerns was the harsh treatment of Afghan women under Taliban rule. This was not an issue, however, that had interested American leaders during the 1980s when they lavishly armed and supported the forces that became the Taliban. During those years, the United States and many of its allies failed to recognize their "responsibilities" to Rwandans, Chiapans, Chechens, Tibetans, Kashmiris, East Timorese, and Palestinians.

No one denies that, in extreme cases, foreign intervention to save innocent lives may be required. The issue is who gets to declare that a military intervention is humanitarian. The International Commission thinks that only the United Nations Security Council should authorize and legalize such activities, whatever the rationale; a self-declaration of humanitarian intervention like that of the United States in Somalia or Serbia thus becomes an act of imperialism. Positing a new, unilateral "responsibility to protect" that is to be the sole responsibility of the world's last great power and then assuming it only when that superpower finds it convenient to do so may actually worsen relations among nations.

Since the September 11, 2001, attacks, our government no longer appears to want Security Council authorization for its foreign wars (if it ever did) and does not seem to think it needs it. President Bush's speech at the United Nations on September 12, 2002, was more ultimatum than request: if the United Nations was not going to act against Iraq, then the United States would do so alone. On March 19, 2003, facing an almost certain veto and probably an outright majoritarian defeat if he had sought Security Council authorization for a war with Iraq, Bush made good on that threat and launched the war himself. Imperialism means, among other things, unilateralism in the decision making and actions of a nation, regardless of any humanitarian or other motives it may put forward. "The Rule of Power or the Rule of Law," a major study by two non-profit research organizations, the Institute for Energy and Environmental Research and the Lawyers' Committee on Nuclear Policy, analyzed the U.S. response to eight major international agreements, including the Nuclear Nonproliferation Treaty, the Comprehensive Test Ban Treaty, and the Anti-Ballistic Missile Treaty. "The United States has violated, compromised, or acted to undermine in some crucial way every treaty that we have studied in detail," says Nicole Deller, coauthor of the report.[14] The United States "not only refuses to participate in newly created legal mechanisms, it fails to live up to obligations undertaken in treaties that it has ratified."

According to the report, the United States is "drifting away from regarding treaties as an essential element in global security to a more opportunistic stand of abiding by treaties only when it is convenient." Its attempt to undermine the International Criminal Court (ICC), the world's first permanent war crimes tribunal, is a vivid example of its unilateralist motives. On December 31, 2000, President Bill Clinton signed the treaty that created the court, originally drafted during multilateral talks in Rome in July 1998 and subsequently signed and ratified by all of America's closest democratic allies. But the administration of the younger George Bush, fearing that someday American high officials might find themselves called before the court (though "safeguards" in the treaty make this an unlikely prospect), not only refused to submit the treaty to the Senate for ratification but, in an unprecedented move, retroactively "unsigned" it. As journalist David Moberg has written, "U.S. rejection of the court is thus mainly a symbolic statement that America is not accountable to anyone. . . . Bush wants the United States to serve as the world's investigator, policeman, prosecutor, judge, and executioner. This is an imperial ideal, not an assertion of sovereignty."[15] The administration simultaneously claimed itself no longer bound by the 1969 Vienna Convention on the Law of Treaties, which requires signatory nations to refrain from taking steps to undermine treaties they sign, even if they do not ratify them. As with the treaty for the ICC, the United States had signed but not ratified the Vienna agreement.

Our government became so paranoid on the subject of the ICC that it attempted to bar former U.S. ambassador to the United Nations Richard Holbrooke from even testifying in the war crimes trial of former Serbian president Slobodan Milosevic before the special U.N. tribunal on war crimes in the Hague. The State Department claimed it feared setting a precedent for cooperation with an international criminal court with jurisdiction over individuals, given that the ICC treaty had been successfully ratified by a sufficient number of nations and had come into being despite American opposition.[16]

On March 11, 2003, the ICC began formal operations in The Hague considering charges of war crimes committed after July 1, 2002. Anticipating that development, both houses of Congress passed the American Services Members' Protection Act, which would, in effect, allow the United States to use military force to free any American citizen held by the court. Dutch politicians, longtime American allies, mystified and outraged by what they saw as senseless grandstanding, sardonically referred to the legislation as the "Hague Invasion Act."[17]

The Bush administration claims it fears "capricious" prosecutions of its officials and military officers by an international prosecutor over whom it has no control, even though the Treaty of Rome contains many safeguards against arbitrary prosecutions, including the right of any nation to precedence over the ICC in trying its own citizens for war crimes. If the United States resists the establishment of a court that can prosecute individuals for war crimes, it is precisely because its global imperialist activities almost inevitably involve the commission of such crimes. The United States is the sole country the old World Court (which can try only nations, not individuals) ever condemned for terrorism— owing to the Reagan administration's covert action to destabilize and destroy the Sandinista government of Nicaragua in 1984.

The administration has always claimed that its opposition to the ICC is rooted in its desire to shield ordinary servicemen and low-ranking officers from war crimes charges, but its real concern clearly has been that the court might try to prosecute President Bush or other prominent civilian and military leaders. Remembering well the impact of Special Prosecutor Kenneth Starr's investigation of former President Bill Clinton for his sexual dalliance with Monica Lewinsky, the administration fears that were an international prosecutor to open a public investigation into the acts of President Bush, it might have a deleterious political impact, even if it never led to an indictment.[18]

These fears are, in some ways, not that far-fetched. After all, General Wesley Clark, commander of the NATO air war against Serbia, is as liable under the Geneva Convention of 1949 for not stopping the illegal bombing of water-treatment plants, hospitals, and schools, which killed almost 2,000 civilians, as Dragan Obrenovic, the Bosnian Serb general who commanded the assault on Srebrenica in July 1995 and subsequently was turned over to the war crimes tribunal in The Hague for trial. Prosecutors in Chile, Argentina, Spain, and France would like to put former Secretary of State Henry Kissinger on trial for his support and sponsorship of the military dictatorships of Brazil, Chile, Uruguay, Paraguay, Bolivia, Argentina, and Ecuador while, in the 1970s, they were killing, torturing, and "disappearing" their own citizens and those of neighboring lands.[19]

Similarly, the newly independent nation of East Timor would like to ask Kissinger under oath what he meant when, the day before Indonesia's 1975 invasion of the former Portuguese territory began, he seemed to give the green light to Indonesian strongman General Suharto. On December 6, 1975, on their way home from a visit to Beijing, President Gerald R. Ford and Kissinger stopped off in Jakarta for a meeting with Suharto. The general told them of his plans to seize the territory against the will of its inhabitants and incorporate it into Indonesia. Even though the Indonesian army was equipped in part with American weaponry, and the use of such arms for domestic purposes is illegal under U.S. law, Kissinger said, "It is important that whatever you do succeed quickly" and asked whether the Indonesians anticipated a "long guerrilla war." General Ali Murtopo, one of the architects of the seizure, replied that "the whole business will be settled in three weeks."[20] The Indonesian army went on to kill some 200,000 East Timorese.

The administration has not only tried to undercut treaties it finds inconvenient but refused to engage in normal diplomacy with its allies to make such treaties more acceptable. Thus, administration representatives simply walked away from the 1997 Kyoto Protocol on global warming that tried to rein in carbon dioxide emissions, claiming that the economic costs were too high. (The United States generates far more such emissions than any other country.) All of the United States's democratic allies continued to work on the treaty despite the boycott. On July 23, 2001, in Bonn, Germany, a compromise was reached on the severity of the cuts in emissions advanced industrial nations would have to make and on the penalties to be imposed if they do not, resulting in a legally binding treaty endorsed by more than 180 nations. The modified Kyoto Protocol is hardly perfect, but it is a start toward the reduction of greenhouse gases.

Similarly, the United States and Israel walked out of the United Nations conference on racism held in Durban, South Africa, in August and September 2001. The nations that stayed on eventually voted down Syrian demands that language accusing Israel of racism be included. In the conference's final statement, they also produced an apology for slavery as a "crime against humanity" but did so without language that would have made slave-holding nations liable for reparations. Given the history of slavery in the United States and the degree to which the final document was adjusted to accommodate American concerns, the walkout seemed a display of imperial petulance—or yet another message that "we" do not need "you" to run this world.

Following the terrorist attacks of September 11, 2001, many domestic and foreign observers expressed hopes that the United States would abandon its imperial unilateralism in recognition that its war against terrorism—or at least its efforts to control the financing of terrorism—required allies and a massive, coordinated international effort.[21] But this hope proved illusory. In the months after 9/11, the Bush administration unilaterally denied rights normally accorded prisoners of war to the fighters it had seized in Afghanistan and was holding at "Camp X-Ray," a complex of open-air wire cages on the old American military base in Guantánamo Bay, Cuba.[22] It unilaterally declared Iran, Iraq, and North Korea to be "rogue states" that constituted an "axis of evil" and reserved the right preemptively to destroy any or all of them or, in fact, any other nation deemed potentially hostile that maintained or planned to acquire "weapons of mass destruction"—nuclear, chemical, or biological weapons. At the same time, the United States endorsed the development of new and more "usable" nuclear weapons of its own and dramatically expanded the circumstances in which the Pentagon would consider "going nuclear" in a future conflict, all this in open violation of its pledge under the Nuclear Nonproliferation Treaty to make an "unequivocal undertaking" to eliminate its nuclear arsenal.[23] The Bush administration has similarly exempted itself from a treaty prohibiting the manufacture of biological weapons because it might have to open "private" pharmaceutical plants to international inspectors.

From evidence of this sort, the late Flora Lewis, longtime *New York Times* analyst of international relations, concluded that "the U.S. is turning its back on any global rules." She was concerned particularly by our attempt to subvert an international agreement to limit the world trade in small arms. In July 2001, John R. Bolton, undersecretary of state for arms control, had declared that the United States intended to thwart any agreement that might constrict the right of its citizens to possess guns.[24] Professor Michael Glennon, a specialist in international law at the Fletcher School of Law and Diplomacy at Tufts University, concludes that the Bush administration's unilateralism and its refusal to be bound by Security Council resolutions means that "the [U.N.] Charter provisions governing the use of force are simply no longer regarded as binding international law. . . . The Charter has, tragically, gone the way of the 1928 Kellogg-Briand pact which purported to outlaw war and was signed by every major belligerent in World War II."[25]

"In half a year [since 9/11], we have reinvented ourselves as the most belligerent people on earth. How did this happen?" asks *Boston Globe* columnist James Carroll. "Because the September attacks were the first massive violence suffered in the continental United States since the Civil War," he answers, "they left us uncertain and afraid. But elsewhere in the world, the devastations of war are all too common. To us they remain abstract. September memories, in fact, underscore how the horrors of modern warfare have never touched the cities of America. That is the only reason we can reorganize U.S. force projection around robot strikes, strategic bombing, and even usable nuclear weapons. All of this represents a failure of the American imagination to grasp the real effect on real people of such assaults. We wage war without knowing war."[26]

As late as 1874, well after the Civil War, our country's standing army had an authorized strength of only 16,000 soldiers, and the military was considerably less important to most Americans than, say, the post office. In those days, an American did not need a passport or governmental permission to travel abroad. When immigrants arrived they were tested only for infectious diseases and did not have to report to anyone. No drugs were prohibited. Tariffs were the main source of revenue for the federal government; there was no income tax.[27]

A century and a quarter later the U.S. Army has 480,000 members, the navy 375,000, the air force 359,000, and the marines 175,000, for a total of 1,389,000 men and women on active duty. The payroll for these uniformed personnel in 2003 was $27.1 billion for the active army, $22 billion each for the navy and air force, and $8.6 billion for the marines. Today, the federal government can tap into and listen to all citizens' phone calls, faxes, and e-mail transmissions if it chooses to. It has begun to incarcerate native-born and naturalized citizens as well as immigrants and travelers in military prisons without bringing charges against them. The president alone decides who is an "illegal belligerent," a term the Bush administration introduced, and there is no appeal from his decision. Much of the defense budget and all intelligence agency budgets are secret. These are all signs of militarism and of the creation of a national security state.

One unusual aspect of American militarism in the twenty-first century is that the government has elaborate plans to exert world dominance not merely through a vast military machine on this planet but through the control of space. The first hint of such aspirations could be found in the aerial bombardment of Serbia from March 24 until June 3, 1999. Pilots, including some in B-2 stealth bombers whose bomb runs took them from Missouri to the Balkans and back, flew more than 38,000 sorties over Serbia. In the course of this campaign only two aircraft were shot down and not a single American combat casualty occurred. General Richard B. Myers, then head of the U.S. Space Command, commented that Kosovo was "a space-enabled war," "a new benchmark" for the future. Military satellites and a space-based global positioning system had allowed U.S. aircraft to launch more or less precise bombing and guided-missile attacks that kept soldiers and airmen far from danger. In August 2001, President George W. Bush named Myers to head the Joint Chiefs of Staff, the first officer from such a background to be entrusted with the nation's highest military post.[28]

The next space-enabled war followed less than a month after the attacks of September 11, 2001. The Americans began high-altitude bombing of Afghanistan, a country already so devastated by over two decades of war that the dislodging of the repressive Taliban regime proved relatively easy. Despite Pentagon reports of only occasional "collateral damage," the United States killed at least as many civilians in Afghanistan as the terrorist attacks had killed at the World Trade Center and the Pentagon.[29] Nonetheless, the military claimed a great victory, with almost no American casualties, and further vindication for its new high-tech, space-based mode of war making.

In 2001, President Bush appointed Peter Teets, former chief operating officer of Lockheed Martin, undersecretary of the air force and director of the National Reconnaissance Office (NRO), in budgetary terms our largest intelligence agency. At the eighteenth annual National Space Symposium in Colorado Springs in April 2002, Teets was joined by General Ed Eberhardt, General Myers's successor at the Space Command, in underscoring the message that the United States can control the world through a planned domination of space and that it intends to ensure that domination.

Teets and Eberhardt emphasized the role of space in the victory over the Taliban, arguing that satellites were heavily used in the war and that they "allowed for extremely precise bombing by fighters and unmanned aerial vehicles in Afghanistan."[30] Eberhardt asserted that the provision of broadband services from space was as important to soldiers as providing them with intelligence. "We in Space Command provided [General] Tommy Franks [commander in Afghanistan] seven times the bandwidth that was provided to [General] Norman Schwarzkopf, and an individual soldier had 322 times the bandwidth that was available in Desert Storm." Jeff Harris, a former director of the NRO and now an executive of Lockheed's Space Systems Company, told the convention, "The U.S. must now act regularly in a preemptive and proactive way around the globe, using space-based resources for local skirmishes. . . . The U.S. military should make all potential adversaries unquestionably afraid of U.S. capabilities." Undersecretary Teets derided any talk of cooperation with NATO or the United Nations or other forms of "burden-sharing" or "multilateralism." The United States, he said, should be proud of its unilateral capabilities and should exploit "our space supremacy, our space dominance, to achieve warfighting success."[31] More than anything else, it is this cybertech military prowess that is fueling a rethinking of the entire military establishment and its missions.[32]

Even prior to the Afghan war, a group of right-wing "defense intellectuals" had started to advocate a comprehensive new strategy for global domination. Many had served in earlier Republican administrations and most of them were again given high appointive positions when George W. Bush became president. They focused on plans for the next decade or two in much the same way that Captain Alfred T. Mahan of the navy, Senator Henry Cabot Lodge, and Assistant Secretary of the Navy Theodore Roosevelt had emphasized sea power, Pacific bases, and a two-ocean navy at the end of the nineteenth century. Rarely taking the public into their confidence, the members of this new clique were masters of media manipulation, something they acknowledged they had "learned" as a result of bitter experience during the Vietnam War. The terrorist incidents of 2001, much like the sinking of the battleship *Maine* in 1898, gave a tremendous boost to their private agenda. It mobilized popular sentiment and patriotism behind military initiatives that might otherwise have elicited serious mainstream doubts and protests.

The determination to militarize outer space and dominate the globe from orbiting battle stations armed with an array of weapons includes high-energy lasers that could be directed toward any target on earth or against other nations' satellites. The Space Command's policy statement, "Vision for 2020," argues that "the globalization of the world economy will continue, with a widening gulf between 'haves' and 'have-nots,'" and that the Pentagon's mission is therefore to "dominate the space dimension of military operations to protect U.S. interests and investments" in an increasingly dangerous and implicitly anti-American world. One crucial goal of policy should be "denying other countries access to space."[33]

Such an aggressive attempt to ensure unilateral military hegemony requires that this country abandon all arms control agreements and constraints, including the 1967 Outer Space Treaty, which placed limits on the militarization of space, since space is inherently global. (Satellites do not remain within national boundaries.) The logic behind the weaponization of space is an ancient one implicit in virtually all imperialist projects—the need to protect some territory or capability whose vulnerability has been exaggerated and where alternatives to military options have not even been considered. The U.S. claim is that it has become militarily dependent on satellite communications and espionage and that an adversary could gain an advantage by deploying antisatellite weapons to disrupt these signals. Much as Britain at the end of the nineteenth century had to make colonies of Egypt and South Africa in order, so it said, to protect the sea approaches to its imperial enclave in India, and then had to conquer Sudan and the upper Nile to protect Egypt and much of sub-Saharan Africa to protect South Africa, the United States now argues that it must totally dominate space to protect its new, casualty-free war-fighting technologies.

But this kind of logic—comparable to the "domino theory" in the Vietnam War—leads to an endless progression of places and commitments that must be protected, resulting inevitably in imperial overstretch, bankruptcy, and popular disaffection, precisely the maladies that plagued Edwardian Britain. Such strategic planning also tends to produce unintended consequences in the form of unjustifiably brutal wars of imperial conquest, such as Britain's against the Boer settlers of South Africa. The Boer War, which lasted from 1899 to 1902, resulted in the deaths of 22,000 British soldiers. In the course of defeating the settlers, who took to guerrilla warfare against their stronger enemy, the British built the world's first concentration camps, where at least 28,000 Boer civilians (mostly women and children) and between 14,000 and 20,000 Bushmen, Zulus, and assorted other tribal peoples died.[34] Deaths in the camps amounted to about 10 percent of the Boer population. The root cause of all this mayhem was not the need to defend India but the urge to dominate globally—in short, imperialism and militarism. Alternative ways to achieve the same objectives—or a decision to abandon those objectives as not worth it—were never seriously considered.

In the contemporary clique of imperialists the main proponents of the militarization of space are Donald Rumsfeld (b. 1932), an old cold warrior and secretary of defense in the Ford administration (1975–77), who was brought back to the Pentagon by George Bush the younger a quarter century later, and Vice President Dick Cheney (b. 1941), President Ford's chief of staff and Bush *père*'s secretary of defense (1989-93). Immediately prior to becoming secretary of defense in 2001, Rumsfeld chaired the Commission to Assess United States National Security Space Management and Organization, whose final report concludes, "It is in the U.S. national interest to . . . use the nation's potential in space to support its domestic, economic, diplomatic, and national security objectives; develop and deploy the means to deter and defend against hostile acts directed at U.S. space assets and against the uses of space hostile to U.S. interests."[35]

Rumsfeld and Cheney have received analytical support from within the Pentagon in the person of Andrew W. Marshall (b. 1921), a former Rand Corporation "thinker about the unthinkable," who has specialized for many years in promoting a "revolution in military affairs," meaning advanced forms of warfare utilizing cybertechnology. Rumsfeld immediately put Marshall in charge of producing a blueprint for the Pentagon's future—and launched a full-scale campaign advocating a new space-based, high-tech grand strategy for transforming the military and securing global dominance for decades to come.[36] In a classic replay of paranoid imperialist thinking, American generals now warn about the country's dependence on satellites and the danger of a "space Pearl Harbor." To avoid this imagined catastrophe, militarists argue, the United States must seize and dominate space as soon as possible. In 2003, the United States created its first military unit intended to defend communications, weather, navigation, and missile-warning satellites from potential "enemy" attacks against ground stations or in space. This is the 614th Space Intelligence Squadron, based at Vandenburg Air Force Base in California. "All smart bombs and smart weapons are controlled by the GPS (global positioning system)," says Major Kurt Gaudette, director of operations for the new squadron. "If those don't work, we don't have any smart bombs anymore. So it's critical that those assets stay up there and are safe."[37]

As a key part of this program, the United States must not only put significant resources into developing "killer" satellites to keep other nations from "inhabiting" space but also build defenses, ultimately space-based ones, against other countries' ballistic missiles. This latter program, the open face of the more secretive project to militarize space, has been the subject of a great deal of presidential and political grandstanding. During 2001, advocating ballistic missile defenses became the primary way for our leaders to show their commitment to "unilateralism," a powerful demonstration of which was the president's decision on December 13, 2001, to withdraw from the 1972 Anti-Ballistic Missile Treaty with the former Soviet Union. He took this action well before the United States had developed any kind of antiballistic missile defenses, much less tested and deployed them, and despite open opposition by Russia, China, and the leading NATO nations.

Not surprisingly, China suspects that ballistic missile defense (BMD) is actually a program aimed at neutralizing its minuscule nuclear deterrent, and most of America's main allies implicitly agree and so have proved reluctant to go along with it, fearing that BMD will unleash a new arms race as challenged nuclear nations like China build more and better missiles to overwhelm such defenses. Nonetheless, the Bush administration is determined to go ahead with this unproven—in fact, still nonexistent—and highly destabilizing system, for which, given the patriotic mania that followed the attacks of September 11, 2001, Congress voted every last dollar the Pentagon requested.

In the process, the Bush administration has done everything in its power to classify and so hide official information on the high probability that the system will malfunction. For example, the Pentagon suppressed a report written in August 2000 by Philip E. Coyle, its own director of operational testing and evaluation, despite six different congressional requests for it. Among other things, Coyle documented how the command and control system for BMD is easily confused and has in the past caused a simulated launch of multiple interceptors against missiles that did not exist. As Representative John Tierney (D-Massachusetts) commented, "One immediate danger in these types of situations is that adversaries may interpret these launches as a hostile first strike and respond accordingly."[38] Defense Secretary Rumsfeld has said that he wants a ballistic missile defense even if it has not been thoroughly tested and is admittedly not able to perform to specifications.

BMD derives some legitimacy within Republican Party circles from former president Ronald Reagan's advocacy of a strategic defense initiative (SDI), which had as its objective the building of a kind of protective electronic astrodome of rockets and lasers over the country, an idea that never proved technically feasible. Reagan undoubtedly thought of SDI as defensive, but both SDI and BMD are in truth offensive concepts. It may be good public relations for its current advocates to imply that BMD is meant only to defend us against what are now called rogue states, places like North Korea and Iran that have not acquiesced in American hegemony and might conceivably be able to produce missiles with an intercontinental range. But no one seriously believes that any nation, small or large, plans to commit suicide by launching anything as traceable as a nuclear missile against the United States. As neoconservative pundit Lawrence F. Kaplan puts it, "Missile defense isn't really meant to protect America. It's a tool for global dominance."[39] Or, in the words of Jim Walsh, a research fellow in science and international affairs at Harvard, "missile defense is more missile than defense."[40]

If BMD were a genuine defensive strategy, it would be subject to the same problems as China's Great Wall, which stopped neither Mongol nor Manchu invaders, or France's Maginot Line, which was supposed to protect the country from a German invasion but failed spectacularly when the Germans simply went around it. Even in the unlikely event that our BMD proved technologically perfect, its very existence would immediately elicit plans to overwhelm it with more missiles than it had interceptors. But that matters little to those planning for our militarized future. For them, BMD is a reasonable cover for the extensive research program required to "weaponize" space, a good conduit for supplying extensive funding to key defense contractors; and finally, a way to complicate the decision making of any opponent who might threaten to "deter" the United States with a nuclear attack. BMD strategists conjecture that such an enemy would have to wonder whether its threat was credible in the face of missile defenses. As *New York Times* columnist Bill Keller puts it, military theorists "fear that any nation with a few nuclear weapons can do to us what we did to the Soviets—deter us from projecting our vastly superior conventional forces into the world."[41] The fact is, missile defense is not about defense. It is about offense, and it offers ample fuel for a new global nuclear arms race while ironically making the United States considerably less secure.

Not surprisingly, the 1998 commission that developed the plans for the present BMD system was headed by Donald Rumsfeld.[42] One of its members, and a figure who typifies this group, was Paul Wolfowitz, who has a Ph.D. in political science but no experience of either war or the military. Wolfowitz has used his many positions in the Reagan and both Bush administrations to push for ever-greater military supremacy over all rivals, including our Cold War allies. In 1992, he argued that the objective of foreign policy should be "to prevent any hostile power from dominating a region whose resources would, under consolidated control, be sufficient to generate global power." These regions, he suggested, included Western Europe, East Asia, the territory of the former Soviet Union, and the Middle East—Africa and Latin America (which we already controlled) excepted, essentially the world. Just before returning to the Pentagon in 2001 as Rumsfeld's deputy, Wolfowitz asserted that his earlier insistence on the need to establish a Pax Americana, although heavily criticized at the time, had become mainstream strategic thought.[43]

Nowhere is this need more strongly felt (and yet more strenuously denied) than vis-à-vis China. Supporters of BMD insist that the system is in no way aimed at China. "We don't think that they should really be concerned about missile defense," commented John Bolton, undersecretary of state for arms control and international security affairs. "It's not directed against them. After all it is defensive."[44] But defensive is precisely what it is not, and the status of Taiwan is at the heart of the BMD plan.

Since the Chinese civil war (1946–49) and the 1950 intervention of Chinese troops in the Korean War, the right wing of the Republican Party has never been able to accept that our wartime ally, Chiang Kai-shek's Kuomintang (Nationalist Party), was defeated by the Communists owing to its hopeless corruption and incompetence. After Chiang retreated with the remnants of his forces to the offshore island of Taiwan, the "China Lobby" pushed for the United States to defend him. It did so until 1971, when a majority vote by the United Nations General Assembly finally dislodged Taiwan from the seat reserved for China in the United Nations Charter. Even after the Carter administration belatedly recognized China in 1978, it continued to arm Taiwan. Congressional supporters of Taiwan have done everything in their power to commit the country to defending Taiwan militarily, even were it to invite Chinese military action by unilaterally declaring its independence.

Throughout the 1990s, official Washington reverberated with anti-Chinese statements, actions, and provocations. These included a May 25, 1999, report of the House Select Committee on U.S. National Security and Military/Commercial Concerns with the People's Republic of China, headed by Representative Christopher Cox (R-California). The Cox Report asserted that espionage had enabled China to achieve a nuclear weapons capacity "on a par" with that of the United States. At the time, China had roughly twenty old, liquid-fueled, single-warhead intercontinental-range missiles, whereas the United States had about 7,150 strategic warheads deliverable against China via missiles, submarines, and bombers. The hysteria the Cox Report generated, however, contributed to a governmental witch-hunt against Wen-ho Lee, an American computer researcher of Taiwanese ancestry at the Los Alamos Nuclear Weapons Laboratory. Lee was accused of being a spy for mainland China and was freed after 277 days of brutal solitary confinement only when a federal judge threw out the government's case and denounced the FBI and the Justice Department for harassing Lee, probably because the officials in charge of the case were racists.[45]

In 2001, with the advent of the latest Bush administration, the Pentagon shifted much of its nuclear targeting from Russia to China. It also began regular high-level military talks with Taiwan over defense of the island, ordered a shift of army personnel and supplies to the Asia-Pacific region, and worked strenuously to promote the remilitarization of Japan. On April 1, 2001, a U.S. Navy EP-3E Aries II electronic spy plane collided with a Chinese fighter off Hainan Island. The American aircraft was on a mission to provoke Chinese radar defenses and then record the transmissions and procedures the Chinese used in sending up interceptors.[46] These flights were ordered by the commander in chief in the Pacific, one of the United States's increasingly independent military proconsuls who are the de facto authors of foreign policy in their regions. While the Chinese jet went down and the pilot lost his life, the American plane landed safely on Hainan Island, and its crew of twenty-four spies were well treated by the Chinese authorities.

It soon became clear that China, after the United States and Britain now the third-largest recipient of direct foreign investment, was not interested in a confrontation. Many of its most important investors have their headquarters in the United States. But it could not instantly return the crew of the spy plane without risking powerful domestic criticism of obsequiousness in the face of provocation. It therefore delayed eleven days, until it received a pro forma American apology for causing the death of a Chinese pilot on the edge of China's territorial air space and for making an unauthorized landing at a Chinese military airfield. Meanwhile, our media promptly labeled the crew "hostages," encouraged their relatives to tie yellow ribbons around neighborhood trees, claimed that the president was doing "a first-rate job," and endlessly criticized China for its "state-controlled media." Washington carefully avoided mentioning that the United States enforces a 200-mile aircraft-intercept zone around the country, which stretches far beyond territorial waters.

On April 25, 2001, during an interview on national television, President Bush was asked whether he would ever use "the full force of the American military" against China for the sake of Taiwan. He responded, "Whatever it takes to help Taiwan defend herself." Some American militarists argue that a missile defense would make this commitment credible by protecting American cities from any Chinese retaliatory attack. After 9/11, as America became preoccupied with al-Qaeda, Afghanistan, and Iraq, China temporarily disappeared from the Pentagon's radar screen. But during 2002–03 the issue of nuclear deterrence arose again in East Asia, not with reference to China but to North Korea.

The diehards of the Republican Party who have never been able to accept that China is not and never will be an American satellite have even greater trouble accepting a small, poverty-stricken, but resolutely defiant regime in North Korea. In his State of the Union address of January 29, 2002, the president famously included North Korea on his short list of countries the United States was thinking of preventively "taking out." With the fall of Baghdad in April 2003, the "shock and awe" and bloody slaughter phase of the American "liberation" of Iraq came to an end. Our full armada of B-1, B-2, and B-52 bombers, five carrier task forces in the Persian Gulf, innumerable surface ships and submarines armed with cruise missiles, and the command and control staffs who fought the war from air-conditioned tents in Qatar were released for redeployment. Flushed with success, they may well choose as their next target—if not the Middle East—North Korea. It seems likely that the North Koreans themselves are thinking along these same lines and believe that George Bush plans to order an attack on them. North Korea illustrates the kinds of explosive situations the United States, in its guise as a New Rome, creates for itself.

A little history may be in order. Back in 1994, the United States discovered that the Pyongyang regime was producing plutonium as a by-product of an old Russian-designed reactor for generating electric power. A crisis over the possibility that North Korea might be able to turn out a few atomic bombs was resolved within the year by the oddly titled "Agreed Framework." In return for Pyongyang's pledge to mothball its old reactor and allow inspections by the International Atomic Energy Agency, the United States and its allies promised to build two new reactors that would not produce weapons-grade fissionable material and to open some form of diplomatic and economic relations with the isolated North. The United States also agreed to supply the North with fuel oil to replace the energy lost by shutting down the reactor (since the country has no independent sources of energy of any sort). For three years the Clinton administration stalled on implementing the agreement, hoping that the highly militarized North Korean regime, its people suffering from starvation, would simply collapse.

By the end of the decade this standoff had degenerated into stalemate. In June 2000, the president of South Korea, Kim Dae-jung, acting on his own initiative and without consulting the United States, undertook a historic journey of reconciliation to Pyongyang, trying to eradicate the last vestiges of the Cold War on the Korean peninsula. His visit produced a breakthrough, and for his efforts he received the Nobel Peace Prize. Even more important, President Kim's initiative caught the imagination of his own people, much as Richard Nixon's 1971 opening to China captured the imagination of millions of Americans.

South Korea has a population of forty-seven million, more than twice the North's twenty-one million, and is twenty-five to thirty times richer than its desolate neighbor. The South's willingness to help the North reflects a growing democratic and economic self-confidence. It is important to remember that South Korea is one of only three countries in East Asia (the others being the Philippines and Taiwan) to have achieved democracy from below. In South Korea and the Philippines, mass movements fought against oppressive dictators imposed and supported by the United States—General Chun Doo-hwan in Seoul and Ferdinand Marcos in Manila.

During 2000, relations between North and South Korea continued to improve, leading to an October visit to Pyongyang by Secretary of State Madeleine Albright. In the early days of the Bush administration, however, these favorable trends in Korea and in Washington came to a halt. On a visit to Washington in March 2001, Kim Dae-jung was rudely brushed off by Bush; the administration began to include North Korea in its increasingly bellicose statements.

In September 2002, when the Bush administration asserted in its National Security Strategy a right to wage "preventive war," this rhetoric gained an almost immediate reality for North Korean leader Kim Jong-il. As the United States began mobilizing a powerful invasion force on the borders of Iraq and then invaded, North Korea prepared to defend itself in the only way it thought the Americans could understand. It withdrew from the Nuclear Nonproliferation Treaty, expelled international inspectors, and restarted its old power reactor.

At first, the Bush administration's response was muted. It was already launching one war. Another in Korea would have threatened the South Korean capital, Seoul, a city of 10.8 million within easy artillery range of the North. Among them were thousands of American troops stationed for decades near the demilitarized zone between the two Koreas as a "tripwire" against an attack from the North. This was meant to ensure, among other things, that, as the first casualties came in, the American people would have no choice but to back the war.

On the other hand, the men (and woman) of the Bush administration made no effort to back down from or soften their positions or offer to negotiate. Kim Jong-il's regime thus reached the almost unavoidable conclusion that it was likely to be the next victim of a bully and began trying to "deter" the Americans. It insisted on a nonaggression treaty with the United States in return for shutting down its dangerous reactor and halting its nuclear weapons development program. At the same time, it offered to allow the expelled inspectors from the International Atomic Energy Agency to return to monitor its nuclear facilities.

After the United States invaded Iraq, North Korea pulled back from even this offer. On April 6, 2003, it announced that only by arming itself with a "tremendous military deterrent" could it guarantee its security. "The Iraqi war shows that to allow disarming through inspection does not help avert a war but rather sparks it. . . . This suggests that even the signing of a nonaggression treaty with the U.S. would not help avert a war." Much like Winston Churchill during the Battle of Britain, North Korea was now telling its citizens, "If you've got to go, take one with you." The places it threatened to take with it were Seoul, some of the thirty-eight American bases on Okinawa, and as many Japanese cities as it could hit (though its nuclear-tipped missiles may not have the capability to reach as far as either Okinawa or the Japanese mainland). The South Koreans estimate that the North possesses 175 to 200 Rodong missiles with a range of 1,300 kilometers, capable of striking anywhere in Japan, and 650 to 800 intermediate-range Scud missiles targeted on South Korea and stored in underground facilities.[47]

Over the previous two years, South Korean public opinion had shifted radically on the issue of North Korea. The prosperous and well-informed people of the South know that their fellow Koreans—hungry, desperate, oppressed, but well armed—are trapped by the ironies of the end of the Cold War and by the harshness of the Kim Jong-il regime but are also being pushed into an exceedingly dangerous corner by the Americans in their newly proclaimed role as the reigning global military colossus. The South no longer much fears the North—at least a North not pushed to extreme acts by Washington. It fears instead the enthusiasm for war emanating from Washington and the constant problems generated by the American troops based in South Korea over the past fifty years.

Here, too, some history is needed of this peninsula where the past is seldom forgotten. Ever since the United States occupied the southern half of it in 1945 and created the "Republic of Korea," it has maintained a strong military presence there. During 2002, the Department of Defense listed among its properties and personnel in South Korea 101 separate military installations manned by 37,605 American troops, 2,875 U.S. civilians working for the military, and 7,027 resident American dependents.[48] The installations include Osan Air Base, known as K-55 during the Korean War, which is the headquarters of the Seventh Air Force, and

Kunsan Air Base on the west coast of the country, which is the main fighter base. Easily the most astonishing facility in South Korea, however, is the Yongsan Army Garrison. A monument to American cultural and historical insensitivity, it is located on the site of Japan's old military headquarters, created in 1894 and a symbol of Japan's hated occupation of Korea. Originally on the outskirts of old Seoul, it occupies 630 prime acres squarely in the center of the densely populated capital. It has been the headquarters for American military operations in Korea since 1945.[49]

Today, Yongsan features the Dragon Hill Recreation Center, "the largest exchange in Korea with shopping arcade," including half a dozen bars and restaurants, a state-of-the-art hotel (with different room rates for different ranks), a fitness center, and numerous other amenities. Dragon Hill is a vacation resort for American officers, servicemen and women, and their families located smack in downtown Seoul, and it is not open to Koreans. This facility has so irritated the Koreans that on April 9, 2003, the United States agreed to move it to some other location, probably to another base located in a remote area. It remains to be seen how expeditiously the U.S. Forces Korea command will actually implement this agreement.

Just forty miles north of the South Korean capital and twelve miles south of the Demilitarized Zone is Camp Casey, the most powerful, forward-deployed location of the army's Second Infantry Division. It houses more than 6,300 troops, a large proportion of the American military personnel in Korea. Casey is a 19,000-acre domain of brick buildings and Quonset hut–like sheds that resembles nothing so much as a penitentiary. Private Kenneth Markle, easily the most notorious American in South Korea because in 1993 he raped and murdered a Korean woman, Kum E. Yoon, was based there. The strangling in 1996 of Lee Ki Sun, another Korean woman, over an argument about paying for sex, by Private Eric Munnich, a twenty-two-year-old soldier, took place in the nearby village of Tongduchon.

On June 13, 2002, a sixty-ton army tracked vehicle from Camp Casey rumbled down a narrow two-lane road through small villages a few miles north of Seoul. The two sergeants manning the vehicle failed to see two thirteen-year-old schoolgirls walking along the road on their way to a friend's birthday party. Both girls were crushed to death. It is not clear whether the two soldiers were operating the vehicle as part of their official duties, whether they failed to see the girls because of equipment faultily mounted on their vehicle, or whether the vehicle's internal communications system malfunctioned or just had not been plugged in properly.

The Korean government demanded that the sergeants be handed over to them to be tried in a Korean court for manslaughter. The United States refused, claiming that right under a status of forces agreement (SOFA) it forced on the country during the Korean War. Instead the men were tried in an American military court for "criminal negligence" and exonerated for the "accidental" deaths. No real prosecution evidence was introduced at the trial, and the men's commanding officer, who was in Korea, was never called to testify on the soldiers' training and supervision. Anti-American riots erupted throughout the South, first calling for the SOFA to be revised and later demanding that American forces get out of the country altogether.[50]

On December 19, 2002, South Korea elected Roh Moo-hyun, a human rights lawyer, to succeed Kim Dae-jung as president. In his campaign, Roh pledged to continue Kim's opening to the North and asked for changes in South Korea's military relations with the United States. His incoming administration is said to have told Bush that South Korea would rather live with a nuclear North than join the United States in another war. On April 9, the day Baghdad fell, the Pentagon and the Roh government entered into negotiations over the future of U.S. forces in the Republic of Korea, and the American delegation suddenly showed extraordinary impatience to move the Second Infantry Division back from the Demilitarized Zone as quickly as possible. One source quoted Admiral Thomas B. Fargo, head of the Pacific Command, as saying, "I'd like to be out yesterday."[51]

As it was no doubt meant to do, the American plan threw fear into both the official South and the southern public. The concern among the Republic of Korea's citizens was that such a sudden redeployment of U.S. troops out of harm's way would not only look to the North like preparations for a preemptive strike but might actually prove to be so. Equally ominous, the Bush administration sent B-1 and B-52 strategic bombers to Guam "in case they might be needed in Korea" and later announced that an undisclosed number of F-117 stealth fighter jets and F-15E Strike Eagles deployed to South Korea for recently concluded military exercises would remain in the country. The radar-evading F-117s would be highly suitable for attacking a broad variety of targets in the North, including the nuclear plant at Yongbyon. The last time F-117s were based in South Korea was in 1994, when the Clinton administration was also contemplating a "surgical strike" on the North. That crisis ended peacefully only when former President Jimmy Carter went to Pyongyang and opened direct negotiations with Kim Il-sung.

As might be expected, the Bush administration sees these developments on the Korean Peninsula as further evidence of the need for a ballistic missile defense—to protect against future nuclear-tipped North Korean Taepodong II missiles. But, in fact, even if such a system succeeded in shooting down a North Korean nuclear warhead, the fallout over South Korea or perhaps Japan and Okinawa might be almost as hazardous as a direct hit. The most serious outcome of this American-generated crisis has been to give great impetus to nuclear proliferation around the world. Smaller nations everywhere now believe that the only way to deter the United States from exercising its imperial will over them is to acquire a nuclear capability.[52] Iraq's problem, from this perspective, was that it really did not have any weapons of mass destruction.

North Korea remains a failed Communist regime with much of its population on the edge of starvation. It has been attempting, fitfully and with great trepidation, to come in from the cold in somewhat the same way China has so successfully over the past twenty years. As Kim Dae-jung understood, the United States and South Korea should be magnanimous winners instead of threatening a renewed use of force. No surrounding nation—not the Republic of Korea, or Japan, or China, or Russia—wants, or sees the need for, a renewed civil war on the Korean Peninsula.

The Bush administration is trying to soothe the South Koreans' fears about a preventive war with talk of America's "precision-guided missiles," its commitment to avoiding civilian casualties, its superbly trained fighting forces, and its conviction that the North Koreans who survive our bombers will hail the Americans and South Koreans as liberators. But the South Koreans know better and are unlikely to go along with American ideas about the need for a preventive war. One certain legacy of the war in Iraq is that American political and military leaders can no longer be believed or trusted.

4

THE INSTITUTIONS OF
AMERICAN MILITARISM

I learned, for example, the secret that contrary to all public declarations, President Eisenhower had delegated to major theater commanders the authority to initiate nuclear attacks under certain circumstances, such as outage of communications with Washington—an almost daily occurrence in those days—or presidential incapacitation (twice suffered by President Eisenhower). This delegation was unknown to President Kennedy's assistant for national security, McGeorge Bundy—and thus to the president—in early 1961, after nearly a month in office, when I briefed him on the issue. Kennedy secretly continued the authorization, as did President Johnson.

DANIEL ELLSBERG,
Secrets (2002)

The army's target for 2002 was to hire 79,500 young adults as new recruits. Demographics and salesmanship matter in trying to raise and retain an all-volunteer army, and, until recently, the main recruiting slogans were "Be all you can be" and "An Army of one" (meaning that the army is a collection of quintessential American individualists). A recent gimmick is a free computer game, called *America's Army,* aimed directly at capturing the hearts and minds of technology-savvy teenagers. By the autumn of 2002, more than 500,000 copies had been downloaded from americasarmy.com, and recruiters now have a two-CD set of the game to give away to likely prospects. During the summer of 2002, many video-game magazines included the CDs with issues.

The game differs from most other combat videos now on the market in that bullet hits are recorded only by little red puffs instead of gushers of blood and flying body parts. The army wants to avoid any suggestion that actual combat might be unpleasant. According to the game instructions, "When a soldier is killed, that soldier simply falls to the ground and is no longer part of the ongoing mission. The game does not include any dismemberment or disfigurement." In "Soldiers," the second part of the game, players progress through a virtual career in the army, serving in a variety of units and improving their ratings in categories like loyalty, honor, and personal courage as they go. Enemies are portrayed as both white- and black-skinned but have one trait in common—nearly all of them are unshaven. The government has so far spent $7.6 million to develop the game, and plans to devote about $2.5 million a year to updates and another $1.5 million to maintaining a multiplayer infrastructure. The army hoped to use it to attract 300 to 400 recruits in 2003.[1]

Another aspect of the attempt to interest adolescent boys in a military career is the army's sponsorship of drag racing. Its twenty-four-foot, 6,000 horsepower dragster "The Sarge" is fueled with nitromethane at thirty dollars a gallon and has emblazoned in gold on its side, "GO ARMY." Anyone who has been to an auto speedway and seen (or heard) the car accelerate from 0 to 200 m.p.h. in 2.2 seconds will appreciate the mechanical machismo the army is using to attract young recruits. In the 1970s, the army had sponsored racing cars with its name on them but gave the effort up as a waste of money. In 1999, it began a new collaboration with the National Hot Rod Association, this time to enter its own car and to install recruiting booths at the racetracks with helicopters and assault vehicles for boys to climb on. In the 2002 season, to compete at twenty-three drag racing events, the army's recruiting command invested about $5.5 million. All the drivers are professionals, though few are veterans of the armed forces. High schools around the country are encouraged to take their pupils out for a "day at the track." In 2001, of some 56,000 young people who were sent to a drag race by their schools, 300 joined the army.[2] One thing that does seem to work in attracting recruits is the military's offer of up to $50,000 in grants to attend college, although few who enlist end up taking advantage of this program.

Video games and hot rods are both very American examples of the art of advertising, but they seem unlikely to change the composition of the armed forces very much. Race, socioeconomic class, and the state of the U.S. economy, as well as the possibility of an upcoming war, influence the decision to sign up, and women do not respond to video games or dragsters in the same way that men do. During the run-up to the second U.S. war with Iraq, military recruiters noted that virtually no one was joining up to serve the nation in an actual war.

A real deterrent to recruitment is the possibility that a new soldier will find himself or herself in combat. Roughly four out of five young Americans who enlist in our all-volunteer armed forces specifically choose non-combat jobs, becoming computer technicians, personnel managers, shipping clerks, truck mechanics, weather forecasters, intelligence analysts, cooks, forklift drivers—all jobs that carry a low risk of contact with an enemy. They often enlist because of a lack of good jobs in the civilian economy and thus take refuge in the military's long-established system of state socialism—steady paychecks, decent housing, medical and dental benefits, job training, and the promise of a college education. The mother of one such recruit recently commented on her nineteen-year-old daughter, who was soon to become an army intelligence analyst. She was proud but also cynical: "Wealthy people don't go into the military or take risks because why should they? They already got everything handed to them."[3]

These recruits do not expect to be shot at. Thus it must have been a shock to the noncombat rank and file when in March 2003 Iraqi guns opened up on an army supply convoy, killing eleven and taking another six prisoner, including Private First Class Jessica Lynch of Palestine, West Virginia, a supply clerk. The army's response has been, "You don't have to be in combat arms [of the military] to close with and kill the enemy." Despite her high-profile story, Jessica Lynch is still the exception to the rule. It is rare for noncombat military personnel to find themselves in a firefight. But that hardly means that soldiers doing noncombat duty are not at risk. What the Pentagon is not saying to the Private Lynches and their families is that all soldiers, regardless of their duties, stand a real chance of injury or death because they chose the military as a route of social mobility.

Our recent wars have produced serious unintended consequences, and these have fallen nearly as heavily on noncombat soldiers as on their frontline compatriots. The most important factor in that casualty rate is the malady that goes by the name Gulf War Syndrome, a potentially deadly medical disorder that first appeared among combat veterans of the 1990–91 conflict with Iraq. Just as the effects of Agent Orange during the Vietnam War were first explained away by the Pentagon as "posttraumatic stress disorder," "combat fatigue," or "shell shock," so the potential toxic side effects of the ammunition now widely used by the armed forces have been played down by the Bush administration. The implications are devastating, not just for America's adversaries or civilians caught in their country turned battlefield but for American forces themselves (and even possibly their future offspring).

The first Iraq war produced four classes of casualties—killed in action, wounded in action, killed in accidents (including "friendly fire"), and injuries and illnesses that appeared only after the end of hostilities. During 1990 and 1991, some 696,778 individuals served in the Persian Gulf as elements of Operation Desert Shield and Operation Desert Storm. Of these, 148 were killed in battle, 467 were wounded in action, and 145 were killed in accidents, producing a total of 760 casualties, quite a low number given the scale of the operations. As of May 2002, however, the Veterans Administration reported that an additional 8,306 soldiers had died and 159,705 were injured or ill as a result of service-connected "exposures" suffered during the war. Even more alarmingly, the VA revealed that 206,861 veterans, almost a third of General Norman Schwarzkopf's entire army, had filed claims for medical care, compensation, and pension benefits based on injuries and illnesses caused by combat in 1991. After reviewing the cases, the agency has classified 168,011 applicants as "disabled veterans." In light of these deaths and disabilities, the casualty rate for the first Gulf War may actually be a staggering 29.3 percent.

Doug Rokke, a former army colonel and a professor of environmental science at Jacksonville University, was in charge of the military's environmental cleanup following the first Gulf War. The Pentagon has since sacked him for criticizing NATO commanders for not adequately protecting their troops in areas where ammunition made from depleted uranium (DU) was used, such as Kosovo in 1999. Rokke observes that many thousands of U.S. troops have been based in and around Kuwait since

1990, and their exposure to DU seems to produce a higher figure than the VA's. He notes that between August 1990 and May 2002, a total of 262,586 soldiers became "disabled veterans" and 10,617 died. His numbers result in a casualty rate for the whole decade of 30.8 percent.[4]

The suggestion that DU munitions are a significant factor in these deaths and disabilities is a hotly contested proposition. Some researchers, often paid for by the Pentagon, argue that depleted uranium could not possibly be the cause of these war-related maladies and that a more likely explanation is dust and debris from the blowing up of Saddam Hussein's chemical and biological weapons factories in 1991, or perhaps a "cocktail" of volatile particles from DU ammunition, the destruction of nerve gas bunkers, and polluted air from burning oil fields. But the evidence— including abnormal clusters of childhood cancers and deformities in Iraq and also in the areas of Kosovo where we used depleted-uranium weapons in our 1999 air war—point toward a significant role for DU. Moreover, simply by insisting on using such weaponry, the military is deliberately flouting a 1996 United Nations resolution that classifies DU ammunition as an illegal weapon of mass destruction.

Depleted uranium, or uranium-238, is a waste product of power-generating nuclear reactors. It is used in projectiles like tank shells and cruise missiles because it is 1.7 times denser than lead, burns as it flies, and penetrates armor easily, but it breaks up and vaporizes on impact— which makes it potentially deadly in unexpected ways. Each shell fired by an American tank includes between three and ten pounds of DU. Such warheads are essentially "dirty bombs," not especially radioactive individually but suspected of being capable in quantity of causing serious illnesses and even birth defects. In 1991, American forces fired a staggering 944,000 DU rounds in Kuwait and Iraq. The Pentagon admits that it left behind at a bare minimum 320 metric tons of DU on the battlefield. One study of Gulf War veterans showed that their children had a higher possibility of being born with severe deformities, including missing eyes, blood infections, respiratory problems, and fused fingers. Rokke fears that because the military relied on DU munitions more heavily in the second Iraq war than in the first, postwar casualties may be even greater. When he saw TV images of unprotected soldiers and Iraqi civilians driving past burning Iraqi trucks destroyed by tank fire or inspecting buildings hit by missiles, he suspected that they were being poisoned by DU.[5]

Young Americans being seduced into the armed forces these days may thus quite literally be making themselves into "cannon fodder," even if they have been able to secure noncombat jobs. These men and women comprise an ethnically heterogeneous group that nonetheless differs, in several important respects, from the population from which it is drawn. Because membership in the armed forces is entirely voluntary, they are no longer in any sense a citizen army, even though the Pentagon pretends otherwise. The contemporary military bears almost no relation to the armies that fought in World War II, Korea, and Vietnam—all made up of conscripts. Nor do our forces resemble armies that are based on a universal obligation to defend the country, as, for example, the Israeli army, from which only the religiously devout are exempt. Because today's soldiers and sailors know that they constitute a special stratum of society, they tend to think of themselves increasingly in distinct, corporate terms—an aspect of militarism—and not as people who expect soon to return to civilian life. Since the military also makes exit easy for those who sign up but find they do not like life in the armed forces, the special subculture of barracks and ships only solidifies further. During 2002, the army was losing 13.7 percent of all recruits during training.

According to the twenty-sixth annual Department of Defense report on "Population Representation in the Military Services," covering fiscal year 1999, the most recent report available, the full-time active-duty military numbered just under 1.4 million.[6] In addition, active reserves—made up of the Army National Guard, the Army Reserve, the Naval Reserve, the Marine Corps Reserve, the Air National Guard, and the Air Force Reserve—totaled just under 871,000. There were also more than 405,000 men and women in the inactive reserve and the inactive National Guard. In fiscal 1999, all the services took in approximately 184,000 new recruits, and nearly 6,000 prior-service members returned to the active-duty ranks. More than 16,000 newly commissioned officers reported for active duty. Also in 1999, about 55,000 recruits without and more than 88,000 with prior military experience enlisted in the reserves. In excess of 17,000 officers entered the National Guard or other active reserve units.

The active-duty military is, of course, much younger than the overall civilian population. Almost half of those in the active-duty enlisted force were seventeen to twenty-four years old, in contrast to about 15 percent of the civilian labor force. Officers were older than those in the enlisted ranks (with a mean age of thirty-four), but they too were younger than their civilian counterparts—college graduates whose mean age was thirty-six. This means that the Americans with whom foreigners come into contact most frequently tend to be late adolescents or twenty-year-old youths, almost totally ignorant of foreign cultures and languages but indoctrinated to think that they represent a nation that President George W. Bush has called "the greatest force for good in history."

In terms of race and ethnicity, African Americans are overrepresented among enlisted ranks. Some 20 percent of 1999 recruits to active duty were African Americans, who constitute 12.71 percent of the nation's civilian workforce of military age. African Americans also have higher retention rates in the armed forces, boosting their representation among active enlisted members to 22.5 percent.

Hispanics were underrepresented, making up only 11 percent of new recruits, whereas they constitute 13 percent of the general population. They contributed 9.5 percent of all active-duty enlisted personnel but were overrepresented in combat positions, where they constituted 17.7 percent of the forces who directly handle weapons. Latino underrepresentation can probably be explained by high dropout rates from high school—recruits must be high school graduates or hold an alternative credential—and the fact that many are living in the country illegally. In border cities like San Diego, army recruiters have occasionally crossed into Tijuana to try to sign up young Mexicans with offers of green cards (legal alien residents' certificates) or possible citizenship after a hitch in the army.[7] The navy and the Marine Corps generally recruit more Hispanics than the army and the air force. The Marine Corps has the highest retention rate for Hispanics. "Other" minorities (Native Americans, Asians, and Pacific Islanders), slightly more than 5 percent of the civilian population, made up a further 7 percent of enlistees. Thus, in 1999, 38 percent of the total active-duty enlisted force were people of color (22 percent African American, 9 percent Hispanic, and 7 percent other).

Among officers the percentages were different. Almost 9 percent of newly commissioned officers were African American, 4 percent Hispanic, and 9 percent other. Within the active-duty officer corps, 8 percent were African Americans, 4 percent Hispanics, and 5 percent other. African Americans thus constituted a much smaller proportion of officers than of enlisted men and women. The same pattern holds for the reserves. All three service academies, West Point for army officers, Annapolis for naval and marine officers, and Colorado Springs for air force officers, implement explicit race-preference policies in their admissions. West Point maintains specific percentage goals. It seeks an entering class of 10 to 12 percent African Americans and normally gets 7 to 9 percent. All three academies actively recruit racial minorities, sending promising but under-qualified candidates to one-year preparatory schools before admitting them. (These policies directly contradict those of the Bush administration, which on January 15, 2003, announced its opposition to the University of Michigan Law School's employment of "affirmative action" to produce a "diverse" student body.)

The military defends its use of race in admissions on the grounds that since 28 percent of air force enlisted personnel and 44 percent of army enlisted personnel are racial minorities, an all-white officer corps would hurt morale, a possibility that also brings to mind fears of the "fraggings" of the Vietnam War era, when enlisted men conscripted into a war they did not support sometimes lobbed or rolled grenades into officers' quarters.[8] In many of the 209 reported fragging incidents in Vietnam, the men who tossed grenades or shot their officers were African Americans and the targets of the attacks were mostly white junior field officers. Racism in the armed forces was clearly a contributing cause. In a January 2003 background briefing at the Pentagon on the all-volunteer force, the issue of fragging came up. "Not a pretty picture," commented the senior defense official who gave the briefing. There was at least one fragging incident, on March 23, during the subsequent war in Iraq.[9]

In 1999, women made up 18 percent of new recruits and 24 percent of new members of the active reserve. Among all enlisted personnel on active duty, 14 percent were women. Some 20 percent of new officers were women, who constitute 15 percent of the overall officer corps. Most significantly, military women, whether in the enlisted ranks, the officer corps, on active duty, or in the active reserve, are more likely to be members of racial or ethnic minority groups than military men. Half the enlisted women in the U.S. armed forces are members of minority groups. African American women made up 35.3 percent of the women in the enlisted force.

Sexual assault remains a pervasive problem for women serving in all branches of the armed forces, including those deployed overseas. According to a report in the *American Journal of Industrial Medicine,* 28 percent of female veterans reported sexual assaults during their careers—MSTs, or "military sexual traumas," as they are called in the Pentagon and Veterans Administration offices. In 1996, the Defense Department surveyed women in the military about their experiences during the previous twelve months, and found that 9 percent in the marines, 8 percent in the army, 6 percent in the navy, and 4 percent in the air force had experienced a rape or an attempted rape that year. Since about 200,000 women serve in the military, these numbers would represent about 14,000 sexual assaults or attempted assaults each year. Few of these, however, are reported. According to the Department of Defense, only twenty-four cases of sexual assault were actually reported during the buildup to and carrying out of the first Persian Gulf War.

Marie Tessier, an authority on violence against women, writes, "The entire military criminal justice system is worlds apart from the civilian world. . . . The most important difference is that decisions about investigation and prosecution are made within the chain of command, not by an adversarial outside agency like a prosecutor's office. This leaves commanders with an inherent conflict of interest."[10] A rape scandal at the Air Force Academy that burst into the open in 2003 exposed just these issues. The air force disclosed to Congress fifty-four reports of rape or other sexual assaults that had occurred there over the previous decade, but Air Force Secretary James G. Roche testified, "There's probably another hundred that we've not seen."[11] The director of the local civilian rape-counseling center said that the most consistent complaint of cadet women coming into the center was their fear that academy officers and investigators would violate their confidentiality. The issue of consent to a sexual encounter is also more complicated in the military than in civilian life because of hierarchy. Both male and female service personnel are indoctrinated to obey the orders of a superior officer or upperclassman.

Today a slight majority of soldiers, sailors, marines, and airmen are married, up from about 40 percent in 1973. Men are more likely to be married than women. In terms of education, the Department of Defense reports that 1999 recruits had a mean reading ability at an eleventh-grade level, whereas the mean for civilian youths in the same age range was tenth grade. The South, in particular the South Atlantic and West South Central states (Texas, Arkansas, Louisiana), had the greatest geographical representation. More than two-fifths of new recruits came from this area. Both the Northeast and North Central regions were underrepresented, while recruits from the West were approximately equal to the percentage of eighteen-to-twenty-four-year-olds in that region's population. Based on a survey of parents' education, employment status, occupation, and home ownership, the 1999 data also showed that both active and reserve recruits came primarily from families in the middle and lower-middle socioeconomic strata. As the report concludes, "Although the force is diverse, it is not an exact replica of the society as a whole. The military way of life is more attractive to some members of society than to others."

The military is founded on the ideals of patriotism, defense of the nation, and loyalty to an abstract set of values often called the "American way of life." Most of its members, however, are motivated by defense-establishment careerism, the possibility of using the military as a way out of racial and economic ghettoes, and a fascination, often media-inspired, with military technology. Young African Americans join the military in large numbers in part to escape from inner-city racial ghettoes and employment in the "informal economy," which frequently leads to prison time. Almost none enlist primarily out of patriotic or public-service motives. In conversation after conversation with journalists, youthful soldiers and sailors referred to the problems of high civilian unemployment, made worse by the shift of entry-level manufacturing jobs abroad and the likelihood of a clash with the law if they tried to make it on their own. One said that if he had not joined the navy, "I would only have ended up in prison."[12] "Probably if I hadn't joined the Army," said a nineteen-year-old woman, "I would be doing the same thing most of my friends are doing, which is working fast food."[13]

Investigative reporter Kevin Heldman, who in 1997 interviewed troops at Camp Casey, twelve miles from the Demilitarized Zone in South Korea, quotes a soldier who was baited by his sergeant for not wanting to reenlist: "What are you going to do when you get out, go work at McDonald's?" The soldier replied, "When I get out, if I am flipping burgers at McDonald's at least I'd be wearing a uniform I was proud of."[14] The case of twenty-three-year-old Private Michael Waldron is typical. He told Heldman he joined the army because "when I got out of high school jobs sucked." He served for two years and extended for six months during the first Gulf War. He left the army, joined the National Guard, married, and lived in a trailer in Georgia, where he worked in construction, roofing, and aluminum siding. He divorced his wife, his car broke down, he failed a police-officer test, moved back in with his parents, and after being off active duty for two years, reenlisted. It is worth noting that many recruits, like Waldron, claim they joined the army as a way of eventually becoming police officers. In many cities, applicants for the police force are allowed to substitute two years of military service for required college credits.

Crime and racism are ubiquitous in the military. Although the military invariably tries to portray all reported criminal or racial incidents as unique events, perpetrated by an infinitesimally small number of "bad apples" and with officers taking determined remedial action, a different reality is apparent at military bases around the globe. Heldman enumerates the best-known cases from the mid-1990s: "Soldiers with white supremacist ties are arrested for killing a Black couple in North Carolina; a soldier is sentenced to death for opening fire on a formation, killing one and injuring eighteen, explaining, 'I wanted to send a message to the chain of command that had forgotten the welfare of the common soldier;' ten Black soldiers at Fort Bragg beat a white GI into a coma off post; a soldier at Fort Campbell [Kentucky] rammed his vehicle into a crowd of fighting soldiers and civilians, killing two people; two soldiers are shot dead, one injured, at Fort Riley, Kansas, the second double homicide at the base in less than a year; fourteen service members are arrested for smuggling cocaine and heroin; twenty-three women working at Fort Bliss [Texas] file a class-action complaint charging that they have been harassed to pose nude or perform sexual acts; in Japan, a service member is accused of exposing himself to a sixth-grade girl; four others are sentenced for raping a fourteen-year-old girl; another service member is arrested for slashing the throat of a Japanese woman and stealing her purse; two marines are arrested for assaulting and robbing another 56-year-old Japanese woman; and a twelve-year-old girl in Okinawa is raped by three servicemen, inciting a protest of more than 50,000 people."[15] In South Korea alone during 1996, there were 861 reported offenses committed by American service members involving Korean civilians.

Only rarely do such incidents make it into the mainstream American press. During the summer of 2002, however, Americans were disturbed to read that within the space of six weeks four elite Special Forces and Delta Force soldiers based at Fort Bragg, North Carolina, murdered their wives. In a fifth murder a Fort Bragg wife managed to shoot her husband, also a member of the Special Forces, first, while he slept. Three of the soldiers had recently returned from service in Afghanistan, leading *U.S. News & World Report* to wonder whether the training of the Special Forces could possibly "prime men for homicide." In the end, it concluded that there simply was no explanation for the murders beyond "the complicated alchemy of military service and the sad mysteries of marriages gone desperately wrong."[16]

According to one 1999 report, the rate of incidents of domestic violence in the military rose from 18.6 per thousand soldiers in 1990 to 25.6 in 1996. During the same period, such incidents within the overall population were actually on the decline. Some studies suggest that the rate of domestic violence in the military is two to five times higher than among civilians.[17] It seems likely that the Fort Bragg killers' experiences in Afghanistan had some effect on their inclination toward violence. Shortly after the murders, *Newsweek* reported in detail on Special Forces and Eighty-second Airborne troops in Afghanistan behaving toward unarmed Afghan civilians in an extremely brutal manner. For example, the soldiers took turns photographing one another holding a rifle to the head of an old Afghan man as he begged for his life on his knees. One report said that the soldiers of the Eighty-second Airborne were so indisciplined that they undid "in minutes six months of community building."[18]

The military is aware of the problem. The Marine Corps canceled its 2002 annual meeting of snipers, to be held at its Quantico, Virginia, base at the end of October, because the entire District of Columbia area was then being stalked by a sniper, who turned out to be an army-trained marksman.[19] During the same month, on the other side of the country, another sniper, a Gulf War veteran who had served eleven years on active duty and had received training in an elite Ranger unit, shot and killed three nursing instructors on the campus of the University of Arizona.[20]

In September 2002, the navy made public a significant series of incidents involving the aircraft carrier USS *Kitty Hawk*, which has its home port at the Yokosuka naval base south of Tokyo, Japan, and served in the Arabian Sea in 2001–02 during the initial assault on Afghanistan. In August 2002, the carrier returned to Japan, where a series of crimes committed by its crew members led to the sacking of the captain for losing control of his ship and its personnel. On August 11, a petty officer assaulted and robbed a sixty-eight-year-old Japanese man and was arrested by the Yokosuka police at the gates of the naval base. Two days later, a nineteen-year-old crew member was arrested for a carjacking after attacking a forty-three-year-old Japanese woman sitting in her automobile at a traffic light. Ten days later, Japanese customs officers arrested a *Kitty Hawk* petty officer as he attempted to smuggle a kilogram of marijuana from Bangkok into Japan through Narita Airport. The publicity in Japan was devastating. Vice Admiral Robert Willard, commander of the U.S. Seventh Fleet, relieved Captain Thomas Hejl and brought in Captain Robert Barabee from a cruiser, the USS *Seattle*, to restore some measure of discipline. (On February 13, 2003, Captain Barabee's superior officer, Rear Admiral Steven Kunkle, head of the Seventh Fleet's Carrier Group Five, organized around the *Kitty Hawk*, was himself relieved of his command for having "an improper relationship with a female naval officer.")

In reporting on the troubled *Kitty Hawk*, two British journalists uncovered institutionalized conditions of racism on the ship similar to those that caused race riots on the same vessel during the Vietnam War.

Roland Watson and Glen Owen wrote of their reactions on visiting the aircraft carrier, "Boarding [the ship] is like entering a time warp back to the former Deep South. In the bowels of the carrier, where the crew are cooped up for six months at a time, manual workers sleep dozens to a room. Most are Black or Puerto Rican, paid $7,000 to $10,000 a year to work in the broiling temperatures of the kitchens and engine rooms. As you move up the eleven segregated levels towards the pilots' quarters beneath the deck, the living quarters become larger, the air cooler, and the skin tones lighter. Officers exist in almost total ignorance of the teeming world beneath them, passing around second-hand tales of murders, gang-fights, and drug abuse. Visitors are banned from venturing down to the lowest decks, which swelter next to the vast nuclear-powered engines. . . . Access to the flight deck, which buzzes with F-14 and F-18 aircraft taking part in exercises, is banned for all except the flight crew."[21] Such situations are commonplace throughout the armed services. In Korea, for example, soldiers have organized their own racial gangs—the NFL ("Niggas for Life") for African Americans, the Wild Ass Cowboys and Silver Star Outlaws for whites, and La Raza for Latinos.[22]

Under these conditions, recruiting and retaining enough people to staff all the outposts and ships of the empire is a full-time job, and the military has become extremely creative in finding ways to lure young men and women into signing up. A standard ploy by recruiters is to obtain the names, addresses, and phone numbers of students in a community's high schools and flood their homes with unsolicited mail, phone calls, prowar videos, and T-shirts emblazoned with slogans. The message is aimed at parents as well as students and stresses the benefits of serving in the armed forces, including possible help toward a college education. When the recruiters get an interview with a prospect, they are obliged to ask whether he or she has ever smoked marijuana. According to many reports, if the student answers yes, they just keep asking the same question until the answer is no and then write that down.[23]

Complaints about harassment by military recruiters in San Diego, California, became so numerous in 1993 that the San Diego Unified School District adopted a policy against releasing student information to recruiters of any kind. From then on, the military mobilized politicians, the chamber of commerce, the superintendent of schools, even the county grand jury to pressure the school board to reverse itself. Yet in those years of "the ban," the Pentagon's message was never absent from the San Diego schools because there are eleven Junior ROTC (Reserve Officer Training Corps) units embedded in the city's high schools that function as permanent on-campus recruiting centers. Finally the military decided to take a national legislative route to force all public high schools to allow recruiters to proselytize under threat of a cutoff of federal funds for education.

In 2000, President Clinton signed a new law promoted by the Pentagon that gave military recruiters the same access to high schools granted to college and business recruiters. This law contained no penalties for refusal, however, and exempted schools wherever an official districtwide policy, as in San Diego, had been adopted restricting military access. To overcome these obstacles, in 2001 the Pentagon engineered an amendment to a new law intended to help disadvantaged students. This amended law, which President Bush called (without apparent irony) his No Child Left Behind Act of 2001, states: "Any secondary school that receives federal funds under this Act shall permit regular United States Armed Services recruitment activities on school grounds, in a manner reasonably accessible to all students of such school." The House of Representatives passed it by a vote of 366-57. The Senate did the same by a voice vote, and on January 8, 2002, President Bush signed it into law. As Representative John Shimkus (R-Illinois) said triumphantly, "No recruiters, no money."[24]

The Pentagon was so pleased by this development that it decided to extend its newly found leverage to the nation's universities and graduate schools, most of which withhold their career placement services from employers that discriminate on the basis of race, sex, religion, national origin, disability, or sexual orientation. Until August 2002, Harvard Law School, for instance, managed to bar recruiters for the Judge Advocate General's Corps of the military because qualified students who wish to serve are rejected if they are openly lesbian, gay, or bisexual. However, the Department of Defense has reinterpreted federal law to say that if any part of a university denies access to military recruiters the entire university will lose all federal funds. Harvard could not afford to risk the loss of $300 million in federal grants and therefore forced its law school to comply. The military says that it will continue to bar openly lesbian, gay, or bisexual lawyers because they allegedly threaten "unit cohesion." As George Fisher, a professor at Stanford Law School, commented, "On the battlefield, this justification is merely improbable; in a JAG Corps law office, it is absurd."[25]

Another aspect of the Pentagon's creative efforts to attract more recruits is its support for pro-war Hollywood films. This is nothing new. The first Hollywood film about aerial combat, made with military advice, personnel, and equipment in return for an advance look at the script and the right to make changes, was *Wings* in 1927. As Lawrence H. Suid, a historian of military films, has written, "*What Price Glory, Wings, Air Force, Sands of Iwo Jima, The Longest Day*, and hundreds of other Hollywood films have created the image of combat as exciting, as a place to prove masculinity, as a place to challenge death in a socially acceptable manner. As a result, until the late 1960s, American war movies have always ended in victory, with our soldiers, sailors, marines, and fliers running faster than their enemy—whether German, Italian, or Japanese. These screen victories reinforced the image of the American military as all-conquering, all-powerful, always right."[26] During and after Vietnam there were some changes—*Patton* (1970) introduced an element of realism into war films and the Pentagon declined to assist *Apocalypse Now*, about one officer in Vietnam sent to kill another, who has gone mad. In the post-Vietnam era, it also did not support films like Demi Moore's *G.I. Jane*, featuring a woman determined to join the all-male SEALs. Soon, however, the old pattern was largely reestablished. Each branch of the military now has a Los Angeles office, and the relationship between producers and Pentagon "project officers" sent on location to watch everything being filmed and offer advice is closer than ever.[27]

A contemporary example of the direct ties between Hollywood and recruiting efforts was Disney Studio's *Pearl Harbor*. The movie premiered on May 21, 2001, with a special showing on the flight deck of the nuclear-powered aircraft carrier USS *John C. Stennis*. Bleachers had been built, a huge screen installed, and the carrier moved (without its aircraft) from its home port in San Diego to Pearl Harbor specifically for this purpose.

The navy and Disney invited more that 2,500 guests to the film's premiere. As the credits reveal, numerous U.S. military commands helped make the movie and in turn extracted changes in the scenario in order to portray the military in a favorable light and promote the idea that service in the armed forces is romantic, patriotic, and fun. According to the *Chicago Tribune,* military recruiters even set up tables in the lobbies of theaters where *Pearl Harbor* was being shown in hopes of catching a few youths on their way out of this three-hour recruiting pitch.[28]

Disney and the Pentagon also worked closely with the media to promote the idea that *Pearl Harbor* recounted the achievements of what the NBC broadcaster Tom Brokaw has called "the Greatest Generation" in his book of that title—as distinct from the Vietnam generation, which the Pentagon would prefer the public to forget. On May 26, 2001, the day after the film opened in theaters, the Disney-owned ABC-TV network ran a one-hour special on the Pearl Harbor attack narrated by David Brinkley, and the next day rival NBC broadcast a two-hour *National Geographic* special on the subject, featuring Tom Brokaw himself. The NBC cable affiliate MSNBC then put on a two-hour program about the survivors of the Pearl Harbor attack narrated by General Norman Schwarzkopf, commander in the Gulf War.[29]

After the September 11 attacks, the Pentagon introduced a short movie advertisement presumably meant to bolster civilian support for the armed forces and designed to be shown before numerous films. Entitled *Enduring Freedom: The Opening Chapter,* the trailer was created by Lieutenant Colonel James Kuhn at a cost of $1.2 million. "Operation Enduring Freedom" was, of course, the title of the military's campaign against Afghanistan. Although some parents objected to attaching the film—which shows scenes of the airplanes ramming New York's World Trade Center—to G-rated children's movies, the public seemed to accept its running with films like *The Four Feathers* or *Sweet Home Alabama.* The military's camera crews shot over 250 hours of footage in making the film—on location with an antiterrorist squad in Kabul, Afghanistan, at the marine base at Twentynine Palms, California, and in the Indian Ocean, Hawaii, Yuma, Arizona, and Norfolk, Virginia. The leftover footage will be made into recruiting commercials and DVDs. In a tie-in with Regal Entertainment Group, the nation's largest theater chain, the Pentagon also planned to show the short before all feature presentations on Regal's 4,000 screens.[30]

Closely related to the Pentagon's film activities are its general public relations operations. These include helping the mass media portray the military in a favorable light, cultivating promilitary civilian groups at public expense, and suppressing information the military does not want Congress or the public to have. As with support for war movies, so the manipulation of the media to whip up pretexts for military action has a long history in the United States. Prowar and anticommunist propaganda has been a constant in public life since the country's entry into World War II. In the 1970s, uniformed and civilian militarists' obsession with closing the Vietnam "credibility gap" spurred a whole new effort. Official lies about military progress during that war and their subsequent exposure by the press caused Pentagon managers to professionalize news management and look for ways to suppress negative aspects of any American military campaign.

"Operation Urgent Fury," the Reagan administration's October 1983 invasion of the small Caribbean island of Grenada, allegedly to rescue some American students, figures prominently in the history of the Pentagon's manipulation of the press. With memories of Vietnam fresh in their minds, Defense Secretary Caspar Weinberger and the commander of the invasion forces, Vice Admiral Joseph W. Metcalf III, banned all reporters from the island. It was the first U.S. conflict from which the media were excluded at the start of military operations. After seizing the island, the military even took a journalist who had been on the island prior to the invasion into custody and transported him to the navy's flagship. More significantly, reporters who tried to get to Grenada independently accused navy aircraft of attacking their boats. The claim by critical reporters that press restraints were designed to hide military embarrassments was almost certainly true given the numerous instances of faulty intelligence, failed communications, and general incompetence during the taking of the largely undefended island.

The invasion force included some 5,000 marines, Army Rangers, and parts of the Eighty-second Airborne Division, plus a navy SEALs team, against an all but nonexistent resistance. On the third day of the five-day campaign, the military allowed a carefully chosen "pool" of reporters to visit Grenada. This was the first use of the pool system, in which a few reporters are grouped together and given an officially escorted tour of the battle area. Until Gulf War II, the pool was the standard way of ensuring that nothing disturbing to the military was reported.

In Afghanistan, the military actually issued laminated cards to all soldiers with instructions on how to deal with journalists. The cards included hypothetical questions and answers, such as "How do you feel about what you're doing in Afghanistan?" Answer: "We're united in our purpose and committed to achieving our goals." "How long do you think that will take?" "We will stay here as long as it takes to get the job done, sir!" To give the feeling of spontaneity, some alternatives were provided. "How do you feel about being here?" "I'm proud to be serving my country, sir. We have a job to do and I'm glad to be part of it." Conversations with reporters at Bagram Air Base near Kabul were so stilted that a BBC journalist finally became suspicious and two GIs showed him their prompt cards.[31]

In preparing for the assault on Iraq in the spring of 2003, the Pentagon invented a new ploy in its unending campaign to control what the public learns and to portray the military in a favorable light. It decided to "embed" (the military's term) some 600 male and female reporters, photographers, and television crews into combat units and allow them to accompany the troops throughout what was expected to be—and largely was—a walkover of a war. All the journalists assigned were given inoculations against smallpox and anthrax, just like the fighting forces, and about half of them completed weeklong training programs—"camps"— at Fort Dix, New Jersey, and other domestic military bases to expose them to "combat conditions," including wearing a gas mask. They were not allowed to carry or fire weapons or to drive their own vehicles. The Pentagon's rules prohibited reporting a continuing action without the permission of the commanding officer or offering the date, time, place, and outcome of a military mission except in the most general terms. In the first Persian Gulf War, the military had relied on the pool system. In the second, it felt more confident that nothing would be on display it did not want reported and that there would be recruitment advantages to bringing one of America's new, antiseptic wars into the nation's living rooms.[32]

In addition to massaging the media to get out its message, the Pentagon tries to cultivate civilian groups who are likely to support it politically or who have vested interests in defense spending. This lobbying went unnoticed until a fatal case of negligence aboard the submarine USS *Greeneville* brought it briefly into the open. On February 9, 2001, the 6,500-ton nuclear-powered attack submarine performed a simulated emergency surfacing off Honolulu, colliding with and sinking the *Ehime Maru*, a 190-foot Japanese high-school training ship, with a loss of nine young Japanese lives.

The *Greeneville* had put to sea solely to give sixteen rich civilian backers of the navy a joyride. It was missing about a third of its crew and was operating close to Waikiki Beach with several pieces of equipment out of commission. Its captain, Commander Scott D. Waddle, initially testified before a court of inquiry that he had not been distracted by the civilians or by a navy captain escort, even though all of them were crowded into the control room. Nonetheless, a collision between a surfacing submarine and another ship could only have been caused by inattention. On April 16, 2001, the *Honolulu Advertiser* reported that Waddle reversed himself. If he were court-martialed for negligence, he said, his main defense would be that he had been ordered to take the civilians on a cruise and that, as he told *Time,* "having them in the control room at least interfered with our concentration."[33] A Texas oil company executive was actually at the controls when the submarine shot to the surface.

To prevent Waddle from repeating his comments for the official record, the navy's court of inquiry did not call for testimony from any of the civilian guests, and Admiral Thomas B. Fargo, commander of the Pacific Fleet, decided against court-martialing him, because it would, he argued, be detrimental to morale.[34] In a court-martial, Waddle would have been able to introduce a defense, which the navy obviously did not want. Instead, Commander Waddle was allowed to retire with full pension benefits. The *Greeneville* case revealed for the first time, however, the extent to which the navy was using its ships and aircraft as public relations props. During 2000, the Pacific Fleet alone welcomed 7,836 civilian visitors aboard its vessels. It embarked on twenty-one voyages using *Los Angeles*–class nuclear attack submarines like the *Greeneville* for 307 civilian guests and another seventy-four with aircraft carriers for 1,478 visitors. No member of Congress was recorded as questioning or even taking an interest in this lobbying by the navy.

By far the most powerful tool of the Department of Defense in promoting its image and protecting its interests from public scrutiny is official secrecy—the so-called black programs paid for through the "black budget." Reliance on a budget that systematically attempts to confuse and disinform the public started during World War II with the Manhattan Project to build the atomic bomb. All funds allocated for nuclear weapons research and development were hidden in fake accounts of the War Department and never made public to Congress or the people. The president and the military made the decision entirely on their own to develop the first "weapons of mass destruction."

With the onset of the Cold War, the Pentagon became addicted to a black-budget way of life. After passage in 1949 of the Central Intelligence Act, all funds for the CIA were (and still are) secretly contained in the Department of Defense's published budget under camouflaged names. As the president, the Pentagon, and the CIA created new intelligence agencies, the black budget expanded exponentially. In 1952, President Truman signed a still-secret seven-page charter creating the National Security Agency, which is devoted to signals and communications espionage; in 1960, President Eisenhower set up the even more secret National Reconnaissance Office, which runs our spy satellites; in 1961, President Kennedy launched the Defense Intelligence Agency, the personal intelligence organization of the Joint Chiefs of Staff and the secretary of defense; and in 1996, President Clinton combined several agencies into the National Imagery and Mapping Agency. The budgets of these ever-proliferating intelligence organizations are all unpublished, but estimates of their size are possible. In August 1994, an internal Pentagon memorandum was accidentally leaked to and published in *Defense Week*, a weapons-trade magazine. According to this memo, the NSA at that time spent $3.5 billion per year, the DIA $621 million, and the NRO $122 million (the CIA was not included).[35]

The official name for the black budget is "Special Access Programs" (SAPs), which are classified well above "top secret." ("SAP" may be a subtle or unintentional bureaucratic reference to the taxpayer.) SAPs are divided into three basic types: weapons research and acquisition (AQ-SAP), operations and support, including much of the funds for the various Special Forces (OS-SAP), and intelligence (IN-SAP). Only a few members of Congress receive briefings on them, and this limited sharing of information itself came about only late in the Cold War, in the wake of the Watergate scandals. Moreover, at the discretion of the secretary of defense, the reporting requirement may be waived or transmitted orally to only eight designated members of Congress. These "waived SAPs" are the blackest of black holes. The General Accounting Office has identified at least 185 black programs and notes that they increased eightfold during the 1981–86 period. There is no authoritative total, but the GAO once estimated that $30 to $35 billion per year was devoted to secret military and intelligence spending. According to a report of the independent Center for Strategic and Budgetary Assessments, black programs requested in President Bush's 2004 defense budget are at the highest level since 1988.[36]

Weapons and operations are identified in the published Pentagon budget by a series of fanciful names—"Grass Blade," "Chalk Eagle," "Dark Eyes," "Guardian Bear," "Senior Citizen," "Tractor Rose," "Have Blue," "Sea Nymph," and many more. Independent analysts of the defense budgets have noticed that in these unclassified nicknames, "Have," "Senior," and "Constant" are frequently used as the first word in air force programs, "Tractor" in army programs, and "Chalk" in navy ones.[37] Black programs that have slowly, usually inadvertently, come to light include a secret flight-test base on the edge of the dry Groom Lake in the desert north of Las Vegas, Nevada, known as Area 51 and carried on the books as part of Edwards Air Force Base, California; three reconnaissance UAVs (unmanned air vehicles) first put on the drawing board in 1994–95—the Predator, Dark Star, and Global Hawk—of which the Predator saw extensive use in the Afghan invasion; and the USAF's space maneuver vehicle (SMV), originated by Rockwell but today a Boeing project. Some of the more interesting black operations include the army's 160th Special Operations Air Regiment, based at Fort Campbell, Kentucky, which supplies helicopters for the Delta Force commando unit, and the air force's 4477th Test and Evaluation Squadron, formally located at Nellis Air Force Base, Nevada. Since the 1970s the 4477th has bought or stolen Soviet combat aircraft for flight testing at Area 51. In 1998, the air force announced that for the first time it had acquired a MiG-29 from the former Soviet republic of Moldava, but all further details remain classified.

The military's extreme fetish for secrecy and disinformation—the dissemination of plausible but false data—makes a farce of congressional oversight. It is impossible for anyone without an extraordinarily high security clearance to make any sense at all of "defense" appropriations. Moreover, the whole system is so compartmentalized that black programs often duplicate one another without anyone's appearing to know what is going on. In a lawsuit over the cancelation of the navy's stealth fighter, the A-12 Avenger II, a black program, the McDonnell Douglas and General Dynamics companies charged that technology developed in other black programs would have solved some of the problems that led to the project's termination but that the people in the A-12 program were not informed about it.[38] Secrecy has been carried to such lengths that at Boeing's aptly named Phantom Works at Palmdale, California, devoted to black projects, background music plays constantly to drown out conversations, which are assumed to be of a secret nature.

If anything, the situation today is worse than ever. A typical recent scandal involves contracts signed between the Defense Department, Lockheed Martin, and Boeing to design and build new rockets to lift heavy satellites into space. The DoD has classified the contracts themselves "to protect the business interests of two of America's biggest defense contractors."[39]

As with the seemingly unstoppable growth of secrecy within the government, so too has there been implacable pressure from the Pentagon to expand its functions and seize bureaucratic turf from other agencies. There are many aspects to this problem, but perhaps the most important politically, and certainly one of the clearest signs of militarism in America, is the willingness of some senior officers and civilian militarists to meddle in domestic policing. The U.S. Constitution establishes a clear separation between the activities of the armed forces in the defense of the country and law enforcement under the penal codes of the various states. James Madison so feared military dominance that he wrote in *The Federalist*, No. 41, "a standing [military] force is a dangerous provision." While this fear was rooted in the political preoccupations of the American Revolution, it did not become a pressing issue until the disputed presidential election of 1876, when troops were dispatched to polling stations in three southern states—South Carolina, Florida, and Louisiana. Rutherford B. Hayes, a northerner from Ohio, won by only one electoral vote in a situation comparable to the disputed Florida election of 2000, when the Supreme Court rather than the military interfered in state affairs.

The purpose of the Posse Comitatus Act of 1878 was to prevent the military from ever again engaging in police activities without the consent of Congress or the president. *Posse comitatus,* Latin for "power of the country," is a medieval term for the English practice of a sheriff summoning citizens to help him arrest a criminal or quell a civil disturbance. In nineteenth-century America, the phrase was shortened simply to "posse." Although the act has been modified many times to allow the military to aid in drug interdiction and help patrol the Mexican border, it still is meant to ensure that the standing army will not have any role in policing American citizens in their own country.

However, the rise of militarism, aided by the attacks of September 11, 2001, has eroded these old distinctions. By expanding the meaning of national security to include counterterrorism and controlling immigration, areas in which it now actively participates, the Pentagon has moved into the domestic policy business. The Department of Defense has, for instance, drafted operational orders to respond to what it calls a CIDCON ("civilian disorder condition"). During the Republican Party's convention in Philadelphia in August 2000, for example, the Pentagon placed on alert in case of a large-scale terrorist incident a "Joint Task Force–Civil Support" based at Fort Monroe, Virginia, and "Task Force 250." Task Force 250 is actually the army's Eighty-second Airborne Division, based at Fort Bragg, North Carolina.[40]

The United States has obviously not proved immune to terrorist attacks—witness the 1993 bombing of the World Trade Center in New York, the blowing up of the Murrah federal office building in Oklahoma City in May 1995, and the assaults on New York and Washington of September 2001. In one way or another—one of the Murrah terrorists was a Gulf War veteran—these incidents all suggest blowback from U.S. government activities in foreign countries. The United States has also seen instances of state terrorism, as in the federal agents' attack on the white supremacist former Green Beret Randy Weaver and his family at Ruby Ridge, Idaho, in 1992 and the FBI's assault on religious dissidents at Waco, Texas, in 1993.[41] It is conceivable that in the future such incidents will bring out the troops. But, more important, "terrorism" is an extremely flexible concept open to abuse by the leaders of an ambitious and unscrupulous military.

During the summer of 2002, the Bush administration directed lawyers in the Departments of Justice and Defense to review the Posse Comitatus Act and any other laws that might restrict the military's ability to participate in domestic law enforcement. At the time, the Defense Department was creating a new regional command to defend North America, comparable to those for Latin America, Europe, the Middle East, and the Pacific. The Northern Command, based at Peterson Air Force Base in Colorado Springs, is intended to better position the military to respond to terrorism close to home and to prevent the introduction of chemical, biological, or nuclear weapons into the United States. (Even during World War II, the federal government did not create a centralized command for the American mainland, because of concerns that it could become the basis for a military dictatorship.) The command's jurisdiction includes the United States, Mexico, Canada, and Cuba. Neither the Mexicans, the Canadians, nor, of course, the Cubans were consulted. This new headquarters, like that of the other regional "CINCs" (commanders in chief), will exist largely outside either the civilian or the military chains of command. CINCs are, in fact, comparable to Roman proconsuls, except that the men assigned to that post in the Roman Republic had already held the highest office in the realm, that of consul, and were deeply trusted civilians and military veterans.

The first CINC of the Northern Command is General Ralph E. Eberhart of the air force, another former head of the Space Command. On his appointment, Eberhart said, "We should always be reviewing things like Posse Comitatus and other laws if we think it ties our hands in protecting the American people."[42] It seemed not to have occurred to Eberhart that the Posse Comitatus Act was intended to protect Americans from generals like himself. Several civilian agencies, including the FBI, the Public Health Service, and the Federal Emergency Management Agency, have expressed dismay at the growing role of the military in their spheres of responsibility. The new Department of Homeland Security, created in 2003, combines many formerly civilian agencies and works closely with the Pentagon and the Northern Command. Its first deputy director is Gordon R. England, a former secretary of the navy and a former executive vice president of General Dynamics Corporation of Fort Worth, Texas, the manufacturer of the military's main fighter plane, the F-16.[43] It is not at all obvious which is a greater threat to the safety and integrity of the citizens of the United States: the possibility of a terrorist attack using weapons of mass destruction or an out-of-control military intent on displacing elected officials who stand in their way.

In addition to setting up the Northern Command and trying to undermine the Posse Comitatus Act, the military establishment is expanding its functions and influence on many other fronts. It has, for instance, directly challenged the Treasury Department with a demand that all significant foreign acquisitions of American companies be subjected to a national security review. The Pentagon wants a much larger voice in the Committee on Foreign Investment in the United States, including compulsory notification from the CFIUS of all takeovers by foreigners worth more than $100 million. Such a demand may be a thinly disguised form of protectionism, but, as the British *Financial Times* observed, "The Pentagon's attempt to extend its influence over inward investment is emblematic of its growing power within the Bush administration."[44]

Equally to the point, during 2003, the administration tucked a surprise proposal into a broader intelligence authorization bill that would give the military (and the CIA) authority to issue subpoenas requiring Internet providers, credit card companies, libraries, and a range of other organizations to produce on-demand materials like phone records, bank transactions, and e-mail logs. This would be a total break with the long-standing requirement that only the FBI can seek such information on American citizens within the United States and then only with judicial authorization, particularly if it plans to use such information in court. The new proposal would allow the military and the CIA to gather intelligence on citizens without ever being subject to judicial oversight.[45]

Rumsfeld's Pentagon has also been active in trying to exempt the military from various environmental protection laws. For example, the Marine Corps has complained that the 1973 Endangered Species Act interferes with its troops' abilities to dig foxholes wherever they want on the 125,000-acre base at Camp Pendleton, California. The Fish and Wildlife Service wants to designate a small part of the base as "critical habitats" for endangered species of birds, including the Western snowy plover and the California least tern. There is already provision within the Endangered Species Act for a national security exemption, but the marines have never used it. They seem less interested in solving the problems of training marines while protecting the environment than in establishing the principle that the military is a law unto itself.[46]

The Pentagon's priority areas for expansion are the diplomatic functions of the State Department and the intelligence and covert-action functions of the CIA. Both the military's Special Forces and the posts of regional commanders in chief have their roots in the disastrous attempt between April 24 and 26, 1980, to rescue American hostages captured in the Iranian seizure of our embassy in Teheran. That failure revealed that the Pentagon needed to be much more serious in training and equipping commandos for "low-intensity warfare" and in providing unified commands that could order up the needed resources without having to fight their way through a labyrinthine chain of command and the inevitable interservice rivalries. Colonel Charlie A. Beckwith, the commander of the army's Delta Force that was destroyed at Desert One, southeast of Teheran, through its own bungling, testified to Congress: "In Iran we had an ad hoc affair. We went out, found bits and pieces, people and equipment, brought them together occasionally and then asked them to perform a highly complex mission. The parts all performed, but they didn't necessarily perform as a team. Nor did they have the same motivation. My recommendation is to put together an organization that contains everything it will ever need, an organization that would include Delta, the Rangers, Navy SEALs, Air Force pilots, its own staff, its own support people, its own aircraft and helicopters. Make this organization a permanent military unit. Give it a place to call home. Allocate sufficient funds to run it. And give it sufficient time to recruit, assess, and train its people. Otherwise, we are not serious about combatting terrorism."[47]

These recommendations slowly led to the empowerment of the regional commanders and the dramatic enlargement, during the 1990s, of the Special Forces, which were used for the "humanitarian interventions" favored by the Clinton administration. In 1997, responsibility for shaping key foreign political and military strategies was officially given to the regional commanders (called commanders in chief, or CINCs, until October 2002, when Defense Secretary Rumsfeld, apparently feeling threatened by their growing power, rechristened them "combatant commanders"). These semiautonomous generals and admirals perform functions that until the 1990s had been handled primarily by civilian officials.

In the Middle East (CENTCOM), the Pacific (PACOM), Europe (EUCOM), and Latin America (SOUTHCOM), the CINCs oversee such things as intelligence, special operations, space assets, nuclear forces, arms sales, and military bases; and they produce what are called "theater engagement plans." These are essentially mini–foreign policy statements for each region and include explicit programs to cultivate close relations with local military organizations.[48] This is done chiefly by deploying approximately 7,000 Special Forces soldiers in 150 countries to train local militaries in what is called "foreign internal defense" (FID)—in many cases merely a euphemism for the techniques of state terrorism. The training missions allow the United States to spy on these countries, sell them weapons, and encourage their armies to carry out policies the Pentagon favors. Everything is done very quietly and with virtually no political oversight.

Over time, the CINCs have become more influential in their regions than ambassadors. When General Anthony C. Zinni of the marines was head of CENTCOM, he had twenty ambassadors serving under him and a personal political adviser with ambassadorial rank. PACOM (also known as CINCPAC) supervises the affairs of forty-three countries. Each CINC has at his disposal virtually unlimited funds, his own airplanes and helicopters, and numerous staff officers. A CINC reports directly to the president and the secretary of defense, avoiding the service chiefs and the normal chain of command.

When, in October 1999, General Pervez Musharraf carried out a military coup d'état in Pakistan, President Clinton telephoned to protest and asked to be called back. Musharraf instead called General Zinni and reportedly began, "Tony, I want to tell you what I am doing."[49] General Zinni ignored the congressional ban on foreign aid to a country that has undergone a military coup and emerged as one of Musharraf's strongest supporters before 9/11. It was also Zinni, and not officials of the State Department, who made the decision to refuel warships in the Yemeni port of Aden, where, on October 12, 2000, suicide bombers attacked the destroyer USS *Cole,* killing seventeen sailors.

The CINCs appear more interested in friendly relations with their foreign military colleagues than in a regime's human rights abuses, regardless of U.S. foreign policy. As CINCPAC, Admiral Dennis Blair was determined to reopen ties with the Indonesian military despite its commanders' having been involved in the massacre of hundreds of unarmed civilians as well as United Nations officials in East Timor. Although our ambassador to Jakarta explicitly objected to his illegal collaboration with Indonesia's military, Blair became the first high-ranking American officer to visit Indonesia after Congress imposed sanctions. Thanks to military intelligence, Blair was well informed about conditions on Timor and the likelihood of violence if its citizens voted for independence, but at no time did he seek to restrain his Indonesian colleagues. Five Indonesian officers, all of them products of American military training, were subsequently charged with crimes against humanity. Senator Patrick J. Leahy (D-Vermont) commented, "For as long as I have been in the Senate, the Pentagon has said that U.S. engagement would professionalize the Indonesian army. That has been disproved time and time again, and the final straw was the debacle in East Timor."[50]

Blair's CINCPAC was not exceptional. The head of CINCSOUTH has gone out of his way to reestablish close ties with the El Salvadoran army, which probably has the worst human rights record of any Latin American military. On October 15, 1979, the United States sponsored a coup by young Salvadoran military officers that led to a vicious war against largely unarmed civilians by army *esquadrones de la muerte* (death squads). They slaughtered some 38,000 people before the Reagan administration sent then Vice President Bush to tell them to stop. In mid-1986, one Pentagon official boasted, "Every soldier in [El Salvador's] army has been trained by us in one way or another."[51] As late as 1989, army Special Forces were still "training" El Salvador's Atlacatl Battalion, which during November of that year murdered six Jesuit priests, their housekeeper, and her young daughter for alleged guerrilla sympathies. It is the officers of El Salvador's army "who have remained close to the U.S. military in the decade since their civil war ended," and who are our allies today in that tiny nation.[52] No country in the CINCSOUTH theater is threatened by a foreign enemy; therefore the purpose of our military presence is purely imperialist.

Leaving foreign policy in the hands of regional proconsuls advances militarism because they inevitably turn to military assets to achieve foreign policy objectives. Under these circumstances, it is hard to see why anyone would want to work for the State Department. The CIA is also being undercut, but here the assault comes not from the CINCs but directly from the Pentagon and the current darlings of the military—the "special forces."

Immediately following the terrorist attacks of September 11—once it had been established that al-Qaeda was the probable terrorist organization responsible—Secretary of Defense Donald Rumsfeld and Deputy Secretary of Defense Paul Wolfowitz ordered Undersecretary of Defense Douglas J. Feith to set up a special intelligence unit within the Pentagon. Its specific purpose was to find links between al-Qaeda and the regime of President Saddam Hussein of Iraq even though the CIA did not believe such links existed. Feith, like his bosses, had held several defense positions in the Reagan administration, including special counsel to then Assistant Secretary of Defense Richard Perle, and was part of a group of officials strongly influenced by Vice President Dick Cheney, the former secretary of defense. From the moment the new Bush administration was formed, this group passionately wanted to go to war with Iraq. Feith had been, in the words of the *New York Times*, "data mining" to find an al-Qaeda connection to Saddam Hussein that would justify an American war against him. Wolfowitz, Feith, and their associates were "intent on politicizing intelligence to fit their hawkish views."[53]

It soon developed that the chief obstacle to these efforts was the Central Intelligence Agency. Its operatives and analysts could find no connection between Iraq and the attacks of September 11. The agency also believed that the secular regime in Iraq was unlikely to have anything to do with the militantly Islamicist al-Qaeda and doubted that Saddam Hussein would supply terrorists beyond his control with any kind of weaponry that could be traced back to him.[54] This difference of opinion soon developed into a full-blown bureaucratic turf war.

In March 2002, a presidential commission led by retired Lieutenant General Brent Scowcroft, the first President Bush's national security adviser, recommended that three key Pentagon-financed intelligence agencies—the National Security Agency, the National Reconnaissance Office, and the National Imagery and Mapping Agency—be placed under the control of the director of the CIA. This was a serious challenge to Rumsfeld's empire. On June 21, 2002, Secretary Rumsfeld responded with what *U.S. News & World Report* called a "brilliant stealth attack." He quietly inserted in a Senate defense bill the authority to create a new undersecretary of defense for intelligence. "The new undersecretary position is a bureaucratic coup that accomplished many Pentagon goals in one fell swoop. . . . [Rumsfeld] is creating another DCI [director of central intelligence] for all practical purposes."[55] The new undersecretary is Rumsfeld's neocon crony Stephen Cambone. He has been given authority over the three nonmilitary intelligence agencies plus the Defense Intelligence Agency. According to Jay Farrar, a former employee in the Defense Department and National Security Council who works with the Center for Strategic and International Studies, a conservative think tank, "It's one more step in the Defense Department seeking to consolidate major control over the intelligence apparatus of the United States." The *New York Times* adds, "Wolfowitz and company disbelieve any analysis that doesn't support their own preconceived conclusions. The CIA is enemy territory, as far as they are concerned."[56]

Secretary of Defense Rumsfeld has also reportedly been "eager to have U.S. special forces usurp the [Central Intelligence] agency's traditional role" in conducting covert operations.[57] There are interlocking reasons for this. The secretary arrived in the Pentagon eager to wean the army away from its commitment to heavy armor and artillery of the sort once aimed at the tank forces of the former Soviet Union. He and other defense planners also believed covert operations were the most logical means of implementing the president's new National Military Strategy of "preventive war." Part of this strategy consists of infiltrating covert operatives into target countries to carry out provocative acts that would supposedly flush out terrorists and provide excuses for military intervention. Under the control of the army, such covert operations were would not have to be reported to Congress as do those conducted by the CIA. The United States would then be able to intervene more easily in targeted countries with even less civilian supervision than if such illegal operations were left to the official clandestine services agency. Above all, a stress on special operations expands the functions of the military into new, previously quasi-civilian-run jurisdictions.

Despite press glorification of special forces as an "elite secret army" and the fact that they received the biggest increase in spending in the 2003 defense budget—a rise of some 20 percent, to $3.8 billion—they do not have a good reputation.[58] In Vietnam, the army's Green Berets were notorious for their brutality as well as their ineffectiveness, and the failure of the First Special Forces Detachment-Delta, as it was formally known, in the Teheran hostage rescue operation led to the first major expansion of special forces during the Reagan administration and the 1981 creation of the army's supersecret Intelligence Support Activity (ISA). As *Philadelphia Inquirer* journalist Tim Weiner has observed, "[The ISA] set up shop all over Central America—El Salvador, Guatemala, Honduras, Nicaragua, Panama—to support the war against the Sandinistas and their left-wing allies. It created private companies to serve as fronts for espionage, including a butcher shop and a meat warehouse in Panama. It set up safe houses, secret airfields and caches for money and weapons, breaking a trail for future operations against the enemy [namely, the elected Sandinista government] in Nicaragua."[59] Very soon, however, its officers also developed reputations for embezzlement, cocaine trafficking, and obstruction of justice. Although the ISA never went completely out of business, by the mid-1980s $324 million of its funds were missing and secret tribunals sentenced several of its officers to long sentences at Fort Leavenworth. During the same period, members of Delta Force were charged with $200,000 worth of double billings for expenses while traveling overseas to protect U.S. ambassadors.[60]

To try to bring some order out of this chaos, Congress, in 1987, created a new Special Operations Command headquartered at MacDill Air Force Base in Tampa, Florida. This umbrella organization, led by a four-star general, finally brought the competing special forces of the army, navy, and air force under a unified command even though intelligence rivalries still persist. The special forces, currently amounting to about 47,000 soldiers, sailors, and airmen, include four army groups—Special Forces (Green Berets), headquartered at Fort Bragg, North Carolina; the Rangers, rapid-reaction units whose primary mission is combat behind enemy lines; Delta Force commandos for hostage rescue operations; and the 160th Special Operations Air Regiment, the helicopter attack squadron that transports Delta operatives into action. The navy contributes the SEALs, reputedly the best trained of all special operations forces, and the air force commits a "special operations wing" with squadrons all over the world responsible for long-range infiltration of special operations forces and rescue missions. Some elements of the Marine Corps were scheduled to join this megagrouping in 2002. In June of that year, Defense Secretary Rumsfeld assigned to the special operations command the primary role in the hunt for al-Qaeda.[61]

In September 2002, the Defense Science Board, a highly respected panel of private industry executives that advises the Pentagon on technologies and policies, issued its report on "Special Operations and Joint Forces in Countering Terrorism." It called for the creation of what it termed a "Proactive Preemptive Operations Group," yet another special force that would devise ways to provoke terrorists into an overt response so they could be targeted and attacked. The report advocated numerous other projects, including assembling a special SWAT team to surreptitiously find and destroy chemical, biological, and nuclear weapons all over the world. The total price tag was an estimated $7 billion a year. Above all, the Defense Science Board advocated authorizing the military to carry out covert operations independent of (and unknown to) other intelligence and police agencies.[62] The recommendations reflected the thinking of the Cheney-Rumsfeld group within the military establishment and would involve a remarkable expansion and centralization of clandestine military services in the hands of the secretary of defense. Some very mainstream observers have urged caution. Two prominent Council on Foreign Relations officials, Lawrence J. Korb, a former assistant secretary of defense, and Jonathan D. Tepperman, an analyst, in an article entitled "Soldiers Should Not Be Spying," condemn the idea— implicit in the new covert operations planning in the Pentagon—of sending special forces into allied countries without informing their governments. They speculate on Germany's probable reaction if Delta Force soldiers were caught raiding an alleged al-Qaeda cell in Hamburg without the approval of the German government.[63] Despite these warnings, the Pentagon has decided to go ahead. It plans to deploy hundreds of spies drawn from all four services under the control of the Defense Intelligence Agency.[64]

These latest proposals threaten to institutionalize the acts behind the Iran-Contra scandals of the 1980s as a way of life. When Congress cut off funding for the CIA-run war in Central America, the military used Oliver North, a marine officer in civilian clothes based in the White House, to raise funds illegally in arms deals with Iran and secretly funnel the money to the Contras, a private army of Nicaraguan counterrevolutionaries. Given the advance of militarism since that time, it is not fanciful to think that this may become a normal method of operations in the future conduct of foreign policy.

5

SURROGATE SOLDIERS AND
PRIVATE MERCENARIES

European soldiers in the tropics, often confined to cantonments, . . .
experienced long periods of inactivity and boredom, were prone to high
levels of drunkenness, and fell sick with "the physical and moral infec-
tion of venereal disease." The answer was to employ indigenous soldiers
who were both cheaper and healthier. The issue, however, was whether
they would prove to be reliable.

DAVID KILLINGRAY,
Guardians of Empire (1999)

The British had their Gurkhas, Sikhs, and sepoys; the French their
Foreign Legion; the Dutch their Amboinese; the Russians their
Cossacks; and the Japanese their puppet armies in Manchuria, China,
Indonesia, and Burma. Among the traditions of imperialism, the hege-
mon recruiting foreigners to do his dirty work certainly stands near the
top of the list. Replacing homeland soldiers with local cannon fodder and
setting one indigenous ethnic or religious group against another have
often made the policing of a subordinate people easier and less expensive.

The Americans tried their hand at it in Vietnam when, in 1962, they
sent some 2,000 Green Berets into the southern highlands to train the Montagnards—mountain people, ethnically distinct from the Vietnamese—
and organize them into a Civilian Irregular Defense Group. Generally
speaking, the Montagnards contributed little to the war effort and their
outposts were easily overrun by the Vietcong whenever it served their
purposes.[1] Nonetheless, like virtually all imperialists before them, the

Americans have never given up hope that they might discover the key to getting locals to do their fighting for them.

Particularly since the end of the Cold War, the military has developed close relations with myriad governments and officer corps in the Third World and has put immense effort into military-to-military training programs. During the 1990s, leaders in both political parties concluded that many foreign policy goals could best be fostered through such military-to-military contacts and weapons sales as opposed to traditional economic and diplomatic ties.[2] One program for implementing such policies, the State Department's International Military Education and Training Program (IMET), has increased fourfold since 1994. In 1990, it was offering military instruction to the armies of 96 countries; by 2002, that already impressive number had risen to 133 countries. There are only 189 countries in the United Nations, which means that this single program "instructs" militaries in 70 percent of the world's nations. In recent years we have been training approximately 100,000 foreign soldiers each year—and here we are ordinarily talking about officers who then can pass on American methods to their troops. In 2001, the military taught 15,030 officers and men in Latin America alone. The Pentagon either brings the trainees to about 150 different military educational institutions in the United States or sends military instructors, almost always army Special Forces, to the countries themselves. The war on terrorism only accelerated these trends. Funding for IMET rose from $58 million in fiscal year 2001 to $80 million for 2003, a jump of 38 percent.

The United States claims that it trains foreign armies as a way of teaching them American values and models of civil-military relations. Pentagon officials regularly assure congressional committees that educating foreign soldiers helps correct the civil rights records of sometimes abusive militaries. However, Lora Lumpe, the leading authority on the subject, concludes, "Most of the programs have had no discernible focus on human rights and have been carried out in a highly, if not completely, unaccountable manner."[3] The Special Forces are anything but impeccable models when it comes to adhering to high standards in the treatment of prisoners or civilians.[4] Such close contact between American military instructors and foreign officers and soldiers also gives the United States an inside track in weapons sales, a form of commerce run directly out of the Pentagon, although private munitions companies can also sell weapons if licensed to do so by the State Department's Office of Defense Trade Controls. Since 1991, the United States has been by far the largest single seller of munitions on earth. From 1997 to 2001, it exported $44.82 billion in arms; the next-biggest supplier, Russia, sold $17.35 billion. Train and sell—it is a closely meshed system to enlist allies and make money from less developed countries.

The main public intent behind foreign military training today is the recruitment of more foot soldiers in the war on terrorism and their preparation for joint operations with American units. Among the hidden motives behind such programs is finding surrogates for American troops in order to avoid casualties that might roil the "homeland." Ever since 1993, when the dragging of the body of Sergeant Randy Shughart through the streets of Somalia's capital, Mogadishu, was televised, causing President Clinton to withdraw our forces from the country four days later, the Pentagon has tried to avoid anything that would turn the public against its plans. As President Bush said in a speech on March 11, 2002, "We will not send American troops to every battle, but America will actively prepare other nations for the battles ahead."[5]

Troop trainers are often sent abroad—ostensibly to learn foreign languages and familiarize themselves with exotic cultures—in order to circumvent congressional bans on official contacts with countries that have bad human rights records. The Pentagon finds it convenient to train foreign military forces and police to carry out secret programs of state terrorism, including the assassination of foreign leaders, without being charged with war crimes and violations of the Geneva Conventions.[6] Foreign military training is also a way to buy political influence. For example, the United States spends $12,000 a year training the military forces of the tiny Pacific island nation of Tuvalu. In return, Tuvalu was one of only four countries that joined the United States and Israel in voting against an October 2000 U.N. General Assembly resolution condemning Israel for its indiscriminate use of force in Palestine.

The United States has two alternative ways of implementing its training programs, each with different unintended consequences. Both have long-standing precedents in the practices of the British Empire, of which the United States has become a dutiful if not particularly inspired pupil. I call these the "sepoy strategy" and the "private military companies strategy." The word *sepoy* probably derives from the Urdu word for "horseman" or "soldier," and the sepoy strategy once involved training "native" troops to serve in regiments commanded by British officers or in imperial Indian regiments thought to be loyal to the British crown, which were normally composed of Sikh and Gurkha mercenaries. In 1857, at the time of the Sepoy Mutiny—which Indian nationalists call their "first war of independence"—Britain deployed an army of 300,000 soldiers in India, 96 percent of whom were sepoys. The fact that, when push came to shove, they proved not to be loyal to Britain highlights one of the major potential pitfalls of this approach.

The classic American example of the employment of sepoys was in the "secret war" in Laos that stretched from 1960 to 1975. Army Green Berets and the CIA supplied clandestine aid to French-trained General Vang Pao of the Laotian army, who, in turn, recruited a 30,000-strong army of Hmong tribesmen to fight the Pathet Lao Communist forces allied with North Vietnam. Vang Pao became a hero to American strategists in Saigon and Washington—the best puppet we ever found in Indochina. Our most important form of aid to him was air power. We backed the Hmong fighters with bombing missions from our bases in Thailand. We also used the CIA's private airline, Air America, to supply the scattered Hmong villages with arms, rice, and other supplies and then transported their main cash crop, opium, to Vang Pao's headquarters in the Plain of Jars. From there the opium went on to supply American troops fighting in Vietnam and, via underworld traffickers, on to the international market.

When, after 1969, the Pathet Lao began to defeat the Hmong guerrillas, Air America evacuated thousands of them to refugee camps under Vang Pao's control and carpet-bombed the Hmong villages that had been overrun. Ultimately, after the collapse of anti-Communist resistance throughout Indochina, the CIA evacuated Vang Pao and thousands of his supporters to the United States, where they now live. Unlike Britain's sepoys, Vang Pao and the Hmong always remained loyal to the CIA. As Alfred McCoy, the leading authority on the opium trade that accompanied this secret war, notes, "While the U.S. military sent half a million troops to fight a conventional war in South Vietnam, this mountain warfare required only a handful of American personnel."[7]

The private military companies strategy is typified by the Vinnell Corporation of Fairfax, Virginia, a subsidiary of the large defense conglomerate Northrop Grumman. Vinnell was created by retired American military officers and, since 1975, has been licensed by the government to train the Saudi National Guard, the 100,000-strong force that protects the monarchy and serves as a counterweight to any threat from the regular armed forces. Over the years Vinnell has constructed, run, written doctrine for, and staffed five Saudi military academies, seven shooting ranges, and a health care system, while training and equipping four Saudi mechanized brigades and five infantry brigades. Saudi Arabia has, in turn, funneled hundreds of millions of dollars into major defense corporations to equip these forces, which briefly saw action in the first Gulf War by recapturing the Saudi town of Khafji, on the Kuwait border, from the Iraqis.[8]

Vinnell is one of about thirty-five private rent-a-trainer, rent-a-mercenary, and rent-a-cop companies whose leaders and employees, mostly retired high-ranking officers and members of the Special Forces, hire themselves out to the government and its foreign allies to perform any number of military tasks, including troop training. Since these companies are private contractors, they are not subject to military discipline and their operations remain the proprietary secrets of the companies, not subject to any form of public oversight. From the 1950s to the 1970s, the British and South Africans created similar companies of mercenaries to train and sometimes fight alongside both governmental and insurgent forces in the Middle East, Angola, and Sierra Leone. The United States also hired private companies to train South Vietnamese military forces and police during the 1960s and 1970s, but to little avail. I will return to the American private companies below, but let us first consider our record with sepoys.

IMET was created in 1976 in the wake of the Nixon Doctrine, that forlorn attempt to "Vietnamize" the Vietnam War—that is, to shift to the principle that "Asian boys should fight Asian wars." IMET's primary mode of operation was—and remains—to pay foreign officers and soldiers to take courses at such places as the National Defense University in Washington, DC; the U.S. Army Intelligence Center at Fort Huachuca, Arizona; the Naval Special Warfare Center (headquarters of the SEALs) at Coronado, California; the Inter-American Air Force Academy at Lackland Air Force Base, San Antonio, Texas; the Air Force Special Operations Command's school at Hurlburt Field, Fort Walton Beach, Florida; and the John F. Kennedy Special Warfare Center at Fort Bragg, North Carolina.

By far the most notorious of these institutions is the Spanish-language School of the Americas (SOA), which, to evade a congressional order that it be closed, in 2000 renamed itself the Western Hemisphere Institute for Security Cooperation (WHISC). This ruse, which fooled no one, nonetheless formally stopped the movement to abolish SOA. Founded in 1946 and situated in the then American colony of the Canal Zone, it was evicted in 1984 by the Panamanian government, whose president, Jorge Illueca, termed it the "biggest base for destabilization in Latin America." SOA/WHISC is now located on the grounds of the army base at Fort Benning, Georgia. Over the years it has trained well over 60,000 Latin American military and police officers, significant numbers of whom have been implicated in cases of torture, rape, massacre, and assassination. Among them was Roberto D'Aubuisson, the leader of El Salvador's right-wing death squads. Lower-level SOA graduates have participated in human rights abuses that include the March 24, 1980, assassination of El Salvador's Archbishop Oscar Romero (in which the CIA may have been implicated) and the December 1981 El Mozote massacre of 900 Salvadoran civilians. As of late 2002, civil war–torn Colombia's army includes some 10,000 SOA/WHISC graduates.

In 1996, the American press discovered that between 1982 and 1991 the SOA adopted as textbooks seven different Spanish-language manuals based on a U.S. Army original that called for "neutralizing [i.e., killing] government officials, political leaders, and members of the infrastructure." These manuals were distributed to thousands of military officers in eleven South and Central American countries. According to a Pentagon spokesman, Lieutenant Colonel Arne Owens, "The problem was discovered in 1992, properly reported, and fixed."[9] WHISC remains the focus of a widespread protest movement led by Father Roy Bourgeois, a former navy officer who is today a Maryknoll priest. He has been arrested many times at Fort Benning. Should he and his supporters ever succeed in closing down the school on U.S. soil, the Bush administration has announced backup plans for a successor in Costa Rica.

The rich rival of the State Department's IMET program is the Pentagon's Foreign Military Financing (FMF), which gives money to countries to buy American weapons and then supplies training in how to use them. Appropriations for IMET in fiscal year 2001 were $57,875,000, with proposed expenditures for 2003 of $80,000,000—whereas the FMF appropriations are in the billions and still rising. In 2001, the Pentagon received $3,576,240,000 and promptly put in a request of $4,107,200,000 for 2003. Such differences between the two programs reflect the fact that the Pentagon's budget is almost twenty times larger than the State Department's. A major portion of the Pentagon's funds traditionally goes to Israel, but the biggest proposed recipients in the FMF 2003 budget were Jordan, at $198 million (plus IMET of $2.4 million); Colombia at $98 million (IMET of $1.2 million); India at $50 million (IMET of $1 million); Pakistan at $50 million (IMET of $1 million); Turkey at $17.5 million (IMET of $350,000); and Uzbekistan at $8.75 million (IMET of $1.2 million). These sums represented the first FMF payments to Colombia, India, and Pakistan in recent years. Uzbekistan, which has one of the worst human rights records anywhere, is a new recipient. The Department of Defense at first proposed that Azerbaijan also receive an IMET grant of $750,000 and a FMF grant of $3 million in 2003 as part of the war on terrorism but later admitted that the funds were actually intended to protect U.S. access to oil in and around the Caspian Sea.

One other Department of Defense training program was created primarily to deceive Congress. From 1950 until November 1991, when the Indonesian army opened fire on and killed 270 unarmed demonstrators in the city of Dili, the capital of East Timor, the government paid for the training of over 7,300 Indonesian officers. After it was discovered that American-trained troops firing American-supplied weapons had carried out the Dili massacre, Congress banned all further military funds to Indonesia. The following year the Pentagon set up a new program, Joint Combined Exchange Training (JCET), which sends Special Forces to various countries allegedly to learn local languages and gain "familiarity" with the local military. It was, however, designed largely to keep military relationships with Indonesia on course. From 1992 to May 1998, without informing Congress, Special Forces units carried out thirty-six training exercises with Indonesian special forces units under cover of JCET.

In 1999, after East Timor gained its independence through a United Nations–sponsored referendum, militias under Indonesian military guidance pursued a relentless campaign of "ethnic cleansing" against the island's civilian population. This time the Clinton administration instituted a ban on all forms of military assistance to Indonesia, a ban still in effect at the time of the September 11, 2001, terrorist attacks. In December 2001, the Pentagon inserted a clause into the Defense Appropriations Act establishing a new "Regional Counter-Terrorism Defense Fellowship Program," worth $17.9 million. Completely independent of IMET, FMF, and JCET, this program now brings Indonesian military officers to the United States for training. The Pentagon uses several other practices to evade congressional restrictions on its relations with foreign militaries, evidence of a mind-set consistent with militarism.

Reminiscent as all this may be of British imperial practices, U.S. military officers may not recall the underside of such training programs—the Sepoy Mutiny. This massive rebellion lasted almost a year from the first outbreak at Meerut on May 10, 1857, until March 1858, when the siege of Lucknow was lifted. For a short period, the mutineers even captured the capital of the British Raj, Delhi. It was one of the few instances in modern history of a genuine clash of civilizations. The British in India had come to think of themselves as a master race and looked down on the native Indians, both Hindu and Muslim, serving in the British army. They even sent Christian missionaries among the troops to try to convert them. In 1857, when the British introduced one of the earliest versions of the Enfield rifle, the bullets came soaked in grease made from animal fat, including fat from cows and pigs. Cows are sacred to Hindus; pigs are repulsive to Muslims. One of the idiosyncrasies of the ammunition for this particular rifle was that a twist of paper attached at one end had to be bitten off before the gun could be used.[10] Rumors quickly spread among the sepoys that the British were trying to humiliate them by forcing them to violate religious taboos. So when one British commander ordered his troops to bite the bullet, a soldier shot him.

The revolt spread like an eruption through the Indian army, and the British struck back with savage brutality. Captured sepoys were bayoneted or sewn into the hides of pigs or cows and fired from cannons. Much as when the Roman Republic suppressed the Spartacist revolt, the road from Kanpur to Allahabad was lined with the corpses of Indian soldiers who had been hanged. England ended the authority of the East India Company, which had employed the sepoys and their officers, and for the next ninety years ruled the country directly as a crown colony. The Indian regiments were abolished and their soldiers absorbed into larger formations that included Englishmen. The operation of artillery was restricted to British soldiers only. With these changes, the British in effect gave up their role as merchants in India and became the unwelcome occupiers of a hostile land.

Something similar happened to the Americans in Afghanistan. Between 1979 and 1989, the CIA supplied *mujahideen* ("freedom fighter") groups with over $2 billion worth of light weapons, including Stinger antiaircraft missile launchers, and offered instruction in how to use them against the Soviet forces occupying Afghanistan. The Americans were uninterested in the religious beliefs, political loyalties, or attitudes toward the West of those they were recruiting, training, and arming.[11] Once the Soviet Union was defeated, the Americans abandoned Afghanistan to its fate and the Afghan freedom fighters, mainly Islamic fundamentalists, turned against the United States. The deployment of thousands of American military forces to Saudi Arabia, site of Islam's two most sacred sites, and support for Israel only increased their resentment. Muslim militants retaliated throughout the 1990s, attacking New York's World Trade Center in 1993, U.S. military apartment towers in Saudi Arabia in 1996, American embassies in Kenya and Tanzania in 1998, and the navy destroyer USS *Cole* in 2000. It is possible to think of the suicidal attacks of September 11 as a contemporary version of the Sepoy Mutiny—even though the Bush administration has done everything in its power to ensure that Americans do not think such things.

America's military trains and equips its sepoys directly, but increasingly it also does so through private companies beyond the knowledge and control of Congress. The top thirty-five of these private military companies are among the most profitable businesses in the country today. The main ones are Vinnell Corporation; Military Professional Resources, Inc., best known by its acronym, MPRI, located in Alexandria, Virginia, and owned by L3 Communications; Kellogg Brown & Root, the legendary Texas company that bankrolled Lyndon Johnson's political career and is today a subsidiary of the Halliburton Corporation; DynCorp of Reston, Virginia, which became notorious during the late 1990s when it was discovered that some of its employees in Bosnia were keeping underaged women as sex slaves and then selling them elsewhere in Europe (DynCorp simply fired these employees); Science Applications International Corporation (SAIC) of San Diego, whose top five executives made between $825,000 and $1.8 million in salaries in 2001 and held more than $1.5 million worth of stock options each; BDM International of Fairfax, Virginia; Armor Holdings of Jacksonville, Florida; Cubic Applications, Inc., of San Diego; DFI International (originally Defense Forecasts, Inc.) of Washington, DC; and International Charter, Inc., of Oregon.[12]

Since the end of the Cold War, in addition to the money spent on IMET, FMF, and JCET, the Department of Defense has hired these and other companies to train the armed forces of more than forty-two countries. (Sometimes the foreign country hires the company, but this still requires an export license from the State Department and approval from the Pentagon's Defense Security Cooperation Agency.) In 1995, for instance, a private company, MPRI, was given the job of training and equipping the armies of Croatia and Bosnia, which then went on to conduct systematic and bloody ethnic exterminations of Serbs, accompanied by many war crimes. MPRI also had a $6 million contract during 2001 to train the Colombian army and police. MPRI and Cubic run programs to prepare some of the former Soviet-bloc countries for membership in NATO. A number of different companies have been involved in the military education of about 120 African leaders and the training of more than 5,500 sub-Saharan African troops in modern military techniques.

DynCorp was hired to provide personal protection for President Hamid Karzai of Afghanistan and will take over the training of the

Afghan army once the Green Berets leave the country. After the United States intervened militarily in Haiti in 1994, DynCorp "trained" that country's police. The company has been so successful that in early 2003 Computer Sciences Corporation of El Segundo, California, bought it. After the second Iraq war, DynCorp won the lucrative contract to provide a thousand advisers to help form Iraq's new police department, judicial branch, and prison system. The Bush administration decided to take the money for the DynCorp contract from the funds allocated for antidrug operations in Afghanistan.

The people who do this sort of training are almost invariably retired military types—soldiers of fortune, war lovers, men who found themselves out of jobs at the end of the Cold War but wanted to keep on doing what they had been doing on active service. Most of the companies for which they now work originated as the brainchildren of recently retired high-ranking officers and Green Berets. The classic example is MPRI, founded by General Carl E. Vuono, the former army chief of staff during the first Gulf War; General Crosbie E. Saint, former commander of the U.S. Army in Europe; General Ron Griffith, a former army vice chief of staff; and other senior generals and admirals. The company's spokesman, Harry E. Soyster, a former director of the Defense Intelligence Agency, is a mere lieutenant general. These men became millionaires in July 2000 when they and about thirty-five other stockholders sold the company to L3 Communications for $40 million cash.

These private military companies are not small organizations. DynCorp has 23,000 employees, Cubic some 4,500, and MPRI about 700 full-time staff members with a roster of 10,000 retired military personnel it can call on. One authority on these new mercenaries, Deborah Avant of the Elliott School of International Affairs at George Washington University, estimates that the revenues of the private military companies, which were at $55.6 billion in 1990, will rise to $202 billion by 2010. The companies even have their own industry trade group, the International Peace Operations Association—a name George Orwell would have cherished.

It is not just foreigners these companies train. Until March 2002, MPRI held the contract to run the Reserve Officer Training Corps (ROTC) programs in some 217 American universities. ROTC offers college money to students in return for taking some military courses, wearing uniforms on campus, training during part of the summer at a military base, and accepting a commission in the army reserve upon graduation. When it lost its bid to continue running the ROTC programs, MPRI picked up a contract to operate the nation's military recruiting stations. Both MPRI and Cubic are active in developing curricula, writing doctrine, and running educational programs for military officers as well as training military press attachés. Much of this privatization of our armed forces is actually deeply disliked by uniformed professionals. As Colonel Bruce Grant notes, "Privatization is a way of going around Congress and not telling the public. Foreign policy is made by default by private military consultants motivated by bottom-line profits."[13]

Private military companies also provide contractor services to repair equipment so complex the military itself simply cannot maintain it. This is an old story. I well recall from my days of military service in the Korean War era—I was the operations officer on a navy amphibious vessel, the USS *LST-883*, in the western Pacific—that the navigational radar on the ship's bridge was forever breaking down. Even our best electronics mates could not fix it and we invariably had to call in a civilian representative of the manufacturer to make repairs. Today, many complex weapons systems are heavily contractor-dependent, including Patriot missiles, Apache helicopters, Paladin artillery pieces, M1A1 Abrams tanks, and virtually all the unmanned aerial vehicles used by the military and the CIA. Some manufacturers even promise the military "factory to foxhole" support.[14]

It has been argued that specialized logistical and support activities diverge too far from the military's main purposes and that the Department of Defense can impose better quality control over a private contractor than over regular military units. During the 1990s, the Pentagon began to contract out every conceivable kind of service except firing a rifle or flying an airplane, spawning a rapidly growing, extremely lucrative new sector of the military-industrial complex. Given the Pentagon's penchant for cost-plus (read "open-ended") contracts, many new so-called base-support contracting firms have come into being. Over time the military has gotten used to contracting out base construction, maintenance, and security. The World War II and Cold War days of KP ("kitchen police"), cleaning barracks and latrines, and guard duty are almost totally unknown to contemporary soldiers.

A notorious example of this change is the superluxurious Camp Bondsteel in the Balkans. Immediately following the end of the American bombing campaign against Yugoslavia in June 1999, the United States simply seized from private owners a thousand acres of farmland at Uresevic in southeast Kosovo, near the Macedonian border. Between July and October 1999, it then proceeded to build Camp Bondsteel in record time. The United States also constructed Camp Monteith, a smaller but similarly luxurious base nearby. Bondsteel was named after Army Staff Sergeant James L. Bondsteel, a Medal of Honor winner in Vietnam; Monteith was named after First Lieutenant Jimmy W. Monteith Jr., a Medal of Honor winner in France during World War II. Bondsteel is the largest and most expensive base constructed since the Vietnam War, costing some $36.6 million to build and approximately $180 million annually to operate.[15] Army wags say facetiously that there are only two man-made objects that can be seen from outer space—the Great Wall of China and the army's Camp Bondsteel.

Kellogg Brown & Root, which built Camp Bondsteel under contract to the army, continues to do everything there except perform military duties. Under one of the costliest contracts in Pentagon history, Brown & Root, as it was originally known, maintains the barracks, cooks the food, mops the floors, transports all supplies, and operates the water and sewage systems. Employing about a thousand former U.S. military personnel and another 7,000 local Albanians, the company delivers 600,000 gallons of water daily, supplies enough electricity for a city of 25,000, washes 1,200 bags of laundry, and cooks and serves 18,000 meals per day. According to a September 2000 report by the congressional budget oversight agency, the General Accounting Office, Brown & Root bought $5.2 million worth of furniture for Bondsteel and Monteith that the army could not find enough space even to store, and the camp was so overstaffed that offices were cleaned four times a day and latrines a mere three times a day. Soldiers serving at Camp Bondsteel say the only patch missing on their camouflage fatigues is one that says, *Sponsored by Brown & Root.* The company provides similar services for many other military bases, including those in Kuwait and Turkey and the new American installation at Khanabad in Uzbekistan.[16]

Brown & Root, long known in Texas for its political connections, was acquired in 1962 by the oil-drilling and construction company Halliburton. Dick Cheney was secretary of defense when Brown & Root first began to supply logistical services to the army. According to an investigative report by Robert Bryce in the *Austin Chronicle*, Cheney is the author of the idea that the military's logistical operations should be privatized. He was trying not so much to increase efficiency as to reward the private sector. He basically asked how private companies could assist the army in cutting hundreds of thousands of jobs. "In 1992, the Pentagon, then under Cheney's direction, paid Brown & Root $3.9 million to produce a classified report detailing how private companies—like itself—could help provide logistics for American troops in potential war zones around the world. Later in 1992, the Pentagon gave the firm an additional $5 million to update its report. That same year, the company won a five-year logistics contract from the Army Corps of Engineers to work alongside GIs in places like Zaire, Haiti, Somalia, Kosovo, the Balkans, and Saudi Arabia."[17]

After the 1992 election, Cheney left the Defense Department, and between 1995 and 2000 he was the chief executive officer of Halliburton. Under his leadership, Brown & Root took in $2.3 billion in government contracts, almost double the $1.2 billion it earned from the government in the five years before Cheney arrived. Halliburton rebuilt Saddam Hussein's war-damaged oil fields for some $23.8 million, even though Cheney, as secretary of defense during the first Gulf War, had been instrumental in destroying them. By 1999, Halliburton had become the biggest nonunion employer in the United States, although Wal-Mart soon replaced it. Cheney also appointed Dave Gibben, his chief of staff when he was at the Pentagon, as one of Halliburton's leading lobbyists. In 2001, Cheney returned to Washington as vice president, and Brown & Root continued to build, maintain, and protect bases from Central Asia to the Persian Gulf.[18]

During Cheney's term as Halliburton's CEO, the company advanced from seventy-third to eighteenth on the Pentagon's list of top contractors.

Its number of subsidiaries located in offshore tax havens also increased from nine to forty-four. As a result, Halliburton went from paying $302 million in company taxes in 1998 to getting an $85 million tax refund in 1999. Following the second Gulf War, while Cheney was vice president, the Army Corps of Engineers awarded the company a no-bid contract to extinguish oil well fires in Iraq. The contract was open-ended, with no time or dollar limits, and was "cost-plus," meaning that the company is guaranteed both to recover costs and then to make a profit on top of that. Such contracts are typical of Brown & Root's operating methods and are worth tens of millions of dollars.[19] On April 4, 2003, in honor of "Big Business Day 2003," Citizen Works, a watchdog organization created by the consumer advocate Ralph Nader, gave Dick Cheney its "Daddy War-bucks" award for eminence in corporate war profiteering.

Kosovo's Camp Bondsteel, a Brown & Root product, is a spooky place, surrounded by a 2.5-meter-high earthen berm and nine wooden guard towers. All trees in the area have been removed to provide open fields of fire. Dominated by a mass of communications antennae, satellite dishes, and hovering attack helicopters, it has a six-mile perimeter and seems too large and permanent an installation merely to meet the requirements of peacekeeping in southern Serbia, a mission that President Clinton asserted would last no longer than six months and that George Bush said in his election campaign he wished to eliminate. More likely, Camp Bondsteel is intended to play a role in a grand strategy to secure for us Middle Eastern and Central Asian oil supplies and to control oil going to other countries.

Camp Bondsteel is actually located astride the route of the proposed AMBO (Albania, Macedonia, Bulgaria Oil) Trans-Balkan pipeline. This $1.3 billion project, if built, will pump Caspian Basin oil brought by tanker from a pipeline terminus in Georgia across the Black Sea to the Bulgarian oil port at Burgas, where it will be piped through Macedonia to the Albanian Adriatic port of Vlore. From there, supertankers would take it to Europe and the United States, thus bypassing the congested Bosporous Strait—as of now the only route out of the Black Sea by ship—where tankers are restricted to 150,000 tons. The initial feasibility study for the AMBO pipeline was done in 1995 by Brown & Root, which updated it in 1999.[20] Bondsteel appears to be a base camp for what the University of Texas political scientist James K. Galbraith has called the "military-petroleum complex," of which Dick Cheney is assuredly a godfather.[21]

Not coincidentally, in February 2003, the United States also began to build two new military bases at Burgas. On November 14, 2001, the Bulgarian parliament ratified an agreement giving the United States over-flight and transit rights for the war in Afghanistan; when Turkey withdrew its support of Washington's 2003 invasion of Iraq, the United States turned to Sofia for a permanent installation, to which the Bulgarians agreed. The air force took over much of Burgas International Airport, one of three commercial airports in Bulgaria, and flew in numerous construction crews to build a garrison at a nearby beach for American military personnel. It is called Camp Sarafovo. The large number of airmen who arrived seemingly overnight are the first foreign troops to commandeer the Burgas airport since the Luftwaffe seized it in 1943. During the second Iraq war, the United States flew KC-10 and KC-135 aerial refueling missions from Burgas to support air operations over Baghdad. The port of Burgas is home to the country's largest oil refinery and, under the terms of the Bulgarian-American agreement, supplies all the fuel required by the air force. Just a few hundred miles up the Black Sea coast, at the Romanian port of Constanta, the air force is building a similar base complex. Constanta is the center of Romania's large oil industry. The Afghan war and second Iraq war turned out to be splendid opportunities for the United States to consolidate its oil strategy for the Balkans, the first stage of which was Camp Bondsteel.[22]

Private military companies and private contractors have become indispensable to the operations of our more than 700 military bases around the world. They supply—for profit—the logistics that keep the empire operating. Camp Doha is a good example of what they supply. It is the major army base in Kuwait and has been in continuous use since the Persian Gulf War of 1991. (Camp Doha, in Kuwait, should be distinguished from the city of Doha, which is the capital of the nation of Qatar.) Camp Doha is a huge complex of heavily defended warehouses some twenty miles into the desert from Kuwait City. It has grown from two small buildings at the time of the first Gulf War into a 500-acre depot.

Since December 1994, it has been the headquarters for Army Forces Central Command–Kuwait (ARCENT-KU). In June 1991, four months after Operation Desert Storm had ended, the Pentagon deployed the Eleventh Armored Cavalry Regiment from Germany to Camp Doha to serve as a rapid response force in case of renewed hostilities with Iraq. Since this unit was at the time the army's only asset in the region, it was maintained at a maximum state of readiness, its tanks "combat loaded" with ammunition. Large numbers of vehicles and enormous backlogs of fuel and ammunition were stockpiled at the base to be used in case of an emergency.

Over the years, Camp Doha has become the army's model ammunition depot, a prototype and paradigmatic example of a forward base for "prepositioning" the equipment, ammunition, and fuel needed for a brigade-sized armored task force. In theory, all the army needs to do is fly in the troops, who then climb into their warmed-up tanks and armored personnel carriers and head for the front lines in the oil lands of our planet. Doha was not, however, always a model base. On the morning of July 11, 1991, a defective heater in an ammunition carrier loaded with 155 mm artillery shells caught fire and exploded. The scattering shells landed on loaded vehicles and ammunition stockpiles, setting off fires and explosions that lasted the rest of the day. No one was killed, although forty-nine soldiers were injured. Among the estimated $14 million worth of ammunition and two dozen buildings destroyed were some 660 rounds of 120 mm depleted uranium shells.[23]

As a result of this accident, the army decided to turn over all maintenance of the stockpiled vehicles and ammunition to private contractors. The company that received the contract to operate Camp Doha in 1991 was DynCorp of Reston, Virginia. By the year 2000, it was number twenty among the top two hundred military contractors. (Halliburton was number twenty-one.)[24] In 1994, the contract for maintaining the prepositioned equipment at Camp Doha passed from DynCorp to the ITT Corporation. The contractor just prior to the second American attack on Iraq was Combat Support Associates of Orange, California, a joint venture of three military suppliers located in California, Colorado, and Texas. The ten-year cost-plus-award fee for all maintenance and operating services

on the tanks and other tracked vehicles at Camp Doha comes to an estimated cumulative total of $546,751,502, an amount the Kuwaiti govern-
ment has pledged to reimburse the U.S. goverment. In late 2002, Combat
Support Associates had 546 American civilians and 747 third-country
nationals working for it at the base.[25] Camp Doha became the jumping-
off point for the American assault forces in the second Iraq war.

Like Camp Doha, the other American military bases in the Persian
Gulf region all depend on private contractors for their defenses, amenities, and operations. The significance of this development for military
effectiveness as well as for the principle of accountable civilian government in the United States is a subject only rarely mentioned either in
Congress or in the press. The use of private contractors is assumed to be
more cost-effective, but even that is open to question when contracts go
only to a few well-connected companies and the bidding is not particularly competitive.

In the long run, one wonders whether these private companies will
be able to recruit employees successfully to work in countries where
American bases are deeply resented. On January 21, 2003, at 9:15 in the
morning, a gunman fired twenty-four bullets from a Kalashnikov at two
American civilians sitting in a Toyota sport utility vehicle at a traffic signal three miles from Camp Doha. He killed Michael R. Pouliot, the executive vice president and cofounder of Tapestry Solutions Corporation, a
small San Diego software development company that produces comput-
erized modeling and simulation exercises for the military. Pouliot's companion, David Caraway, was wounded six times but survived in critical
condition. He is a senior software engineer for the company.

A few months later, on May 12, 2003, just after the end of fighting in
the second Iraq war, terrorists blew up three foreign housing compounds
in Riyadh, Saudi Arabia, killing thirty-four, including eight Americans.
One of the main targets was an apartment building for some seventy Vinnell Corporation employees—military mercenaries hired to train the
Saudi National Guard. Fortunately for Vinnell, fifty members of its staff
were away on a "training exercise" at the time of the bombing. It was
widely speculated that the attack was a response to the American con-

quest of Iraq. Vinnell has about 800 employees in Riyadh, of whom 300 are Americans.

A large number of military contractors work in Kuwait and Saudi Arabia on various chores, including helping the army operate and maintain its equipment and training and equipping local militaries. After the Camp Doha killing, a spokesman for the army, Major Steve Stover, merely commented that "the world is a dangerous place, especially for Americans abroad."[26]

6

THE EMPIRE OF BASES

The presence of American forces overseas is one of the most profound symbols of the U.S. commitments to allies and friends. Through our willingness to use force in our own defense and in defense of others, the United States demonstrates its resolve to maintain a balance of power that favors freedom. To contend with uncertainty and to meet the many security challenges we face, the United States will require bases and stations within and beyond Western Europe and Northeast Asia, as well as temporary access arrangements for the long-distance deployment of U.S. forces.

"The National Security Strategy of the United States,"
September 17, 2002

During the Cold War, standard military doctrine held that overseas bases had four missions. They were to project conventional military power into areas of concern to the United States; prepare, if necessary, for a nuclear war; serve as "tripwires" guaranteeing an American response to an attack (particularly in divided "hot spots" like Germany and South Korea); and function as symbols of American power.[1] Since the end of the Cold War, the United States has been engaged in a continuous search for new justifications for its ever-expanding base structure—from "humanitarian intervention" to "disarming Iraq."

I believe that today five post–Cold War missions have replaced the four older ones: maintaining absolute military preponderance over the rest of the world, a task that includes imperial policing to ensure that no part of the empire slips the leash; eavesdropping on the communications of citizens, allies, and enemies alike, often apparently just to demonstrate that no realm of privacy is impervious to the technological capabilities of our government; attempting to control as many sources of petroleum as possible, both to service America's insatiable demand for fossil fuels and to use that control as a bargaining chip with even more oil-dependent regions; providing work and income for the military-industrial complex (as, for example, in the exorbitant profits Halliburton has extracted for building and operating Camps Bondsteel and Monteith); and ensuring that members of the military and their families live comfortably and are well entertained while serving abroad.

No one of these goals or even all of them together, however, can entirely explain our expanding empire of bases. There is something else at work, which I believe is the post–Cold War discovery of our immense power, rationalized by the self-glorifying conclusion that because we have it we deserve to have it. The only truly common elements in the totality of America's foreign bases are imperialism and militarism—an impulse on the part of our elites to dominate other peoples largely because we have the power to do so, followed by the strategic reasoning that, in order to defend these newly acquired outposts and control the regions they are in, we must expand the areas under our control with still more bases. To maintain its empire, the Pentagon must constantly invent new reasons for keeping in our hands as many bases as possible long after the wars and crises that led to their creation have evaporated. As the Senate Foreign Relations Committee observed as long ago as 1970, "Once an American overseas base is established it takes on a life of its own. Original missions may become outdated but new missions are developed, not only with the intention of keeping the facility going, but often to actually enlarge it. Within the government departments most directly concerned—State and Defense—we found little initiative to reduce or eliminate any of these overseas facilities."[2] The Pentagon tries to prevent local populations from reclaiming or otherwise exerting their rights over these long-established bases (as in the cases of the Puerto Rican movement to get the navy off Vieques Island, which it used largely for target practice, and of the Okinawan movement to get the marines and air force to go home—or at least go elsewhere). It also works hard to think of ways to reestablish the right to bases from which the United States has withdrawn or been expelled (in places like the Philippines, Taiwan, Greece, and Spain).

Given that many of our bases around the world are secret, that some are camouflaged by flags of convenience, and that many consist of multiple distinct installations, how can anyone assess accurately the scope and value of our military empire? It is not easy. If the Secretary of Defense were to ask his closest aides with the highest security clearances how many bases abroad he had under his control, they would have to reply, using an old naval officers' cop-out, "I don't know, sir, but I'll find out."

To begin to answer this question two official sources of data must be explored; both are of major importance although they differ in their standards of compilation. The Department of Defense's *Base Structure Report* (BSR) details the physical property owned by the Pentagon, while the report on *Worldwide Manpower Distribution by Geographical Area* (Manpower Report) gives the numbers of military personnel at each base, broken down by army, navy, marines, and air force, plus civilians working for the Defense Department, locally hired civilians, and dependents of military personnel.[3]

Both reports are supposed to be issued quarterly but actually appear intermittently. Neither report is inclusive, since many bases are cloaked in secrecy. For example, Charles Glass, the chief Middle East correspondent for ABC News from 1983 to 1993 and an authority on the Israeli-Palestinian conflict, writes, "Israel has provided the U.S. with sites in the Negev [desert] for military bases, now under construction, which will be far less vulnerable to Muslim fundamentalists than those in Saudi Arabia."[4] These are officially nonexistent sites. There have been press reports of aircraft from the carrier battle group USS *Eisenhower* operating from Nevatim Airfield in Israel, and a specialist on the military, William M. Arkin, adds, "The United States has 'prepositioned' vehicles, military equipment, even a 500-bed hospital, for U.S. Marines, Special Forces, and Air Force fighter and bomber aircraft at at least six sites in Israel, all part of what is antiseptically described as 'U.S.-Israel strategic cooperation.'"[5] These bases in Israel are known simply as Sites 51, 53, and 54. Their specific locations are classified and highly sensitive. There is no mention of American bases in Israel in any of the Department of Defense's official compilations.

The Manpower Report is the more complete of the two in its worldwide coverage, but the BSR is critically important for two reasons. First, for every listed site it gives an estimated "plant replacement value" (PRV) in millions of dollars. Second, it gives details on some 725 foreign bases in thirty-eight countries, of which it defines 17 as "large installations" (having a PRV greater than $1.5 billion), 18 as "medium installations" (having a PRV between $800 million and $1.5 billion), and 690 as "small installations" (having a PRV of less than $800 million). According to the Department of Defense, "The PRV represents the reported cost of replacing the facility and its supporting infrastructure using today's costs (labor and material) and standards (methods and codes)."

Although one must doubt the accuracy of any such estimates, particularly given the Pentagon's record of incompetent accounting, they are nonetheless useful for making comparisons. Thus, according to Pentagon specialists, Ramstein Air Force Base near Kaiserslautern, Germany, the largest NATO air base in Europe, has a PRV of $2,458.8 million; whereas Kadena Air Force Base in Okinawa, the largest U.S. facility in East Asia, has a PRV nearly twice as large, at $4,758.5 million (and its adjoining Kadena Ammunition Storage Annex adds another $964.3 million). These are astronomical sums even though they probably underestimate real replacement values. In its detailed reports by country, the BSR lists foreign bases only if they are larger than ten acres and have a PRV greater than $10 million. Sites that do not meet these criteria are aggregated for each country as "other." Only places with null or zero PRVs are not counted at all. These include small sites such as single, unmanned navigational aids or air force strategic missile emplacements. The 725 foreign bases, including the installations listed as "other," have a total replacement value, according to the Pentagon, of $118 billion. This is a mindboggling aggregation of foreign real estate and buildings possessed by the United States.

By contrast, the DoD's Manpower Report does not list individual bases, only countries. It found that in September 2001, the United States was deploying a total of 254,788 military personnel in 153 countries. When civilians and dependents are included, the number doubles to 531,227. Since the Manpower Report does not say what the assignments are within a particular foreign country, one cannot distinguish between a country with American bases and a country with merely some embassy guards, a few special forces on a training mission, and perhaps some communications clerks. Therefore, it seems useful to consider only those countries with at least a hundred active-duty military personnel. These are likely to be assigned to bases. The total then, according to the DoD's Manpower Report, is thirty-three, which comes close to the BSR's list of significant bases in thirty-eight countries.

There are some major discrepancies between the BSR and the Manpower Report that are not easily explained. To give one important example, the BSR for September 2001 does not have any entries for Bosnia-Herzegovina or for Yugoslavia, Serbia, or Kosovo. The Manpower Report for the same month gives 3,100 for the number of army troops in Bosnia and 5,675 for the number of army troops in the Serbian province of Kosovo. It is possible that Camp Eagle in Bosnia (built in 1995–96) and Camps Bondsteel and Monteith in Kosovo (both of which went up in 1999) were omitted intentionally in order to disguise their purpose—of protecting oil pipelines rather than contributing to international peace-keeping operations.

With such caveats, the table on pages 156–160 offers a snapshot of the American empire in terms of military personnel deployed overseas just before September 11, 2001. In the months following, the United States radically expanded its deployments everywhere but particularly in Afghanistan, elsewhere in Central Asia, and in the Persian Gulf.

Numerous bases are "secret" or else disguised in ways designed to keep them off the official books, but we know with certainty that they exist, where many of them are, and more or less what they do. They are either DoD-operated listening posts of the National Security Agency (NSA) and the National Reconnaissance Office (NRO), both among the most secretive of our intelligence organizations, or covert outposts of the military-petroleum complex. Officials never discuss either of these subjects with any degree of candor, but that does not alter the point that spying and oil are obsessive interests of theirs.

The United States operates so many overseas espionage bases that Michael Moran of NBC News once suggested, "Today, one could throw a dart at a map of the world and it would likely land within a few hundred miles of a quietly established U.S. intelligence-gathering operation. . . .

FOREIGN DEPLOYMENTS OF U.S. MILITARY PERSONNEL AT THE TIME OF THE
TERRORIST ATTACKS ON THE WORLD TRADE CENTER AND THE PENTAGON

By Region and Country
September 2001

Only those countries with at least 100 active-duty U. S. military personnel are listed. Totals of the listed countries do not add up to the regional totals because the latter include all countries with any U.S. troops, regardless of the size of the contingent.

	Army	Navy	Marines	Air Force	Military Total	Department of Defense U.S. civilians	U.S. dependents	Total
EUROPE	68,640	12,474	3,368	33,623	118,105	23,346	136,807	278,258
Belgium	894	105	30	549	1,578	634	2,827	5,039
Bosnia and Herzegovina	3,100	10	5	1	3,116	6	1	3,123
Germany	55,149	322	279	15,248	70,998	16,488	97,571	185,057
Greece	71	283	84	68	506	104	98	708

Greenland	0	0	0	153	153	3	0	156
Iceland	3	1,022	48	670	1,743	277	1,465	3,485
Italy	2,326	5,174	149	4,055	11,704	2,406	12,804	26,914
Macedonia (formerly Yugoslav Republic of Macedonia)	350	0	0	1	351	1	3	355
Netherlands	360	23	12	281	676	298	1,283	2,257
Portugal (including Azores)	15	58	7	925	1,005	164	1,302	2,471
Serbia (including Kosovo)	5,675	1	1	2	5,679	13	0	5,692
Spain	38	1,554	141	257	1,990	406	1,938	4,334
Turkey	172	26	196	1,759	2,153	399	2,195	4,747
United Kingdom	410	1,217	165	9,526	11,318	2,084	14,905	28,307
Afloat	0	2,632	2,071	0	4,703	0	0	4,703

Army	Navy	Marines	Air Force	Military Total	Department of Defense U.S. civilians	U.S. dependents	Total
FORMER SOVIET UNION (*including Armenia, Azerbaijan, Belarus, Georgia, Kazakhstan, Kyrgyzstan, Moldova, Russia, Tajikistan, Turkmenistan, Ukraine, and Uzbekistan*)							
39	6	81	25	151	3	49	203
EAST ASIA AND PACIFIC							
30,584	19,110	20,157	21,819	91,670	9,457	50,283	151,410
Australia							
8	61	663	71	803	9	218	1,030
Japan (including Okinawa)							
1,827	6,189	19,073	13,128	40,217	6,431	42,653	89,301
Republic of Korea (South Korea)							
28,654	327	110	8,514	37,605	2,875	7,027	47,507
Singapore							
8	92	16	44	160	48	111	319
Thailand							
42	9	30	32	113	3	64	180
Afloat							
0	12,382	196	0	12,578	0	0	12,578
MIDDLE EAST (including NORTH AFRICA and SOUTH ASIA)							
2,945	16,159	409	7,365	26,878	833	927	28,638

Bahrain							
38	1,843	157	27	2,065	286	543	2,894
Diego Garcia							
4	557	0	29	590	5	44	639
Egypt							
341	30	57	72	500	67	110	677
Kuwait							
2,150	7	41	2,010	4,208	98	5	4,311
Oman							
0	122	7	544	673	5	16	694
Qatar							
97	3	2	14	116	19	4	139
Saudi Arabia							
285	29	47	4,444	4,805	305	43	5,153
United Arab Emirates							
0	7	7	190	209	5	8	217
Afloat							
0	13,546	0	0	13,546	0	0	13,546
SUB-SAHARAN AFRICA							
46	6	209	18	279	7	138	424
WESTERN HEMISPHERE							
307	12,560	764	384	14,015	300	1,064	15,379

Army	Navy	Marines	Air Force	Military Total	Department of Defense U.S. civilians	U.S. dependents	Total
Canada							
13	53	9	88	163	21	203	387
Chile							
5	5	319	8	337	0	39	376
Cuba (Guantánamo)							
6	419	132	0	557	201	475	1,233
Honduras							
176	1	11	206	394	20	31	445
Afloat							
0	12,014	0	0	12,014	0	0	12,014
WORLD TOTALS							
102,561	60,315	24,988	63,234	251,098	33,946	189,268	474,312

SOURCE: U.S. Department of Defense, Washington Headquarters Services, Directorate for Information, Operations, and Reports, *Worldwide Manpower Distribution by Geographical Area*, September 30, 2001, on line at <http://web1.whs.osd.mil/DIORCAT.HTM#M05>.

America's surveillance network has grown so vast and formidable that in some respects it is feared as much as U.S. weaponry itself."[6] Because of secrecy the total number of these bases is impossible to know, but we are able to gain some idea of their extent and identify the most important ones. They are almost invariably located on foreign military installations, staffed by our military personnel but disguised as belonging to the country in which they are sited. They are normally listening and retrieval posts that transmit raw intercepts back to NSA headquarters at Fort George Meade, Maryland, or to the NSA's top spy base, RAF Menwith Hill, located on the moorlands near Harrogate in North Yorkshire, England ("the largest spy station in the world," as the Campaign for Nuclear Disarmament calls it).

There are three main forms of telecommunications. The first consists of telephone calls, faxes, e-mail, Internet connections, telegrams, and telexes sent and received via communications satellites owned and operated by the International Telecommunications Satellite organization (Intelsat), which is a treaty-based international organization. These satellites are in geostationary orbits so that they always maintain the same position in space relative to the earth. Created in 1964, Intelsat orbited its first satellite in 1967; as of 1999, it operated nineteen satellites. By 2002, 24 percent of its stock was owned by the Lockheed Martin Corporation. It is fairly simple, if expensive, to train an antenna from a ground listening post on an Intelsat or other communications satellite and eavesdrop on what it is sending and receiving. To get full coverage, however, listening posts need to be placed at strategic points all over the globe.

The volume of messages thus intercepted is huge. According to the director of the NSA, Lieutenant General Michael V. Hayden of the air force, during the 1990s international telephone traffic rose from an already impressive 38 billion minutes a year to over 100 billion a year. During 2002, the world's population will spend over 180 billion minutes on the phone in *international calls* alone.[7] All these messages can easily be intercepted, but voice-recognition technology remains unreliable. More commonly, spying is done by monitoring particular telephone numbers.

In contrast to these messages, a second form of telecommunications, shortwave and VHF (very high frequency) radio signals, carry only about two hundred miles at the most before being shielded by the curvature of the earth. Ground-based monitoring stations have difficulty intercepting them. During the 1960s, the United States installed monstrous antennas 400 meters in diameter to listen to high-frequency radio signals at such places as RAF Chicksands Priory, near Bedford, thirty-five miles north of London; San Vito dei Normanni, near Brindisi in the "heel" of Italy; Ayios Nikolaos, in eastern Cyprus; Misawa Air Force Base, Japan; Elmendorf Air Force Base, Alaska; Udorn, Thailand; and Karamursel, Turkey. Their targets were Soviet and Warsaw Pact air force communications and diplomatic messages from all countries on earth.

Today the NSA listens to such messages—including mobile phones and city-to-city microwave radio transmissions—from space. For this purpose the National Reconnaissance Office launches spy satellites into stationary orbits strung out along the equator. There they serve as "electronic vacuum cleaners," intercepting and beaming back to earth a huge array of messages. These satellites also take photographs, keep the oceans under surveillance, detect nuclear blasts, warn of missile launches and record the telemetry of their flights, transmit highly encrypted messages between NSA stations, and keep track of radar emanations. They require large arrays of antennas on earth to receive their output in intercepted messages.

Among the main American stations for downlinks from spy satellites are RAF Menwith Hill; RAF Morwenstow, in Cornwall, England; the air force base at Bad Aibling, near Augsberg, Germany; Pine Gap, near Alice Springs in central Australia (which also operates CIA satellites); Sabana Seca, Puerto Rico; "Summit Communications," located in the suburbs of Taipei, Taiwan; and the Naval Air Facility within the U.S. Air Force Base at Misawa, Aomori prefecture, in northern Japan.[8] Geopolitical analyst Paul Rogers of Opendemocracy.net revealed on November 29, 2002, that Pine Gap and Menwith Hill had been designated to pick up signals from a new Space-Based Infrared System (SBIRS) of satellites, which give an immediate indication of missile launches anywhere on earth and are key components in the Bush administration's ballistic missile defense scheme.

In 1975, Australia's Labor Party prime minister, Gough Whitlam, wanted to close the then-secret satellite intelligence base at Pine Gap. He threatened to reveal that the base, which except for its antennas is mostly underground, was a wholly American-run military operation under the command of a CIA officer, facts that had been kept hidden from him. On November 11, 1975, in Australia's greatest constitutional crisis, the governor-general of Australia, Sir John Kerr, after being briefed by the CIA, obligingly fired Whitlam and appointed opposition leader Malcolm Fraser as caretaker prime minister until elections could be called. Fraser was prepared to mobilize the army to maintain order, and Australia teetered close to revolution. In 1977, Warren Christopher, then assistant secretary of state for East Asia and later secretary of state, promised the deposed Whitlam that the United States would never again interfere in Australian domestic politics. But, of course, Pine Gap was not closed or brought under Australian government control.[9]

A third type of communications is via copper cables or high-capacity optical fiber networks. Unlike messages sent via cell phones and microwaves, which leak or bounce into the atmosphere and become interceptable, messages over cables can be spied on only if a physical tap is placed on the cable itself. The security of ordinary copper cable ended in October 1971 when an American submarine, the USS *Halibut,* put a tap on a Soviet military cable going to the Kamchatka Peninsula. Many other taps have been placed by the navy since then. In 1999, Congress authorized some $600 million to modify one of the newest nuclear submarines, the USS *Jimmy Carter* (named after the only president ever to serve on a submarine), to enable it to tap underwater fiber-optic cables. According to the *Wall Street Journal,* the *Jimmy Carter* "will be the premier U.S. spy sub . . . [with] state-of-the-art technology for undersea fiber-optic taps."[10] Bases for tapping into these cables include the submarine pens at Diego Garcia in the Indian Ocean; White Beach, Okinawa; La Maddalena Island, off Sardinia opposite Naples; Holy Loch, Scotland; and Rota, near Cádiz, Spain. The navy lobbies for more submarines, saying that they are needed for spy missions, but at roughly $2.3 billion each they are an expensive way to gather intelligence.[11] Still, most experts believe that fiber-optic cables are harder to tap than copper and that they remain the most secure mode of communication—except, of course, for human messengers and homing pigeons. Planning for the 1998 Indian nuclear weapons tests was, for example, done over fiber-optic lines, which is evidently why the U.S. intelligence community failed to gain prior knowledge of them. The Chinese are among the biggest purchasers of fiber-optic cable on earth.

Sigint (signals intelligence) bases designed to intercept the first two types of communications are quite conspicuous because they involve fields full of antennas covered in hard plastic domes to protect them from the weather and hide the direction in which they are pointed. There are, for example, over twenty telltale satellite dishes at Menwith Hill and fourteen at Misawa. With their covering domes, they look like huge golf balls. Sigint bases in England are disguised as Royal Air Force (RAF) stations even though there are few if any British personnel assigned to them. For example, Chicksands Priory, created in 1941 by the RAF for electronic spying on northern Germany and Poland during World War II, was turned over to the U.S. Air Force in 1950. Ever since, the United States has operated Chicksands for its exclusive use, not even sharing the information gathered there with NATO. These arrangements reflect the historical fact that the two governments never entered into any formal agreements on American bases in England. Parliament has, moreover, never taken a vote on the matter. What exists are letters dating from the early Cold War era drafted by British civil servants and countersigned by the American ambassador giving the United States the right to use RAF bases.[12] For these reasons, it has never been possible to say with precision how many U.S. bases there are in Britain (although one well-informed source claims there were 104 by the end of the Cold War).[13]

Much information about the disguised American bases in Britain comes from peace activists like Lindis Percy, coordinator of the United Kingdom's Campaign for the Accountability of American Bases, who has been arrested many times for breaking into them. One recent escapade occurred at RAF Croughton, twenty-five miles southwest of Stratford-upon-Avon, where Percy was charged with "aggravated trespass." She then revealed to the press that the RAF designation was phony and that Croughton is actually a U.S. Air Force base. One authoritative but unofficial source says that the base's active-duty personnel include 400 Americans and 109 employees of the British Ministry of Defense.[14] Its function is communications with U.S. Air Force aircraft, including nuclear bombers. The Americans dropped charges against Percy to prevent "embarrassing evidence" from being presented in open court.[15] In June 2002, she had five injunctions against her for entering such bases, including Menwith Hill.

Since 1948, a highly classified agreement among the intelligence agencies of the United Kingdom, the United States, Canada, Australia, and New Zealand allows them to exchange information not just about target countries but also about one another. This arrangement permits the United States's National Security Agency, Britain's Government Communications Headquarters (GCHQ), Canada's Communications Security Establishment, Australia's Defense Signals Directorate, and New Zealand's General Communications Security Bureau to swap information with one another about their own citizens—including political leaders—without formally violating national laws against domestic spying. Even though the U.S. government, for example, is prohibited by law from spying on its own citizens except under a court-ordered warrant, as are all the other countries in the consortium, the NSA can, and often does, ask one of its partners to do so and pass the information its way. One former employee of the Canadian Communications Security Establishment revealed that, at the request of Prime Minister Margaret Thatcher of Britain, the GCHQ asked the Canadians to monitor certain British political leaders for them.[16]

Since at least 1981, what had once been an informal covert intelligence-sharing arrangement among the English-speaking countries has been formalized under the code name "Echelon." Up until then the consortium exchanged only "finished" intelligence reports. With the advent of Echelon, they started to share raw intercepts. Echelon is, in fact, a specific program for satellites and computers designed to intercept nonmilitary communications of governments, private organizations, businesses, and individuals on behalf of what is known as the "UKUSA signals intelligence alliance." Each member of the alliance operates its own satellites and creates its own "dictionary" supercomputers that list key words, names, telephone numbers, and anything else that can be made machine-readable. They then search the massive downloads of information the satellites bring in every day. Each country exchanges its daily intake and its analyses with the others. One member may request the addition to another's dictionary of a word or name it wants to target. Echelon monitors or operates approximately 120 satellites worldwide.

The system, which targets international *civil* communications channels, is so secret that the NSA has refused even to admit it exists or to discuss it with delegations from the European Parliament who have come to Washington to protest such surveillance. France, Germany, and other European nations accuse the United States and Britain, the two nations that originally set up Echelon, with commercial espionage—what they call "state-sponsored information piracy."[17] There is some evidence that the United States has used information illegally collected from Echelon to advise its negotiators in trade talks with the Japanese and to help Boeing sell airplanes to Saudi Arabia in competition with Europe's Airbus. In January 1995, the CIA used Echelon to track British moves to win a contract to build a 700-megawatt power station near Bombay, India. As a result, the contract was awarded to Enron, General Electric, and Bechtel. During October 1999, European activists and government officials held a "Jam Echelon Day," spending twenty-four hours sending as many messages by e-mail as possible with words like *terrorism* and *bomb* in them to try to overload the system.

Echelon's existence has given great impetus to more or less unbreakable systems of encryption, such as what are called random one-time pads. These use keys known only to sender and receiver and are secure against all forms of cryptanalysis. The plaintext message is encrypted using computer-generated random numbers and never used again. The sender and the receiver must use the same key, the weak point being getting the key to the recipient via some tamperproof channel, commonly a CD sent through the mail.[18] One-time pads are a development to which the NSA is extremely hostile. However, knowing that the NSA has access to all forms of electronic communications, users seeking privacy have naturally turned to coded messages. The NSA, in turn, is reported to be trying to get Microsoft to include secret decoding keys known only to it in all its software.

The problem with Echelon is not just that nations occasionally use it to promote their commercial activities, or simply that it is a club of

English speakers, or even that it can be defeated by fiber-optic cables and encryption. The fatal flaw of Echelon is that it is operated by the intelligence and military establishments of the main English-speaking countries in total secrecy and hence beyond any kind of accountability to representatives of the people it claims to be protecting. Among the resultant travesties was the case of a woman whose name and telephone number went into the Echelon directories as those of a possible terrorist because she told a friend on the phone that her son had "bombed" in a school play.[19] According to several knowledgeable sources, the British government has included the word *amnesty* in all the system's dictionaries in order to collect information against the human rights organization Amnesty International. Even though the governments of the world now know about Echelon, they can do nothing about it except take defensive measures on their messaging systems, and this is but another sign of the implacable advance of militarism in countries that claim to be democracies.

As I have said, no single purpose can possibly explain the more than 725 American military bases spread around the world. But the government's addiction to surveillance certainly explains where some of them are and why they are so secret. Another explanation for some of the bases is the staggering level of American dependence on foreign sources of oil, which grows greater by the year. Many garrisons are in foreign countries to defend oil leases from competitors or to provide police protection to oil pipelines, although they invariably claim to be doing something completely unrelated—fighting the "war on terrorism" or the "war on drugs," or training foreign soldiers, or engaging in some form of "humanitarian" intervention. The search for scarce resources is, of course, a traditional focus of foreign policy. Nonetheless, the United States has made itself particularly dependent on foreign oil because it refuses to conserve or in other ways put limits on fossil fuel consumption and because multinational petroleum companies and the politicians they support profit enormously from Americans' profligate use. A year after the 9/11 attacks, General Motors's sales of its 5,000-pound gas-guzzling Chevrolet Suburban SUV, which gets thirteen miles to the gallon, had doubled.[20]

Starting with the CIA's 1953 covert overthrow of the government of Iran for the sake of the British Petroleum Company, American policy in the Middle East—except for its support of Israel—has been dictated by oil. It has been a constant motive behind the vast expansion of bases in the Persian Gulf. America's wars in the oil lands of the Persian Gulf are the subject of a later chapter; what I want to explore here are some other cases in which oil is the *only* plausible explanation for acquiring more bases. In these cases, the government has produced elaborate cover stories for what amounts to the use of public resources and the armed forces to advance private capitalist interests. The invasion of Afghanistan and the rapid expansion of bases into Central and Southwestern Asia are among the best examples, although there are several instances from Latin America as well.

Oil is a very old subject around the Caspian Sea and especially in the city of Baku, capital of Azerbaijan, itself located on the Apsheron Peninsula that juts into the Caspian from its western shore. In the thirteenth century, Marco Polo commented on springs in the region giving forth a black fluid that burned easily and was useful for cleaning the mange of camels. Baku was also the site of the "eternal pillars of fire"—obviously oil-fed—worshiped by the Zoroastrians. In the nineteenth and early twentieth centuries, it was the place where the Nobel brothers, Robert and Ludwig, revolutionized oil-drilling techniques and methods of transporting oil to world markets, thereby laying the foundations for their own vast fortune and that of the Rothschild family of Paris. In the patent of a third Nobel brother, Alfred, the inventor of dynamite and later the creator of the Nobel Prize, lay the roots of the successes of the DuPont company in the United States and of Royal Dutch Shell in the Netherlands. Baku's oil was Hitler's target in the Caucasus until his armies were stopped and defeated at Stalingrad.

In 1978, while traveling in Azerbaijan, Armenia, and Georgia, I took a swim in the Caspian and could not help noticing its slightly oily texture and smell. At that time, however, the region was better known for Beluga sturgeon and caviar, since during the years when only two nations, the USSR and Iran, bordered on the Caspian Sea, the oil and gas of the basin remained largely underdeveloped. The Soviets preferred to invest in their vast Siberian oil fields and left the Muslim areas of the Caspian to produce primarily for local markets. Iran, of course, has its own oil fields.

After the breakup of the USSR in 1991, five independent nations suddenly bordered the sea—Russia, Iran, Azerbaijan, Kazakhstan, and Turkmenistan—and the modern race to control the oil and gas resources of the region began. It was led by American-based multinational oil companies, soon to be followed by the U.S. military in one of its more traditional and well-established roles: protector of private capitalist interests. As retired Marine Lieutenant General Smedley Butler, winner of two congressional Medals of Honor, wrote way back in 1933, "I spent thirty-three years and four months in active military service. . . . And during that period I spent most of my time as a high-class muscle-man for big business, for Wall Street, and the bankers. . . . Thus, I helped make Mexico and especially Tampico safe for American oil interests in 1914. I helped make Haiti and Cuba a decent place for the National City Bank boys to collect revenues in. I helped in the raping of half a dozen Central American republics for the benefit of Wall Street. . . . In China I helped to see to it that Standard Oil went its way unmolested."[21] During the 1990s and especially after Bush's declaration of a "war on terrorism," the oil companies again needed some muscle and the Pentagon was happy to oblige.

Nobody knows exactly how much oil and gas there is in the Caspian Basin, since it has been poorly surveyed. The Energy Information Administration of the U.S. Department of Energy conservatively estimates that proven reserves in Azerbaijan, Kazakhstan, and Turkmenistan are just under 8 billion barrels but that possible reserves may well reach over 200 billion barrels. Natural gas reserves are, for Turkmenistan, 101 trillion cubic feet proven and 159 trillion cubic feet probable and, for Kazakhstan, 65 tcf proven and 88 tcf probable. Turkmenistan may have the eighth-largest gas reserves in the world. (The agency defines proven reserves as oil and natural gas deposits that are 90 percent probable and possible reserves as deposits that are 50 percent probable.)[22] The Bush administration's national energy policy document of May 17, 2001, known as the Cheney Report, notorious because one of its chief sources of information was the chairman of the now discredited and bankrupt Enron Corporation, suggests that "proven oil reserves in Azerbaijan and Kazakhstan are about twenty billion barrels, a little more than the North Sea."[23] These proven reserves, whose value hovers between $3 trillion and $5 trillion, might supply all of Europe's petroleum needs for eleven years.[24] Two other elements add to the prospects of great profits: labor costs are extremely low and environmental standards nonexistent.

Even if the Caspian Basin is not the El Dorado that some claim, it is the world's last large, virtually undeveloped oil and gas field that could for a time compete with the Persian Gulf in supplying petroleum to Europe, East Asia, and North America. It seems to have about 6 percent of the world's proven oil reserves and 40 percent of its gas reserves.[25] China, which has the world's fastest-growing economy, became a net oil importer in November 1993 and continues to try to negotiate a possible pipeline from Kazakhstan to Shanghai via Xinjiang Province. China is also attempting to obtain oil from Russia via a pipeline that would stretch from Angarsk in Siberia to the Daqing oil field in Manchuria.[26]

Imagining the five Central Asian republics that became independent when the USSR broke up in 1991 as potential suppliers of oil to the United States, however, involves numerous problems. Kazakhstan (by far the largest in terms of land area), Kyrgyzstan, and Tajikistan all share frontiers with China. Turkmenistan borders on Iran. Uzbekistan, in the center, is the only one that abuts all the others plus Afghanistan. All except one are ruled by former Communist Party apparatchiks. Only President Askar Akayev of Kyrgyzstan was not a former Soviet boss, and he has arranged for all fuel for the military jets flying out of the U.S. base in Kyrgyzstan, the biggest American garrison in Central Asia, to be supplied by a firm owned by his son-in-law.[27]

All the leaders of these Central Asian republics have hopeless human rights records, the two worst being the president of Uzbekistan, where the big U.S. air base at Khanabad is located, and the president for life in Turkmenistan, who has established a personality cult surpassing that of Stalin and who has placed all oil revenues in an offshore account that only he controls. Even Kazakhstan, which is relatively developed and sophisticated—the famous Russian Cosmodrome that launched the world's first space missions is located at Baykonur in south-central Kazakhstan and the country has a population that is 35–40 percent Russian—is hardly a model republic. Its foreign minister revealed that in 1996 President

CENTRAL ASIA

Nursultan Nazarbayev moved $1 billion in oil revenues to a secret Swiss bank account without informing his parliament.[28]

These countries are also among the premier suppliers of narcotic drugs to world markets, and their repressive, monopolistic regimes have proved powerful breeding grounds for Islamic militants. Their "Kalashnikov cultures" make ordinary business dealings close to impossible. President George W. Bush told *Washington Post* assistant managing editor Bob Woodward that he loathed North Korean dictator Kim Jong Il because Kim starves his people, breaks up families, and tortures dissidents.[29] The records of the Central Asian autocrats bear an uncomfortable likeness to those of Kim, but Bush has entertained President Islam Karimov of Uzbekistan, President Akayev of Kyrgyzstan, and President Nazarbayev of Kazakhstan in the Oval Office. Moreover, Defense Secretary Donald Rumsfeld and Central Command chief General Tommy Franks have called on each of them, including the Stalinist President Saparmurat Niyazov of Turkmenistan, to thank them profusely for allowing our planes to use their airspace and for their support for "humanitarian" aid to Afghanistan.[30]

The biggest problem of all, however, is simply that the Central Asian republics are landlocked. Oil and gas must be transported to market through exposed pipelines, and on none of the proposed routes to market can security be fully guaranteed. Chechen rebels, Armenian irredentists, Iranian mullahs, and Afghan and Kurdish guerrillas threaten all known paths west and south from Baku.[31] The only pipelines currently in operation connect the Caspian Basin north to Russia. International consortia have been created to lay pipelines on the bottom of the Caspian Sea but the five nations bordering on the sea do not have a legal agreement on how rights to the sea should be divided. Prior to the American attack on Afghanistan, the big American petroleum companies active in the area—Chevron (now ChevronTexaco), Union Oil Company of California (Unocal), Amoco (now British Petroleum–Amoco), Exxon (now ExxonMobil), and a few others—had all tried to get concessions from and strike pipeline deals with Azerbaijan, Kazakhstan, and Turkmenistan with little success. Only after the Americans started to build a complex of military bases in at least four different countries—Afghanistan, Kyrgyz-

stan, Pakistan, and Uzbekistan—did the situation begin to improve for
these companies.

The pipeline race began in 1993 when Chevron entered into a forty-
year deal with the government of Kazakhstan to exploit the Tengiz oil
field and export its oil through a proposed new pipeline complex across
the Caspian Sea to Baku and from there to the Russian Black Sea port of
Novorossiisk.[32] The obstacles to this project, in which Chevron has
invested several billion dollars, have so far proved insuperable. The Western portion of the pipeline, which is complete, has two sections. One
passes through Chechnya, where an anti-Russian rebellion is ongoing,
and the other through Dagestan to the north, only slightly more settled
politically. These are very difficult pipelines to protect from sabotage.
Nor is export by ship from the Black Sea particularly profitable because
the Turks have placed heavy constraints on the use of supertankers in the
narrow Bosporus Strait into the Mediterranean to protect against a disastrous oil spill off Istanbul. The pipeline section from Kazakhstan to Baku
across the Caspian remains in legal jeopardy because of conflicts over
who owns the sea bottom. The project is also a joint venture with Russia,
an arrangement that irritates the U.S. government, which wants to see
oil and gas leaving Central Asia without passing through either Russia
or Iran.

The list of people who backed the Kazakhstan pipeline reads like a
who's who of Republican oil politicians. Chevron's chief adviser was
Condoleezza Rice, then a Stanford University professor who joined the
Chevron board in 1991 after serving for a year on Bush Senior's National
Security Council. She received a $35,000 annual retainer, plus generous
stock options and other perks, and stepped down a decade later, just days
before becoming Bush Junior's national security adviser. The press often
refers to her as Chevron's "main expert on Kazakhstan" although she has
never published anything about Central Asia. (The only book she has
ever written without a collaborator is her doctoral dissertation, *The
Soviet Union and the Czechoslovak Army, 1948–1983: Uncertain Allegiance*
[1984].) Chevron was nonetheless so pleased with her role that it named
a 129,000-ton Bahamian-registered supertanker after her. In late April
2001, the company quietly renamed the ship the *Altair Voyager* "to eliminate

the unnecessary attention caused by the vessel's original name."[33] Although sailors regard it as a bad omen to rechristen a ship, the vessel is, at least, a double-hulled tanker.

Dick Cheney, Bush Senior's secretary of defense and Bush Junior's vice president, helped broker the deal, while out of office, between Chevron and Kazakhstan as a member of Kazakhstan's Oil Advisory Board. James A. Baker III, former secretary of state, mastermind of the scheme to get the Supreme Court to appoint Bush Junior president in 2001, and senior partner of the Houston and Washington law firm of Baker Botts, had a hand in the negotiations. Baker's firm maintains an office in Baku staffed by five attorneys. He is a member of the U.S.-Azerbaijan Chamber of Commerce's advisory council, as is Cheney. During the 1990s, the council's cochairman was Richard Armitage, a veteran administrator of the American-sponsored anti-Soviet war in Afghanistan during the 1980s and undersecretary of state in the second Bush administration. Brent Scowcroft, Rice's boss and mentor when he was Bush Senior's national security adviser, is a member of the board of Pennzoil, an active investor in the Caspian Sea oil consortia.

The pipeline project currently most favored by our government is a 1,091-mile-long conduit that would begin at Baku and head in a northwesterly direction, passing through Azerbaijan just north of the rebellious Armenian enclave of Nagorno-Karabakh (not perhaps a wise place to put an oil pipeline bound for Turkey since the Armenians hate the Turks), through Georgia to its Black Sea port of Batumi, and then southwest across volatile Turkish Kurdistan, to Turkey's deep-water Mediterranean port of Ceyhan. The cost of building it would be in the neighborhood of $3 billion. The United States likes this project because it avoids Russia and Iran while reaching the Mediterranean without passing through the Bosporus Strait and the Dardanelles. Even if it can be built and American troops can protect it, however, the pipeline would serve only Europe, a mature market with limited prospects for growth, whereas the real markets for Central Asian oil and gas are in East Asia. In addition, for the Baku-Ceyhan project to prove profitable, oil prices must remain above twenty dollars per barrel, a level that may not prove realistic.

Nonetheless, both the Clinton and the Bush administrations have vigorously supported this pipeline, and it is going ahead. In September 2002, U.S. Energy Secretary Spencer Abraham stopped briefly in Azerbaijan to officiate at a groundbreaking ceremony for its construction, and at the end of November the Georgian government approved routing it through the Borjomi valley, one of the country's most scenic regions and a source of mineral water, which is a prime Georgian export. An official from a mineral water company protested that the plan was like building a pipeline "next to a Perrier or Evian reserve in France."[34]

The Clinton administration, which was an enthusiastic supporter of the Baku-Ceyhan project as well as of a proposed trans-Afghan pipeline discussed below, put American military forces in Central Asia to try to drive a wedge between the new Central Asian republics and Russia. In 1997, the United States dispatched 500 paratroopers from the Eighty-second Airborne Division in North Carolina to Kazakhstan to train Kazakh and other Central Asian troops. This was deemed so successful that the following year the United States did the same in Uzbekistan using U.S. troops from the Tenth Mountain Division. It then formalized these ties into a kind of military version of the "sister city" relationships so beloved by municipal chambers of commerce. The Department of Defense gave various state National Guard units training missions in Central Asia and responsibility for instructing troops from Central Asian lands that visited the United States. The Arizona National Guard got Kazakhstan, the Montana National Guard teamed up with Kyrgyzstan, and the Louisiana National Guard worked with soldiers from Uzbekistan. Two of these Central Asian nations are today sites of major permanent American military bases.[35] The Tenth Mountain Division from Fort Drum, New York, is itself back in force at Khanabad, Uzbekistan.

Without question, the key post–9/11 military deployment supporting the Baku-Ceyhan pipeline was the dispatch in February 2002 of approximately 150 Special Forces and ten combat helicopters to the Republic of Georgia in the Caucasus. The cover story for this operation was that they were preparing Georgian forces to fight Chechen rebels with alleged al-Qaeda connections hiding out in the Pankisi Gorge of northeastern Georgia. But on February 27, 2002, Georgian Defense Ministry official Mirian Kiknadze told Radio Free Europe, "The U.S. military will train our rapid reaction force, which is guarding strategic sites in Georgia—particularly oil pipelines."[36] The Russians were seriously irritated by the American military presence in an area they regard as their sphere of influence, and two breakaway regions of Georgia—Abkhazia and South Ossetia—instantaneously decided to seek closer relations with Russia.

A third big U.S. project in Central Asia has been proposed: dual oil and gas pipelines from Turkmenistan south through Afghanistan to the Arabian Sea coast of Pakistan. Support for this enterprise appears to have been a major consideration in the Bush administration's decision to attack Afghanistan on October 7, 2001. The Taliban government in Afghanistan had so blocked development of the pipelines under American auspices that removal of the Taliban became the secret casus belli of the "war on terrorism" following the attacks of September 11, 2001. As the journalist Patrick Martin has commented, "If history had skipped over September 11 and the events of that day had never happened, it is very likely that the United States would have gone to war in Afghanistan anyway, and on much the same schedule."[37]

The original idea of tapping the vast gas reserves of Turkmenistan belongs to Carlos Bulgheroni, the hard-driving, ambitious chairman of the Argentine company Bridas, the third-largest oil and gas company in Latin America. In 1993, he negotiated an agreement with President Saparmurat Niyazov of Turkmenistan and Benazir Bhutto, then prime minister of Pakistan, to build separate oil and gas pipelines across Afghanistan to Pakistan's Arabian Sea port of Gwadar. Bridas was, however, not big enough to cover all the costs, estimated at $2 billion for the 918-mile natural gas line and $4 billion for the 1,005-mile oil line, and so sought to create a consortium with the Union Oil Company of California (Unocal). Notorious and often in legal trouble for its flouting of environmental regulations in California, its collaboration in an oil deal with the murderous generals of Burma, and its indifference to the human rights of its employees in its many oil concessions, Unocal was so attracted to the idea that it went directly to Turkmenistan and Pakistan and negotiated a new agreement that froze Bridas out. Bulgheroni promptly sued Unocal in a Texas court for the theft of his idea, but the case was dismissed for lack of jurisdiction. Having learned that bigness matters, Bridas, in 1997, merged with the giant American company Amoco and the following year Amoco merged with British Petroleum, producing Britain's largest company. But by then BP-Amoco was no longer interested in what was becoming one of the riskiest oil ventures of modern times.

The problem, of course, was the endless civil war in fragmented Afghanistan. In the mid-1990s, Unocal needed a government in Kabul it could deal with in obtaining transit rights. Moreover, the international financing necessary to build such pipelines would not be forthcoming until the United Nations, the United States, and many other nations had a government in the Afghan capital to recognize. In this context, the United States and Pakistan decided that an unusual offshoot of the anti-Soviet *mujahideen* ("freedom fighters") of the 1980s was their best bet to end the war and obtain international legitimacy. They sponsored and supported a new organization calling itself the Taliban (Students of Islam). It would be hard to overstate the disasters that have befallen Afghanistan as a result of the "help" it has received from Americans, including the creation and subsequent destruction of the Taliban. During the almost decade-long Soviet military occupation of that country and our recruitment and arming of Islamic militants from around the world to fight the Russians, one-third of the population fled the country. (At one point, Pakistan and Iran sheltered more than six million Afghan refugees, and even in 1999, some 1.2 million Afghan refugees remained in Pakistan and about 1.4 million in Iran.) After the Soviet Union withdrew in 1989 and until Unocal came along, Afghanistan spiraled downward into one of the most brutal civil wars of modern times, becoming in the process by far the world's largest producer of opium poppies. Narcotics trafficking became its major source of revenue.

The Taliban, composed mostly of ethnic Pushtuns from around Kandahar, launched a war against the hopelessly corrupt Tajik and Uzbek warlords of the "Northern Alliance." War-weary Afghans often supported Taliban victories because its fundamentalist leaders did at least stamp out corruption, restore law and order (even if the law was an extreme version of medieval Islamic practice), and allow some semblance of normality to return to parts of the country. On September 27, 1996, the Taliban captured the capital, Kabul, and continued to drive the warlords north toward the borders of Tajikistan and Uzbekistan. Both Unocal and the U.S. government were convinced that they could work with the Taliban and that its harsh treatment of women and criminals was no worse than that of America's Afghan allies during the 1980s.

The United States began to help in every way it could. Deployments of American troop trainers to various Central Asian republics from 1997 on was a signal that Unocal, the American entry in the race for pipeline rights, was the company to back. Even after the Saudi extremist Osama bin Laden returned to Afghanistan in 1996 as a "guest" of the Taliban and after al-Qaeda's attacks of August 7, 1998, on the American embassies in Kenya and Tanzania, neither the Clinton nor the Bush State Departments ever designated Afghanistan a terrorist-sponsoring nation, since that would have ended any possibility of international funding for the pipelines. Both administrations were willing to accept the Taliban regime, despite its sponsorship of terrorism, so long as it cooperated with plans to develop the oil and gas resources of Central Asia.

A remarkable group of Washington insiders came together to promote the Unocal project. Unocal itself hired former national security adviser Henry Kissinger as a consultant in its negotiations with Turkmenistan, Afghanistan, and Pakistan. Kissinger then worked with Turkmenistan's chief consultant, General Alexander Haig, his former assistant in the White House and later Ronald Reagan's secretary of state. (Amoco, meanwhile, hired another former national security adviser, Zbigniew Brzezinski, who had helped instigate the Afghan-Soviet war of the 1980s.) Unocal also paid for the services of Robert Oakley, a former U.S. State Department coordinator for counterterrorism and a former ambassador to Pakistan, Zaire, and Somalia.[38]

Most creatively, Unocal employed two well-connected Afghans to help influence the Taliban in its favor—a naturalized U.S. citizen, Zalmay Khalilzad, a Pushtun with a 1979 Ph.D. from the University of Chicago, and Hamid Karzai, a Pushtun from Kandahar with links to the former Afghan king, Zahir Shah, then living in Quetta, Pakistan. In 1991 and 1992, George Bush Senior had appointed Khalilzad deputy undersecretary of defense for policy planning, working under Paul Wolfowitz, with whom he became closely associated. While at the Pentagon Khalilzad was also noticed by then Secretary of Defense Dick Cheney, who in 2001 named him to head the Bush Junior transition team for defense. On May 23, 2001, President Bush appointed Khalilzad to the National Security Council staff working under Condoleezza Rice, and on December 31, 2001, Khalilzad became the United States's "special envoy" (that is, unofficial ambassador) to Afghanistan only nine days after the U.S.-backed interim government of Hamid Karzai took office in Kabul. In 1996, Khalilzad and Karzai were both pro-Taliban, thinking of the new government as Unocal's best hope for "stability." In November of the following year, Khalilzad participated in a major Unocal effort to entertain and impress a delegation of Taliban officials whom the company had invited to its engineering headquarters in Houston (with a side trip to the NASA Space Center thrown in). The continued collaboration of Khalilzad and Karzai in post–9/11 Afghanistan strongly suggests that the Bush administration was and remains as interested in oil as in terrorism in that region.[39]

In the mid-1990s, Unocal put together the Central Asia Gas and Pipeline Consortium (CentGas), made up of the government of Turkmenistan, the Delta Oil Company of Saudi Arabia, Indonesia Petroleum, Itochu Oil Exploration Company of Japan, Hyundai Engineering and Construction Company of South Korea, the Crescent Group of Pakistan, and Gazprom, the Russian natural gas behemoth. Delta was included because it was close to King Fahd of Saudi Arabia, and Unocal's advisers thought that he might help legitimize Unocal with the Taliban. (The only countries ever to recognize the Taliban government were Saudi Arabia, Pakistan, and the United Arab Emirates.) Gazprom was brought in to neutralize any Russian opposition. Unocal held 46.5 percent of the shares, Delta 15 percent, and the government of Turkmenistan 7 percent. According to the preeminent authority on the politics of Central Asia, the Pakistani journalist Ahmed Rashid, by 1996, "strategy over pipelines had become the driving force behind Washington's interest in the Taliban."[40]

Unocal's scheme looked good on paper, but it didn't fly. The Taliban was split between pro-Bridas and pro-Unocal factions, and it kept asking the CentGas consortium for more money and investments in roads and other infrastructure projects. Rumors suggest that Osama bin Laden favored working with Bridas rather than Unocal, in part because he did not like seeing his militant colleagues collaborating with Americans. The company was also encountering resistance from a quarter it normally did not deign to notice. Unocal's indifference to the Taliban's human rights record deeply offended the American women's movement. An organization called the Feminist Majority Foundation of Los Angeles petitioned the state of California to revoke Unocal's charter, and in June 1998, Mavis Leno, wife of Jay Leno, the host of TV's *The Tonight Show,* attended a Unocal stockholders' meeting and denounced the company for its willingness to cooperate with the Taliban.[41] Then, on August 7, 1998, Osama bin Laden's terrorists attacked the American embassies in East Africa, and on August 20, President Clinton retaliated by ordering Tomahawk cruise missiles fired into bin Laden's training camps in Afghanistan. The next day Unocal suspended work on the pipeline until the United States recognized the government of Afghanistan, and on December 4, it formally withdrew from the CentGas consortium, claiming that world oil and gas prices were too low to make it profitable. Most analysts concluded that no other major oil company would take its place and that the project was dead.

But the U.S. government was not ready to give up. Its purpose was not just to make money but to establish an American presence in Central Asia. It was pleased with the Taliban's crackdown on Afghan poppy production and wanted the Taliban to turn over Osama bin Laden. The Taliban was also winning the war against the Northern Alliance and consolidating its rule throughout the country. It was, however, getting deservedly awful press. In November 1999, the United Nations imposed sanctions against Afghanistan because of its human rights abuses, and on March 1, 2001, the Taliban provoked international outrage by blowing up two monumental ancient Buddhist statues at Bamiyan. The United States lost patience and concluded that "regime change" was in order.

As *Alexander's Gas & Oil Connections* reported in February 2002, "Plans to destroy the Taliban had been the subject of international diplomatic and not-so-diplomatic discussions for months before September 11. There was a crucial meeting in Geneva in May 2001 between U.S. State Department, Iranian, German, and Italian officials, where the main topic was a strategy to topple the Taliban and replace the theocracy with a 'broad-based government.' The topic was raised again in full force at the Group of Eight (G-8) summit in Genoa, Italy, in July 2001 when India— an observer at the summit—contributed its own plans."[42] Further meetings took place after the G-8 session in Berlin among American, Russian, German, and Pakistani officials, and Pakistani insiders have described a detailed American plan of July 2001 to launch military strikes against the Taliban from bases in Uzbekistan and Tajikistan before mid-October of that year. It should be recalled that "Bush's favorite Afghan," Zalmay Khalilzad, joined the National Security Council on May 23, 2001, just in time to work on an operational order for an attack on Afghanistan. On August 2, 2001, Assistant Secretary of State for South Asian Affairs Christina Rocca, a former CIA officer, held the United States's last official meeting with the Taliban in Islamabad.

In light of this trajectory, it would appear that the attacks of September 11 provided an opportunity for the United States to act unilaterally to remove the Taliban, without assistance from Russia, India, or any other country. In the weeks following 9/11, the Pentagon's formidable public relations apparatus went into top gear to describe to a public almost totally ignorant of Afghanistan and of Central Asian oil politics generally how we proposed to smash Osama bin Laden and his al-Qaeda organization. The secretary of defense, Donald Rumsfeld, became something of a stand-up comic in his daily press conferences, quipping about how the United States wanted bin Laden dead or alive and was "smoking out" al-Qaeda operatives, who were said to be "on the run." The primary strategy, however, was to reopen the Afghan civil war by having the CIA spread some $70 million in cash among the Tajik and Uzbek warlords that the Taliban had defeated.[43] The reemergence of the Northern Alliance, backed by massive American air power, resulted in the almost instantaneous collapse of the Taliban regime, leaving Afghanistan to revert to fighting among local satraps and the cultivation of opium poppies.

With astonishing speed and efficiency, the U.S. military managed to use the war to obtain the rights to military bases in Afghanistan and surrounding countries. For its immediate military operations, which were largely over by the beginning of 2002, it occupied three main sites within

Afghanistan itself—Mazar-i-Sharif airport in the extreme north of the country, Bagram Air Base in the suburbs of Kabul, and Kandahar International Airport in the south. It also placed troops in Kabul to provide immediate security for Hamid Karzai's newly installed government, whose powers hardly extended beyond Kabul, much less the rest of the country. For the first few weeks, all of these places were occupied by Special Forces, marines, and frontline army troops, but as the Taliban collapsed and al-Qaeda dispersed into the countryside and across the Pakistan border, these combat forces were replaced with army units engaged in establishing semipermanent garrisons. In August 2002, Central Command chief General Tommy Franks commented that U.S. soldiers would be in Afghanistan for "a long, long time" and compared the situation to South Korea, where army and air force troops had been based for more than half a century.[44]

In addition to occupying strategic points in Afghanistan, the Bush administration entered into an agreement with General Pervez Musharraf, the president of Pakistan, to take over three important bases of the Pakistan Air Force: Jacobabad, 300 miles northeast of Karachi; Pasni, 180 miles west of Karachi on the Arabian Sea coast; and Dalbandin, 170 miles southwest of Quetta and only 20 miles from the Afghan border. It was from these Pakistani bases that the United States sent its CIA operatives and Special Forces into Afghanistan and launched its AC-130 gunships and Predator drones. All told, the United States flew as many as 57,800 sorties against Afghan targets from bases in Pakistan or crossing its airspace. At Jacobabad, the United States quickly undertook a major program to improve the runways, install air-traffic-control radar, and air-condition offices and living quarters. Dalbandin airstrip had been built in the late 1980s with Saudi Arabian money to allow Saudi and Persian Gulf princes to fly in for falconing and bird-hunting expeditions. The CIA found its location near the Afghan border very convenient. In January 2002, however, with the threat of another war with India looming, Pakistan moved its forces south from that border and reoccupied Jacobabad and Pasni. Though displeased, the Americans had little choice but to share the facilities.[45]

All these Afghan and Pakistani bases, plus some small CIA camps on the Tajik-Afghan border for liaison with the Northern Alliance warlords, directly supported the short military campaign of the fall and winter of 2001 that overthrew the Taliban. But the bases that were built in Kyrgyzstan and Uzbekistan are another matter. Less than a month after September 11, 2001, the United States negotiated long-term leases with both countries—reacting incredibly fast for a government responding to an unexpected event.

These bases did not extend the reach of American air power in Afghanistan to any appreciable degree. Aircraft carriers in the Arabian Sea were just as close to targets in southern Afghanistan and much cheaper to operate. Nor were these bases meant for the deployment of large numbers of ground forces. The Kyrgyzstan base was 620 miles from the Afghan border, and Washington's strategy in the war did not involve the use of large concentrations of American troops. In fact, the Kyrgyz and Uzbek bases were brought to bear only tangentially during the war, and they were too far from Iraq to be of much use in the war already being planned against Saddam Hussein's regime. Nor were they intended to supply significant amounts of humanitarian aid to Afghanistan, since that remained largely in the hands of the United Nations and nongovernmental organizations like the Red Cross, which are not normally allowed to use U.S. bases.[46] Nor were they there to protect the local regimes from Islamic militants since these governments would not entrust that mission to Americans and have agreements with the Russians to deal with such problems. (The Russians, for instance, have deployed some 20,000 troops in Tajikistan for that purpose.)

According to the *New York Times*, the Kyrgyz and Uzbek facilities are virtual copies of Camp Bondsteel in Kosovo. "Their function may be more political than actually military," acknowledged Deputy Secretary of Defense Paul Wolfowitz in an interview, but he did not specify what that political function might be.[47] The biggest of the bases is located on thirty-seven acres at the formerly civilian Manas International Airport, nineteen miles west of Bishkek, the capital of Kyrgyzstan. The Americans have renamed it Chief Peter J. Ganci Jr. Air Base after the highest-ranking officer of the New York Fire Department to perish in the collapse of the World Trade Center towers. Kyrgyzstan initially leased Manas for a year, but President Akayev assured American officials that he was willing to renew the lease for as long as necessary. American military headquarters in Kyrgyzstan are not actually located at the base but in downtown Bishkek at the local Hyatt Regency, where the military also set up an employment office to hire local workers. The base houses some 3,000 servicemen and women and includes a recreation and fitness center, live American sports programming on wide-screen TVs, and an Internet cafe. French air force pilots and their Mirage jet fighters, as well as British and Danish troops, are also stationed at Manas. Instead of using either of the two industrial-sized kitchens provided by the United States, however, the French have set up their own cooking facility, catering to French tastes. One airman told the *New York Times,* "I could tell from the start that this would be one of the better bases."[48]

In Uzbekistan, the twin of Manas is located at an old Soviet air base at Khanabad, near the city of Karshi, about a hundred miles north of the Afghan border. By May 2002, a thousand American soldiers from the Tenth Mountain Division and a squadron of F-15E fighter jets were deployed there. Russian sources claim that Uzbekistan has leased the base to the United States for twenty-five years. The Pentagon denies this but refuses to say how long the lease actually is. The president of Uzbekistan, Islam Karimov, declined to publish this agreement because it reportedly pledged him to "intensify the democratic transformation of society."[49] The Pentagon has given Vice President Cheney's old company, the Kellogg Brown & Root subdivision of Halliburton, an open-ended contract to provide logistics for the Khanabad base—everything from cooking the meals to fueling the aircraft, the same services Halliburton supplies so profitably to Camp Bondsteel and many other military facilities around the world.

Elsewhere in the Central Asian republics, the Bush administration has said it will build at least one base in Tajikistan but has not yet specified where. It already has overflight agreements with Azerbaijan and Kazakhstan and is sending Kazakh officers to America for training. Kazakhstan has given permission for the airfield in its former capital city, Almaty, to be used in case of emergency, and the United States is negotiating for basing rights on the Caspian shore of Kazakhstan. The only Central Asian republic that has denied the United States bases or overflight rights is

Turkmenistan, which adopted a policy of neutrality toward the struggle in Afghanistan.

The assistant secretary of state for European and Eurasian affairs, who was sworn in on May 31, 2001, is a career diplomat, Elizabeth Jones. She speaks Russian, German, and Arabic and was, from 1995 to 1998, ambassador to Kazakhstan. She used to drive around the Kazakh capital with a yellow bumper strip on her car that read, "Happiness Is Multiple Pipelines." In December 2001, at a press conference in Almaty, she promised, "When the Afghan conflict is over, we will not leave Central Asia. We have long-term plans and interests in this region."[50] As I hope to show, there is ample reason why we should believe her.

7

THE SPOILS OF WAR

Over the years, the real purposes of many of these overseas bases has changed from tactical and strategic locations of military value to elaborate American housing and logistic installations away from home. They provide locations and facilities for some units that would have no reason for existence if based in the United States, and they furnish justification for interesting and attractive overseas travel and adventure for the troops and their families.

COLONEL JAMES A. DONOVAN, USMC (RET.),
Militarism, U.S.A. (1970)

Wars and imperialism are Siamese twins joined at the hip. Each thrives off the other. They cannot be separated. Imperialism is the single-greatest cause of war, and war is the midwife of new imperialist acquisitions. Wars usually begin because political leaders convince a people that the use of armed force is necessary to defend the country or pursue some abstract goal—Cuban independence from Spain, preventing a Communist victory in a Korean civil war, keeping the banana republics of Central America in the "free world," or even bringing democracy to Iraq. For a major power, prosecution of any war that is not a defense of the "homeland" usually requires overseas military bases for strategic reasons. After the war is over, it is tempting for the victor to retain such bases and easy to find reasons to do so. Commonly, preparedness for a possible resumption of hostilities will be invoked. Over time, if a nation's aims become imperial, the bases form the skeleton of an empire. In recent centuries, wars launched from such bases have been the primary means through which imperialism has prospered and expanded, although an induced economic dependence can sometimes achieve the same effect. Since the end of World War II, American governments have offered many rationales for the bases they were collecting around the world, including containing Communism, warding off the "domino theory," fighting "ethnic cleansing," and preventing the spread of "weapons of mass destruction."

From the time of the Romans and the Han dynasty Chinese to the present, all empires have had permanent military encampments, forts, or bases of some sort. These were meant to garrison conquered territory, keeping restless populations under control, and to serve as launching points for further imperial conquests. What is most fascinating and curious about the developing American form of empire, however, is that, in its modern phase, it is solely an empire of bases, not of territories, and these bases now encircle the earth in a way that, despite centuries-old dreams of global domination, would previously have been inconceivable.

Yet, although our own nation is filled with military installations—there are 969 separate bases in the fifty states—ours has, oddly enough, never been a warrior culture.[1] Our people are largely not in uniform, nor (until the recent "war on terrorism") were military uniforms common in our cities and airports; our streets seldom see a military parade; our concerts are rarely filled with martial music; and yet ours is also a thoroughly militarized empire—though our model of a warrior seems most likely to be a military bureaucrat. The modern American empire can only be perceived, and understood, by a close look at our basing policies, the specific way we garrison the earth. To trace the historical patterns of base acquisition and to explore our basing systems worldwide is to reveal the sinews of what has until very recently, for most Americans, been a largely hidden empire.

Our imperial history is littered with bases on foreign soil. Our foreign policy is now largely made in the Pentagon and implemented by commanders who spend their lives cloistered in our myriad outposts, which constitute a deeply interconnected world with its own customs, habits, and ways of living as well as its own hierarchies and professional classes who are increasingly detached from the rest of us. It is hard even to remember that on the eve of World War II our regular army was a mere 186,000 men. Now, the 1.4 million-strong "peacetime" military, funded by a defense budget larger than most national budgets, is made up of both men and women living in a closed-off, self-contained base world serviced by their own airline—the Air Mobility Command, with its fleet of long-range C-17 Globemasters, C-5 Galaxies, C-141 Starlifters, KC-135 Stratotankers, KC-10 Extenders, and C-9 Nightingales—that links outposts from Greenland to Australia. Starting with our turn-of-the-century imperial beginnings, I want to explore here how that world of bases was assembled to become an imperial motor driving the United States on to ever more wars.

Though, as I said earlier, we were already a great continental empire by 1898, the Spanish-American War first set us on our modern path of imperialism. Some of the bases we acquired at that time—Guantánamo Bay, Pearl Harbor, Guam—are still overseas military outposts or are on territories that we later directly annexed. Under the influence of Wilsonian idealism, we did not follow our British, French, and Japanese allies in exploiting victory in World War I to acquire new colonies. It was not until World War II that our empire of bases achieved its global reach, and the United States still seems to regard its continuing occupation of the territory of its former Axis foes as something akin to a natural birthright. The Korean War, though ended in stalemate, nonetheless projected us onto the Asian mainland. After Vietnam, our base numbers were cut—not just in Southeast Asia but in other places where our defeat emboldened governments or peoples to oppose our military presence in their countries; the three most important such cases were Spain, Greece, and the Philippines. With the end of the Cold War, we resumed our march toward empire. Our 1999 war against Serbia, our two wars with Iraq, and our war against the Taliban and al-Qaeda in Afghanistan allowed us to expand our empire of overseas bases into the broad southern Eurasian region stretching from the Balkans in the west to the Chinese border in the east, an oil-rich area that opened up to our imperial dreams after the demise of the Soviet Union. Iran is now the only serious obstacle to our military domination of the whole region.

As mentioned in the last chapter, the Pentagon calculates "plant replacement values" in U.S. dollars for all the overseas bases whose existence it publicly acknowledges. The total value of these 725 recognized overseas military bases as of September 11, 2001, was $117,838.5 million (c. $118 billion). Of this $118 billion, the bases acquired from the vanquished of World War II and still in our possession were said to be worth $78 billion—$38 billion in Germany and $40 billion in Japan, or 66 percent of the total. The Pentagon prices the garrisons it established in Korea as a result of the Korean War at $11.5 billion. In other words, according to the Department of Defense's calculations, in "value" terms World War II and Korea accounted for three-quarters of our contemporary empire of bases. The Pentagon does not, however, include in its calculations any of our recent bases in the Balkans, the Persian Gulf, or Central Asia. Plant replacement values have not been published for these areas because our government is reluctant to admit that they are actually imperial outposts. (In some cases, too, Islamic governments in the Persian Gulf do not want to publicize our "footprint" there.) But the fact is, we vastly enlarged and consolidated our Persian Gulf bases in preparation for the renewed war against Iraq, a development discussed in the next chapter. But first some groundwork.

The Spanish-American War and Our Latin American Bases

Most of our bases in Latin America derived from the Monroe Doctrine of 1823 and the Spanish-American War of 1898. Following the American declaration of independence from the British Empire in 1776, Americans generally thought of their new country as the quintessential anti-imperialist state. For its first century there was some basis for this belief, so long as one was willing to regard the lands of Native Americans and Mexicans as essentially uninhabited. The American Revolution inspired a wave of uprisings across the Caribbean and South America that led to the independence of almost all the Spanish and Portuguese colonies. These rebellions in turn provoked the Monroe Doctrine, through which—according to the official account to be found in American textbooks—the United States appointed itself the protector of the nations of the Western Hemisphere against further European incursions.

The Monroe Doctrine itself actually reflected the ideas of John

Quincy Adams, a member of the Federalist Party, not President James Monroe, a Republican. When Adams decided in 1823 to run as a Republican in the upcoming presidential election, he needed to counter suspicions that he had "pro-British" leanings, and the Monroe Doctrine was designed to this end.[2] By the time it was actually proclaimed a fundamental principle of our foreign policy, during the presidency of James K. Polk (1845–49), who added more territory to the United States than any president other than Thomas Jefferson, its effect was already imperialist. It was first invoked in a dispute with Britain over the Oregon Territory and again to warn off any European powers that might care to interfere in the controversies that led to the Mexican War of 1846–48.

Traditional interpretations of American imperialism follow a vein already familiar from writings about British imperialism—namely, we "conquered half the world in a fit of absence of mind," were "reluctant imperialists," and lacked "rationality of purpose" in what we were doing.[3] As the international relations analyst Ronald Steel has remarked, "The theme of reluctance is one of the most pervasive explanations found in the histories of colonialism."[4] In addition to arguing that we never really intended to become imperialists, American historians divide U.S. actions to conquer other peoples into a continental strand and a maritime strand, maintaining that only the maritime strand constituted "real" imperialism. The continental strand—the westward movement of conquest over indigenous peoples and Mexicans—is usually considered mere "expansionism," as if some inexorable pressure beyond planning or will forced us on.

The shift from the continental to the maritime strand at the end of the nineteenth century was, according to Frederick Jackson Turner's famous thesis of 1893, caused by the closing of the frontier. Serious scholarship has long ago revealed the ideological intent of Turner's thesis, but his was certainly one of the more sophisticated defenses of America's turn to overseas expansion. Even so, prominent American historians like Yale University's Samuel Flagg Bemis have argued that the imperialism that began in 1898 was "a great aberration in American history," one that in his view would ultimately be corrected by twentieth-century liberal political leaders such as Woodrow Wilson and Franklin Roosevelt.[5]

The Monroe Doctrine assumed ever-new opportunistic forms. In December 1904, President Theodore Roosevelt enunciated the Roosevelt Corollary to it, calling for intervention throughout the Americas to suppress political movements that might interfere with the payment of Latin American debts. Because the United States was a "civilized nation," Roosevelt wrote, it had a duty to exercise "an international police power" to stop "chronic wrongdoing" wherever it occurred among America's neighbors to the south. Theodore Roosevelt's successor as president, William Howard Taft, the former governor of the Philippines, proclaimed something he called "dollar diplomacy"—another euphemism for imperialism—and invoked Roosevelt's Corollary to promote and protect American business interests overseas, particularly in the Caribbean and Central America.[6] Between 1898 and 1934, the United States sent marines to Cuba four times, Honduras seven times, the Dominican Republic four times, Haiti twice, Guatemala once, Panama twice, Mexico three times, Colombia four times, and Nicaragua five times (where they built bases and maintained an uninterrupted presence for twenty-one years except for a short period in 1925).[7] As the political scientist David Abernethy observes, "The country that had proclaimed the Monroe Doctrine to protect the independence of Spanish-speaking countries on the New World mainland now found itself in the anomalous position of replacing Spain as a colonial ruler and repressing national independence movements."[8] The Roosevelt Corollary was supplanted only in 1934, by President Franklin Roosevelt's Good Neighbor Policy.

The first war devoted explicitly to creating military bases outside mainland North America was the Spanish-American War. Though officially it was launched to assist Cuban rebels against Spanish rule and avenge the sinking of the USS *Maine,* the actual reason was to establish military and naval bases in the Caribbean and the Western Pacific, in accordance with plans of then Assistant Secretary of the Navy Theodore Roosevelt, Secretary of State John Hay, several leading Republican senators, including Henry Cabot Lodge and Albert Beveridge, naval theorist Captain Alfred T. Mahan, and various other supporters like Brooks Adams and Elihu Root. As a result of victory in that war, Puerto Rico, Guam, and the Philippines were made colonies, Hawaii and the Panama

Canal Zone (in which numerous military bases were located) were annexed, and a military base was established in Cuba.

After World War II, we gave the Philippines its independence but, until the Philippine Senate expelled us in 1992, we maintained two of our largest overseas bases there—Clark Air Base at Angeles City and Subic Bay Naval Base at Olongapo, both on the island of Luzon. Ever since 1992, the Pentagon has been trying to find a way to reestablish a military presence in the islands, whether by exaggerating the threat of China, through military "exchanges" under so-called visiting forces agreements, or more recently under the rubric of the "war on terrorism." During 2002, the Bush administration succeeded in reintroducing forces into the Philippines to train Filipinos to fight Muslim guerrillas in the southern islands.

WORLD WAR II AND THE GERMAN BASES

World War II fatally weakened all the major colonial empires and simultaneously left the United States as the most powerful nation on earth, indeed an imperial power of the first order. With the onset of the Cold War, America decided not just to hang on to its wartime territorial gains but to expand them into a huge ring of bases reaching from Iceland to Japan that would completely surround the USSR and China, whose Communist Party had emerged victorious from a bitter civil war.

Whether or not most of these bases would have proved of real importance in a Soviet-American war, their possession was justified as a crucial part of a policy of "containing" Communism. It was sometimes argued as well that the bases needed to be retained just to keep them out of Soviet hands. Containment and strategic denial became the rationales for a new version of imperialism that replaced the old and discredited practice of colonialism. Military bases, vaguely legitimized through alliances and mutual security pacts, became the institutional form this new imperialism took. Even in Latin America, where the United States had for over a century maintained a more traditional form of political and economic domination, using older imperial explanations for its acts, it now began to apply Cold War ideology, claiming that the overthrow of elected governments in Guatemala, Chile, and Nicaragua and the training of thousands of Latin American military officers in the techniques of domestic repression were an essential part of containing Communism and Soviet influence in the hemisphere.

The two biggest prizes of World War II were Germany and Japan. The American army occupied all of Japan, while the standoff between the United States and the USSR in Germany, where the two victorious armies had met at the Elbe River in 1945, became the supreme symbol of the Cold War. In the four-power division of occupied Germany, the United States controlled the southern and central states of Bavaria, parts of what is today Baden-Württemberg, and Hesse. France occupied the western regions, Britain the north, the USSR the eastern half of the country, and all four powers jointly governed the capital, Berlin. Facing the USSR from Germany's south-central quarter, a territory about the size of the state of Oregon, some 285,000 U.S. combat troops, armed with nuclear weapons, were deployed at just under 800 bases. Across the artificial border created where the armies stopped, the USSR stationed approximately 380,000 troops and some 20,000 tanks, one of the largest land armadas ever assembled. Initial NATO military planning for repelling a Soviet invasion contemplated a defensive line at the Rhine River; therefore the main NATO command and air bases were located behind the Rhine, in France. But in May 1966, at the height of the Vietnam War, the French government, led by former General Charles de Gaulle, declared its intention to regain "full sovereignty [over] French territory." It would no longer "accept the presence of foreign units, installations, or bases in France falling in any respect under the control of authorities other than French authorities."[9] France opted out of NATO because, as supreme commander, an American general dominated it. (In 1993, France rejoined.)

On April 1, 1967, NATO was evicted from France, and Supreme Headquarters, Allied Powers Europe (SHAPE) moved to Brussels. Major U.S. Army commands relocated to Stuttgart and Heidelberg, and south-central Germany became even more congested with American military bases. Even though the threat of war with the USSR was already receding, the United States developed a new "defensive" strategy, placing its air bases as close to the French border as possible. American strategists put six combat airfields (Bitburg, Hahn, Ramstein, Sembach, Spangdahlem, and Zweibrüchen) in the small German state of Rhineland-Palatinate, which became, as it remains today, an American sphere of influence. U.S. commanders posited that a Soviet invasion, if it came, would be launched through a gap between the Rhön and Vogelsberg Mountains where the terrain was advantageous for invading tanks. The small central German city of Fulda, only twenty miles from the East German border, was directly in the path of the projected invasion. The army therefore created a "military community" in Fulda that occupied the city center and twenty-two other sites around the town, all part of the 104th Area Support Group headquartered in nearby Hanau. With the reunification of Germany in 1990, the city's importance vanished overnight. The last U.S. soldiers said good-bye to Fulda in the summer of 1994.

Many bases in Germany are actually made up of numerous separate minibases or "sites," a fragmentation that multiplies the effects of our military presence on surrounding civilian communities. The Department of Defense likes to count only major bases in its reports, thereby understating their numbers, whereas people who live near them think that counting "sites" is what matters. Keith B. Cunningham and Andreas Klemmer, researchers with the Bonn International Center for Conversion, have studied the economic effects of base closings in Germany and the longer-term implications of continuing to maintain American bases in Central Europe that have no military functions. According to them, at the time of German unification, the United States had forty-seven major military bases in Germany (thirty-seven "military communities" and ten air bases).[10] But a shift in the terms of calculation, they write, reveals that "the United States maintained 285,000 troops in Germany at almost 800 discrete sites. By 1995, those numbers had fallen to approximately 94,000 troops at about 260 sites."[11]

What the army calls a military community exists only in Germany. In the United States, major military bases are normally large, self-contained reservations more or less separated from civilian urban areas and often constituting the equivalent of small or medium-sized towns or cities in their own right. For example, Fort Hood, Texas, sixty miles northeast of Austin, occupies 217,337 contiguous acres and has a population of about 130,000 people. By contrast, "each [German] Military Community consists of one or more barracks, or *Kasernen,* near the city center which acts as the administrative and social center of the community. The soldiers and their families may live in nearby U.S.-operated 'family housing complexes' or find their own housing within neighboring German communities. Most Military Communities also operate training ranges and airfields outside the city center. Additionally, the community likely supports a number of other, isolated sites such as radio stations, depots, warehouses, and hospitals. All of this causes the average community to operate more than seventeen different sites in at least two different German cities. . . . Shortly after the end of the Cold War, the Military Communities were reorganized under the command umbrella of Area Support Groups (ASGs) to facilitate consolidation. Thirteen ASGs were established in Germany in 1991, containing a total of thirty-four Military Communities."[12]

It is doubtful that any American city or town, with the possible exception of Honolulu, would put up with what the Germans, the Koreans, the Okinawans, and many others have experienced for more than half a century. The American film and television producer Michael Goldfarb caught the atmosphere of Cold War Germany in a description of a 1970 drive through Frankfurt: "At a red light an American Army jeep pulls up with a bunch of G.I.'s. We keep driving around the city trying to find the Department of Motor Vehicles or the German equivalent and at every red light there are jeeps with American soldiers. It seems like there are more jeeps than police cars, more American soldiers on the streets than German policemen. The war was over a quarter of a century ago. Surely the ratio of American G.I.'s to German cops should have skewed in favor of the Germans. We are long past the point of occupation and pacification. The phrase 'Roman Legionnaires' goes through my brain as another jeep passes us."[13]

As late as September 1991, the 103rd ASG, containing the military communities of Frankfurt—its headquarters—plus Darmstadt and Wiesbaden, with 25,598 military personnel, occupied 4,783 acres spread around seventy different sites. The Twenty-sixth ASG had its administrative center in the old university city of Heidelberg, which was also the headquarters of the U.S. Army Europe, the Seventh Army, and the V Corps. The Heidelberg ASG included the cities of Heilbronn, Karlsruhe, Mannheim, and Worms, with a total of 36,014 military personnel, occupying 18,312 acres at seventy-eight separate sites. The current public affairs officer of the Twenty-sixth ASG notes that the "community" encompasses over twelve separate installations in and around the city of Heidelberg and adds laconically that the military "shopping center complex [is] within walking distance of Campbell and Patton Barracks."[14]

The main offices of these military communities are usually in the middle of town because in 1945 the army simply moved its offices into the old German military barracks, often architecturally imposing edifices dating from the nineteenth century. The various family housing units of the military communities have been given colorful American names like Pattonville in the Stuttgart military community and Mark Twain Village Family Housing at Heidelberg. One of the most desirable military communities is Garmisch, located in the Bavarian Alps near Hitler's old retreat, Berchtesgaden. It is home to many hotels, bachelors' quarters, a shopping center, a golf course, and a skeet-shooting range, all named after famous American generals. It is, in fact, the Armed Forces Recreational Center for Europe—that is, an official ski resort for the military. Just so the brass can pretend to be working while visiting Garmisch, it also includes the George C. Marshall European Center for Security Studies, a think tank. The military has not found a need to downsize the 543rd ASG, which includes Garmisch.[15]

Garmisch is but the tip of the recreational iceberg when it comes to base life in Germany. In December 2002, the army committed $375,000 for improvements to the Rheinblick Golf Course in Wiesbaden, $9 million for a bowling and entertainment center in Baumholder, $16 million for a physical fitness center in Bamberg, and $290,000 for a "kids' zone" restaurant and entertainment center at the Pulaski Barracks—and these projects were just for the 104th Area Support Group in Hanau. All the other ASGs had similar expansion plans. It is possible, however, that none of these projects will be built thanks to the Bush administration's pique over Germany's refusal to fall in line behind its war on Iraq.

Contrary to the general rule that, once opened, an overseas base is never closed, after the collapse of the Warsaw Pact in 1990 it was no longer possible even for the army to pretend that a huge military force was needed in Central Europe. The Pentagon therefore cut forces in Germany by about two-thirds, transferring them to new bases then being established in the Balkans and the Persian Gulf. The most astonishing aspect of the German downsizing, however, is the number of bases the United States decided to *retain*—some 325, according to the September 2001 *Base Status Report,* occupied by 70,998 soldiers and airmen, 16,488 civilian Department of Defense employees, and 97,571 dependents. Since there is no credible use for these forces in Europe, they simply live there waiting for "out-of-area operations." In the forty-one years from 1948 to 1989, we deployed army troops stationed in Germany outside their area of operations just eighteen times. During the four years after Operation Desert Storm, however, the Pentagon sent German-based soldiers on forty-nine out-of-area missions.[16]

Germany has become a European version of Okinawa, a staging area for imperial activities in the Mediterranean, the Middle East, and Central Asia. As in Okinawa, the areas around our bases are constantly exposed to environmental pollution, the noise of warplanes, a high incidence of sexual crimes, and disputes about who has legal jurisdiction over the large number of Americans living in the host society. The first serious signs that Germany was getting tired of its semicolonial status came in the general elections of September 2002, when Gerhard Schröder was reelected chancellor on an explicit plank of dissociating Germany from American plans for a war against Iraq. The increasing tension between the two countries over our global aspirations may result in large-scale transfers of military personnel from Germany to the ex-Communist East European countries and to newly created Iraqi and Central Asian bases. Many in the Bush administration, including NATO commander General James L. Jones, have called for a radical reduction of American bases of Germany.

WORLD WAR II AND JAPAN

Japan offers many similarities to Germany, except that no Soviet-American confrontation took place on Japanese territory and that a much higher level of protest against the stationing of foreign troops was apparent from the beginning. Because of the devastation of the war and the atomic bombings, Japan became an intensely pacifist country. In rewriting the Japanese constitution, the Allied occupation added an explicitly pacifist clause, article 9, whereby Japan renounced forever the use of force in international relations. The considerable idealism behind this provision appealed to many Japanese, and although the antiwar sentiment of the immediate postwar years has faded, a large portion of the electorate still accepts the idea that Japanese armed forces should be maintained only for defensive purposes.

With the onset of the Cold War in East Asia, however, the Pentagon decided that it needed large numbers of military bases in Japan, which was deemed a "secure rear area" in the struggle to contain Communism. This plan ran counter to prevailing sentiment in Japan and to the formal stipulations of the new constitution. Moreover, after regaining its independence in 1952, Japan had renounced forever the use of nuclear weapons and formally prohibited the United States from stockpiling them at its bases in the country. Early in the postwar period, therefore, Pentagon strategists concluded that they would have to find a place in Japan not bound by government policies. The result was the virtual annexation of Okinawa, the southernmost major island in the Japanese chain and the scene of exceedingly bloody fighting and kamikaze suicide attacks in 1945.

From 1945 to 1972, the United States held on to the island as a colony directly governed by the Pentagon. During this period, the 1.3 million Okinawans became stateless, unrecognized as citizens of either Japan or the United States, governed by an American lieutenant general. They could not travel to Japan or anywhere else without special documents issued by American military authorities. Okinawa was closed to the outside world, a secret enclave of military airfields, submarine pens, intelligence facilities, and CIA safe houses. Some Okinawans who protested these conditions were declared probable Communists and hundreds of them were transported to Bolivia, where they were dumped in the remote countryside of the Amazon headwaters to fend for themselves.[17] During the height of the Cold War, Congress was not interested in what went on in Okinawa and exercised minimal oversight of army rule.

By the early 1970s, Okinawans were in open revolt against the use of the island as a bomber base for the Vietnam War, incensed by revelations that the military was storing nerve gas and nuclear weapons there without even warning the local population of the dangers involved. Reluctantly, the United States agreed to a pro forma "reversion" of Okinawa to Japanese sovereignty so long as the Japanese government allowed us to keep our bases there. Reversion was a convenient way to perpetuate the status quo while transferring responsibility for the Okinawan people to Japan.

Over the years, the Japanese government has done everything it could to keep the American military confined to Okinawa. Some 75 percent of our bases in Japan are located on the island even though it constitutes less than 1 percent of the total Japanese land area and is the poorest of all Japanese prefectures. The island's relationship to Japan is very similar to that of Puerto Rico to the United States. The government in Tokyo likes this arrangement because it knows that the public will tolerate American troops on Japanese soil only if they are kept out of sight. Ever since Japan forcibly annexed the Ryukyu kingdom (of which Okinawa is the largest island) in the late nineteenth century, its people have discriminated against the culturally distinct Okinawans.[18] The semicolonial conditions there have not changed. In 2002, the Japanese government agreed to build for American use yet another air base on the island, one that will destroy a sensitive coral reef and endangered species that depend on it.

In imposing military colonialism on the Okinawans, our senior leaders were always aware that they were violating the United Nations Charter, our own proclaimed objectives in fighting World War II, and virtually all the political ideals and values the United States has espoused as a nation. The lack of due process of law in the military's seizure of land from Okinawan farmers to build huge base complexes helped compromise our attempt to promote democracy in postwar Japan and elsewhere in East Asia. Numerous high-ranking American officials have acknowledged that in keeping Okinawa for twenty years after the 1952 peace treaty with Japan and giving it up only under intense pressure, they were making a mockery of the pledge in the Atlantic Charter of August 1941 that the United States sought "no aggrandizement, territorial or other," in World War II.[19] Former ambassador to Japan and Undersecretary of State

U. Alexis Johnson admitted that giving Okinawa to the military in the late 1940s was simply the price of getting the Pentagon to go along with the peace treaty, which restored Japanese sovereignty over the four main islands but kept Okinawa under American military rule.[20]

Okinawa is not the only place in Japan with American bases; it just has more of them. The old Japanese naval base at Yokosuka, south of Yokohama, is the home port of the navy's Seventh Fleet, and a full carrier task force is permanently stationed there. When the aircraft carrier enters port, the navy flies its aircraft off to Atsugi Naval Air Station in nearby, heavily populated Kanagawa Prefecture, where protests by residents about the noise of takeoffs and landings have become a permanent feature of local politics. The navy operates another major harbor for aircraft carriers and submarines at Sasebo, near Nagasaki, on the southern island of Kyushu. The air force, in addition to its huge facility at Kadena in Okinawa and Yokota Air Force Base in Tokyo, headquarters of U.S. Forces Japan, also operates Misawa Air Force Base, located in the most northerly prefecture of the main island of Honshu. It is home to a fighter wing of F-16s, the "Ripsaw Range" for target practice, and numerous espionage listening posts run by the navy.

The Marine Corps operates the majority of bases on Okinawa. The Third Marine Division, whose headquarters are there, is the only marine division based outside the United States. The Marine Corps also operates the big Iwakuni Air Station on southern Honshu, where for many years we illegally stored nuclear weapons on the USS *San Joaquin County*, moored a short distance offshore. The ship remained at the base without ever getting under way for at least six years during the 1960s, an important fact since in a secret agreement with Japan, the United States in 1960 had promised not to store nuclear weapons at its bases but adopted the position that nuclear weapons on naval vessels were merely in transit and had not actually been introduced into the country. The Japanese government went along with this ruse until June 1981, when former American ambassador Edwin O. Reischauer revealed the existence of the secret agreement in an interview in the *Washington Post*. An uproar ensued, during which the Pentagon neither affirmed nor denied the presence of nuclear weapons anywhere in Japan and the Japanese simply said that they trusted the United States to abide by the agreement.[21] Certainly no one raised the possibility of calling in U.N. weapons inspectors.

According to the Pentagon's September 2001 *Base Status Report*, the United States has seventy-three bases in Japan. (A careful and well-documented analysis by Japanese antibase activists gives the number as ninety-one.)[22] These bases house some 40,217 uniformed service personnel, plus 6,431 civilian employees of the Department of Defense and 42,653 dependents. They also employ 29,205 Japanese and Okinawans to mow the lawns, repair the plumbing, wait on tables in officers' clubs, operate motor pools—and translate Japanese-language books and magazines as well as communications intercepts for U.S. intelligence agencies. The Japanese government pays us some $4 billion per annum to help defray the costs of these services, making Japan perhaps the only country that pays another country to carry out espionage against itself. The troops on these bases have no military functions. They have been held in reserve for deployment elsewhere in Asia—in Afghanistan, the Persian Gulf, the Philippines, East Timor, and other places—as the need (or opportunity) arises. The United States does not have to consult the Japanese government about their use.

In 1950, when the Korean War began, Japan was still under our military occupation and served as the main staging area and privileged sanctuary for our forces. This pattern was repeated during the Vietnam War, when Okinawa was still an American colony and could be used as a bomber base and supply center, despite considerable opposition. But today it seems unlikely that the United States could use any of its bases directly in a war that did not involve Japan—especially if the Bush administration went to war with North Korea over its nuclear program or with China over Taiwan—and not provoke violent resistance.

South Korea's extensive network of American bases, established in the years of the Korean War and detailed in chapter 3, are a cross between those in Cold War Germany and present-day Japan, being located in a sovereign country, not a neocolonial enclave like Okinawa, but more hated than those in Germany. Despite an artificially maintained military standoff with North Korea, the large numbers of troops based all over South Korea have had nothing to do since the armistice of 1953. They spend their days mostly dozing in their tanks and their evenings in the arms of prostitutes. Between 1961 and 1993, the United States backed or installed a series of military dictators in South Korea, and even today representatives of the military, commanders and staff officers of the Eighth Army, by their very presence, make South Korean efforts toward a peaceful reconciliation with the North more difficult. South Korea is the only place where at the height of the Cold War the United States twice sent ambassadors who were former high-ranking officials of the CIA.

Post-Vietnam Fallout

America's defeat in Vietnam highlighted our tendency to build bases in and give military support to countries where militarists, fascists, or right-wing dictators prevailed, sometimes after these had first been installed by our military or CIA. There is virtually no case in Asia, Europe, or Latin America where in making a decision to establish bases we gave any consideration to whether or not a government was democratic. The new bases set up in 2001 in Kyrgyzstan and Uzbekistan illustrate that this general rule still holds since both countries have atrocious human rights records. The military, of course, argues that it has to deal with regimes as it finds them and that the presence of a base does not necessarily constitute an endorsement. But, as a matter of fact, in Asia alone the United States was directly responsible for helping to bring to power and sustain brutally repressive military governments in Indonesia, South Vietnam, South Korea, Taiwan, Cambodia, and the Philippines. At one time or another, we had extensive military bases in each of them except Cambodia and Indonesia.

When in 1975 North Vietnamese forces finally conquered South Vietnam's regime despite its lavish American backing, other countries felt emboldened to deal with their own potentially lethal combinations of American-backed indigenous rightists and military bases on their soil. The death of Francisco Franco in Spain on November 20, 1975, brought an end to the last of the fascist dictatorships that had dominated Europe during the 1930s. He had been the right-wing victor in the Spanish Civil War of the late 1930s, an ally of the Nazis, and the notorious *Caudillo de*

España (as is still inscribed above his tomb at the Valle de los Caidos near Madrid). The United States liked him because he was, of course, anti-Communist.

Franco had leased us for indefinite use Torrejón Air Base near Madrid, Zaragoza Air Base with its 13,000-foot runways for B-52s, Morón Air Base near Seville, and Rota Naval Base just west of the Strait of Gibraltar. The democratic government that succeeded him set out at once to rene-gotiate all these agreements. In the ensuing discussions, we ultimately retained some but not all of these sites, primarily because Spain was also seeking belated integration into Europe, including membership in NATO, and this would have been threatened had they simply thrown the Americans out wholesale. But ever since the death of Franco, the Spanish bases have been hostage to Madrid's latent anti-Americanism because of the long-term support we once gave the dictator. Only Morón and Rota are still open at the beginning of the twenty-first century.

In the case of Spain there is some plausibility to the argument that the United States had to deal with the leader it found there, even if he hap-pened to be a fascist. But the story was different in Greece. We helped bring the militarists to power there, and the legacy of our complicity still poisons Greek attitudes toward the United States. There is probably no democratic public anywhere on earth with more deeply entrenched anti-American views than the Greeks.[23] The roots of these attitudes go back to the birth of the Cold War itself, to the Greek civil war of 1946–49 and the U.S. decision embodied in the Truman Doctrine to intervene on the neofascist side because the wartime Greek partisan forces had been Communist-dominated. In 1949, the neofascists won and created a bru-tal right-wing government protected by the Greek secret police, com-posed of officers trained in the United States by the wartime Office of Strategic Services and its successor, the CIA.

During the 1950s, George Papandreou, the future prime minister, was fond of saying that Greece was an American puppet state and its officials "exercised almost dictatorial control, . . . requiring the signature of the chief of the U.S. Economic Mission to appear alongside that of the Greek Minister of Coordination on any important documents."[24] Under these conditions, we faced no difficulties in building naval bases and airfields at Souda Bay and Iraklion on the island of Crete, Hellenikon Air Base near Athens, and Nea Makri Communications Station at Marathon Bay, northeast of Athens.

In February 1964, George Papandreou was elected prime minister by a huge majority. He tried to remain on friendly terms with the Americans, but President Lyndon Johnson's White House was pressuring him to sacrifice Greek interests on the disputed island of Cyprus in favor of Turkey, where the United States was also building military bases. Both Greece and Turkey had been members of NATO since 1952, but by the mid-1960s the United States seemed more interested in cultivating Turkey. When the Greek ambassador told President Johnson that his proposed solution to the Cyprus dispute was unacceptable to the Greek parliament, Johnson reportedly responded, "Fuck your parliament and your constitution. We pay a lot of good American dollars to the Greeks. If your prime minister gives me talk about democracy, parliament, and constitutions, he, his parliament, and his constitution may not last very long."[25] And they did not.

The CIA, under its Athens station chief, John Maury, immediately began plotting with Greek military officers they had trained and cultivated for over twenty years. In order to create a sense of crisis, the Greek intelligence service, the KYP, carried out an extensive program of terrorist attacks and bombings that it blamed on the left. Constantin Costa-Gavras's 1969 film, *Z*, accurately depicts those days. On April 21, 1967, just before the beginning of an election campaign that would have returned Papandreou as prime minister, the military acted. Claiming they were protecting the country from a Communist coup, a five-man junta, four of whom had close connections with either the CIA or the U.S. military in Greece, established one of the most repressive regimes sponsored by either side during the Cold War.

The "Greek colonels," as they came to be known, opened up the country to American missile launch sites and espionage bases, and they donated some $549,000 to the 1968 Nixon-Agnew election campaign.[26] The U.S. Senate suspected that this was CIA money coming home from

Greece to influence domestic politics, but Henry Kissinger, President Nixon's national security adviser, urgently requested that any congressional investigation be canceled. Since 1995, the State Department has had ready for publication a book of documents concerning U.S.-Greek relations for the years 1964–68 in its legally mandated historical series *Foreign Relations of the United States,* but the CIA has prevented its release.[27]

The leader of the junta, Colonel George Papadopoulos, was an avowed fascist and admirer of Adolf Hitler. He had been trained in the United States during World War II and had been on the CIA payroll for fifteen years preceding the coup. His regime was noted for its brutality. During the colonel's first month in power some 8,000 professionals, students, and others disliked by the junta were seized and tortured. Many were executed. In 1969, the eighteen member countries of the European Commission on Human Rights threatened to expel Greece—it walked out before the commission could act—but even this had no effect on American policies.

On July 15, 1974, after seven years of misrule, the Greek junta, in league with militarist colleagues on the island of Cyprus, attempted a coup d'état against Cypriot president Makarios, who was simultaneously primate and archbishop of the Greek Orthodox Church and a person who had promoted peaceful coexistence between the Greek and Turkish communities on the island. On July 20, Turkey responded by invading the island and dividing it into a Turkish-dominated north and a Greek-dominated south. The only country ever to recognize the Turkish Republic of North Cyprus is Turkey. In Athens, largely because the Turkish assault was an embarrassing defeat for Greece, the junta collapsed.[28] It was replaced by a civilian government under a conservative politician, Constantine Karamanlis, which withdrew Greek troops from NATO's military wing but continued to cooperate diplomatically with the United States—until the elections of 1981.

Andreas Papandreou, the son of George Papandreou, had been in exile in Sweden and Canada during the reign of the colonel. In August 1974, after the fall of the junta, he returned to Athens and created a new political party, the Panhellenic Socialist Movement (PASOK). Reflecting the events of the previous decade as well as the Communist victory in Vietnam, its platform was explicitly anti-American: get the bases out of Greece and get Greece out of NATO. In 1981, PASOK won a landslide victory and Andreas Papandreou became prime minister. The party repeated this success in the elections of June 1985. Papandreou never fully delivered on all his promises, but when it came to the bases, he did: there are only two small detachments of U.S. Air Force and Navy technical personnel left in Greece, both on Greek military bases.

THE PHILIPPINE BASES

The Spanish-American War created the Philippine bases, and the outcome of the Vietnam War started a process that in 1992 brought them to an end. America's almost century-long record in the Philippines is one of colonialism, neocolonialism, and sponsorship of a hated dictator, which ultimately led to a successful anti-American revolution. The Philippine case is comparable to what happened in Greece except that the bases had been in existence for a much longer time and we took the Filipinos even more for granted than we did the Greeks. In 1946, at the same time that our government gave the Philippines their "independence," it took measures to ensure that the islands remained indefinitely under our control. The Philippines were severely damaged during World War II and desperately in need of economic assistance; the new Philippine government had little choice but to accept the strings attached to the grant of independence. The resulting neocolonial system proved even more unfavorable to the Philippines than colonialism itself, crippling their capacity for democratic development for forty years—until the revolution of February 1986 drove Ferdinand Marcos from power and led to the closing of all U.S. military bases.

Three American initiatives in 1946 and 1947 rendered Philippine independence virtually meaningless. These were the Bell Act of 1946; the Military Bases Agreement of March 14, 1947; and the Military Assistance Pact of March 21, 1947. The Bell Act forced the Filipinos to modify their 1935 constitution, which stipulated that all corporations in the Philippines be 60 percent owned by Filipinos. It demanded "parity," meaning that Americans would have the same rights and privileges as Filipinos to possess and exploit Philippine companies. It established "free trade" between the two countries for ten years, thereby eliminating the Philippines' capacity to control American imports. It also allowed Americans to own and operate public utilities in the country. The effect was to tie the Philippines, in the words of journalist William J. Pomeroy, "to the old colonial trade pattern of being a supplier of raw agricultural products and mineral ores to the United States in exchange for U.S. manufactured goods."[29] The Bell Act effectively prevented industrialization in the islands despite abundant supplies of coal, iron ore, alloy metals, hydroelectric power, and a large labor force. To this day, the Philippines resemble Okinawa far more than they do Taiwan, which has become one of the richest and most industrialized nations in East Asia. Taiwan is an example of what Okinawa and the Philippines might have become had the United States not played a neocolonial role.

The United States made all payments to the Philippines for war damages dependent on the Filipinos' acceptance of the Bell Act. A majority of the Philippine Congress deeply opposed a constitutional amendment granting parity, but the Americans and their local supporters worked behind the scenes to get eight representatives and three senators expelled for alleged fraud and terrorism, thereby achieving—by subtraction—the minimum number of votes needed to pass it.

Three days after amending the constitution, the Philippine government signed a military bases agreement giving the United States ninety-nine-year leases to twenty-three sites, sixteen active and seven held in reserve. The agreement authorized the United States to use these bases as it saw fit. Since Filipino public land laws specify that government leases cannot be longer than twenty-five years, the terms of the bases agreement immediately set off a popular protest movement. Successive American administrations stalled for nineteen years, until in 1966, the Johnson administration traded a new twenty-five-year lease agreement for Manila's willingness to send a military contingent to Vietnam. The two most important installations were Clark Air Force Base, second in size only to Vandenberg in California, and Subic Bay, the Seventh Fleet's main operational and repair facility in the western Pacific. Clark Field sprawled over ten thousand acres, larger than Singapore, and was enclosed by a twenty-two-mile security fence. The right to go through its garbage gave rise to two new villages, named appropriately after two Philippine presidents, Macapagal and Marcos. On June 15, 1991, Mount Pinatubo volcano, located ten miles away, erupted for the first time in six hundred years, covering the air field in ash and rendering it a total loss. Leases to the deep-water bay and drydock facilities at Subic Bay were thus the main points of contention in the final 1991 Philippine-American base negotiations.

A week after the original 1947 base agreement was signed, the Philippine government entered into still another treaty, the Military Assistance Pact, which established a Joint U.S. Military Advisory Group (JUSMAG) in Manila. This organization, composed of American military officers, was authorized "to assist and advise the Republic of the Philippines on military and naval matters," including supplying the Philippine army with weapons and ammunition, and so essentially reestablished a military overlordship like that of the colonial era. On August 30, 1951, the United States and the Philippines signed a Mutual Defense Treaty (although there was nothing "mutual" about it), and on September 8, 1954, the United States, the Philippines, and other nations signed a treaty establishing the Southeast Asia Treaty Organization (SEATO). Both treaties turned effective control of the Philippine armed forces over to the United States via the JUSMAG, which with the CIA's help handpicked a former army captain and ruling party congressman, Ramón Magsaysay, as a compliant secretary of national defense. In 1953, he became the third president of the Republic of the Philippines. With the United States now in control of the Philippine economy and military, and our own military properties secure, we were able to dictate huge military budgets that the Philippines could ill afford and to involve their armed forces in the Korean and Vietnamese Wars. The Philippine bases became critical staging areas for the American war in Vietnam, and the United States also used its installations on Luzon to carry out CIA plots against Indonesia in 1958 and 1965.

In November 1965, Ferdinand Marcos, a Manila trial lawyer, was elected president. At first, he seemed a dynamic leader devoted to public works and intent on moving the rigged Philippine economy toward greater development. In November 1969, he won a second four-year term, the first president to be reelected in the Philippines' short democratic history. But Marcos was interested primarily in lining his own pockets—his biographers all point out that he is in *The Guinness Book of Records* as the greatest thief of all time—and in the late 1960s the quality of Philippine life began to deteriorate in a serious way. Inspired by the Vietnamese liberation fighters and Chinese propaganda about "people's war," guerrilla insurgencies broke out throughout the main islands. Some were led by the New People's Army (NPA), the military arm of the Communist Party of the Philippines. On the southern island of Mindanao, Muslim secessionists organized under the banner of the Moro National Liberation Front. In August 1969, Marcos launched major military campaigns against both the NPA and the Moros.

By 1972 the situation had so worsened that Marcos faked an assassination attempt against his defense minister, Juan Ponce Enrile, in order to have an excuse to declare martial law. He then arrested and detained opposition politicians (including his likely successor, Senator Benigno "Ninoy" Aquino), reporters, students, and labor leaders. He closed newspapers and outlawed demonstrations, strikes, and boycotts. Assuming dictatorial powers, Marcos suspended the constitution, which permitted presidents only two terms, and in 1973, he introduced a new constitution that allowed him to stay in office indefinitely and to rule by decree. He made his wife, Imelda, governor of Manila and minister of "human settlements and ecology."

None of this occurred in a vacuum. As Alva Bowen, a career U.S. naval officer and researcher for the Congressional Reference Service, has acknowledged, "By 1975 the United States had been kicked out of Vietnam, and all the countries of Southeast Asia were taking another look at their security arrangements. The Philippines was one of the first to ask for a review of the security treaties. In 1975, just a few months after the U.S. departure from Saigon, President Gerald Ford visited the Philippines and came to an agreement with President Ferdinand Marcos that the 1947 accord on the U.S. use of the Philippine military bases would be revised, this time with a clear recognition of Philippine sovereignty."[30]

The Ford-Marcos agreement represented a slight improvement but the old problems still festered. Conditions around Clark Field and Subic Bay inflamed Filipino nationalism. The bases had given rise to a huge drug and sex industry employing thousands of poor Filipino women. Angeles City, home of Clark Field, was in the 1980s the most drug-afflicted city in the Philippines. Meanwhile, under martial law Marcos vastly expanded and politicized his own military establishment, appointing cronies who were personally loyal to him and giving the army unrestricted powers to arrest civilians. "Disappearances" and murders of anyone taking an interest in politics became common. Marcos also nationalized many manufacturing and business enterprises and gave them to his relatives. They proceeded to siphon off profits for their personal enrichment while the United States looked on with a blind eye.

In 1983, after three years in exile, the opposition politician Benigno Aquino returned to the Philippines to try to rally opposition to the Marcos regime. Minutes after landing at Manila airport on August 21, he was shot dead and his assassin, in turn, was shot and killed on the spot. Marcos claimed a Communist had been responsible for the murder, but a subsequent official commission of inquiry found that it was the work of a military conspiracy. Marcos rejected this finding and released the conspirators. Aquino's widow, Corazon Cojuangco Aquino, became the leader of the opposition, as hundreds of thousands of people attended her husband's funeral procession in Manila. It was the largest demonstration in the history of the Philippines and the beginning of a movement that would be dubbed "People Power." Filipino People Power was never as explicitly anti-American as the Iranian version against the Shah or the Papandreou campaign against the Greek junta, but the presence of our bases and Washington's blatant support for Marcos certainly helped mobilize the public.

In late 1985, in an attempt to acquire greater legitimacy and ensure continued American support, Marcos announced that a presidential election would be held in February 1986. Corazon Aquino declared her candidacy. After the balloting, the Catholic Church, in the person of Cardinal Jaime Sin, denounced Marcos for widespread voter fraud and intimidation and challenged his claim to victory. The Reagan administration agonized over its friend's difficulties and vacillated about recognizing the validity of Corazon Aquino's election. In the meantime, in the face of continuous street demonstrations against Marcos, the Philippine armed forces abandoned him, either supporting the Aquino forces or refusing to act when ordered to fire on unarmed protesters.[31]

On February 25, 1986, after over twenty years in power, Ferdinand and Imelda Marcos fled Malacañang Palace for Clark Air Force Base and then exile in the United States. When he arrived in Hawaii, Marcos was reportedly carrying suitcases containing jewels, gold bars, and certificates for billions of dollars' worth of gold bullion. Aquino's successor government estimated that Marcos had stashed away at least $3 billion in Swiss bank accounts, but some analysts put the figure as high as $35 billion. None of this money was ever recovered. Marcos died in Honolulu on September 28, 1989.

On February 2, 1987, the Filipino public overwhelmingly ratified a new national constitution. Its article 2, entitled "Declaration of Principles and State Policies," started a process that led to the termination of the bases agreement with the United States. Sections 2 and 3 read as follows: "The Philippines renounces war as an instrument of national policy, adopts the generally accepted principles of international law as part of the law of the land and adheres to the policy of peace, equality, justice, freedom, cooperation, and amity with all nations. Civilian authority is, at all times, supreme over the military. The armed forces of the Philippines is the protector of the people and the State. Its goal is to secure the sovereignty of the State and the integrity of the national territory." All Filipinos believed the United States kept atomic weapons ready for use at Subic and Clark. Section 8 of the state policies was the death knell for the bases: "The Philippines, consistent with the national interest, adopts and pursues a policy of freedom from nuclear weapons in its territory." On June 6, 1988, by a vote of nineteen yes, three no, and one abstention, the Philippine Senate passed the Freedom from Nuclear Weapons Act, implementing the constitutional mandate. The government of the Philippines now had something serious to talk about when the leases on the bases expired in 1991.

Totally misreading the post-Marcos political climate, the American negotiators badly bungled their attempt to extend the base leases. According to Roland G. Simbulan of the University of the Philippines, an adviser to the Philippine Senate, the United States "tried to bully its way through. Former Health Secretary Alfredo Bengzon, who served as vice chairman of the Philippine negotiating panel, later confirmed in a published article the 'narrow and arrogant mindset of the U.S. negotiators, led by [Richard] Armitage during the negotiations. They tried to force a prolonged treaty of extension,' Bengzon said."[32] Armitage, President George H. W. Bush's special representative for the Philippine military bases agreement, was a former CIA official. (He would later become deputy secretary of state in the Bush Junior administration.)

The Americans believed that the Filipinos were too poor to evict them and that conservatives in the Philippine Senate would support them. However, after Mount Pinatubo destroyed Clark air base, the United States cut its offer of assistance to the Philippines from about $700 million to $203 million; and on September 16, 1991, irritated by America's tight-fistedness and its refusal to undertake a cleanup of the pollution at Clark Field, the Philippine Senate, by a vote of twelve to eleven, rejected the proposed renewal of the 1947 bases agreement.[33] Although the event was barely noted in the United States, all its military forces were completely withdrawn by November 24, 1992.

Since its expulsion, the United States has tried various stratagems to reintroduce its forces into the Philippines, always offering much-needed hard currency as an inducement. Early in 2002, we sent about a thousand Special Forces and supporting troops to help Filipinos fight the Abu Sayyaf, a Muslim "terrorist gang" on the southern island of Basilan with a record of kidnapping and extortion but not of political terrorism.[34] The main U.S. goal in the Philippines has been to negotiate a "Mutual Logistics Support Agreement" that would allow us access to Philippine bases for refueling, reprovisioning, and repairing ships without a case-by-case debate. On August 3, 2002, in Manila, Secretary of State Colin Powell said that "the United States is not interested in returning to the Philippines with bases or a permanent presence," but it is unlikely that there was a single person in East Asia who believed him.[35] On February 20, 2003, the Pentagon announced that it was sending a new contingent of nearly 2,000 troops to the Philippines in an operation against "terrorists" that "has no fixed deadline."[36]

FROM WAR TO IMPERIALISM

As the American empire grows, we go to war significantly more frequently than we did before and during the Cold War. Wars, in turn, promote the growth of the military and are a great advertising medium for the power and effectiveness of our weapons—and the companies that make them, which can then more easily peddle them to others. According to the journalist William Greider, "The U.S. volume [of arms sales] represents 44 percent of the global market, more than double America's market share in 1990 when the Soviet Union was the leading exporter of arms."[37] As the military-industrial complex gets ever fatter, with more overcapacity, it must be "fed" ever more often. The creation of new bases requires more new bases to protect the ones already established, producing ever-tighter cycles of militarism, wars, arms sales, and base expansions.

After the collapse of the Soviet Union, we began to wage at an accelerating rate wars whose publicly stated purposes were increasingly deceptive or unpersuasive. We were also ever more willing to go to war outside the framework of international law and in the face of worldwide popular opposition. These were de facto imperialist wars, defended by propaganda claims of humanitarian intervention, women's liberation, the threat posed by unconventional weapons, or whatever current buzzword happened to occur to White House and Pentagon spokespersons. In each war we acquired major new military bases that in terms of location or scale were disproportionate to the military tasks required and that we retained and consolidated after the war. After the attacks of September 11, 2001, we waged two wars, in Afghanistan and Iraq, and acquired fourteen new bases, in Eastern Europe, Iraq, the Persian Gulf, Pakistan, Afghanistan, Uzbekistan, and Kyrgyzstan. It was said that these wars were a response to the terrorist attacks and would lessen our vulnerability to terrorism in the future. But it seems more likely that the new bases and other American targets of vulnerability will be subject to continued or increased terrorist strikes.

Following our usual practice, we established our bases in weak states, most of which have undemocratic and repressive governments. Immediately after our victory in the second Iraq war, we began to scale back our deployments in Germany, Turkey, and Saudi Arabia, where we had become much more unpopular as a result of the war. Instead, we shifted our forces and garrisons to thinly populated, less demanding monarchies or autocracies/dictatorships, places like Qatar, Bahrain, Oman, the United Arab Emirates, and Uzbekistan.[38]

A new picture of our empire has begun to emerge. We retain our centuries-old lock on Latin America and our close collaboration with the single-party government of Japan, although we are deeply disliked in Okinawa and South Korea, where the situation is increasingly volatile. Our lack of legitimacy in the war with Iraq has undercut our position in what Secretary of Defense Donald Rumsfeld disparagingly called "the old Europe," so we are trying to compensate by finding allies and building bases in the much poorer, still struggling ex-Communist countries of Eastern Europe. In the oil-rich area of southern Eurasia we are building outposts in Kosovo, Iraq, Afghanistan, Pakistan, and Central Asia, in an attempt to bring the whole region under American hegemony. Iran alone, thus far, has been impervious to our efforts. We did not do any of these things to fight terrorism, liberate Iraq, trigger a domino effect for the democratization of the Middle East, or the other excuses proffered by our leaders. We did them, as I will show, because of oil, Israel, and domestic politics—and to fulfill our self-perceived destiny as a New Rome. The next chapter takes up American imperialism on the current battleground of global power, the Persian Gulf, a region where we have a long history.

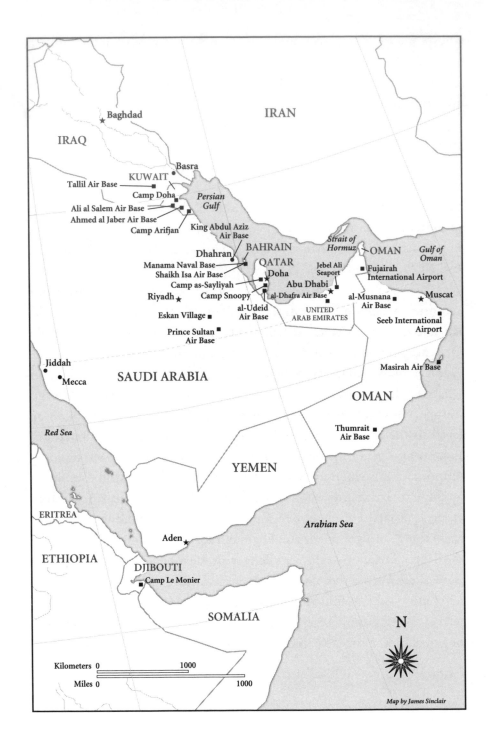

PERSIAN GULF

8

IRAQ WARS

"From a marketing point of view," said Andrew H. Card, Jr., the White House chief of staff on the rollout this week of the campaign for a war with Iraq, "you don't introduce new products in August."
New York Times, September 7, 2002

After all, this is the guy [Saddam Hussein] who tried to kill my dad.
PRESIDENT GEORGE W. BUSH,
at Houston, September 26, 2002

The Persian Gulf, a 600-mile-long extension of the Indian Ocean, separates the Arabian Peninsula on the west from Iran on the east. At the head of the gulf is Iraq, whose access to the waterway is largely blocked by Kuwait. Along the gulf's western coast, from Kuwait to Oman, lie what in the nineteenth century were known as the "trucial states," tribal fiefdoms that then lived by piracy and with whom Britain signed "truces" that turned them into British protectorates. The British were chiefly interested in protecting the shipping routes to their empire in India and so were ready to trade promises from local tribal leaders to suppress piracy for British guarantees to defend them from their neighbors. In this way, Britain became the supervisor of all relations among the trucial states as well as all their relations with the world outside the Persian Gulf.

Prior to World War II, the gulf area was thus a focus for British imperialism. Only in Saudi Arabia did events take a different turn when, in May 1933, the Standard Oil Company of California obtained the right to drill in that country's fabulously oil-rich eastern provinces. In return for a payment of 35,000 British pounds, Standard of California (SoCal), known today as Chevron, obtained a sixty-year concession from King Ibn Saud to develop and export oil. Since British influence in the region was paramount, the Americans surely would not have gained a foothold had it not been for one of history's most unusual figures, H. St. John Philby, Ibn Saud's adviser and a specialist in Arabian matters. (He was also the father of Kim Philby, the British intelligence official who secretly went to work for the Soviet Union and became, after his defection to that country, the most notorious spy of the Cold War era.) Disturbed by the grossly imperialist practices of British oil companies in Iran, Philby persuaded King Ibn Saud to throw in his lot with the Americans. SoCal started oil production in Saudi Arabia in 1938. Shortly thereafter, the company and the monarchy formalized their partnership by creating a new entity, the Arabian-American Oil Company (Aramco), and brought in other partners—Texaco, Standard Oil of New Jersey (Exxon), and Socony-Vacuum (Mobil). Aramco has been described as "the largest and richest consortium in the history of commerce."[1] Its corporate headquarters are still located at Dhahran, Saudi Arabia.

From the beginning, Aramco did everything in its power to avoid the arrogance associated with British imperialism in the Middle East. Its employees enjoyed no immunity from strict Saudi laws, and the company worked hard to bring benefits to the underpopulated country, including roads, power plants, and badly needed water wells. It responded quickly when Saudi rulers asked for more money or cooperation on projects of primary interest to them. The United States has always been exceedingly careful about its Saudi Arabian connection. In February 1943, in a letter to Undersecretary of State Edward Stettinius, President Franklin Delano Roosevelt wrote, "I hereby find the defense of Saudi Arabia is vital to the defense of the United States."[2] From World War II on, Aramco also collaborated informally with the Office of Strategic Services—the CIA's predecessor—and later with the CIA itself. Washington was always kept well informed about Aramco's view of the Middle East and the world beyond. So long as the CIA had a Board of National Estimates, a retired high-ranking Aramco executive was always a member.

Approximately thirty years ago, Saudi Arabia began to loosen some of these ties. In 1972, it bought a 20 percent stake in Aramco and, in 1980, acquired 100 percent of Aramco's shares. At the same time, it authorized the Aramco partners to continue to operate and manage the Saudi oil fields. Finally, in 1988, by royal decree and in a remarkably friendly act of expropriation, Saudi Arabia took over the management and operation of all its oil and gas resources. Aramco became Saudi Aramco.

On the basis of this long and extremely lucrative relationship, the United States built the first pillar of its Persian Gulf policy—close ties with Saudi Arabia. Perhaps the high point of American policy in the region, from the Arab point of view, was reached in 1956, when the United States sided with Egypt against Britain, France, and Israel, who had gone to war to stop Egypt's president, Gamal Abdel Nasser, from nationalizing the Suez Canal. This crisis marked the beginning of British decline east of Suez and earned the United States praise throughout the Middle East.[3] In 1968, the British made the decision to withdraw over time from all their outposts east of Suez. The true arbiters of policy in the region during these years were, in fact, the multinational oil companies, which, prior to the creation of the Organization of the Petroleum Exporting Countries (OPEC) in 1960, exerted great influence over both the British and the American governments.

One of our prime political and military concerns has always been to ensure that no other power, friendly or not, interferes with Saudi oil resources. In August 1945, the Army Corps of Engineers began work on an airfield at Dhahran, next door to Aramco's headquarters. From 1952 to 1963, the United States leased this airfield from the Saudis and based a Strategic Air Command squadron of nuclear-armed bombers there. In 1963, becoming concerned about the size of the American presence in his country, King Faisal ordered the air force to leave Dhahran, which was promptly renamed King Abdul Aziz Air Base of the Saudi Arabian Air Force. The Saudis, however, allowed the U.S. military to use it on a case-by-case basis until the Gulf War, when it was again turned over for operations to expel Iraq from Kuwait. Dhahran proved by far the most important Allied airfield in the American-led 1991 blitzkrieg against Iraq. Of some 7,248 aircraft arriving in Saudi Arabia between August 7, 1990, and March 26, 1991, 6,755 landed at Dhahran.[4]

From 1953 to 1979, the second great pillar of America's Persian Gulf policy was Iran, then the second-largest exporter of crude petroleum and possessor of the world's third-largest oil reserves. The British, who had been pumping oil from Iran since 1908, operated the world's largest refinery there. The Anglo-Persian Oil Company (after 1935, the Anglo-Iranian Oil Company) had provided the British treasury with 24 million pounds sterling in taxes and 92 million pounds in foreign exchange. The British had no intention of seeing their lucrative oil company national-ized, and the American oil majors sympathized with them. So, in 1953, the British gained the cooperation of the new Eisenhower administration in a blatantly illegal plan to overthrow an Iranian government that wanted a fairer share of the country's oil revenues.

Eisenhower ordered the CIA to help the British protect their assets, and the Americans in turn redefined the Anglo-Iranian oil crisis as a case of "free world" resistance to the threat of Communism in the Middle East. CIA operatives guided Iranian army officers in ousting Prime Min-ister Mohammad Mossadeq, a patrician politician known for his incor-ruptible defense of the country's national interests, and replaced him with the young shah Mohammed Reza Pahlavi, whose reign Mossadeq had interrupted. Although the shah claimed to be a nationalist, he was much more willing than Mossadeq to cooperate with Britain and the United States, seeing them as counterweights to the influence of the Soviet Union on Iran's northern border. After the successful coup, the new Iran-ian government awarded concessions to a consortium of major Western oil companies. In this consortium, 40 percent of the shares went to the Anglo-Iranian Oil Company, renamed British Petroleum, and 14 percent to its ally Royal Dutch Shell, thereby ensuring that Britain retained a majority vote. A group of American firms received 40 percent, a reward for American participation in the coup, and the French state company 6 percent.[5]

America's position in the world's richest oil region thus depended on its close relations with the Persian Gulf's two largest countries. So long as British military forces were still in place and effective, our government sought bases in the area only for its navy. In 1948, the United States had negotiated an informal agreement with Britain to use harbor facilities of the long-established British naval base (and airfield) at Manama on the island of Bahrain, the largest of the thirty-three islands in its colony Bahrain; in 1949, the U.S. Middle East Force was established there under a navy captain, upgraded in 1951 to a rear admiral. On August 15, 1971, Bahrain obtained its independence from Britain, and the United States concluded an executive agreement to retain its naval access in return for a payment of $4 million a year.[6]

Before the 1991 Gulf War, the only other territory in the region securely in American military hands was the Indian Ocean island of Diego Garcia. Along with Mauritius, Diego Garcia had been a British possession since England seized it from France during the Napoleonic Wars. The United States wanted to build a naval communications facility there, as Cold War radio and espionage bases in western Australia could not cover the full ocean. In 1965, Britain split Diego Garcia off from Mauritius, setting it up as the "British Indian Ocean Territory" and then "loaning" it to the United States rent-free for fifty years, although it was understood that the Americans would simultaneously waive payment on $14 million worth of Polaris submarine missiles heading for England.

American officials like to brag that Diego Garcia is "immune to local political developments"—for a very good reason. The British deported the island's entire population to Mauritius and the Seychelles, where they continue to live in conditions of poverty and racial discrimination. London paid Mauritius £650,000 to take the Diego Garcians, but decades later the refugees are still challenging their resettlement before London courts, which have already ruled the deportation illegal. Meanwhile, in 1974, the United States converted its communications station into a full-blown naval base, extended the airport runway to 12,000 feet, deepened the lagoon to accommodate a carrier task force, and stored a thirty-days' supply of fuel there for ships and aircraft. In 2001, the Department of Defense said that there were more buildings on Diego Garcia than military personnel—654 to be exact—and that the facility had a plant replacement value of $1,917.8 million.[7] It served as the main platform for the B-52s that bombed Afghanistan during 2001–02. Late in 2002, the Pentagon built four maintenance hangars at a cost of $2.5 million designed to house as many as sixteen out of the total fleet of twenty-one B-2 stealth bombers. Along with B-52s and B-1s, Diego Garcia's B-2s led the "shock and awe" bombing attacks on Baghdad on March 22, 2003, dropping 4,200 pound "bunker busters" on the essentially undefended city. It was the first time in history that all three types of American long-range strategic bombers targeted the same place at the same time—an experiment comparable to Hitler's 1937 bombing of the Spanish village of Guernica. Diego Garcia is 3,340 miles from Baghdad, the farthest away of any of the American bases in South Asia.

During the 1970s, Britain's departure from the region threatened to leave the area without imperialist supervision, a growing concern of the United States. Kuwait had been independent since 1961; Bahrain and Qatar both gained their independence in 1971. On December 2, 1971, one day after the British officially withdrew from the area, the six remaining sheikdoms, including the two richest, Abu Dhabi and Dubai, created a sovereign confederation known as the United Arab Emirates. Britain delayed its withdrawal from Oman until 1977 because of serious internal disunity there. The United States now had to deal with these new entities on its own and without the century and a half of experience of the British. It did not attempt to acquire American bases from any of them until the Gulf War provided a splendid opportunity.

Before that happened, however, the placid world of the Persian Gulf changed radically in 1979, a year almost as momentous for American foreign policy as 1949, when the Communists came to power in China, the USSR detonated its first atomic bomb, and the NATO alliance was formed. In 1979, one of the twin pillars of American policy collapsed. In January, a popular revolution against the shah's repressive rule forced him into exile and brought to power a fundamentalist Islamic regime under the Ayatollah Khomeini; in November, the revolutionaries seized the American embassy, taking all its employees hostage and holding them until January 1981. Complicating things even further, in December 1979, the Soviet Union invaded Iran's neighbor, Afghanistan, in an attempt to protect a leftist regime there. This elicited a huge CIA operation in Pakistan and throughout the Islamic world to recruit and arm Muslim "freedom fighters" to join the anti-Soviet guerrilla resistance.

In this context, in October 1979, the Carter administration set up what it called a Rapid Deployment Force to protect American interests in the Persian Gulf. Having no bases in the area, it located the force's head-quarters at MacDill Air Force Base in Tampa, Florida. On January 23, 1980, just before leaving office, President Carter proclaimed the Carter Doctrine: "Any attempts by any outside force to gain control of the Gulf region will be regarded as an assault on the vital interests of the United States of America, and such an assault will be repelled by any means nec-essary, including military force." This was at the time far easier to say than to do, and the United States set out to find a replacement for the Iranian pillar. On January 1, 1983, the Reagan administration converted the Rapid Deployment Force (still based in Florida) into the U.S. Central Command (CENTCOM), the first regional command created in thirty-five years.

In July 1979, Iraq also acquired a new leader, Saddam Hussein al-Tikriti of the Ba'ath Party. Slightly more than twenty years earlier, in 1958, Iraqi military officers, inspired by Gamal Abdel Nasser's nationalist revolt in 1952 against the British-backed monarchy in Egypt, had seized power and taken the country in a Soviet-leaning direction. The leader of the coup, General Abdel-Karim Kassem, proclaimed a republic, with-drew from the anti-Soviet Baghdad Pact, legalized the Communist Party, decreed wide-ranging land reform, and even granted autonomy to the Kurds in the north. These shifts, coming at the height of the Cold War, were too much for the United States—CIA director Allan Dulles publicly called Iraq "the most dangerous spot in the world"—and in 1963, the CIA supported the anti-Communist Ba'ath Party's efforts to bring Kassem's republic to an end. Ba'ath activists, including a youthful Saddam Hussein, gunned down Kassem and many others on a list the CIA supplied. The plotters were able, however, only to create a coalition government. In 1968, the CIA again fomented a palace revolt in which the Ba'athists eliminated their coalition partners and assumed direct control. According to Roger Morris, a staff member of the National Security Council during the John-son and Nixon administrations, "It was a regime that was unquestionably midwived by the United States and the CIA's involvement there was really primary."[8] In July 1979, the same year as the anti-American revolution in

Iran, Saddam Hussein replaced his mentor, Ahmad Hasan al-Bakr, as president, a position he held until 2003. He was, like many other famous beneficiaries of American political intrigue before and since, a CIA "asset."

In September 1980, Saddam, fearing Iranian influence among Iraq's majority Shi'ites, invaded Iran. When, in early 1982, Iranian forces gained the upper hand on the battlefield, the United States launched another covert operation to arm and aid Saddam. NSDD (National Security Decision Directive) 114 of November 26, 1983, is one of the few important Reagan-era foreign policy decisions that still remain classified. The only line from the text that has ever been leaked said that the United States would do "whatever was necessary and legal" to prevent Iraq from losing the war. The Reagan administration soon abandoned its scruples about what was legal.[9] It began clandestinely to supply Saddam with satellite intelligence on Iran's deployments. As much as $5.5 billion in fraudulent loans to help Iraq buy arms was channeled through the Atlanta branch of an Italian Bank (Banca Nazionale del Lavoro), all of it guaranteed by the Commodity Credit Corporation "to promote American farm exports." Weapons were also sent via CIA fronts in Chile and Saudi Arabia directly to Baghdad. Between 1986 and 1989, some seventy-three transactions took place that included bacterial cultures to make weapons-grade anthrax, advanced computers, and equipment to repair jet engines and rockets. In December 2002, when Iraq was forced to deliver to the U.N. Security Council an 11,800-page dossier on the history of its weapons programs in accordance with resolution 1441, officials of the Bush administration hurried to New York to take possession of it before any other member could have a look. They then excised and suppressed 8,000 pages that detailed the weapons and dual-use technologies American and other Western companies had sold to Iraq prior to 1991. The American companies included Honeywell, Unisys, Rockwell, Sperry, Hewlett-Packard, DuPont, Eastman Kodak, and many others.[10]

The United States had not had diplomatic relations with Iraq since the 1967 Arab-Israeli war. In December 1983, however, President Reagan sent his personal envoy, former secretary of defense in the Ford administration Donald Rumsfeld, to Baghdad to meet with Saddam Hussein. Rumsfeld returned to Iraq in March 1984, precisely when both Iran and the United Nations were accusing Saddam's regime of using chemical weapons in an increasingly brutal war. Rumsfeld, however, made no reference to the Iraqi gas attacks. Instead, he declared that "the defeat of Iraq in the three-year-old war with Iran would be contrary to U.S. interests."[11] In November 1984, Washington restored full diplomatic relations with Baghdad and stepped up the sales to Saddam of a range of munitions, including helicopters used in subsequent gas attacks. One of these assaults was the March 1988 gassing of Kurds in the village of Halabja that killed some 5,000 people. The United States maintained friendly relations with Iraq right up until the moment that Saddam revived Iraq's old territorial claims on Kuwait and on August 2, 1990, carried out his surprise attack against that country. It was barely two years since the end of Iraq's bloody war with Iran.

In response, the United States at first seemed indecisive. President Bush and Prime Minister Margaret Thatcher of Britain were attending a conference in Colorado shortly after the attack. According to those in attendance, Bush muttered something like, "It's all right going in, but how are we going to get out?" and commented that most Americans couldn't find Kuwait on the map. At this point, Thatcher allegedly took the microphone and said, "Look, George, this is no time to go wobbly. We can't fall at the first fence." Nonetheless, the evidence suggests that the administration allowed Saddam to invade and then rebuffed all efforts by other Middle Eastern nations and the United Nations to resolve the issue peacefully. Bush contended that it was his responsibility to maintain human rights in Kuwait and elsewhere in the Middle East, despite the fact that Kuwait's record on human rights is hardly admirable.

The United States assembled a coalition force of more than 600,000 ground, sea, and air force personnel (573,000 of whom were American) in Saudi Arabia and on January 16, 1991, launched Operation Desert Storm to "liberate" Kuwait. By February 28, 1991, the operation was declared over. The United States had flown some 110,000 sorties against Iraq, dropping 88,500 tons of bombs, including cluster bombs and depleted uranium devices. It destroyed water-purification plants, food-processing plants, electric power stations, hospitals, schools, telephone exchanges, bridges, and roads throughout the country. Iraqi forces were definitively expelled from Kuwait and decimated in the field (thousands of retreating soldiers were slaughtered in what American pilots referred to as a "turkey shoot"), but the coalition did not press on to Baghdad and attempt to capture or oust Saddam Hussein.

Instead, the period between the two Iraq wars—from January 16, 1991, when General Norman Schwarzkopf launched his assault, to March 19, 2003, when General Tommy Franks ordered the start of the Anglo-American invasion of Iraq—saw a vast expansion of our empire of military bases in the Persian Gulf region. After the truce following the first war, we consolidated the bases we had acquired in Kuwait and Saudi Arabia and prepositioned the tanks and ammunition that would be needed if we reopened hostilities. In the middle of this period, around 1995, a series of terrorist incidents led us to move much of our armor, aircraft, and troops into hardened or extremely remote sites, such as Prince Sultan Air Base in Saudi Arabia. In the late 1990s, during the second Clinton administration, the Pentagon began seriously to prepare for a renewed war with Iraq. The Joint Chiefs of Staff's *Strategic Assessment 1999* specifically said that an "oil war" in the Persian Gulf was a serious contingency and that "U.S. forces might be used to ensure adequate supplies."[12] It was reasoned that a new war would eliminate once and for all the influence of Saddam Hussein, gain control of his oil, and extend our influence into the vacuum created in the oil-rich lands of southern Eurasia by the demise of the Soviet Union.

As we have already seen, this renewed interest in Central, South, and Southwest Asia included the opening of military-to-military ties with the independent Central Asian republics of Kyrgyzstan and Uzbekistan and support for a Taliban government in Afghanistan as a way to obtain gas and oil pipeline rights for an American-led consortium. But the jewel in the crown of this grand strategy was a plan to replace the Ba'ath regime in Iraq with a pro-American puppet government and build permanent military bases there. In preparation for the military campaign, the Pentagon made huge efforts in all its client states surrounding the Persian Gulf to isolate our bases from the predominantly anti-American peoples living there and get them ready to support an expeditionary force for the conquest of Iraq. The terrorist attacks of 9/11, the war against the Taliban, and Bush's "war on terror" merely provided further impetus for a plan that had been in the works for at least a decade.

In the hours following the September 11, 2001, attacks, Secretary of Defense Donald Rumsfeld asked for an immediate assault on Iraq. The following day, in a cabinet meeting at the White House, Rumsfeld again insisted that Iraq should be "a principal target of the first round in the war against terrorism."[13] The president reportedly was advised that "public opinion has to be prepared before a move against Iraq is possible" and instead chose Afghanistan as a much softer target.

These statements and their timing are noteworthy because at that point the United States had not even determined that the suicide bombers came from Osama bin Laden's al Qaeda network and, though the president would later damn Saddam Hussein as an "ally" of al-Qaeda, the Bush administration never provided any evidence substantiating that connection. In fact, the 2001 edition of the Department of State's annual *Patterns of Global Terrorism* listed no acts of global terrorism linked to the government of Iraq. On September 22, 2001, Secretary of State Colin Powell promised to release proof that al-Qaeda and Osama bin Laden were guilty of planning and executing the attacks on New York and Washington, and only after that did national security adviser Condoleezza Rice tell CNN, "Clearly, we do have evidence, historical and otherwise, about the relationship of the al-Qaeda network to what happened on September 11." Such evidence has never actually been forthcoming. Until passenger manifests revealed that the airliner hijackers were mostly from Saudi Arabia, I myself thought that the attacks could be blowback from American policies in any number of places, including Chile, Argentina, Indonesia, Greece, all of Central America, or Okinawa, not to mention Palestine and Iran. Rumsfeld's early targeting of Iraq therefore suggests that the Bush administration and the Pentagon had long had a hidden agenda involving a "regime change" there.

Ever since the first American war against Iraq, the Gulf War of 1991, a number of the key people who planned and executed it in the White House and the Pentagon have wanted to go back and finish what they started. They said so in reports written for then Secretary of Defense Cheney in the last years of the first Bush administration; and during the period from 1992 to 2000, when they were out of power, they drafted extensive plans for what should be done if the Republicans retook the White House. In the spring of 1997, they organized themselves as the Project for the New American Century (PNAC) and began to lobby vigorously for aggression against Iraq and the remaking of the Middle East.

In a letter to President Clinton dated January 26, 1998, they called for "the removal of Saddam Hussein's regime from power," and in a letter dated May 29, 1998, to Speaker of the House Newt Gingrich and Senate majority leader Trent Lott, complaining that Clinton had not listened to them, they reiterated their recommendation that Saddam be overthrown. As they put the matter, "We should establish and maintain a strong U.S. military presence in the region, and be prepared to use that force to protect our vital interests in the [Persian] Gulf—and, if necessary, to help remove Saddam from power." These letters were signed by Donald Rumsfeld; William Kristol, editor of the right-wing *Weekly Standard* magazine and chairman of PNAC; Elliott Abrams, a convicted Iran-Contra conspirator who would be named in 2002 as director of Middle Eastern policy on the National Security Council; Paul Wolfowitz, who would become Rumsfeld's deputy at the Pentagon; John Bolton, who would become undersecretary of state for arms control and international security in the Bush *fils* administration; Richard Perle, who would become chairman of the Defense Science Board; William J. Bennett, President Reagan's education secretary; Richard Armitage, who would become Colin Powell's deputy at the State Department; Zalmay Khalilzad, a former Unocal consultant who would become Bush's "ambassador" to Afghanistan and later the chief liaison with the Kurds and anti-Saddam exiles in Iraq; and several other prominent American militarists. In addition to the letter signatories, PNAC included Vice President Dick Cheney; I. Lewis Libby, Cheney's chief of staff; and Stephen Cambone, a Pentagon bureaucrat in both Bush administrations. They have made their ideas readily available in a report issued in September 2000 entitled *Rebuilding America's Defenses: Strategy, Forces, and Resources for a New Century* and in a book edited by Robert Kagan and William Kristol, *Present Dangers: Crisis and Opportunity in American Foreign and Defense Policy.*[14]

After George W. Bush became president, ten of the eighteen signers of the letters to Clinton and Republican congressional leaders became members of the administration. They bided their time for nine months. In the words of the PNAC's *Rebuilding America's Defenses*, they were waiting for a "catastrophic and catalyzing event—like a new Pearl Harbor" that would mobilize the public and allow them to put their theories and plans into action. September 11 was, of course, precisely what they were looking for. Within days, Condoleezza Rice called together members of the National Security Council and asked them "to think about 'how do you capitalize on these opportunities' to fundamentally change American doctrine, and the shape of the world, in the wake of September 11th." She said, "I really think this period is analogous to 1945 to 1947," referring to the years when fear and paranoia led the United States into its cold war with the USSR.[15]

Still, the Bush administration could not just go to war with Iraq without tying Saddam Hussein's regime in some way to the 9/11 attacks. It therefore first launched an easy war against Afghanistan because there was a connection between Osama bin Laden and the Taliban regime, even though the United States had contributed more to Osama's development as a terrorist than the extremist Afghan group ever did. The strategy of that war was to rely on massive American bombing and, using suitcases full of money, to recruit the forces of the Northern Alliance warlords, whom the Taliban had defeated, to do the actual fighting as our sepoys. Meanwhile, the White House launched one of the most extraordinary propaganda campaigns of modern times to convince the public that an attack on Saddam Hussein should be an essential part of America's "war on terrorism." This calculated attempt to whip up war fever, in turn, elicited an outpouring of speculation around the world on the true motives of the American president and his evident obsession with Iraq.

The first and most obvious ploy of the warhawks was to claim, in the words of President Bush, that "[Saddam] possesses the most deadly arms of our age." The only problem with this argument was that it probably was not true. Iraq certainly had such weapons of mass destruction (WMDs) at one time, but between 1991 and 1998 a combination of the first Gulf War, U.N. sanctions, and the U.N. inspectors appears to have destroyed most or all of them as well as Iraq's capability to produce more.

As Scott Ritter put it, "I bear personal witness through seven years as a chief weapons inspector in Iraq for the United Nations to both the scope of Iraq's weapons of mass destruction programs and the effectiveness of U.N. weapons inspectors in ultimately eliminating them."[16] Never one to give up on any ploy that might help his cause, Rumsfeld replied that "the absence of evidence is not evidence of absence." This issue led to the return of U.N. weapons inspectors, but not, as it turned out, to international support for the White House's war plans. PNAC was, in any case, never much interested in Saddam's WMDs except as a convenient excuse. "While the unresolved conflict with Iraq provides the immediate justification," wrote the authors of *Rebuilding America's Defenses*, "the need for a substantial American force presence in the Gulf transcends the issue of the regime of Saddam Hussein."[17] Bush did not hedge his bets. As late as a March 6, 2003, press conference in the East Room of the White House, he exclaimed, "Saddam Hussein is not disarming. This is a fact. It cannot be denied."

The administration's harping on the danger that Saddam might give unconventional weapons to "evildoers" rang a familiar bell for those who remember the propaganda that accompanied the prologue to the first Iraq war. Then, the mobilizing tale of the administration of Bush Senior was that Iraqi soldiers had pulled babies from Kuwait's hospital incubators and, in Bush's words, "scattered them across the floor like firewood." The president repeatedly referred to "312 premature babies at Kuwait City's maternity hospital who died after Iraqi soldiers stole their incubators and left the infants on the floor." According to Dr. Mohammed Matar, director of Kuwait's primary care system, and his wife, Dr. Fayeza Youssef, who ran the obstetrics unit at the maternity hospital, there were only a handful of incubators in all of Kuwait and few if any babies in them at the time of the Iraqi invasion. Bush made these comments a few days before the United Nations, on November 29, 1990, authorized the use of "all means necessary" to eject Iraq from Kuwait. After the war it was revealed that Kuwait had hired the big Washington public relations firm of Hill & Knowlton to peddle this story, and on October 10, 1990, arranged for an "eyewitness" to testify before Congress that it had indeed happened. That witness, who turned out to be the daughter of the

Kuwaiti ambassador to Washington, had not been anywhere near a hospital in Kuwait City in August 1990. Other "witnesses" who claimed to have seen Iraqi atrocities later acknowledged that they had all been coached by Hill & Knowlton.[18]

On October 7, 2002, President Bush *fils* contributed what was surely the weirdest of his homicidal-dictator-with-WMDs rationales for a war with Iraq. In a speech in Cincinnati, after noting that "Saddam Hussein is a homicidal dictator who is addicted to weapons of mass destruction," he warned that "Iraq has a growing fleet of manned and unmanned aerial vehicles that could be used to disperse chemical and biological weapons across broad areas. We're concerned that Iraq is exploring ways of using these [unmanned aerial vehicles] for missions targeting the United States." Presumably Bush was here referring to the Czech L-29 jet training aircraft, 169 of which Iraq had bought in the 1960s and 1980s. The L-29 is a single-engine, dual-seat plane intended as a basic flight trainer for novices. It was the Soviet bloc's version of America's Cessna, with a range of about 840 miles and a top speed of around 145 miles per hour. There is some evidence that before the Gulf War Iraq had experimented with converting these aircraft into unmanned aerial vehicles—but they may have only been intending to use them as crop dusters.[19] In any case, the president did not explain how these slow-moving aircraft could reach Maine, the nearest point on the U.S. mainland to Iraq, some 5,500 miles away, or why they would not be shot down the moment they crossed Iraq's borders.

Another major claim in the Bush administration's march to war was that Saddam had backed the al-Qaeda terrorist attacks of September 11. In August 2002, Rumsfeld told Tom Brokaw on NBC News that "there are al-Qaeda in Iraq." On September 26, 2002, he said that the government had "bulletproof" confirmation of links between Iraq and al-Qaeda members, including "solid evidence" that members of the terrorist network maintained a presence in Iraq (but not in Pakistan, our soon-to-be ally). Rumsfeld went on to suggest that Iraq had offered safe haven to bin Laden and the Taliban leader Mullah Mohammed Omar. In an October 11, 2002, speech, President Bush said, "Some al-Qaeda leaders who fled Afghanistan went to Iraq." Since the "solid evidence" was never released, one must assume that Rumsfeld and Bush were referring to about 150 members of a group called Ansar al Islam ("Supporters of Islam") who took refuge in the Kurdish areas of northern Iraq. The problem is that America's would-be Kurdish allies controlled this area, not Saddam. There was no evidence of actual links between Saddam and Osama bin Laden, a point often made by the CIA, and such cooperation would in any case have been implausible given Osama's religious commitments and Saddam's ruthlessly secular regime.

The only instance of Saddam's support for anti-American terrorism was his alleged attempt to assassinate George H. W. Bush during the former president's victory tour of Kuwait in mid-April 1993—the origin of his son's comment in a 2002 campaign speech that Saddam "tried to kill my dad." On June 26, 1993, two and a half months after the attempt, President Clinton retaliated by firing cruise missiles into Baghdad, killing several innocent bystanders. The evidence strongly indicates, however, that not only did the assassination attempt never occur but Kuwaiti intelligence probably was covering up its discovery of a smuggling ring working on the Iraq-Kuwait border by claiming that they were after W's daddy.[20]

Perhaps the least convincing of the official reasons for wanting to get rid of Saddam was the contention that he had no respect for U.N. resolutions. On September 30, 2002, Rumsfeld staged a show at the Pentagon featuring gun-camera footage of Iraqi antiaircraft artillery firing at American and British warplanes patrolling the "no-fly zones" of northern and southern Iraq. "With each missile launched at our air crews," he claimed, "Iraq expresses its contempt for the U.N. resolutions—a fact that must be kept in mind as their latest inspection offers are evaluated." But Secretary Rumsfeld certainly knew that no U.N. resolution (or other international authority) existed to legitimate the no-fly zones. The United States, Britain, and France created them unilaterally in March 1991, theoretically to protect rebellious Kurds in the north and Shi'ites in the south who had risen in revolt against Saddam after the first Gulf War. Although they did indeed stop Saddam from using his air power, the first Bush administration had already stood idly by as he crushed the uprisings—undoubtedly fearing a radically Islamic Iraq and a Kurdish bid for independence that would destabilize an American ally, Turkey, which had long engaged in a ruthless suppression of its own Kurdish minority. France soon dropped out of the no-fly zone enforcement, but the United States and Britain continued, slowly escalating their air attacks right up to the eve of the second Iraq war, even though these were clearly illegal under international law.[21]

Then there was the administration's assertion that overthrowing Saddam would bring democracy to Iraq and other countries around the Persian Gulf. In an interview with the *Financial Times* of London, Condoleezza Rice commented that freedom, democracy, and free enterprise did not "stop at the edge of Islam" and that, after toppling Saddam through the use of military force, the United States would be "completely devoted" to the reconstruction of Iraq as a unified, democratic state.[22] Even then, this sounded a bit like the military's claim, after pulverizing Afghanistan through high-altitude bombing, that it had really arrived to liberate Afghan women from the Taliban. Of course, had the United States truly been interested in democracy in the gulf states, it might have begun long ago in Saudi Arabia or any of the feudal monarchies like Kuwait, Bahrain, Qatar, the United Arab Emirates, and Oman in which it has built major military garrisons.

Since none of the administration's rationales for its belligerence toward Iraq made much sense, some observers around the world looked elsewhere for its true motives. One prominent theory concerned Iraq's oil. Its reserves are the second largest on earth, after those of Saudi Arabia. Given that both the president and the vice president were former oil company executives and that the president's father, also a former president, was the founder, in 1954, of the Zapata Offshore Oil Company, it was reasonable to assume that they were at least very familiar with Iraq's oil wealth. The Zapata Company drilled the first well off Kuwait. In 1963, Bush Senior merged Zapata with another firm to create the oil giant Pennzoil, and in 1966, he sold off his shares, becoming a multimillion-aire in the process. As late as 1998 and 1999, when Dick Cheney was still president of the Halliburton Company of Houston, it sold Saddam some $23.8 million of oil-field equipment. Perhaps Bush Junior's obsession with Iraq, according to this line of thought, was his desire to seize its oil.

The United States needs a lot of oil for its huge and, in the case of SUVs and Humvees, ever more gas-guzzling automotive sector. It also would like strategically to control the oil lands of the Middle East and Central Asia in order to oversee the shipments to regions increasingly dependent on imported petroleum, which might someday challenge American global predominance. Europe and China are the obvious potential challengers. As Anthony Sampson, an oil expert and the author of the classic book on the major oil companies, *The Seven Sisters,* observes, "Western oil interests closely influence military and diplomatic policies, and it is no accident that while American companies are competing for access to oil in Central Asia, the U.S. is building up military bases across the region."[23]

The strongest evidence that oil was a prime motive was the behavior of the American troops in Baghdad after they entered the city on April 9, 2003. They very effectively protected the headquarters of Iraq's Ministry of Oil but were indifferent to looters who spent two days ransacking the National Museum of its priceless antiquities and burning the National Archives and the city's famed Quranic Library. The same thing happened to the National Museum in Mosul. While the marines defaced some of the world's most ancient walls at the site of the Sumerian city of Ur, near Nasiriya, the army was already busy building a permanent garrison at the adjacent Tallil Air Base to protect the southern oil fields.[24]

Another popular theory has been that the Likud Party of Israel was and continues to be the primary influence on the Bush administration's thinking about the Middle East and that the desire to oust Saddam reflected the long-range interests of Israeli rightists who want to ensure their country's continuing regional military superiority. Many of the key figures in the second Bush administration and in PNAC have intimate connections with Ariel Sharon and Likud. Among these are chairman of the Defense Policy Board Richard Perle, Deputy Secretary of Defense Paul Wolfowitz, Undersecretary of Defense for Policy Douglas Feith, and David Wurmser, special assistant to a PNAC founder, John Bolton, who is undersecretary of state for arms control. Michael Ledeen, a former Iran-Contra conspirator and a member of the board of the Jewish Institute for National Security Affairs of Washington, DC, cooperates closely with his colleagues at the American Enterprise Institute to promote Israeli causes. All these men have long records of opposing peace initiatives and accords between Israel and the Palestinians and of calling for American wars not just against Iraq but also against Syria, Lebanon, and Iran—indeed, for a remaking of the whole region that would only benefit Israel.

Perle is a member of the board of the conservative *Jerusalem Post* and author of the chapter "Iraq: Saddam Unbound" in the PNAC book *Present Dangers*. In private life, Feith is a partner in a small Washington law firm that specializes in representing Israeli munitions makers seeking ties with American weapons industries. Before going to the State Department, Wurmser was head of Middle Eastern projects at the right-wing American Enterprise Institute. He is the author of the AEI-published book *Tyranny's Ally: America's Failure to Defeat Saddam Hussein* (1999), whose foreword is by Perle. During the Reagan administration, Feith served as special counsel to Perle, who was then assistant secretary of defense for international security affairs. Another influential figure, Meyrav Wurmser, David Wurmser's wife and cofounder of the Middle East Media Research Institute (Memri), translates and distributes stories from the Arab press that invariably portray Arabs in a bad light.

In July 1996, these four wrote a position paper for Israel's incoming prime minister, Benjamin Netanyahu of the Likud Party, entitled "A Clean Break: A New Strategy for Securing the Realm." It called on Israel to repudiate the Oslo Accords and the underlying concept of "land for peace" and to permanently annex the entire West Bank and Gaza Strip. It also recommended that Israel advocate the elimination of Saddam Hussein as a first step toward regime changes in Syria, Lebanon, Saudi Arabia, and Iran. In November 2002, Prime Minister Sharon echoed these ideas when he urged the United States to turn to Iran as soon as it finished with Saddam. Many other officials and hangers-on of the second Bush administration hold these or similar views. Given their well-known sympathies, it is not implausible to think that they have been attempting to implement them under cover of the "war on terror."[25]

Still another reasonable theory was that America's war fever was stoked by shrewd political operators in the White House and that the campaign against Saddam Hussein was mainly meant to influence domestic politics—both the 2002 midterm election and the 2004 presidential one. Several commentators called this the use of "weapons of mass distraction."[26] Among its goals were to bolster George W. Bush's dubious legitimacy as president and to divert voters' attention from his less than sterling domestic achievements in his first two years in office. Faced with 2002 midterm elections, the leaders of the Republican Party were desperate to keep discussion away from issues such as the president's and vice president's close ties to the corrupt Enron Corporation, the huge and growing federal budget deficit, the looting of workers' pension funds by highly paid CEOs, vast tax cuts that favored the rich, a severe loss of civil liberties under Bush's attorney general, and, in the foreign sphere, the embarrassing fact that, despite the war in Afghanistan, al-Qaeda and Osama bin Laden evidently remained at large and potent.

In this view, key political advisers in the White House such as Karl Rove and Chief of Staff Andrew Card had far more influence with the president than either Secretary of Defense Rumsfeld or Secretary of State Powell. Just as, during the Vietnam War, Presidents Kennedy, Johnson, and Nixon had to a surprising degree based key foreign policy decisions on domestic political considerations rather than on grand strategy or intelligence estimates, the evidence suggests that it was Rove who overruled the unilateralist hawks in the Pentagon and sent the president to the United Nations for his September 12, 2002, speech in which he called for renewed inspections in Iraq. Rove had discovered that domestic opinion was lukewarm on waging a war in the Middle East without allies.[27] For George W. Bush, the strategy worked. After two years in office, the party holding the White House increased its strength in Congress, gaining control of both houses, a genuine rarity in modern political history.

It would be hard to deny that oil, Israel, and domestic politics all played crucial roles in the Bush administration's war against Iraq, but I believe the more encompassing explanation for our second war with Iraq is no different from that for our wars in the Balkans in 1999 or in Afghanistan in 2001–02: the inexorable pressures of imperialism and militarism. Jay Bookman, a columnist at the *Atlanta Journal-Constitution*, asked the relevant question months before the war began: "Why does the administration seem unconcerned about an exit strategy from Iraq once Saddam is toppled? Because we won't be leaving. Having conquered Iraq, the United States will create permanent military bases in that country from which to dominate the Middle East, including neighboring Iran."[28]

Already, between the defeat of Iraq in 1991 and the renewal of hostilities in March 2003, the United States began to acquire and build bases in the area, first by consolidating and enlarging the facilities it had used, especially in Saudi Arabia and Kuwait, during the war. The decision to stay on in Saudi Arabia turned out to have serious unintended consequences, particularly for New York City. A number of influential young Saudis resented what they saw as the highlighting of the U.S.-led coalition and its commander, General Norman Schwarzkopf, to the detriment of his Saudi counterpart, Lieutenant General Khalid Al Saud, who commanded units from twenty-four non-Western countries and yet was generally ignored by the Western allies. These Saudis felt that it would have been better if Arab and Persian Gulf countries had been entrusted with the leading role in disciplining Saddam Hussein instead of having to rely on Americans and Europeans, even though the capability of Saudi Arabia and its allies to assume that role was probably a fantasy. Far more important, some of them also came to believe that the Saudi monarchy wanted the American military forces to remain in Saudi Arabia primarily to safeguard it in the face of growing demands for a more modern, less repressive regime. Since the Saudi monarchy is entrusted with the defense of Mecca and Medina, the most sacred sites in the Muslim world, other Saudi dissidents (but hardly democrats) argued that the presence of so many infidels in the country was an affront not just to Saudi nationalism but to Islam itself.

At first, there were only a few anti-American incidents. In February and March 1991, shots were fired at U.S. military vehicles and an attempt was made to burn a bus. Matters became more serious in 1994, with increasing reports of terrorist threats. On November 13, 1995, dissidents exploded a 220-pound car bomb in the capital city of Riyadh, killing five Americans and two Indians. Its target was the U.S. Military Training Mission to the Kingdom of Saudi Arabia, which was under the direct control of the Central Command at MacDill Air Force Base, Florida, but was actually subcontracted to the Vinnell Corporation, a firm of military mercenaries. In May 1996, the Saudi government convicted and beheaded four Muslim militants for the crime.

During the first Gulf War, the Saudis installed several hundred American, British, and French military commanders and their staffs in the Khobar Towers, a group of eight-story apartment buildings at Dhahran on the periphery of King Abdul Aziz Air Base. The Americans instantly placed Patriot air defense missile batteries around the compound and neighboring Dhahran airfield. In July 1992, after the war was over and the Saudis agreed to allow American military forces to remain, the Army Forces Central Command–Saudi Arabia (ARCENT-SA) established its headquarters in the Khobar Towers. On June 25, 1996, just outside a chain-link fence surrounding the apartment buildings, anti-American terrorists detonated a powerful truck bomb that killed nineteen American airmen and injured hundreds more. Despite the carnage, rather than pull back from Saudi Arabia, now seen as key to our whole Persian Gulf strategy, the White House and the Pentagon decided to dig in deeper but isolate themselves as much as possible from Saudi society.

In the wake of the Khobar Towers attack, the Pentagon relocated some 6,000 military personnel to distant and more easily protected locations. All the senior command units—ARCENT-SA, the Military Training Mission, and other operations—were ordered to move their offices and living quarters from Dhahran and downtown Riyadh to Eskan Village, a compound about fifteen miles outside the capital, surrounded by Patriot missile batteries. The air force transferred its personnel and equipment to Prince Sultan Air Base, located at al Kharj on an unmarked road seventy miles southeast of Riyadh in the open desert. It is a sprawling 230-square-mile compound the size of metropolitan Chicago but not marked on any map. Under Saudi-imposed rules, no photos can depict anything that reveals the presence of American troops at Prince Sultan—no landmarks, no signs, no Saudis walking in the background to show that what's depicted is even in Saudi Arabia, no vehicles with Saudi license plates. All snapshots are reviewed and those that contain anything more than a bland background are confiscated.[29]

The Saudi government built Eskan Village in 1983 to provide housing for one of Saudi Arabia's many nomadic Bedouin tribes, who decided that they preferred living in their traditional tents in the desert. The housing complex was never occupied. It is actually a small, self-contained town consisting of 836 "villas" and thirty-seven high-rise towers. From the Gulf War to the Khobar Towers bombing, Eskan Village was strictly a housing estate for American military personnel working in the Saudi capital or at Riyadh Air Force Base. From 1996 through Gulf War II, it became home and work all wrapped in one. The average villa—five bedrooms, three baths, a living room, and a kitchen—comes fully equipped with a stove, TV, and washing machine. Only villas housing female personnel have clothes driers (in deference to Saudi sensitivities about seeing female underwear flapping on an outdoor clothesline). Eskan Village has become a completely American community, with dining halls, medical and dental clinics, a basketball court, volleyball courts, a miniature golf course, a "Pizza Inn," a Chinese fast-food restaurant, and a "club" with swimming pool.[30] Liquor of any sort, however, is prohibited.

The amenities and scope of Eskan Village paled in comparison with those of Prince Sultan Air Base, for over a decade the largest military facility used by the United States in the Persian Gulf area, approximately the same size as the entire country of Bahrain and a mere 620 miles from Baghdad. The government of Saudi Arabia planned Prince Sultan prior to the first Gulf War but had built only the massive 15,000-feet-long runway plus taxiways and parking aprons. There were as yet no buildings in October 1990, when the U.S. Air Force dispatched one of its 435-person Red Horse squadrons ("Rapid Engineer Deployable Heavy Operational Repair Squadron Engineers") from Aviano Air Force Base in Italy to make the place operational. Created during the Vietnam War, Red Horse squadrons, sometimes used to disable enemy airfields, as they did in Iraq during the Gulf War, specialize in making repairs to airfields during combat. They are fully armed. At Prince Sultan they worked throughout the winter of 1990 on more than twenty-five major projects, at a cost of more than $14.6 million. By January 1991, Prince Sultan Air Base started to receive aircraft, and by the beginning of the Gulf War it held some 4,900 air force personnel and was capable of housing, servicing, and arming five fighter squadrons of aircraft and their supporting personnel (a typical American squadron consists of twenty-four aircraft).

With the end of the fighting in 1991, it was allowed to go fallow until the Khobar Towers bombing put it back on the map.

Prince Sultan, surrounded by flat desert with open lines of fire, was a perfect spot to "hide" the American presence. In addition, the air force assigned 10 percent of the 6,000 troops based there after 1996 to "perimeter security." Even so, F-15s and F-16s on takeoff were under orders to climb as fast as possible to avoid potential attack by surface-to-air missiles. The American troops who served on ninety-day tours almost never left the base. The transfer of U.S. operations to Prince Sultan cost some $500 million. Both before and during the second Iraq war, it was the main base for American surveillance operations using AWACs (airborne warning and control) aircraft and U-2 spy planes.

From the summer of 1996 to 2002, construction at Prince Sultan was continuous. In 1997, the Saudi Ministry of Defense and Aviation awarded Northrop Aviation's Electronic Sensors and Systems Division a contract worth $60.7 million to set up and integrate new air traffic control, navigation, meteorological, and communications systems. In early 1999, the troops, who had been living in air-conditioned tents, moved into a new 4,257-bed housing facility two miles from the base. The Saudi government paid $112 million for it; hence it remained Saudi government property even when run and maintained by the U.S. Air Force. Facilities included community dining halls with names like Camel Lot and Mirage, a base theater, a gymnasium, a recreation center, an outdoor swimming pool permanently *cooled* to 82 degrees (the air temperature at Prince Sultan is normally in the range of 110 to 115 degrees Fahrenheit), and the Prince Sultan Health Center (cost $5.87 million), which Prince Sultan himself dedicated on June 22, 1999. The total cost of the air base, from its inception in the late 1980s, has been estimated at around $1.07 billion. In the years leading up to the second Iraq war, the air force flew a total of 286,000 missions from Prince Sultan and other Persian Gulf bases to enforce the no-fly zone in southern Iraq. The same operations for northern Iraq were launched from Incirlik Air Base in Turkey.

The major new military construction at Prince Sultan, completed just prior to the war in Afghanistan, was a Combined Air Operations Center (CAOC) with state-of-the-art command and control systems and a Joint

Intelligence Center, including three different Internet networks—for unclassified, secret, and allied forces traffic. The air force dedicated the center in June 2001, and in October the Saudi government permitted its use in coordinating air operations against targets in Afghanistan. The hypersecret Air Force Communications Agency supervised its design and installation. The new CAOC at Prince Sultan coordinated air operations with new air bases the United States was just then building in Kuwait, Qatar, and the United Arab Emirates. But as the second Iraq war approached, it became unclear whether and for what functions the Saudi government would allow the Americans to use Prince Sultan, so the Pentagon promptly built an elaborate alternative air command center at al-Udeid Air Base in Qatar.[31]

Typical of life in the spreading empire of bases in the oil lands, days at Prince Sultan were often spent swimming and watching football on TV when not working. Still, the isolation did not necessarily go down well with the troops. In one notorious instance, Lieutenant Colonel Martha McSally, the highest-ranking female pilot in the air force, took the Defense Department to court for requiring her to put on an *abaya*—the total body covering devout Saudi women wear in public when off the base. This, she claimed, was an unconstitutional infringement of the rights of American women. She won (in Washington, DC), and Central Command withdrew the requirement.[32]

The U.S. government has always understood that the presence of our forces in Saudi Arabia was a root cause of al-Qaeda's terrorist activities against both the monarchy and American targets within and outside the country. Rather than move those forces promptly after 9/11, however, the Bush administration waited until it could disguise what it was doing under cover of normal military redeployments. On April 29, 2003, Defense Secretary Donald Rumsfeld and his Saudi counterpart, Prince Sultan bin Abdul Aziz, finally announced in Riyadh that the fall of Saddam Hussein meant that America's military mission in the country was over and that "all combat forces" would be withdrawn. Even so, the Bush administration seemed to have delayed too long. On May 12, 2003, terrorists attacked four walled and guarded compounds for foreigners in Riyadh, killing over thirty Americans and Saudis. Moreover, the United

States is not actually leaving Prince Sultan or the country—it has retained a small maintenance unit at the air base and the Vinnell Corporation's training of the Saudi National Guard continues. The U.S. withdrawal was announced with great fanfare on Saudi television, but it is unlikely that anyone believed that American imperialists had actually lost interest in the world's richest oil-producing nation. As the English historian of imperialism Niall Ferguson observed in an interview with the *New York Times*, "From 1882 until 1922, the British promised the international community sixty-six times that they would leave Egypt, but they never did."[33]

Prince Sultan was for some years the base of bases in the Middle East, but the United States had built such a military overcapacity in the gulf region that the post–Iraq war decision to withdraw almost all military personnel from Saudi Arabia had little effect on America's war-making capability. The proliferation of bases in neighboring Kuwait, Bahrain, and Qatar alone exceeds any military need the United States might face. And there are still more bases in Oman, the United Arab Emirates, Turkey, Egypt, Israel, and Djibouti, plus those recently acquired in Afghanistan, Pakistan, Kyrgyzstan, and Uzbekistan. Before 2003 is over, there will probably be four new American bases in Iraq. The navy also can deploy up to five carrier battle groups, each with approximately seventy-five aircraft, cruise missiles, and atomic weapons, in the Arabian Sea, the Red Sea, and the Persian Gulf. A carrier battle group is composed of the aircraft carrier itself, two cruisers, two to three destroyers, a frigate, an attack submarine, and a combat support ship and is, in essence, a floating base.

On the eve of the second Iraq war, Camp Doha, the army's major base in Kuwait, was the jumping-off point for a huge ground force waiting for orders to surge across the Iraq border, including the army's V Corps from Heidelberg, Germany; the First Marine Expeditionary Force from Camp Pendleton, California; the Third Infantry Division (Mechanized) from Fort Stewart, Georgia; three squadrons of Apache attack helicopters; a Special Forces unit; and an advance party of the British First Armored Division. The principal weaponry of these units were 230 Abrams main battle tanks, 120 Bradley fighting vehicles, and 40 Paladin self-propelled

155 mm artillery pieces. General Dynamics manufactures the Abrams tank, which weighs 68.7 tons and costs $4.3 million each. The Bradley vehicle is a 50,000-pound armored "battle taxi" equipped with modern machine guns, antitank rockets, and smoke grenades that is used to ferry troops into combat behind the tanks. The Paladin is the most advanced gun in the army's arsenal, weighing some 32 tons.

Since the Khobar Towers bombing, one of the army's main goals has been to replace Camp Doha, which is too close to the capital, Kuwait City, with a more modern prepositioning facility fully protected from possible terrorist attacks. In July 1999, the government of Kuwait began work on that new base, a $200 million facility named Camp Arifjan, located in the desert south of the capital. During 2002, about 10,000 noncombat army personnel were transferred there from Camp Doha. At Arifjan, virtually all the prepositioned equipment for a full army brigade is stored in large warehouses rather than exposed to the desert environment, as at Camp Doha. The Army Corps of Engineers designed the base, which includes modern barracks with shatterproof Mylar glass on all windows and special maintenance bays for tanks. Most of Camp Arifjan was completed during 2002, with only some roads and utilities still to be built. Camp Doha, continuously in use since the first Gulf War, was always understood to be a temporary facility, but Arifjan is evidence that the Americans intend to stay a long time.

Throughout the late 1990s, the army flew a new brigade from the United States or Europe into Kuwait every four months for training. The airfield it used was Ahmed al Jaber Air Base, located just seventy-five miles south of the Iraq border; although the base belongs to the Kuwait air force, it has an area set aside only for U.S. Air Force operations. Until late 1996, our air force deployed its F-15 and F-16 fighters at Kuwait City's international airport, but after the terrorist attacks in Riyadh and Dhahran, it moved everything to what the troops inevitably call "the Jab." According to the Global Security Organization, "Ahmed al Jaber Air Base is one hard target. The Air Force uses every means available, from physical barriers to high-tech sensors and infrared cameras, to keep people deployed to al Jaber safe. And an alert and overwhelming security force subjects even the most innocuous happenings to stern scrutiny."[34] The air force contracts out almost all services for the several thousand U.S. troops at al Jaber.

Another American military facility in Kuwait, the Ali al Salem Air Base, only thirty-nine miles from the Iraqi border, was until recently a hard-duty post, devoted to radar surveillance of Iraqi air space. One description of Ali al Salem notes that "the weather is about as hot here as any place you've ever been in your life."[35] During mid-2000, work began on new buildings and security devices to make Ali al Salem a permanent base. Services here, too, are provided under contract.

Americans like to think that Kuwait is indebted to the United States because we came to its aid in 1991 and therefore welcomes permanent military bases on its soil. This is a mistake. Kuwait has not proved a particularly friendly ally. As an Arab nation, Kuwait opposes American support for Israeli expansionism and its double standard for Palestinian terrorists and Israeli soldiers, both of whom kill defenseless civilians. The Kuwaitis are also no more happy with foreign troops living among them than any other nation might be, particularly foreigners who are disrespectful toward their religion. Nonetheless, Kuwait has accepted American protection and pays for it.

The situation is more complex in the other gulf states. Qatar and Oman are small nations, scared to death of their larger neighbors, Iran, Iraq, and Saudi Arabia. They have invited the Americans into their countries as a form of protection, much as their ancestors accepted the British. In return, the Americans demand military bases, preferably in highly secure areas away from population centers. The Pentagon knows that it is not particularly welcome in the area and that the gulf governments prefer not to talk about American bases or acknowledge their presence more than absolutely necessary. Oman is probably the most tolerant of the gulf states toward the Americans, the United Arab Emirates the least. Each risks the wrath of its own people for collaborating with the United States.

Bahrain is a good example. It remained a rather quiet place until July 1995, when the navy moved the headquarters of its Fifth Fleet there, together with some 4,200 military personnel. As the Global Security Organization notes, "The current ASU [naval administrative support unit] bears little resemblance to the small, 10-acre compound it was as recently as 1991. In the past seven years, this 'sleepy hollow' has expanded to 62 acres with $36.5 million worth of new construction, including new transient bachelor quarters, a medical and dental clinic, a racquetball court, a chapel, a post office and several multi-purpose sports fields."[36] Many American servicemen regard duty in Bahrain as the best posting in the gulf. Unlike in Saudi Arabia, which is connected to Bahrain by the King Fahd causeway, Americans can drink alcohol in Bahrain. But even though Manama, Bahrain's capital, is a city made up primarily of foreigners—and not just American foreigners—and the kingdom has a population of only about 660,000, the navy has placed many hotels and bars off-limits to its personnel as a precaution against terrorist attacks.

Bahrain goes out of its way not to appear subservient to the Americans. The Bahrainis are rich and lead comfortable lives, but they nonetheless demonstrate against the United States at the slightest provocation. To keep political matters in balance, during August 2002, King Hamad bin Issa al-Khalifa of Bahrain crossed the gulf and paid a formal visit to Iran, where he was welcomed by President Mohammad Khatami. His visit was the first to Teheran by a Bahraini head of state since the Iranian revolution of 1979.[37] Fifth Fleet or no Fifth Fleet, Bahrain was clearly unimpressed by President George Bush's statement of January 2002 naming Iran as part of an "axis of evil."

The navy inherited the British base at Manama, and military ships are therefore a familiar presence. The air force is another matter. In 1987, the Bahrain air force began to build a massive air base on Bahrain Island, about twenty miles from Manama. The Shaikh Isa Air Base was intended for its one and only fighter wing. The base was still unfinished four years later at the time of the first Gulf War, when the marines took it over, and Navy SeaBees completed it. During the mid-1990s, the air force further enlarged the base, and, in 1997, it flew in the 366th Air Expeditionary Wing from Mountain Home Air Force Base, Idaho, with 1,200 personnel and such advanced aircraft as B-1B bombers, F-15 and F-16 fighters, and KC-135 aerial-refueling tankers. To protect the wing's forty-four aircraft, the Pentagon also transferred in elements of a Patriot antimissile battalion from Fort Bliss, Texas. By 2000, both the marines and the air force were permanent fixtures at Shaikh Isa Air Base, even though their presence was a subject the government of Bahrain had no desire to talk about.

Just south of Bahrain is the rich country of Qatar, about the size of Connecticut and Rhode Island combined. The head of state, the emir, is directly accountable to no one. He is constrained only by tribal tradition and Islamic law and works primarily to preserve the feudal and financial interests of his family. This is not easy, however, given the contemporary pressures on Qatar, which has a population of slightly over 800,000, 80 percent of whom are foreign workers, mostly highly literate Arabs, Pakistanis, Indians, and Iranians. Thanks to great oil wealth and stupendous reserves of natural gas, Qataris in the year 2000 enjoyed a per capita income of about $20,300, equal to that of the most developed countries. The high standard of living among a general population that lacks any firm ties to Qatar or its ruling family means there is constant agitation from below to end autocracy and open up the political system to social change.

Qatar was part of the anti-Iraqi coalition during both Gulf Wars. In June 1992, it granted the United States basing and weapons-prepositioning rights in return for an implicit guarantee of aid if Qatar were attacked. Qatar's fears are not abstract. Although the country is several times larger and much richer than Bahrain, genuine Qataris constitute such a small minority that the country has been ripe for an external takeover, internal revolution, or both. It shares a disputed land border with Saudi Arabia, fought Baghdad during both Gulf Wars, and often feuds with Iran. It hopes that by unobtrusively supporting the United States while publicly criticizing it and denouncing Israel while publicizing its large monetary donations to the Palestinians, it can contain popular indignation. The goal is to keep the dictatorial powers of its small ruling elite intact as long as possible.

After the young emir Sheikh Hamad bin Khalifa al-Thani deposed his conservative father in a bloodless coup in June 1995, he made one significant gesture toward openness, if not democracy. He agreed to sponsor what would become the single most influential source of news in Muslim countries, the cable-news network al-Jazeera (meaning "the peninsula," i.e., Qatar), whose studios are located in Doha, Qatar's capital. In April

1996, Saudi Arabia had thrown the BBC out of the country for reporting on such controversial issues as beheadings and Saudi dissidents. A few months later, the new emir hired most of the BBC's Arabic Service editors, reporters, and technicians and set them up as the nucleus of al-Jazeera. His intent seems to have been to end censorship in Qatar and thereby relieve some of the pressure for more openness without destabilizing the country. The emir has subsequently given his TV network almost complete journalistic freedom. So far, al-Jazeera has been criticized by virtually every Islamic country from Saudi Arabia to Algeria and, of course, by Israel. In October 2001, Secretary of State Colin Powell and national security adviser Condoleezza Rice demanded that the emir censor interviewees who contended that American foreign policy was responsible for the terrorist attacks of September 11, 2001. The following month, the United States bombed al-Jazeera's office in Kabul, Afghanistan, as it would bomb the network's Baghdad studio during the second Iraq war. The emir still backs al-Jazeera to the tune of $100 million a year— corporate advertisers are hard to come by—and the station continues to report world news. The only matters that are off-limits are interviews with Qatari political dissidents and details of U.S. basing policy in the emirate.[38]

Among the Qatari bases the Pentagon has appropriated is one of the best airfields in the gulf, nineteen miles southwest of Doha in the open desert. During the late 1990s, the government of Qatar actually built al-Udeid Air Base at a cost of $1.4 billion with the thought that it might attract the Americans, who clearly were not going to hold on to their Saudi bases forever, and perhaps bribe them into becoming the country's protector. It is the only base in Qatar that the authorities allow to be mentioned in the press. Its 14,760-foot runway is one of the longest in the gulf, greatly exceeding the needs of Qatar's dozen or so fighter aircraft. The airfield has hardened concrete bunkers for as many as 120 warplanes.

The air force enthusiastically took the bait. Al-Udeid is the site for prepositioned air force weapons, fuel, medical supplies, and munitions— the army's site is elsewhere in Qatar. In March 2002, the air force began to build there a combined air operations center that, although not as advanced as Price Sultan Air Base in Saudi Arabia, could serve as an alternative. Following the assault on Afghanistan, the air force put up its own money to complete all the facilities at al-Udeid as fast as possible. In March 2002, Vice President Dick Cheney visited the site, and in June the U.S. secretary of defense did the same. The main air force unit based there is the 379th Air Expeditionary Wing, composed of F-15E and F-16 fighters and KC-10, KC-130, and KC-135 aerial tankers. Al-Udeid played an important role in the Afghan war as the main base for refueling warplanes on their way to and from Afghanistan. The air force estimates that the tankers of the 379th delivered more than 220 million pounds of fuel over Afghanistan, about half of all refueling undertaken during the war.[39]

Al-Udeid also played a key role in the 2003 assault on Iraq, hosting some 6,500 airmen with a planned eventual population of 10,000. They live in a large desert tent city that the air force calls Camp Andy, after Master Sergeant Evander Andrews, the first U.S. casualty of the Afghanistan operation, who died as a result of a forklift accident. It is hard to know whether the officials who supply these names are being intentionally saccharine or are running out of genuine heroes. A permanent housing complex, rechristened Expeditionary Village, is to open on the 3,000-acre base late in 2003. During the summer of 2002, according to one informed source, the first swimming pool at al-Udeid had already been completed, usually a sign that the air force plans a long stay.[40] DynCorp of Reston, Virginia, is responsible for providing this and other amenities and for accepting, storing, maintaining, and protecting the prepositioned war material, the same services it performs at air bases in Oman and Manama, Bahrain.

Two other installations in Qatar are Camp as-Sayliyah, located in the outskirts of Doha, and Camp Snoopy, at Doha International Airport, both army prepositioning sites for tanks and other fighting vehicles, together with their fuel and munitions for a full armored brigade. These are state-of-the-art facilities completed in the summer of 2000. While most other bases in the Persian Gulf region are paid for by the host countries, Congress actually put up a total of $110 million for these. The government of Qatar contributed only the land and utilities.

During the second Iraq war, Camp as-Sayliyah was the forward headquarters of commander in chief General Tommy R. Franks, who, in

December 2002, under cover of a military training exercise, moved about 750 staff officers from MacDill Air Base, Florida, to direct the war in front of banks of computers and video displays located in air-conditioned tents. The base was also the site of the $1.5 million, made-for-TV "Coalition Media Center," where Brigadier General Vincent Brooks, the six-foot-plus, Hollywood-handsome African American spokesman for Central Command, gave hundreds of journalists his daily edited video presentations.[41] Reporting the war from Qatar for *New York* magazine, Michael Wolff described Camp as-Sayliyah as "pure moonscape. Not a tree, not a bush. Hardly a structure. Just a horizon of flat limestone. And then you come upon the U.S. base—really just a ring of wire and then a no-man's-land behind which there is a base. The lack of cover in every direction must provide a high security level, but, in addition, the base is fortified with all other maximum-paranoia, extra-protection measures. It's hunkered down. Not just defended, but defensive." Both the high-tech war and the extreme attention to controlling media coverage were the latest in American-style militarism and imperialism.

As-Sayliyah is said to be the army's largest locale of prepositioned war material in the world. Camp Snoopy is a logistics facility at Qatar's main commercial airport, responsible for shipping food and other supplies to bases throughout the gulf. Whereas a high inner wall and .50-caliber machine guns defend as-Sayliyah's 36.3 acres and twenty-seven warehouses, Snoopy is defended only by guard towers. In May 2003, following the defeat of Iraq, General Richard B. Myers, chairman of the Joint Chiefs of Staff, said that Snoopy was no longer needed and would be eliminated. The number of troops there had already dropped from 1,800 during the war to around 800.

The gulf state least attracted to the United States's imperial presence is undoubtedly the United Arab Emirates. Lying east of Qatar, it is unusual in that it has a good seaport on the Persian Gulf and also one near the Strait of Hormuz on the Gulf of Oman. Yet for all its advantages, the UAE in 1994 concluded a defense cooperation agreement with us, giving the air force access to al-Dhafra Air Base, about an hour outside the capital of Abu Dhabi. The United States has used this facility for launching manned

U-2 and pilotless Global Hawk reconnaissance aircraft against Iraq, Iran, and Afghanistan, and it bases there the 763rd Expeditionary Air Refueling Squadron's KC-10 tanker aircraft.

When the air force first deployed to the UAE, its personnel lived in downtown Abu Dhabi, one of the more sophisticated cities in the region, in an apartment building called the Sahara Residency. But after the terrorist attacks in Saudi Arabia, the Pentagon moved all its personnel from Abu Dhabi to al-Dhafra Air Base. American meals at the airfield, including box lunches for the air crews, are supplied under contract by the local Holiday Inn. In May 2003, the Army Corps of Engineers invited bids from contractors on a headquarters building, dormitories, dining, gym, and medical facilities, and roads and parking at al-Dhafra, again an indication that the Pentagon planned to stay a long time.[42]

The UAE is also familiar to crews of major navy vessels since Jebel Ali, the seaport for the city of Dubai, is the navy's most frequented port outside the United States. Carrier battle groups on patrol in the Persian Gulf call there regularly for fuel, supplies, and shore leave. Perhaps the most important commercial center on the Persian Gulf, Jebel Ali has the largest man-made harbor in the world, with sixty-seven berths and extensive dry docks. It is connected by a good road straight across the UAE to the port of Fujairah on the Gulf of Oman. Most military cargoes from Japan and Diego Garcia are unloaded at Fujairah and trucked to Jebel Ali or flown to Bahrain. This route allows for the resupply of forces in the Persian Gulf even if the Strait of Hormuz should be closed. Neither of these UAE ports has a permanent U.S. naval presence but officers are based in both to assist military ships in transit.

The last and least typical of the Persian Gulf states, to the east of the UAE, is Oman. With a per capita income of $7,700 and a population of 2.5 million, a half million of whom are nonnationals, it is the poorest of the smaller gulf states. It has no arable land and only about 5 percent of its territory serves as pasture. Oil sales make up 80 percent of its export earnings and 40 percent of its gross domestic product. Oman's oil was discovered in commercial quantities only in 1962, later than in any of the other gulf states, and the cost of extracting it is well above that of its neighbors. It is not a member of the Organization of the Petroleum

Exporting Countries, which pleases the United States. One of the reasons Oman accepts the presence of American military bases is because they generate substantial income and help diversify the economy. Moreover, the British foreign intelligence service, MI6, entrenched in Oman for decades, recommended the U.S. military to the sultan.

The Oman of today is a remnant of an old Arabian empire that once extended as far south as Zanzibar on the African coast. Located directly across the Strait of Hormuz from Iran, it has long, undefined borders with the UAE, Saudi Arabia, and Yemen. The first American ambassador arrived in Oman's capital, the old city of Muscat, only in 1972. In 1980, as a consequence of the fall of the shah in Iran and the Soviet invasion of Afghanistan, Oman negotiated a security agreement with the United States. In 1990, this military cooperation agreement was expanded and renewed. Until recently, Oman purchased most of its air force's aircraft from British manufacturers, and in September 2001, following through on arrangements unrelated to that month's terrorist attacks in New York and Washington, carried out a large-scale joint exercise in the desert with 22,000 British troops. In October 2001, it signed a contract with the Department of Defense to buy twelve advanced F-16C/D fighters for $1,120 million. The Omani public does not like the government's military subservience to the United States, but the sultan shrewdly supplies new jobs and benefits whenever internal tensions begin to look dangerous.

Oman is an important location for prepositioned war-fighting equipment and supplies, and the army, navy, and air force all use its four major airfields for aerial refueling, logistics, and intelligence operations in the Persian Gulf and Arabian Sea. Oman's royals claim that there are no foreign military bases in the country and that the Americans are present only as "guests." However, Oman is building a new, highly secret air base at al-Musnana, eighty miles west of Muscat in the desert, at a cost of $120 million. The United States is paying for the base, which will feature a runway able to accommodate the most advanced American bombers, fighters, and cargo aircraft. Al-Musnana will also provide air command and control facilities. When it is completed, the Omani air force will transfer its fighters from Seeb, the international airport for the capital, to al-Musnana, and Seeb will be expanded to handle more civilian traffic.[43] This American buildup in Oman could be a sign of hostile intent toward Iran.

In the far south of the country, in Dhofar, not far from the Yemeni border, Thumrait Air Base is a site for U.S. prepositioned war material and also the home of the British-built Hunter and Jaguar aircraft belonging to the Omani air force. During the 1991 Gulf War, the USAF's 1660th Tactical Airlift Wing was located at Thumrait. In April 1996, the United States sent a Red Horse squadron to expand the runway and aprons, and in November 1998, the Pentagon posted the USAF's Twenty-eighth Air Expeditionary Group from Ellsworth Air Force Base, South Dakota, to Thumrait. After the October 12, 2000, terrorist bombing of the USS *Cole* in Aden harbor in Yemen, the 219 surviving sailors were flown out through Thumrait, which is a relatively short distance north of Aden.

A fourth Omani airfield is located on Masirah Island in the Arabian Sea. Oman has allowed the United States to use Masirah Air Base since World War II, and today it is one more site for prepositioned war equipment and home to a navy patrol squadron flying P-3 Orion surveillance aircraft and EP-3E Aries II spy planes, such as the one that was forced to land on China's Hainan Island on April 1, 2001. It is one of only four sites in the world that houses a permanent navy espionage squadron operating P-3 aircraft; the others are located at Manama, Bahrain; Kadena Air Force Base, Okinawa; and Diego Garcia. Masirah Island is remote and considered a hardship post.

This compilation of American military bases in the Persian Gulf region is by no means complete. Since December 2002, the United States has been building a new base for its Special Forces in the former French colony of Djibouti, separated by only a twenty-mile strip of water from the port of Aden, at the entrance to the Red Sea. We have long deployed several thousand personnel at Incirlik Air Base in Turkey, as well as around fifty F-15 and F-16 fighters and A-10 tank busters, although in the wake of Turkey's refusal to let the United States use its territory for the 2003 assault on Iraq, the Pentagon quickly withdrew most of them. We have also stationed dozens of aircraft at two bases close to the Iraqi border in Jordan and have often used "Cairo West" air base in Egypt for refueling and airlift operations.

Most of these Middle Eastern military bases were hardened and out-fitted specifically for the second war with Iraq and then used during that war. Iraq, however, is but part of a larger picture. Over the past half century the United States has been inexorably acquiring permanent military enclaves whose sole purpose appears to be the domination of one of the most strategically important areas of the world. Of course the United States has an interest in the oil of the region, but the carrier task forces that have already turned the Persian Gulf into an American lake would be sufficient to protect those interests.

The permanent deployment of American soldiers, sailors, and airmen whose culture, lifestyles, wealth, and physical appearance guarantee con-flicts with the peoples who live in the Middle East, is irrational in terms of any cost-benefit analysis. In fact, given the widespread political unrest and a strong revival of militant Islam, the United States seems inexpli-cably intent on providing future enemies with enough grievances to do us considerable damage. One need only recall the arming of Saddam Hussein or the Stinger shoulder-launched missiles that the United States gave so freely to Afghan "freedom fighters" and that were ultimately turned against us. The question is: Have these bases become ends in themselves? Does their existence cause the United States to look for ways to use them? Was the assault against Iraq driven by Iraq's actions or by military capabil-ities in American hands? It may be that the ultimate causes of twenty-first-century mayhem in the Middle East are American militarism and imperialism—that is, our empire of bases itself.

9

WHATEVER HAPPENED TO
GLOBALIZATION?

All warfare is based on deception. Hence, when able to attack, we must seem unable; when using our forces, we must seem inactive; when we are near, we must make the enemy believe that we are away; when far away, we must make him believe we are near. Hold out baits to entice the enemy. Feign disorder, and crush him.

Sun Tzu,
The Art of War (500 BC)

In accordance with the logic of Sun Tzu, Bill Clinton was actually a much more effective imperialist than George W. Bush. During the Clinton administration, the United States employed an indirect approach in imposing its will on other nations. The government of George W. Bush, by contrast, dropped all legitimating principles and adopted the view that might makes right. History tells us that an expansive nation must at least attempt to disguise what it is doing if it wants to consolidate its gains. It must pretend that its exploitation of the weak is in their own best interest, or their own fault, or the result of ineluctable processes beyond human control, or a consequence of the spread of civilization, or in accordance with scientific laws—anything but deliberate aggression by a hyperpower.

Clinton camouflaged his policies by carrying them out under the banner of "globalization." This proved quite effective in maneuvering rich but gullible nations to do America's bidding—for example, Argentina—or in destabilizing potential rivals—for example, South Korea and Indonesia in the 1997 economic crisis—or in protecting domestic economic interests—for example, in maintaining the exorbitant prices of American pharmaceutical companies under cover of defending "intellectual property rights." During the 1990s, the rationales of free trade and capitalist economics were used to disguise America's hegemonic power and make it seem benign or, at least, natural and unavoidable. The main agents of this imperialism were Clinton's secretary of the Treasury, Robert Rubin, and his deputy (today, president of Harvard University), Lawrence Summers. The United States ruled the world but did so in a carefully masked way that produced high degrees of acquiescence among the dominated nations.

George W. Bush, by contrast, turned to a frontal assault based on the use of America's unequaled military power. Even before 9/11, the Bush administration had unveiled its unilateral approach to the world. It withdrew from important international treaties, including those seeking to ban antiballistic missile weapons, control the emission of greenhouse gases, and create a court to try perpetrators of the most heinous war crimes. Bush also proclaimed openly his adherence to a doctrine of preventive war. The United States said it was a New Rome, beyond good and evil and unrestrained by the established conventions of the international community. In its spring 2003 attack on Iraq, it affirmed that it no longer needed (or cared about) international legitimacy, that it had become a power answerable only to itself, and that internal forces of militarism were dictating foreign policy. These policies produced international isolation and a global loss of confidence in the American foreign policy establishment. Two and a half years into the Bush administration, most of our allies had left us, our military was overstretched, and no nation on earth doubted our willingness to employ military power to solve any and all problems.

By the end of the Clinton administration, globalization was under sustained political attack by its victims and their allies. Many of its once prominent supporters, such as the international currency speculator George Soros or the former chief economist of the World Bank, Joseph E. Stiglitz, were intellectually undercutting its major tenets. Globalization, however, was not dead. The world—including the Bush administration—still pretended that the World Trade Organization mattered, that free trade would end poverty in the Third World, and that the International

Monetary Fund and the World Bank were functioning as they were supposed to. Bankers, industrialists, and economists still went to their annual conclave in Davos, Switzerland, but protectionism by rich countries and poverty for most of the people of the world were ascendant.

The aftermath of September 11, 2001, more or less spelled the end of globalization. Whereas the Clinton administration strongly espoused economic imperialism, the second Bush government was unequivocally committed to military imperialism. The Bush administration's adoption of unilateral preventative military action undercut the international rules and norms on which commerce depends. Increasingly, even people who believed in globalist solutions to international economic and environmental problems threw up their hands in despair. At the August 2002 world summit on sustainable development in Johannesburg, the delegates wore badges asking, "What do we do about the United States?"

"The central political idea of imperialism," wrote the political philosopher Hannah Arendt, is "expansion as a permanent and supreme aim of politics."[1] This is true of all empires—witness the endless wars of ancient Rome, the subjugation of Asia by the Mongols and Ottoman Turks, Spain's rape of the Western Hemisphere, Napoleon's ambitions to unite Europe under the French flag, Britain's search for new investment opportunities for its capitalists, the Third Reich's attempts to seize lebens raum for its racially defined nation, and now an insatiable American appetite for ever more military bases. Imperialism cannot exist without a powerful military apparatus for subduing and policing the peoples who stand in its way and an economic system for financing an expensive and largely unproductive military establishment. Thus far in this book I have dealt primarily with the military side of American imperialism. Now I turn to America's attempted *economic* hegemony over much of the world. My intent is to examine the elaborate ideology of "neoliberalism" that has obscured America's international endeavors before the triumph of unilateral militarism and to reveal how militarism has displaced and discredited America's economic leadership. Ironically, it is in this economic sphere that the overstretched American empire will probably first begin to unravel.

Following World War II, America's military might and economic assets were so great that it met with very little resistance of any sort, except from the Soviet Union and its allies and satellites. From the onset of the Cold War until about 1980, those countries that chose to belong to neither the Communist nor the capitalist camps—the so-called Third World—had room to maneuver by playing one superpower against the other. The superpowers, even though they possessed weapons of mass destruction, were often hesitant to exert direct imperial control over these contested nations because they feared that any of them might then bolt to the other camp. The nonaligned countries also had some freedom to experiment with different paths and arrangements that might lead toward "economic development" in accordance with their own cultural traditions and whatever norms they chose of distributive justice. These nations were said to be "underdeveloped," meaning that they had little industry or technology but instead supplied agricultural products and raw materials to the developed countries of the north. In theory, this was to be a mutually beneficial trade that would eventually lead to the industrialization of the Third World, bringing it wealth and true sovereignty.

This situation started to change in the early 1980s. The threat of a superpower war receded as the United States and the USSR became accustomed to their respective roles in the elaborate pas de deux of détente and arms control. Both countries also began to show signs of economic fatigue as the Cold War ground on. The USSR, much poorer than the United States, was by far the more seriously affected as the rigidities of its economic doctrine stood in the way of most forms of entrepreneurship and industrial innovation. Still a mighty military power, the USSR became increasingly bifurcated economically into an authorized and an informal, or "underground," sector. Without the latter it would have collapsed much sooner than it did. From the mid-1980s on, Premier Mikhail Gorbachev sought to reform the ailing economy, but he was ultimately undercut by deeply entrenched vested interests. The United States knew about these problems but pretended in its intelligence estimates not to notice so that it could continue to pour money into its own military machine.

Even though the Soviet Union had lost its potency as an economic challenger, the United States and its allies had for some time been worried by other trends. The General Agreement on Tariffs and Trade (GATT), the rules governing the opening of trade drawn up by the United States and Britain late in World War II and subsequently signed by some twenty-one other nations, had ensured spectacular growth in international trade. (The purpose of GATT was to prevent a recurrence of the economic nationalism and the collapse of international trade that had caused the Great Depression and contributed directly to the emergence of totalitarian regimes in Europe and Asia.) Between 1948 and 1995, when GATT was replaced by the World Trade Organization, international trade expanded from about $124 billion to $10,772 billion.[2] This pattern was fine with the United States so long as its trade balance remained favorable and it could dictate the terms on which others participated in the good times.

The 1970s, however, had already ushered in a period of questioning about where the capitalist world was heading. The American and British economies were plagued by "stagflation" (high rates of inflation combined with low economic growth), high rates of unemployment, large public-sector deficits, two major oil crises as producer nations sought to influence the policies of consuming nations, racial strife, and, for the United States, defeat in Vietnam. Equally ominous, by the mid-1980s, Japan had displaced the United States as the world's leading creditor nation, while America's fiscal deficits and its inability to cover the costs of products imported from foreign countries turned it into the world's largest debtor.

These circumstances allowed for the rise of conservative political parties and leaders—Ronald Reagan and Margaret Thatcher—in the United States and Britain. To revive international trade and, more important, put the United States back in charge of it, the new governments committed themselves to a rebirth of nineteenth-century capitalist fundamentalist theory. This meant withdrawing the state as much as possible from participation in the economy, opening domestic markets at least in principle to international trade and foreign investment, privatizing investment in public utilities and natural resources, ending most protective labor laws, enacting powerful domestic and international safeguards for private property rights, including, above all, "intellectual property rights" (that is, patents of all sorts), and enforcing conservative fiscal policies even at the expense of the public's health and welfare. This program, which soon became Anglo-American mainstream economic thought, was supposed to deliver "a widespread improvement in average incomes," as Bruce R. Scott of the Harvard Business School puts it. "Firms will reap increased economies of scale in a larger market," the thinking went, "and incomes will converge as poor countries grow more rapidly than rich ones. In this 'win-win' perspective, the importance of nation-states fades as the 'global village' grows and market integration and prosperity take hold."[3]

Because the ideas of eighteenth- and nineteenth-century Scottish and English economists like Adam Smith and David Ricardo, from whom the new orthodoxy derived, were associated with the political movement in Britain called "liberalism," the new economic dispensation was often called "neoliberalism." In policy circles it became known as the "Washington consensus," in academic life as "neoclassical economics," and in public ideology as "globalism" or, more proactively, "globalization." One of the leading academic specialists on globalization, Manfred Steger, says that it amounted to "a gigantic repackaging" of two centuries of classical liberalism, relabeled "the new economy." Steger writes: "Globalization's claims and political maneuvers remain conceptually tied to a . . . nineteenth-century narrative of 'modernization' and 'civilization' that presents Western countries—particularly the United States and the United Kingdom—as the privileged vanguard of an evolutionary process that applies to all nations."[4]

Perhaps the most deceptive aspect of globalization was its claim to embody fundamental and inevitable technological developments rather than the conscious policies of Anglo-American political elites trying to advance the interests of their own countries at the expense of others.[5] In its spurious scientificity, globalism has proved similar to Marxism, whose roots lie in the same intellectual soil. As Steger points out, "While disagreeing with Marxists on the final goal of historical development, globalists nonetheless share with their ideological opponents a fondness for such terms as 'irresistible,' 'inevitable,' and 'irreversible' to describe the projected path of globalization."[6] In 1999, President Bill Clinton told an audience, "Today we must embrace the inexorable logic of globalization—

that everything from the strength of our economy to the safety of our cities, to the health of our people, depends on events not only within our borders, but half a world away." At other moments, he indeed emphasized that globalization was "irreversible."[7] His successor, George W. Bush, continued to promote these same nostrums to a reluctant Latin America under a scheme he called the "Free Trade Area of the Americas."[8]

The upside-down Marxism of U.S.-sponsored globalism has been noted by the distinguished diplomat Oswaldo de Rivero, the Peruvian ambassador to the World Trade Organization. He has written, "The ideological war between capitalism and communism during the second half of the twentieth century was not a conflict between totally different ideologies. It was, rather, a civil war between two extreme viewpoints of the same Western ideology: the search for happiness through the material progress disseminated by the Industrial Revolution."[9] As a government official from a part of the world devastated by globalization, de Rivero concluded that "the cost of the Soviet version of development was shortages and lack of freedom; today, that of the neoliberal, capitalist variant is unemployment and social exclusion."[10]

Proponents of globalism, particularly American academic economists and political scientists, cling to it with religious fervor. The theologian Harvey Cox has drawn attention to this devotion in an article entitled "The Market as God."[11] Many otherwise sober business and political leaders in the United States have been carried away by globalization's messianic claims. This phenomenon, too, is not new. Classical liberalism blinded no small number of Englishmen to the racism, genocide, and ruthless exploitation that accompanied the growth of the British Empire. As Hannah Arendt remarked about that earlier period of market worship: "The fact that the 'white man's burden' is either hypocrisy or racism has not prevented a few of the best Englishmen from shouldering the burden in earnest and making themselves the tragic and quixotic fools of imperialism."[12]

It is critically important to understand that the doctrine of globalism is a kind of intellectual sedative that lulls and distracts its Third World victims while rich countries cripple them, ensuring that they will never be able to challenge the imperial powers. It is also designed to persuade the new imperialists that "underdeveloped" countries bring poverty on themselves thanks to "crony capitalism," corruption, and a failure to take advantage of the splendid opportunities being offered. The claim that free markets lead to prosperity for anyone other than the transnational corporations that lobbied for them and have the clout and resources to manipulate them is simply not borne out by the historical record. As even the Nobel Prize–winning economist Joseph Stiglitz, a former director of research at the World Bank, has come to acknowledge, "It is now a commonplace that the international trade agreements about which the United States spoke so proudly only a few years ago were grossly unfair to countries in the Third World. . . . The problem [with globalists is] . . . their fundamentalist market ideology, a faith in free, unfettered markets that is supported by neither modern theory nor historical experience."[13] It must be added that, until November 1999, when 50,000 protesters confronted the World Trade Organization in Seattle and began forcing a reluctant First World to acknowledge its exploitation and hypocrisy, statements like Stiglitz's were not "commonplace," nor had "modern" academic economic theory come to grips with the real nature of globalism.

There is no known case in which globalization has led to prosperity in any Third World country, and none of the world's twenty-four reasonably developed capitalist nations, regardless of their ideological explanations, got where they are by following any of the prescriptions contained in globalization doctrine. What globalization has produced, in the words of de Rivero, is not NICs (newly industrialized countries) but about 130 NNEs (nonviable national economies) or, even worse, UCEs (ungovernable chaotic entities).[14] There is occasional evidence that this result is precisely what the authors of globalization intended.

In 1841, the prominent German political economist Friedrich List (who had immigrated to America) wrote in his masterpiece, *The National System of Political Economy,* "It is a very common clever device that when anyone has attained the summit of greatness, he kicks away the ladder by which he has climbed up, in order to deprive others of the means of climbing up after him."[15] Much of modern Anglo-American economics and all of the theory of globalization are attempts to disguise this kicking away of the ladder.

Leaving aside the former Soviet Union, the main developed countries—Britain, the United States, Germany, France, Sweden, Belgium, the Netherlands, Switzerland, Japan, and the East Asian NICs (South Korea, Taiwan, and Singapore)—all got rich in more or less the same way. Regardless of how they justified their policies, in actual practice they protected their domestic markets using high tariff walls and myriad "nontariff barriers" to trade. Britain, for example, did not accept free trade until the 1840s, long after it had become the world's leading industrial power. Between 1790 and 1940, the United States was probably the most highly protected economy on earth. In the 1970s and 1980s, the only country in the world without a single Japanese car in it was South Korea, because it was nurturing its own automobile industry. All these "developing" nations begged, bought, or stole advanced technology from the countries that first pioneered it and then, through reverse engineering and targeted investment, improved on it. They used state power to support and protect efficient capitalists within their own national boundaries who had the potential to become exporters. They poured subsidies into uncompetitive industries in order to substitute domestically produced goods for imports, often at almost any price. Some of them captured overseas markets through imperial conquest and colonialism and then defended these markets from other would-be conquerors, using powerful navies and armies. Even when defeated, like Japan after World War II and the USSR and the ex-Communist countries of Eastern Europe after the Cold War, they used every device and all the artifice in their power to subvert the economic reform programs that American economists applied to try to turn them into textbook capitalist economies.[16] They understood, as the academicians did not, that a premature introduction of American economic norms was much more likely to produce mafia capitalism than development, as it did in Russia.

In short, the few successful economies on earth did exactly the opposite of what the gurus of globalization said they should have done. In places where economic managers had no choice but to follow the guidelines of globalization—"free" trade, sell-offs of public utilities, no controls over capital movements, the end of all national preferences—the results have been catastrophic. In de Rivero's own Peru, in the twenty-four years preceding the great outburst of terrorist violence by the Shining Path and Tupac Amaru guerrillas, the average yearly per capita income growth rate was 0.1 percent, while the yearly population increase was more than 2.3 percent. In all of Latin America and the Caribbean between 1960 and 1980, gross domestic product grew by 75 percent per person, but over the next twenty years—the high tide of globalization—GDP rose only 6 percent.[17]

Starting in approximately 1981, the United States introduced, under the cover of globalization, a new strategy intended to accomplish two major goals: first, to discredit state-assisted capitalism like Japan's and prevent its spread to any countries other than the East Asian NICs, which had already industrialized by following the Japanese model; and second, to weaken the sovereignty of Third World nations so that they would become even more dependent on the largesse of the advanced capitalist nations and unable to organize themselves as a power bloc to negotiate equitably with the rich countries.

The United States's chosen instruments for putting this strategy into effect were the World Bank and the International Monetary Fund (IMF). Like the General Agreement on Tariffs and Trade, the World Bank and the IMF were created after World War II to manage the international economy and prevent a recurrence of the beggar-thy-neighbor policies of the 1930s. What has to be understood is that both the fund and the bank are actually surrogates for the U.S. Treasury. They are both located at 19th and H Streets, Northwest, in Washington, DC, and their voting rules ensure that they can do nothing without the approval of the secretary of the Treasury. The political scientist Thomas Ferguson compares the IMF to the famous dog in the old RCA advertisements listening to "his master's voice"—the Treasury—on a Victrola.[18]

In addition to GATT, the IMF, and the World Bank, the postwar economic reformers created a truly innovative system of fixed exchange rates among the currencies of all the capitalist nations, so that, for example, from 1949 until 1971 one U.S. dollar could be exchanged for exactly 360 Japanese yen. This system was made credible by tying the value of each currency to the U.S. dollar and by an American guarantee that it would ultimately be willing, on request, to exchange all dollars for gold. Fixed exchange rates expanded international business by making trade stable and predictable, and they formed a major obstacle to the return of the ruinous speculation that had led to the Great Depression.

In this system, the IMF was charged with making loans to redress occasional imbalances between one nation's currency and that of its trading partners (or, rarely, to help alter a fixed exchange rate in the direction of realism); and the World Bank was given responsibility for making developmental loans to countries that needed to invest in their infrastructures and infant industries in hopes of bringing them up to the level of the advanced nations. John Maynard Keynes, the English economic theorist and historian, first formulated the ideas behind these institutions, and at the end of World War II the leading Allies thrashed out compromises to bring them to life. The United States did not accept all of Keynes's proposals, and its objections prevailed largely because of its immense wealth and power, but both the United States and Britain were agreed on a world economic order maintained by enlightened governments. The market was not "king." It was only a widely accepted conventional means for individuals, households, and enterprises to exchange goods and services with one another at mutually acceptable prices. The system of fixed exchange rates, a currency adjustment agency, and a lender to the poor for economic development produced marvelous results during their first twenty years.

By 1971, however, the United States was no longer able to guarantee the fixed value of the dollar in gold. It had ruined its public finances by lavish spending on the Vietnam War, on nuclear weapons and their delivery systems, and on payments to countries that it feared might join the Communist camp or "go neutralist" if the United States stopped bankrolling them. In order to staunch the hemorrhaging of dollars, President Richard Nixon closed the American "gold window" by ending the system of fixed exchange rates. From then on, the currencies of the various nations were allowed to "float," their values being set daily by supply and demand in international currency markets. With floating exchange rates, the market did indeed become king and governments took a backseat. The IMF and the World Bank were left with little to do for the rest of the decade.

The end of fixed exchange rates encouraged risky investments and speculation. Because profits could be huge and costs were low, American banks began to make large "overloans" (that is, loans well beyond the collateral on offer or their own reserves) to Third World countries. Banks like Citicorp and Bankers Trust were soon bringing in almost 80 percent of their revenue from risky overseas transactions.[19] Many loans went to dictatorial or corrupt regimes, with little likelihood of ever being repaid. The banks nonetheless assumed that the governments of "developing countries" were not likely to go broke or, if they did, that some international institution would bail them out.

Thus was born the weird phenomenon of "moral hazard," meaning American bankers could make outrageously irresponsible loans without any risk of having to absorb the loss or make good the money they had mismanaged. Before it was over, the 1970s loan bonanza produced a disaster of exactly the sort Keynes and the reformers at the end of World War II had sought to avoid. Virtually every country in Africa and Latin America was deeply in debt. In August 1982, Jésus Silva Herzog, the Mexican minister of finance, announced that his country was bankrupt and would no longer be able to pay interest on any of its loans. Just as the bankers had assumed, the U.S. government stepped in—not to save Mexico but to ensure that American banks did not collapse. At no time, then or later, did our government suggest that the people who made the bad loans bore some responsibility for the results.

In the early 1980s, following the international loan debacle, the United States put the IMF and the World Bank in charge of the Third World debt problem and essentially instructed them to do two things: keep the debtor countries paying something so that official defaults could be avoided and squeeze as much money out of them as possible. The two semimoribund institutions accepted their new role with alacrity, delighted to act as collection agencies for banks that had made bad loans. Thus were born the World Bank's "structural adjustment loans" and the IMF's "structural adjustment programs."

Under structural adjustment, the World Bank lends funds to a debtor nation so that the nation can continue to "service" its debts in small, pro forma ways. As a condition for the loan, however, the IMF imposes a drastic socioeconomic overhaul of the country in accordance with the neoliberal agenda. If a debtor nation does not accept these terms, all access to international capital is denied it, thereby destabilizing its economy still further and perhaps setting it up for a CIA-abetted coup d'état. The overthrow of Salvador Allende in Chile in 1973 and the installation of the military dictatorship of General Augusto Pinochet were an early and classic example of this process, but there have been many others since. The entire Third World very quickly came under the supervision of the IMF's economic ideologues, and by the late 1990s, close to ninety countries were being "structurally adjusted" by means of shock therapy ordered up in Washington.[20]

In a typical structural adjustment program, the IMF and World Bank require that a country "liberalize" trade—that is, give foreigners free access to its economy. The country is also forced to reduce spending on social programs such as health care and education in order to release public funds to repay debts to foreign banks and transnational corporations. Subsidies to local agriculture are eliminated, usually rendering it unprofitable, while subsidies to agrobusinesses growing export crops such as flowers and fruits are increased. The IMF insists that the country drop all controls over the movements of capital and allow foreign investors and businesses to buy state-owned enterprises, such as electric power, telephone, transportation, natural resources, and energy companies. Perhaps most important, a country receiving a World Bank loan has to agree to maintain the convertibility of its currency—that is, it cannot prohibit the exchange of its own money for that of another country's, which would temporarily halt the outflow of capital. Instead, maintaining free convertibility regardless of the exchange rate makes speculation about a currency's future value possible. What a country gets out of such a mélange of "reforms" is not economic recovery, long-term growth, or stability but a government so weakened that it usually declines into a kleptocracy, experiences periodic economic collapses precipitated by rampant speculation (Mexico, 1994–95; Thailand, South Korea, and Indonesia, 1997; Brazil and Russia, 1998; Argentina, 2000; Venezuela, 2002), and is forced to rely on U.S. corporations to provide virtually all consumer products, employment, and even public services.[21]

The United States was the architect of and main profiteer from these efforts. From 1991 to 1993, Lawrence Summers was the chief economist at the World Bank and the man who oversaw the tailoring of "austerity measures" to each country that needed a loan. He decided exactly what a country had that Washington wanted to open up. On December 12, 1991, Summers became notorious for a leaked memo to senior officials of the bank encouraging polluting industries in the rich nations to relocate to the less developed countries. He wrote, "I think the economic logic behind dumping a load of toxic waste in the lowest wage countries is impeccable and we should face up to that." Brazil's secretary of the environment, Jose Lutzenburger, replied, "The best thing that could happen would be for the Bank to disappear."[22]

Meanwhile, across town in Washington, at the Department of Commerce, Jeffrey Garten, undersecretary of commerce in the Clinton administration and another author of these schemes, explained, "We had a mission: [Ron] Brown [secretary of commerce] called it 'commercial diplomacy,' the intersection of foreign policy, government power, and business deals. We used Washington's official muscle to help firms crack overseas markets. The culture was electric: we set up an economic 'war room' and built a 'trading floor' that tracked the world's largest commercial projects." Garten acknowledged that many of the business deals, often involving insider trading by high-level government officials, were probably crooked, but he justified them on these grounds: "If you open a wild bazaar, as we did, you have to expect the occasional pickpocket."[23]

What these pickpockets achieved can be illustrated by the plight of the Philippines. Between 1980 and 1999, the country received nine structural adjustment loans from the World Bank and six different balance-of-payments loans from the IMF. Between 1983 and 1993, it recorded exactly zero average growth in GNP.[24] Two decades after the first structural adjustment program, the World Bank gave up on the loans for the straightforward reason that, in the words of Walden Bello of the University of the Philippines, "failure, spectacular failure, could no longer be denied at the pain of totally losing institutional credibility."[25]

What began as a poorly conceived program of emergency measures for debtor countries early in the 1980s slowly matured into the hard orthodoxy of the "Washington Consensus" in the 1990s. The U.S. government became determined to impose neoliberal economics on every country on earth. To do so, it unveiled its master plan, the "Uruguay Round" of international trade negotiations (1986 to 1994), and its crown jewel, created on January 1, 1995, the World Trade Organization (WTO). Acting in compliance with a seemingly innocent effort to create a common set of trade rules for all and to bring agriculture under such rules for the first time, "many developing countries discovered that in signing on to the WTO, they had," as Bello put it, "signed away their right to development."[26]

It should be understood that there was no need to create the WTO. There was no crisis in international commerce between 1986 and 1994 that required rectification. International trade was expanding nicely under the GATT formula. The WTO was created because the United States discovered that it could be created. Concretely, it had two objectives: to try to manage the growing trade rivalry among the leading industrial countries, particularly the United States, the European Union, and Japan, and to ensure that the Third World was prevented from using trade as a legitimate instrument for its industrialization, thereby threatening the neoliberal global economic structure. The United States achieved the latter objective through the Agreement on Agriculture and the Trade-Related Intellectual Property Rights Agreement, two of the pacts that the Uruguay Round delivered in 1995 to the WTO to enforce.

Prior to the World Trade Organization, agriculture had for all intents and purposes been outside the purview of GATT because the United States had long threatened to withdraw if it was not allowed to continue protecting domestic sugar, dairy products, and other agricultural commodities. To head off an explosion, GATT simply decided not to enforce any rules on agriculture. By the 1970s, however, Europe had become a net food exporter, and competition between the two agricultural superpowers, the European Union and the United States, was growing ever fiercer. Both wanted to force open the Third World as a new market for agricultural exports. To do this, they had to put the farmers of poor countries out of business and replace them with giant agrobusinesses. In the Uruguay Round of agricultural negotiations, the European Union and the United States excluded all representatives of the Third World and agreed between themselves on rules covering agriculture. In the Blair House Agreement of 1992–93, they prohibited the Third World from protecting its agriculture but exempted their own subsidies because these were already in place before the agreement was concluded. Unsurprisingly, a huge surge of agricultural imports then poured into developing countries without a commensurate increase in their exports. This intrusion produced a flight into Third World cities by displaced agricultural workers, an ever-greater concentration of land holdings, and a marked rise in rural violence as local farmers tried to protect their way of life.

In the late 1990s, under the European Union's Common Agricultural Program, the fifteen EU countries spent $42 billion annually subsidizing their farmers, while they allocated to the Third World only $30 billion in developmental aid for all purposes. The level of overall subsidization of agriculture in Western countries rose from $182 billion in 1995, when the WTO was born, to $280 billion in 1997, and $362 billion in 1998. By 2002, European Union subsidies to agriculture were six times the total amount of foreign aid that all rich countries gave to the poor.[27] The result in the First World was the overproduction of a vast range of agricultural products, including cereals, beef, pork, milk, butter, tomatoes, sunflower oil, and sugar. These commodities were then unceremoniously "dumped" (that is, sold below the costs of production) in developing countries. Joseph Stiglitz's conclusion is unavoidable: "The well-to-do countries that officially praise free trade frequently use tariffs and subsidies to limit imports from poor countries, depriving them of the trade they need to relieve poverty and pursue their own economic growth."[28]

Having deprived the Third World countries of access to agricultural subsidies and crippled their ability to build competitive industries, the WTO proceeded to prevent them from using the foreign technology employed by the industrialized nations and to lock in the monopoly profits of companies that owned patents on indispensable products such as medicines. The Trade-Related Intellectual Property Rights Agreement (TRIPS), which instituted these barriers, proved to be a gold mine for transnational corporations. Its purpose was to prevent developing countries from copying or stealing proprietary technology in the same manner the currently advanced countries had done in their processes of economic growth. The agreement provides transnational corporations with a minimum patent protection of twenty years and places the burden of proof in a dispute on the presumed violator. It is a clear example of the rich nations kicking away the ladder to keep poor nations from catching up.

The chief profiteers have been American and European pharmaceutical companies and agrobusiness conglomerates. On the drug front, Third World countries have demanded that they be allowed to import or manufacture cheap generic copies of patented medicines to deal with acute public health problems, something currently barred by the WTO. All members of the WTO except the United States have in fact favored relaxing a strict interpretation of TRIPS for medicines. The United States instead demands that exemptions be restricted to treatments for AIDS, malaria, tuberculosis, and a few tropical diseases, claiming that the pharmaceutical industry must continue to receive high prices in order to finance future research.[29] With regard to agriculture, the TRIPS system has for the first time given corporations the right to patent life-forms, particularly seeds. Companies that produce genetically modified food (what the Europeans call "Frankenfood") lobbied strenuously for this provision. Monsanto, for example, holds the patent on Roundup Ready soybean seeds, which, until recently, tolerated Monsanto's weed-killing herbicide Roundup.[30] Monsanto is a major player in the corn and soybean markets in North America, Latin America, and Asia and in the European wheat market; one of the ways it and other companies, such as Novartis and DuPont, use the TRIPS system is to develop and patent genetically modified plants that will not produce seeds for succeeding years' crops and that must be fertilized with expensive products made by those same companies. These corporations are thus in a position to extract monopoly profits from poor countries by dominating their agricultural sectors and dictating what they will eat, if they eat at all.

Another abuse of the TRIPS system has come to be called "biopiracy." In this practice, some firms and universities obtain patents on plants that Third World countries have known about and used, often for centuries, and then extract royalties if these countries want to continue growing them. A classic case was the 1997 attempt of RiceTec, Inc., of Alvin, Texas, to patent a hybrid of India's basmati rice, which has been harvested for two centuries throughout the subcontinent; so far its patent is good only in the United States and has been universally denounced by the Third World.[31] Given these abuses of medical and agricultural technology, even some supporters of the WTO now argue that it would have been better not to include agriculture in its purview and not to extend patent rights over life-forms.

In all, the WTO system that came into being in 1995 is a deceptive but extremely effective tool of economic imperialism wielded by rich nations against poor ones. Within a few years after it was launched, however, the system started to fall apart. Post–September 11, the overemphasis on militarism and unilateralism in the United States has radically weakened the effectiveness of international law, eroding the facade of legality that supports the WTO rules. At the same time, the interests of American militarists and economic globalists have begun to clash, particularly over the rise of an obvious future superpower—China. The economic globalists have invested more heavily in manufacturing in China than in any other place outside the Anglo-American world. The militarists, on the other hand, are already plotting to contain China, militarily if necessary, to decide future global supremacy.

Moreover, as the Bush administration declared "war on terrorism," it discovered that globalization was as helpful to terrorists trying to launder their money and finance their militants as it was to capitalist speculators. So it began to tighten its grip on, restrict, or close down various channels of American economic interaction with the rest of the world, including access to our universities by students from the Third World. This trend suggests that globalization, at least as it was promoted in the 1990s, may enjoy a rather short life.

Perhaps the first clear sign that globalization and the WTO were in trouble was the Asian financial collapse of 1997. The Clinton administration had put the smaller economies of East Asia under tremendous pressure to accept neoliberalism, particularly to open up their financial sectors to foreign participation. None of the East Asian countries truly believed this was a good idea, and none of them realized what was necessary in the way of bank supervision and regulation of capital markets in order to operate an American-style economy and prevent a crash, but favorable credit ratings and access to markets required cooperation with Washington. Moreover, foreign investors did not care about the outcome; after the U.S. government's bailout of Mexico in 1994–95, most investors concluded that the U.S.-IMF combination would not permit major defaults in emerging markets, and so capital poured in from all over the world.

Once these smaller nations were loaded up with debt and announced that they would have trouble meeting their repayment schedules, the foreign capital fled even faster than it had arrived. Starting with Thailand, then proceeding to Indonesia and South Korea, most of Asia's economies suddenly were teetering on the edge of default and had to implore the IMF for help. The IMF imposed draconian reforms as a precondition for its loans, prompting a full-blown political crisis that led to the revolutionary overthrow of the government of Indonesia. A permanent and deep-seated hostility to the IMF, the World Bank, and the United States spread slowly and quietly across East Asia.³² American globalists did everything in their power to divert blame for the East Asian collapse away from its proxies, the IMF and World Bank, and to keep it from tarnishing globalization itself. They argued that the cause of the collapse was Asian corruption, which they termed crony capitalism—meaning insider dealing and a lack of transparency—a phrase originally invented by the Filipinos to describe their own Marcos regime.

One of the few East Asian countries to emerge from the crisis unscathed, indeed in better shape, was Malaysia, and its success in standing up to Washington's neoliberal "remedies" helped discredit globalization still further. Mahathir Mohamad, the Malaysian prime minister, resisted the demands of the IMF and quickly restored capital controls over his economy. The fraternity of international economists declared that he was committing commercial suicide. He, in turn, accused Western powers and speculators like George Soros of manipulating markets and currencies in order to destroy healthy East Asian economies. This charge greatly irritated Thomas Friedman, a columnist for the *New York Times* and author of a best-selling paean to globalization, *The Lexus and the Olive Tree*. Friedman gibed, "Excuse me, Mahathir, but what planet are you living on? You talk about participating in globalization as if it were a choice you had. Globalization isn't a choice. It's a reality. . . . And the most basic truth about globalization is this: *No one is in charge.* . . . We all want to believe that someone is in charge and responsible. But the global marketplace today is an Electronic Herd of often anonymous stock, bond, and currency traders and multinational investors, connected by screens and networks."[33]

Two years later in Seattle, to the apoplectic fury of Friedman and other neoliberal apologists, a coalition of nongovernmental organizations began to put names and faces on this electronic herd of politicians and IMF and World Bank officials who were responsible for globalization and who, they argued, ought to be held accountable for its consequences.

Even more disconcerting to Anglo-American globalists, Third World poverty grew faster after the creation of the WTO. Corruption was certainly one factor. For example, Raul Salinas, the brother of the former president of Mexico, siphoned $87 million out of his country through Citibank accounts in New York, Switzerland, and London. Sani Abacha, Nigeria's former dictator, looted his nation of $110 million, also laundered for him by Citibank. One authority estimates that Carlos Menem, president of Argentina from 1989 to 1999, collected close to $1 billion in bribes during his two terms in office.[34] The poor countries' domestic and administrative structures were another factor; these nations lacked, according to Peru's de Rivero, "both the middle class and the national market they needed in order to be governable and viable."[35]

In 1999, at the WTO's third ministerial conference in Seattle, a coalition of people with experience in Third World development programs—environmentalists, trade unionists, anarchists, and some Americans concerned about the role of the "sole remaining superpower"—advanced an alternative explanation for Third World poverty, finally unmasking the imperial, expansionist motives behind neoliberal theory. They emphasized the absence of democracy within the IMF, the World Bank, and the WTO: IMF voting rules, they pointed out, are rigged so that only the richest countries have any influence; the United States reserves the right to name the president of the World Bank; and the WTO takes decisions based on "consensus" whereby any rich nation that does not join the consensus has a de facto veto.[36]

The protesters' demands for reform resonated strongly around the world, and the movement rapidly gained more adherents. By 2002, international meetings of the globalizing powers were drawing protests half a million strong. By and large the globalists, assisted by the big media corporations, chose to vilify the protesters. Prime Minister Tony Blair of Britain declared them to be "anti-democratic hooligans" and a "travelling circus of anarchists."[37] Robert Zoellick, U.S. trade representative in the second Bush administration, compared the protesters to the September 11 terrorists by archly suggesting, "It is inevitable that people will wonder if there are intellectual connections with others who have turned to violence to attack international finance, globalization, and the United States."[38] Writing in the *New York Times*, Thomas Friedman declared that the Seattle demonstrators were "a Noah's ark of flat-earth advocates, protectionist trade unions, and yuppies looking for the 1960s fix." After 9/11, Italian Prime Minister Silvio Berlusconi called them "Talibanized hordes."[39] At the same time, the WTO and the G8 nations took to holding their meetings in ever less accessible places, such as Doha, Qatar, or Kananaskis in the Canadian Rockies. In a cosmetic attempt to improve its image—and in tacit acknowledgment that the ragtag protesters were in fact unnerving the globalists—the IMF changed the name of its "structural adjustment facility" to the more protester-friendly "poverty reduction and growth facility."

Prior to September 11, 2001, three other major developments occurred to further discredit globalization. In March 2000, the Meltzer Report, mandated by the U.S. Congress, concluded that the IMF had "institutionalized economic stagnation" and that the World Bank was "irrelevant rather than central to the goal of eliminating global poverty." Several years earlier, the U.S. Treasury had asked Congress to increase U.S. guarantees to the IMF by $18 billion. In light of the developmental disasters then occurring in East Asia, Brazil, and Russia, Congress set up an International Financial Institutions Advisory Commission to investigate the records of the IMF and the World Bank, under the chairmanship of neoconservative Alan Meltzer of Carnegie Mellon University and the American Enterprise Institute. The findings of the "Meltzer Report" were already common knowledge in the Third World, but this was the first time they were put forth by a reputable figure within the Washington consensus. Meltzer wrote, "Both institutions are driven to a great extent by the interests of key political and economic institutions in the Group of Seven (G7) countries—particularly, in the case of the IMF, the U.S. government, and U.S. financial interests." When it came to addressing its avowed goal of eliminating global poverty, the World Bank's performance, he concluded, was "miserable."[40]

Soon after, Argentina's economy collapsed disastrously, further evidence of IMF and World Bank incompetence. Argentina had faithfully followed the free-market ideas of neoliberalism and the prescriptions of the IMF, even selling off its banking sector to foreigners, who, by 1998, owned 80 percent of the country's banks, and pegging the peso at parity to the value of the dollar, meaning that one peso was worth one dollar and both currencies circulated freely in the country. By 2002, Argentina held the unenviable record of having accumulated the largest amount of public debt by any single country in history—some $160 billion.[41] Its national income shrank by nearly two-thirds in the space of a year; more than half of its largely middle-class population found itself living below the poverty line; and no politician of any orientation dared appear on the streets for fear of public lynching.

The IMF agreed to help the Argentine government meet its debt service payments and then made exactly the same mistake it had in 1997 in East Asia. As a condition for its loans, it demanded an austerity budget that involved firing large numbers of government workers, cutting pensions, reducing wages, and eliminating fringe benefits. Rioting and a fierce police reaction brought the country to a standstill. In December 2000, the IMF provided nearly $40 billion to Argentina on the condition that the government continue to pay foreign debts by intensifying its squeeze on the poorest elements of the society. No government could meet these terms and avoid revolution. Argentina went through five governments and six economic ministers in fourteen months, but the IMF decided that the country was still not being tough enough and was, in any case, of little strategic importance to the United States. It therefore pulled the plug and refused to supply any more loans. Double-digit monthly inflation resulted, the peso fell in value by 220 percent, and social order collapsed. Argentina, once the most prosperous country in Latin America, became a basket case—thanks to neoliberalism, globalization, and the IMF.

The third event that helped discredit globalization was the disclosure of major malfeasance at Enron and other multinational corporations based in the United States. When the agents of globalization, the corporations themselves, are revealed as criminal conspiracies to defraud both their customers and their own employees and their governments, not just the practice but the whole idea of globalization becomes farcical. Evidence that this might be the case was already accumulating in the months leading up to September 11. After the attacks, when the United States shifted decisively from economic to military imperialism, globalization stood revealed in all its predatory nakedness.

Following 9/11, munitions and war profiteering replaced the blatantly illegal or crony capitalism deals of the late 1990s as the best way for politically well-connected capitalists to make money. The military-industrial complex and its protector, the Pentagon, have always played powerful roles in the post–World War II economy, but after 9/11 they became the economy's stars. Arms manufacturing, however, does not follow the rules of globalization. Normally it has only one customer and is not subject to market discipline. Risks of profit and loss are simply not taken into account by governments when national security is an issue. Munitions making is an example not of "free enterprise" but instead of state socialism.

The United States is officially and explicitly opposed to "industrial policy," which is said to subvert the free market in order to produce a governmentally desired outcome. Anathema to orthodox Anglo-American economics, industrial policy is outlawed by the WTO under provisions addressing nontariff barriers to trade. There is, however, a glaring exception to this rule—the production and sales of weapons. The United States has long run one of the world's most highly developed industrial policies through its defense sector. It is illegal, for example, for the United States openly to subsidize Boeing's 747 jumbo jets for export (as the European Union does for Airbus's airliners), but the government has found numerous ways around this restriction, for decades financing technological innovation in universities and enterprises under the cover of national defense needs. Foreign military sales are often financed by Pentagon loans and concessions, and the privatization of numerous activities formerly performed by the armed forces serves the interests of privately owned companies. Given recent trends toward militarism, the United States has become a de facto industrial-policy superpower.

The original GATT Treaty of 1947 treated military subsidies as different from all others under a "national security exception" that became part of every trade treaty negotiated since then. This exception allows states to underwrite production, promote sales, and impose trade embargoes if they do so in the name of national security. Moreover, all structural adjustment programs of the IMF and World Bank include a security exception. This means that although the IMF may impose an austerity budget on a country seeking an emergency loan, it permits the purchase of weapons from a foreign power, usually the United States, even as jobs and health benefits are being slashed. In 1997, when South Korea buckled under its burden of debt, the IMF suggested that it suspend buying military equipment until it had recovered, but the U.S. government overruled this directive. Similarly, Turkey has for years relied on IMF loans to keep its financial system functioning while it has sheltered some 14 percent of its gross domestic product from IMF-required reductions by putting the endangered expenditures into its military budget.

In 1993, the Clinton administration came up with a great new corporate welfare idea—giving defense contractors tax breaks if they would merge into bigger, more diversified agglomerations. For example, the Pentagon supplied the Lockheed Aircraft Corporation and Martin Marietta with $1.2 billion in tax relief when in 1995 they merged to form Lockheed Martin, the world's largest weapons manufacturer. Similarly, after the Cold War ended, Boeing began to move away from arms production—until the tax breaks were announced. Then it reversed course, bought up McDonnell Douglas and parts of Rockwell International, and became one of the world's largest arms exporters.

A further expansion of the military economy is made possible by interpreting the war on drugs as an element of national security. While the U.S. Export Import Bank is prohibited from financing military sales, an exception is made if the weapons are to be used in drug interdiction. The bank has therefore been a prime financier of Sikorsky's sale of nineteen Black Hawk helicopters to Colombia, allegedly to be used in its drug war. In 1996, in order to get around the remaining restrictions on lending Ex-Im Bank funds for military purchases, the government went a step further and created a new agency called the Defense Export Loan Guarantee Fund. It disbursed nearly $8 billion to U.S. companies in its first year of operations.[42]

War profiteering is usually thought of as something done by greedy civilians. But this view understates the role of uniformed military officers in hawking weapons to foreigners. In countless cases, it is a Pentagon-led high-pressure campaign that closes a sale. In April 2002, for example, the United States played the hardest of hard ball with South Korea. It demanded that Seoul award its $4.46 billion contract for forty multirole fighter aircraft to Boeing for its F-15K rather than to France's Dassault for its Rafaele. Leaks from the Korean Defense Ministry indicate that the state-of-the-art Rafaele outperformed the F-15K in every area and was $350 million cheaper. Nonetheless, Deputy Secretary of Defense Paul Wolfowitz told the Koreans that if they went ahead with the French purchase, the United States would refuse both to install cryptographic systems that allow aircraft to identify one another and to supply the Raytheon-built AIM 120B AMRAAM air-to-air missiles the plane uses.[43] Dassault countered that it could easily outfit the Rafaele with an advanced electronic identification system and that missiles were available from several sources. South Korea nonetheless chose Boeing, claiming that it did so to ensure "interoperability" of its weapons with those of its ally. It is worth noting that the United States's closest ally, Britain, does not have a single American combat aircraft in the Royal Air Force but routinely deploys its airplanes and helicopters alongside American-made ones.

U.S. pressure on Latin American countries to buy weapons is blatant. In October 2002, the Colombian Defense Ministry wanted to buy forty Super Tucano light attack aircraft from Embraer of São Paulo, Brazil's largest exporter. The deal was worth $234 million. Instantly, General James T. Hill, head of the U.S. Southern Command, sent a letter to Bogotá warning that the purchase of Brazilian airplanes would have a "negative influence" on congressional support for future military aid to Colombia. Hill recommended that Colombia instead spend its money modernizing its fleet of C-130s, airplanes manufactured by Lockheed Martin in Georgia.[44] The deal with Brazil fell through.

The first sign of resistance to these strong-arm tactics came in the wake of Luiz Lula da Silva's election as president of Brazil, also in October 2002. The previous Brazilian government had been negotiating with both France and the United States to buy as many as twenty-four new fighter planes for the Brazilian air force. In June, the Pentagon tried to sweeten its offer by promising to sell air-to-air missiles with the aircraft, the first time it would have done so in Latin America. However, when Lula da Silva was sworn in on January 1, 2003, he canceled the deal and transferred $750 million from the defense budget to hunger-eradication projects.[45]

The new focus on military imperialism has been a boon to U.S. defense contractors. In the months following 9/11, Boeing went to two shifts of workers making its Joint Direct Attack Munitions, a "smart bomb" heavily used in Afghanistan and Iraq, and Raytheon operated three shifts to produce its Tomahawk cruise missiles.[46] The problem was how to sustain these levels of activity. In November 2002, in a foreign policy decision dictated significantly by the promise of arms sales, the North Atlantic Treaty Organization brought seven Eastern European and Baltic nations into the alliance. The United States had worked for at least six years to achieve this enlargement. It immediately signed up Poland to buy forty-eight Lockheed F-16 fighter aircraft, manufactured in Texas, in order to bring the Polish air force up to NATO standards, and lent it $3.8 billion on concessionary terms to help pay for them. Pentagon planners hoped that the sales of arms and munitions to new NATO members might amount to $35 billion over ten years.[47]

Another way of keeping up armaments sales is through wars. They have the desirable features of depleting stocks and demonstrating to potential customers around the world the effectiveness of new generations of American weapons. The military-industrial complex warmly welcomed the wars against Yugoslavia, Afghanistan, and Iraq as good for business. Actions just short of war, such as bombings and missile strikes, are also, in the words of Karen Talbot, for twenty years the World Peace Council's representative to the United Nations, "giant bazaars for selling the wares of the armaments manufacturers."[48] The military incessantly peddles the latest gadgetry to Taiwan, for instance, even though the Pentagon's efforts to spark a war with China are of declining effectiveness as the mainland and Taiwan begin to integrate their economies. Israel, however, remains one of the Pentagon's oldest and most faithful customers and seems likely to continue to be in the future.

As the United States devotes ever more of its manufacturing assets to the arms trade, it becomes ever more dependent on imports for the nonmilitary products that its citizens no longer manufacture but need in order to maintain their customary lifestyles. With a record trade deficit for 2002 of $435.2 billion and a close-to-negligible savings rate, Americans may end up owing foreigners as much as $3.5 trillion in the next few years alone. As the economic analyst William Greider concludes, "Instead of facing this darkening prospect, [President George W.] Bush and team regularly dismiss the worldviews of these creditor nations and lecture them condescendingly on our superior qualities. Any profligate debtor who insults his banker is unwise, to put it mildly. . . . American leadership has . . . become increasingly delusional—I mean that literally—and blind to the adverse balance of power accumulating against it."[49]

Our government seems not to grasp the relationship between its military unilateralism and the collateral damage it is doing to international commerce, an activity that depends on *mutually beneficial* relationships among individuals, businesses, and countries to function well. If foreign creditors conclude that the United States is no longer a defender of international law, they may lose interest in investing in such a country. Our version of unilateralist military imperialism undercuts international institutions, causes trade to dry up, distorts the availability of finance, and is environmentally disastrous. While the globalization of the 1990s was premised on cheating the poor and defenseless and on destroying the only physical environment we will ever have, its replacement by American militarism and imperialism is likely to usher in something much worse for developed, developing, and underdeveloped nations alike.

10

THE SORROWS OF EMPIRE

Although tyranny, because it needs no consent, may successfully rule
over foreign peoples, it can stay in power only if it destroys first of all the
national institutions of its own people.

HANNAH ARENDT,
The Origins of Totalitarianism (1951)

With the fall of Baghdad on April 11, 2003, America's dutiful Anglophone allies, the British and Australians, were due for their just rewards—luncheons for Prime Ministers Blair and Howard with the boy emperor at his "ranch" in Crawford, Texas. We fielded an army of 255,000 in Iraq, the British added 45,000, and the Australians 2,000 specialists. It was not much of a war, though it confirmed the antiwar forces' contention that dealing with the menace of Saddam Hussein did not require a largely unchallenged slaughter of Iraqis and a Mongol-like sacking of an ancient city. But the war, paradoxically, did leave us and our two coalition nations much weaker than before—the Western alliance of democracies was fractured; the potential for British leadership of the European Union went up in smoke; Pentagon plans to make Iraq over into a client state quickly foundered on Sunni, Shi'ite, and Kurdish realities; and the very concept of "international law," including the Charter of the United Nations, was grievously compromised. Why the British and Australians went along with this fiasco when they could so easily have stood for something other than "might makes right" remains a mystery.

As I have shown, the United States has been inching toward imperialism and militarism for many years. Our leaders, disguising the direction they were taking, cloaked their foreign policies in euphemisms such as "lone superpower," "indispensable nation," "reluctant sheriff," "humanitarian intervention," and "globalization." With the advent of the George W. Bush administration and particularly after the assaults of September 11, 2001, however, these pretenses gave way to assertions of the second coming of the Roman Empire. "American imperialism used to be a fiction of the far-left imagination," wrote the English journalist Madeleine Bunting, "now it is an uncomfortable fact of life."[1]

During 2003, the Bush administration took the further step of carrying out its first "preventive" war—against Iraq, a sovereign nation one-twelfth the size of the United States in population terms and virtually undefended in the face of the Pentagon's awesome array of weaponry and military power. Conducted with few allies and no legal justification and in the face of worldwide protest, this war brought to an end the system of international order that persisted throughout the Cold War and traced its roots back to seventeenth-century doctrines of sovereignty, nonintervention, and the illegitimacy of aggressive war.

From the moment we took on a role that included the permanent military domination of the world, we were on our own—feared, hated, corrupt and corrupting, maintaining "order" through state terrorism and bribery, and given to megalomanic rhetoric and sophistries that virtually invited the rest of the world to unite against us. We had mounted the Napoleonic tiger. The question was, would we—and could we—ever dismount?

During the Watergate scandal of the early 1970s, the president's chief of staff, H. R. Haldeman, once reproved White House counsel John Dean for speaking too frankly to Congress about the felonies President Nixon had ordered. "John," he said, "once the toothpaste is out of the tube, it's hard to get it back in." This homely metaphor by a former advertising executive who was to spend eighteen months in prison for his own role in Watergate also describes the situation of the United States on the day our invasion of Iraq began.

For us, the sorrows of empire may prove to be the inescapable consequences of the path our elites chose after September 11, 2001. Militarism and imperialism always bring with them sorrows. The ubiquitous symbol of the Christian religion, the cross, is perhaps the world's most famous reminder of one sorrow that accompanied the Roman Empire. It represented the most atrocious death Roman proconsuls could devise to keep subordinate peoples in line, as empires invariably discover they must do. From Cato to Cicero, the slogan of Roman leaders was "Let them hate us so long as they fear us" (*Oderint dum metuant*).

Roman imperial sorrows mounted up over hundreds of years. Ours are likely to arrive with the speed of FedEx. If present trends continue, four sorrows, it seems to me, are certain to be visited on the United States. Their cumulative impact guarantees that the United States will cease to bear any resemblance to the country once outlined in our Constitution. First, there will be a state of perpetual war, leading to more terrorism against Americans wherever they may be and a growing reliance on weapons of mass destruction among smaller nations as they try to ward off the imperial juggernaut. Second, there will be a loss of democracy and constitutional rights as the presidency fully eclipses Congress and is itself transformed from an "executive branch" of government into something more like a Pentagonized presidency. Third, an already well-shredded principle of truthfulness will increasingly be replaced by a system of propaganda, disinformation, and glorification of war, power, and the military legions. Lastly, there will be bankruptcy, as we pour our economic resources into ever more grandiose military projects and shortchange the education, health, and safety of our fellow citizens. The future, of course, is as yet unmade. All these trends can be resisted and other—better—futures can certainly be imagined. But it is important to be as clear-eyed as possible about what the present choices and the present path of our imperial leaders portend. So let me briefly assess the ramifications of each of these sorrows and try to estimate how far they have advanced.

In the wake of the al-Qaeda attacks of September 11, 2001, President Bush declared that our policy would be to dominate the world through absolute military superiority and to wage preventive war against any possible competitor. He began to enunciate this "doctrine" in a June 1, 2002, speech to the cadets of the U.S. Military Academy at West Point.

The White House billed his speech as an explicit prelude to an "overall security framework," which on September 20, 2002, was spelled out in an official document, the "National Security Strategy of the United States."[2]

At West Point, the president stated that we had a unilateral right to overthrow any government in the world we deemed a threat to our security. He argued that we must be prepared to wage a "war on terror" in many countries if weapons of mass destruction are to be kept out of terrorists' hands. "We must take that battle to the enemy, disrupt his plans and confront the worst threats before they emerge." Americans must be "ready for pre-emptive action when necessary to defend our liberty and to defend our lives. . . . In the world we have entered, the only path to safety is the path of action. And this nation will act." Although Bush did not name any countries in the speech, it turned out he had a hit list of sixty possible targets, an escalation over Vice President Dick Cheney's November 2001 identification of "forty or fifty" countries we would consider placing on our attack roster after eliminating the al-Qaeda terrorists in Afghanistan.[3] The historian Arthur Schlesinger Jr., former special assistant to President John F. Kennedy, was so appalled that he wrote, "The president has adopted a policy of 'anticipatory self-defense' that is alarmingly similar to the policy that imperial Japan employed at Pearl Harbor on a date which, as an earlier American president said it would, lives in infamy. Franklin D. Roosevelt was right, but today it is we Americans who live in infamy."[4]

At West Point, the president justified his proposed massive military effort in terms of alleged universal values: "We will defend the peace against threats from terrorists and tyrants. We will preserve the peace by building good relations among the great powers. And we will extend the peace by encouraging free and open societies on every continent." He added an assertion that is demonstrably untrue but that, in the mouth of the president of the United States on an official occasion, amounted to an announcement of a crusade: "Moral truth is the same in every culture, in every time, in every place." The preamble to the National Security Strategy document that followed claimed that there is "a single sustainable model for national success"—ours—that is "right and true for every person in every society. . . . The United States must defend liberty and justice because these principles are right and true for all people everywhere."

Paradoxically, this grand strategy may prove more radically disruptive of world order than anything the terrorists of September 11, 2001, could have hoped to achieve on their own. Through its actions, the United States seems determined to bring about precisely the threats that it says it is trying to prevent. Its apparent acceptance of a "clash of civilizations" and of wars to establish a moral truth that is the same in every culture sounds remarkably like a jihad, especially given the Bush administration's ties to Christian fundamentalism. The president even implicitly equated himself with Jesus Christ in repeated statements (notably on September 20, 2001) that those who are not with us are against us, a line clearly meant to echo Matthew 12:30, "He that is not with me is against me."[5]

Analysts familiar with the history of international relations reacted to the Bush administration's strategy report with a chorus of skepticism. International relations theorist Stanley Hoffmann declared it "breathtakingly unrealistic," "morally reckless," and "eerily reminiscent of the disastrously wishful thinking of the Vietnam War."[6] The inventor of "world systems theory," Immanuel Wallerstein, noted that the new strategy has brought into being something American foreign policy historically sought to avoid—namely, the possibility of a coalition involving France, Germany, and Russia. It also stands to alienate the only country in the world, Saudi Arabia, that by turning off its oil supply could transform the United States into a huge junkyard (more on this subject under the sorrow of bankruptcy). "When George Bush leaves office," Wallerstein predicted, "he will have left the United States significantly weaker."[7]

In late February 2003, John Kiesling, a senior diplomat then serving at the American embassy in Greece, resigned and wrote to the secretary of state, "The policies we are now asked to advance are incompatible not only with American values but also with American interests. . . . We have begun to dismantle the largest and most effective web of international relationships the world has ever known. Our current course will bring instability and danger, not security."[8]

Implementation of the new National Security Strategy is considerably

more problematic than its promulgation and presents blowback possibilities galore. By mid-2003, our armed forces were seriously overstretched
and we were going deeply into debt to finance our war machine. Already,
93 percent of budgetary allocations dedicated to international affairs
were going to the military and only 7 percent to the State Department.[9]
During 2003, the Pentagon deployed a quarter of a million troops against
Iraq while several thousand soldiers were engaged in daily skirmishes in
Afghanistan, countless navy crews were manning ships in the waters off
North Korea, a few thousand marines were in the southern Philippines
assisting local forces in fighting an Islamic separatist movement with
roots a century old, and several hundred "advisers" were involved in what
might someday become a Vietnam-like insurgency in Colombia (and
possibly elsewhere in the Andean region). We had a military presence in
153 of the 189 member countries of the United Nations, including large-
scale deployments in twenty-five of them. We had military treaties or
binding security arrangements with at least thirty-six countries.[10]

Aside from the financial costs of all this, another constraint exists. The
American people have, since Vietnam, proved unwilling to accept large
numbers of casualties in our imperial wars. To produce what military
analyst William Arkin calls a "painless dentistry" approach to warfare or
what retired Russian major general and specialist on future wars Vladimir
Slipchenko refers to as "no-contact war," the Pentagon has committed
itself to a massive and very expensive effort to computerize the battlefield.[11] It has spent lavishly on smart bombs, battlefield sensors, computer-
guided munitions, and technologically complex high-performance aircraft
and ships, without comparable efforts to train and retain personnel capable of using them. The result, as any computer owner can guess, is that
these devices often break down. Lieutenant Colonel John A. Gentry, U.S.
Army Special Forces (ret.), writing in the Army War College's journal
Parameters, details a three-day failure of the National Security Agency's
computers in January 2000 that was so threatening to national security it
was immediately classified at the highest level. He describes the incred-
ible complexity of the Pentagon's 1.5 million individual computers—
which are organized into some 10,000 systems, of which 2,300 are "mission

critical"—and the ease with which adversaries could hack into, jam, or deceive our cyberwarfare technology.[12]

The main reason for the emphasis on the highest of high-tech warfare is to keep our troops out of the line of fire. Many soldiers being sent into what bloviating senators like to call "harm's way" are now in considerably less danger than they would be in their automobiles at home. Working in front of computer screens in air-conditioned tents miles from the battlefield or at 35,000 feet in a B-2 bomber, they have no more sense of combat than teenagers in a video arcade. Colonel Gentry deplores "the debilitating effects on military ethics resulting from the technologists' promises of easy victories and comfortable lives."[13]

But there is another problem as well. Operation Anaconda in Afghanistan in March 2002 was supposed to be a showcase for "the miracle of modern technology as applied to combat, with an array of sensitive surveillance platforms to pinpoint the enemy and then precision-bomb him out into the open."[14] An investigation by the Army War College's Strategic Studies Institute, however, discovered that more than half of the enemies' positions went undetected by our eyes in the sky and many precision-guided bombs missed their targets. The operation was a failure as large numbers of al-Qaeda terrorists escaped. A month later, on April 17, 2002, one of our F-16 fighters mistakenly bombed a group of Canadian soldiers, killing four and injuring eight—a typical incident caused by inappropriately high-tech equipment (overly fast aircraft on a ground support mission) and failures of command and control communications. The Pentagon, as usual, dismissed it as just another "tragic" case of friendly fire.

When cyberwarfare munitions do work, they often kill so many noncombatants that their use constitutes a war crime. Although air power can be utterly devastating to all forms of life on earth, it has never once won a war alone. Yet the military remains committed to the most devastating forms of terror bombing with only a pretense of "precision" targeting of militarily significant installations. This strain of current military thinking can be found in the writing of Harlan Ullman, a former high-ranking Pentagon adviser and protégé of General Colin Powell, who advocates that the United States attack its enemies in the same way it defeated Japan in World War II. "Super tools and weapons—information age equivalents of the atomic bomb—have to be invented. As the atomic bombs dropped on Hiroshima and Nagasaki finally convinced the Japanese Emperor and High Command that even suicidal resistance was futile, these tools must be directed toward a similar outcome." Ullman is the author of the idea that the United States should "deter and overpower an adversary through the adversary's perception and fear of his vulnerability and our own invincibility." He calls this "rapid dominance" or "shock and awe." He once suggested that it might be a good idea to use electromagnetic waves to attack people's neurological systems and scare them to death.[15]

In the interest of avoiding military casualties altogether, our government has even declared that it must resume nuclear testing, acquire an array of new "low yield" nuclear weapons, and deal with nuclear proliferation not by trying to control the spread of nuclear devices through treaties and international pressure but through "counter-proliferation," or what commentator Jonathan Schell has called "disarmament wars." The administration's March 2002 Nuclear Posture Review identified Russia, China, North Korea, Iraq, Iran, Syria, and Libya as potential targets for nuclear weapons, and it laid out plans to build a nuclear "robust earth penetrator" as well as a new plant to manufacture nuclear weapons, a new intercontinental ballistic missile, a new submarine-launched missile, and a new bomber. In a leaked document of January 2003, the Pentagon revealed its desires to acquire "mini-nukes" of under one kiloton of explosive power (the Hiroshima bomb was a twenty-kiloton weapon) and neutron bombs; it wants a "future arsenal panel" to study "what forms of testing these new designs will require."[16]

Although our government was an active promoter of the Nuclear Nonproliferation Treaty of 1970, the Bush administration's weapons proposals are open violations of that treaty's article 6, which "requires that the original five nuclear weapon states pursue effective nuclear disarmament measures." Any use of nuclear weapons is also a prima facie violation of the 1948 United Nations Convention on the Prevention and Punishment of the Crime of Genocide, to which the United States is an adherent. Nonetheless, in a 1995 statement to the International Court of Justice, the United States defended the use of nuclear weapons, arguing that "the deliberate killing of large numbers of people" counts as genocide only if the aggressor sets out to destroy "in whole or in part, a national, ethnical, racial, or religious group, as such."[17]

High-tech warfare invites the kind of creative judo the terrorists of al-Qaeda utilized on September 11. Employing domestic American airliners as their weapons of mass destruction, they took a deadly toll of innocents. The United States worries that terrorists might acquire or be given fissionable material by a "rogue state," but the much more likely source is via theft from the huge nuclear stockpiles of the United States or the far less well guarded ones Russia inherited from the USSR. The weapons-grade anthrax used in the September 2001 terrorist attacks in the United States almost certainly came from the Pentagon's own biological stockpile, not from some poverty-stricken Third World country.[18]

The government has other ways to implement its new world strategy without getting its hands dirty, including what it (and its Israeli allies) call "targeted killings." During February 2003, the Bush administration sought the Israeli government's counsel on how to create a legal justification for the assassination of suspected terrorists. In his 2003 State of the Union speech, President Bush said that some terrorism suspects who were not caught and brought to trial had been "otherwise dealt with," and he observed that "more than 3,000 suspected terrorists have been arrested in many countries, and many others have met a different fate. Let's put it this way: they are no longer a problem to the United States and our friends and allies."[19]

If the likelihood of perpetual war hangs over the world, the situation in the United States is hardly better. Militarism and imperialism threaten democratic government at home just as they menace the independence and sovereignty of other countries. Whether George Bush and his zealots can bring about "regime change" in a whole range of other countries may be an open question, but they certainly seem in the process of doing so within the United States. In the second presidential debate, on October 11, 2000, Bush joked, "If this were a dictatorship, it'd be a heck of a lot easier, just so long as I'm the dictator." A little more than a year later, in response to a question by *Washington Post* journalist Bob Woodward, he said, "I'm the commander—see, I don't need to explain—I do not need to explain why I say things. That's the interesting thing about being president. Maybe somebody needs to explain to me why they say something, but I don't feel like I owe anybody an explanation."[20]

Bush and his administration have worked tirelessly to expand the powers of the presidency at the expense of the other branches of government and the Constitution. Article 1, section 8 of the Constitution says explicitly, "The Congress shall have the power to declare war." It prohibits the president from making that decision. The most influential author of the Constitution, James Madison, wrote in 1793, "In no part of the Constitution is more wisdom to be found than in the clause which confides the question of war or peace to the legislature, and not the executive department. . . . The trust and the temptation would be too great for any one man."[21] Yet, after September 11, 2001, President Bush unilaterally declared that the nation was "at war" more or less forever against terrorism, and a White House spokesman later noted that the president "considers any opposition to his policies to be no less than an act of treason."[22]

During October 3 to 10, 2002, Congress's "week of shame" (in the phrase of military affairs analyst Winslow T. Wheeler), both houses voted to give the president open-ended authority to wage war against Iraq (296 to 33 in the House and 77 to 23 in the Senate). The president was also given the unrestricted power to use any means, including military force and nuclear weapons, in a preventive strike against Iraq whenever he— and he alone—deemed "appropriate." There was no debate. Congressional representatives were too politically cowed even to address the issue. Instead, Senator Pete Domenici (R-New Mexico) extolled the 4-H Club, a kind of fraternity for budding young farmers, on its hundredth anniversary; Senator Jim Bunning (R-Kentucky) discussed the Future Farmers of America in his state; and Senator Barbara Boxer (D-California) offered her colleagues a brief history of the city of Mountain View, California (even though she voted against the resolution). As Wheeler concluded, all that the public owed their representatives after such a debacle was "the fare for a trip to the dustbin of history."[23]

The Bush administration also arrogated to itself the power unilaterally to judge whether an American citizen is part of a terrorist organization and could therefore be stripped of all constitutional rights, including the Sixth Amendment guarantees of a speedy trial before a jury of peers, the assistance of an attorney in offering a defense, the right to confront one's accusers, protection against self-incrimination, and, most critically, the requirement that the government spell out its charges and make them public. The key cases here concern two native-born American citizens— Yasir Esam Hamdi and Jose Padilla.

Hamdi, age twenty two, was born in Baton Rouge, Louisiana, but raised in Saudi Arabia. The Pentagon at first claimed he was captured fighting for the Taliban in Afghanistan. In a more detailed submission it later acknowledged that he surrendered to the Northern Alliance forces, the warlords paid to fight on our side, without having engaged in any form of combat. Handed over to the U.S. military, Hamdi was transferred to the detention camp in Guantánamo, Cuba, where many foreign nationals captured on foreign soil are now sequestered. Discovering that Hamdi was an American citizen and fearing intervention by the courts, prison officials flew him to a naval prison in Norfolk, Virginia, where he was held incommunicado. As a citizen, he should be covered by the due process guarantees of the Constitution, but the Department of Justice contends that, having been designated an "enemy combatant" by the president, he can be held indefinitely without a lawyer merely on the president's say-so.

On June 19, 2002, representatives of the Bush administration and the Pentagon outlined to the Fourth Circuit Court of Appeals a claim of presidential power that in its breathtaking sweep is unsupported by the Constitution, law, or precedent. "The military," they argued, "has the authority to capture and detain individuals whom it has determined are enemy combatants . . . including enemy combatants claiming American citizenship. Such combatants, moreover, have no right of access to counsel to challenge their detention." They went on to contend that "the court may not second-guess the military's enemy combatant determination" because by doing so they would intrude on "the president's plenary authority as commander in chief," which supposedly includes the power to order "the capture, detention, and treatment of the enemy and the collection and evaluation of intelligence vital to national security." The courts should defer to the military "when asked to review military decisions in time of war."

Since only Congress can declare war, however, the president's personally declared "war on terror" is merely a rhetorical device. There is no legally valid war on terrorism. Moreover, the president does not enjoy "plenary" (absolute or unqualified) authority in his role as commander in chief, since both he and the military theoretically exercise their powers subject to the budgetary authority of Congress. The claim that a military commander, acting under presidential orders, can be "the supreme legislator, supreme judge, and supreme executive" within his area of responsibility was struck down by the Supreme Court following the Civil War. In *Ex Parte Milligan* (1866), the Court held that "martial rule can never exist where the courts are open and in the proper and unobstructed exercise of their jurisdiction."[24] The federal judge hearing the Hamdi case challenged everything the government asserted, but the solicitor general's representative merely replied, "The present detention is lawful." The judge then asked, "So the Constitution doesn't apply to Mr. Hamdi?" He got no answer. Hamdi remains in military confinement until the Supreme Court, the same court that intervened in the 2000 election to appoint Bush president, hears his appeal—if it ever does.

Padilla's case is similar. A Brooklyn-born American of Puerto Rican ancestry, Padilla (known as Abdullah al-Muhajir after his mid-1990s conversion to Islam) was arrested by federal agents on May 8, 2002, at O'Hare Airport, Chicago, as he stepped off a flight from Pakistan. He was held for a month without charge or any contact with an attorney or the outside world. Finally, on June 10, while visiting Russia, Attorney General John Ashcroft made the sensational announcement that Padilla had been plotting with al-Qaeda to detonate a "dirty bomb" somewhere in the United States. On the eve of Padilla's appearance in federal court in New York, however, he was hastily transferred to a military prison in Charleston, South Carolina, while President Bush publicly designated him "a bad guy" and an "enemy combatant." No charges were brought against him, and attempts to force the government to make its case via writs of habeas corpus have been routinely turned down on the grounds that the courts have no jurisdiction over a military prisoner.[25]

The government may have resorted to these procedures because its only evidence against Padilla seems to consist of statements by prisoners at Guantánamo whom it knows to be untrustworthy. Attorney General Ashcroft, a notorious Washington "camera moth," may have used his announcement simply to gain some personal publicity, as he has done in the past. Even the administration's hardest of hard-liners, Deputy Defense Secretary Paul Wolfowitz, said to CBS News, "I don't think there was actually a plot beyond some fairly loose talk and Padilla's coming in here obviously to plan further deeds."[26] Meanwhile, Padilla remains in a military prison—uncharged, unrepresented, unfree.

The Bush administration has expanded presidential power at the expense of the constitution in another area, thanks to the little-known and totally secret Foreign Intelligence Surveillance Court, which threatens to turn into an American version of the Star Chamber, Henry VIII's personal tribunal for bringing actions against his opponents and having them whipped, pilloried, or branded. The court came into being following the Watergate scandal. For decades up until then, the Federal Bureau of Investigation and the Central Intelligence Agency had illegally wiretapped the telephone calls of citizens, opened their mail, and surreptitiously entered their homes to snoop for information that might be used to blackmail or smear them. The Senate committee investigating these matters after Richard Nixon's resignation from the presidency revealed that between 1953 and 1973 the Postal Service in New York City had illegally made more than twenty-eight million letters available to the CIA.

In one of the few concrete cases that came to light, the FBI admitted using such illegally obtained information to concoct a piece it planted in *Newsweek* magazine that defamed the then-pregnant actress Jean Seberg, who committed suicide as a result. Her death led fifteen months later to the suicide of her husband, French novelist and diplomat Romain Gary. The intent of the story, partially based on illegally obtained information, was to "cause her embarrassment and serve to cheapen her image with the public."[27] In 1974, that public learned for the first time that the FBI had illegally spied on over 10,000 U.S. citizens, including virtually all national politicians as well as public figures like Martin Luther King.

To bring the FBI and CIA under some semblance of control, Congress passed the Foreign Intelligence Surveillance Act (FISA), which President Jimmy Carter signed into law on October 25, 1978. This act allowed the FBI and the National Security Agency to continue to conduct intelligence operations against American citizens within the United States but only under the supervision of a new secret federal tribunal known as the Foreign Intelligence Surveillance Court (FISC). In snooping on suspected criminals in cases not involving intelligence, the FBI must go before an ordinary federal judge and obtain a warrant. It must also meet the "probable cause" standard by providing a judge with evidence that an individual is committing, has committed, or is about to commit a crime. The Fourth Amendment states unambiguously: "The right of the people to be secure in their persons, houses, papers, and effects, against unreasonable searches and seizures, shall not be violated, and no warrants shall issue, but upon probable cause, supported by oath or affirmation, and particularly describing the place to be searched, and the persons or things to be seized." In setting up the Foreign Intelligence Surveillance Court, Congress reasoned that monitoring spies might not be the same as catching thieves but that some form of judicial supervision should still exist to keep federal investigators and voyeurs in line. It has not worked out that way.

The court was originally made up of seven federal judges appointed by the chief justice of the Supreme Court; the USA Patriot Act of 2001 expanded that number to eleven. The judges' identities are secret. They meet in total privacy behind a cipher-locked door in a windowless, bugproof, vaultlike room guarded twenty-four hours a day on the top floor of the Justice Department's building in Washington, DC.[28] Everything they do is "top secret." Since the court was created in 1978, the FBI and the NSA have requested some 13,000 warrants to spy electronically or physically on citizens, and the court has granted all but one of them. The judges hear only the government's side. The court makes annual reports to Congress, normally just two paragraphs long, that give only the total number of warrants it has approved. Beyond that, there is no congressional oversight of the court's activities whatsoever. Patrick S. Poole, an authority on the court, concludes, "The FISC has been nothing but a rubber-stamp court."[29]

Since September 11, 2001, the situation has actually gotten worse. In the original Foreign Intelligence Surveillance Act, law enforcement officials could seek a FISA warrant only if gathering intelligence was the *primary* purpose of the investigation. But the USA Patriot Act, hastily passed by votes of 98 to 1 in the Senate and 357 to 66 in the House and signed into law by President Bush on October 26, 2001, allows FISA warrants if gathering intelligence is merely a *significant* purpose of the investigation.[30] The Patriot Act also allows the government to spy on Internet surfing by Americans, including to collect the terms they enter into search engines such as Google. The person spied on does not have to be the target of the investigation, and the government is not obligated to report to the court or tell the person involved what it has done.

In the past, FISA warrants were issued only to gather raw intelligence data. Under no circumstances was this information ever to be divulged to federal prosecutors, who might then use it to bring a criminal indictment, since this is precisely what the Fourth Amendment forbids. Under the Patriot Act, however, information gathered under a FISA warrant is routinely passed on to prosecutors. Many observers suspect that U.S. attorneys have for years been using the FISA routinely to subvert constitutional protections. The FISA law also allows for "emergency searches" that the attorney general can sign on his own authority without the approval of any court, so long as he justifies the search to the FISC within seventy-two hours. Between September 11, 2001, and early 2003, Attorney General John Ashcroft authorized over 170 such emergency searches, more than triple the 47 authorized by all other attorneys general over the preceding twenty years.[31]

On May 17, 2002, an unusual occurrence for the first time gave outsiders a glimpse into this secret world. Ashcroft asked the FISC to allow him to blur the distinction between monitoring spies and catching criminals even more than the Patriot Act allows—and the court turned him down. It also sent a copy of its opinion to the Senate Judiciary Committee, which on August 22, 2002, released it to the public. In this opinion, the judges of the court unanimously criticized FBI agents for misleading them in some seventy-five different eavesdropping cases and barred one FBI agent—the supervisor in charge of surveillance involving the Palestinian organization Hamas in this country—from ever appearing before them again. Their rebuke was one of the harshest any court has ever delivered to the FBI.

The attorney general appealed this decision to an even more obscure court—the FISA Court of Review—a special three-judge panel created by the FISA that is supposed to oversee the surveillance court. This court had never met. Ashcroft's appeal was the first case ever brought before it in its twenty-three-year history. It is composed of three semiretired judges whose names—unlike those of the FISC judges—have been revealed to the public; all three judges are Republicans appointed to the federal bench by President Ronald Reagan and then to seven-year terms on the special review court by Supreme Court Chief Justice William Rehnquist. Not surprisingly, the FISA Court of Review overruled the FISC and granted Attorney General Ashcroft the additional authority he wanted.[32] The conclusion is unavoidable: a year and a half after September 11, 2001, at least two articles of the Bill of Rights, the fourth and the sixth, were dead letters, and the second half of Thomas Jefferson's old warning "that when the government fears the people, there is liberty; when the people fear the government, there is tyranny" clearly applied.

On February 7, 2003, Justice Department spokeswoman Barbara Comstock said to the press, "The department's deliberations are always undertaken with the strongest commitment to our Constitution and civil liberties."[33] This statement brings us to the third sorrow that accompanies imperialism and militarism—the replacement of truth by propaganda and disinformation and an acceptance of hypocrisy as the norm for declarations coming from our government.

Official lying increases exponentially as imperialism and militarism take over. Our military sees propaganda as one of its major new functions. During the autumn of 2001, Defense Secretary Donald Rumsfeld created within the Pentagon an "Office of Strategic Influence" with the function of carrying out what defense planners call "information warfare"—disinformation and propaganda against foreign enemies as well as domestic critics who do not support presidential policies. Only when it became clear that the new office's operations would include funneling false stories to the American news media did Rumsfeld say that perhaps it was all a mistake and officially shut the operation down.

Nonetheless, the idea did not go away. In the autumn of 2002, Rumsfeld created a new position, deputy undersecretary of defense for "special plans" (a euphemism for "deception operations"). These missions go beyond traditional military activities like jamming enemy radars or disrupting command and control networks. Deception operations include managing (and restricting) public information, controlling news sources, and manipulating public opinion. As the air force explained, the military must prevent "the news media going to other sources [such as an adversary or critic] for information. . . . U.S. and friendly forces must strive to become the favored source of information." "Information warfare," writes military analyst William M. Arkin, "includes controlling as much as possible what the American public sees and reads."[34] In January 2003, the White House followed up by forming its own version of Rumsfeld's Pentagon propaganda agency, the "Office for Global Communications." Its officials seem to spend their time auditioning generals to give media briefings and booking administration stars on foreign and domestic news shows. Its stated purpose is to see that "any war commentary by a U.S. official is approved in advance by the White House."[35]

Typical information-warfare operations range from the trivial to major projects like inventing pretexts for war. An example of the former occurred on January 27, 2003, when the government arranged to have a large blue curtain placed over a tapestry reproduction of Pablo Picasso's *Guernica* hanging near the entrance to the United Nations Security Council. Guernica, a small Basque village in northern Spain, was the site Adolf Hitler chose on April 27, 1937, to demonstrate his air force's new high-explosive and incendiary bombs. He was then allied with the Spanish fascist dictator Francisco Franco. The hamlet burned for three days, and sixteen hundred civilians were killed or wounded. Picasso's famous depiction of this atrocity is perhaps modern art's most powerful antiwar statement. The government decided that the carnage wrought by aerial bombing was an inappropriate backdrop for its secretary of state and its ambassador to the United Nations when they made televised statements that might lead to the bombing of Iraqi cities.

Other typical information-warfare operations included the February 2003 efforts of Bruce Jackson, a former Department of Defense official and subsequently head of a "Committee for the Liberation of Iraq." He played a "considerable role" in drafting a statement "supporting" the United States in its plans to invade Iraq and then in getting ten small European countries, the so-called Vilnius Ten—Albania, Bulgaria, Croatia, Estonia, Latvia, Lithuania, Macedonia, Romania, Slovakia, and Slovenia— to sign it. President Jacques Chirac of France was so infuriated by this meddling in European affairs that at a European Union summit meeting in Brussels on February 17, 2003, he threatened to block their member-ships in the union.[36]

Another function of information warfare is to decontaminate as best as possible incidents of blowback or incidents that could lead to blow-back that cannot be denied but are embarrassing. Decontamination tech-niques include bald-faced lying, classifying relevant documents, refusing requests under the Freedom of Information Act, stonewalling, and obfus-cating (as in the cases, for instance, of the Agent Orange and Gulf War Syndrome sicknesses). One particular strategy is the coining of new terms that make it sound like the Pentagon has always had a situation under control or that give the embarrassing event or act or phenomenon a spuriously scientific aura or downplay its significance. A classic example is the term "collateral damage" for the killing of innocent bystanders in a military attack. The newest term for incidents like the Reagan adminis-tration's selling weapons of mass destruction to Saddam Hussein is "mis-sion myopia," meaning that hardworking officers were so focused on the task at hand they did not bother to try to imagine its repercussions down the road.[37] Secretary of Defense Donald Rumsfeld is particularly fond of neologisms such as "forward deterrence" and "unwarned attacks," which he seems to think are strategic innovations. Perhaps he is merely trying to disguise their more familiar names: "aggression"—that is, what Nazi Ger-many did to Russia on June 22, 1941—and "surprise attack"—what the Japanese did to us at Pearl Harbor on December 7, 1941.

Probably the most corrupt function of information warfare is to fabricate intelligence to justify the policies of a president and his staff. This is a criminal offense, even if it is rarely prosecuted. It involves a conspiracy among technical experts, field agents, supervisors, and leaders to counterfeit evidence and foist it onto sometimes unwitting politicians, complicit or timorous journalists, and a trusting public. When it is exposed, it inevitably undermines the credibility of government officials and the agencies that perpetrated the fraud. It also makes it likely that subsequently, if intelligence should reveal a genuine impending threat to the nation, the public will not believe the president when he warns them about it.

Over the years many governments have manufactured pretexts for going to war. Perhaps the classic instance was the German invasion of Poland on September 1, 1939—Germany claimed that it was avenging attacks by Polish soldiers, who it said had seized a German radio station and broadcast hostile statements. After the war it was revealed that the "raiders" were actually German SS troops dressed in Polish uniforms. The U.S. government also has a long, sad record of inventing pretexts for military action, ranging from the manufactured hysteria over the 1898 sinking of the battleship *Maine* in Havana harbor to President Lyndon Johnson's use of a nonexistent attack on a U.S. destroyer in the Gulf of Tonkin in 1965 to get Congress to endorse a massive bombing campaign against North Vietnam.

During the 1960s, the Joint Chiefs of Staff actually delivered to Secretary of Defense Robert McNamara a proposal, dubbed Operation Northwoods, that the military clandestinely shoot innocent people on American streets, sink boats carrying refugees from Cuba, and carry out terrorist attacks in Washington, Miami, and elsewhere and then pin the blame on Cuban agents. The intent, after the failed Bay of Pigs operation, was to provide an excuse for a new invasion of Cuba. Every member of the Joint Chiefs signed off on it. McNamara silently refused to act on it and a few months later forced the retirement of General Lyman Lemnitzer, then chairman of the Joint Chiefs.[38]

On February 5, 2003, Secretary of State Colin Powell went before the U.N. Security Council to set the stage for war by presenting what he called "definitive" American secret intelligence proving the existence of chemical, biological, and nuclear weapons in Iraq. The secretary of state even went out of his way to try to emulate the famous occasion in 1962 when U.N. ambassador Adlai Stevenson introduced photographs taken by a low-flying U-2 spy plane showing Russian nuclear missile emplacements in Cuba. Powell came with his own blowups of satellite reconnaissance photos. Apparently to add to the credibility of his presentation, Powell placed the director of central intelligence, George Tenet, in a chair directly behind him. Tenet appeared in all television pictures of Powell speaking. He made no comment, but his presence seemed to imply that what Powell had to say came with the full backing of the CIA.

In his statement to the Security Council, Powell pointed to a satellite photograph dated November 10, 2002, and said, "Look at the image on the left. On the left is a close-up of one of the four chemical bunkers. . . . The truck you also see is a signature item. It's a decontamination vehicle in case something goes wrong. This is characteristic of those four bunkers." Powell showed another photo of U.N. vehicles arriving at the same site on December 22, 2002, and said that "the signature trucks are gone. . . . Iraq had been tipped off to the forthcoming inspections." On February 14, 2003, chief United Nations weapons inspector Hans Blix directly countered this testimony, commenting that his inspectors had visited the site in the Powell photo often and that the truck was just a truck. He also said, "Since we arrived in Iraq, we have conducted more than 400 inspections covering more than 300 sites. All inspections were performed without notice, and access was almost always provided promptly. In no case have we seen convincing evidence that the Iraqi side knew in advance that the inspectors were coming."[39]

At the United Nations, Powell claimed, "It took years for Iraq to finally admit that it had produced four tons of the deadly nerve agent VX. A single drop on the skin will kill in minutes. Four tons. The admission only came out after inspectors collected documentation as a result of the defection of Hussein Kamel, Saddam Hussein's late son-in-law." Similar statements had been made by President Bush in an October 7, 2002, speech and by Vice President Cheney in an August 27, 2002, speech. What all three knew was that Lieutenant General Hussein Kamel had also said,

"After the Gulf War, Iraq destroyed all its chemical and biological weapons stocks and the missiles to deliver them." A military aide who defected with him backed his assertions. Kamel was debriefed in Jordan by the CIA, British intelligence (MI6), and the head of the U.N. inspection team at the time, Rolf Ekeus. All three agreed to keep Kamel's statements secret, allegedly to prevent Saddam Hussein from finding out how much they had learned. On February 26, 2003, a complete copy of the transcript of Kamel's statements was obtained from U.N. sources by Glen Rangwala, a Cambridge University specialist in Middle Eastern affairs. In the transcript, Kamel says bluntly, "All weapons—biological, chemical, missile, nuclear—were destroyed."[40] This is what Scott Ritter, a senior American member of the team of U.N. weapons inspectors in Iraq during the 1990s, had said all along.[41]

Hussein Kamel, who defected from Iraq in August 1995, was easily the single most important source of intelligence on Iraq since the first Gulf War. In a January 25, 1999, letter to the U.N. Security Council, Rolf Ekeus reported that the entire eight years of disarmament work since the end of that war "must be divided into two parts, separated by the events following the departure . . . of Lt. Gen. Hussein Kamel." As Saddam Hussein's son-in-law, Kamel was for ten years the man in charge of Iraq's nuclear, chemical, biological, and missile programs. When he defected to Jordan, he took with him crates of secret documents in the apparent belief that his revelations would lead to Saddam's overthrow and that he would then replace him. After six months, he concluded that his plan was not working and returned to Baghdad to try to reconcile with his father-in-law. Instead, Saddam had him executed. Since 1995, any number of American officials have cited information Kamel gave to Western intelligence without ever including the fact that he offered equally compelling evidence that Saddam's weapons no longer existed.

Among Secretary of State Powell's numerous statements on February 5, 2003, he incautiously complimented British intelligence for coming up with a dossier on how Saddam Hussein was concealing his weapons. "I would call my colleague's attention," he said, "to the fine paper that the United Kingdom distributed . . . which describes in exquisite detail Iraqi deception activities." Two days after Powell spoke, the British press, acting on a tip from Rangwala of Cambridge University, reported that the document Powell praised had been plagiarized from articles published in *Jane's Intelligence Review*, one of them six years old, and from a paper written by Ibrahim al-Marashi, an American student of Iraqi Shi'ite ancestry at the Monterey Institute for International Affairs, a small graduate school in California. Marashi published his article in the September 2002 issue of the *Middle East Review of International Affairs*, an Israeli scholarly journal. British intelligence not only quoted verbatim from these previously published sources, without attribution, but even repeated typographic and punctuation mistakes in the originals.[42]

Following his less than sterling performance before the U.N. Security Council, Secretary Powell insisted to Peter Jennings, the anchor of ABC News, "I think I have better information than the inspectors, I think I have more assets available to me than the inspectors do."[43] One of these assets proved to be some letters between Iraq and the Central African country of Niger purporting to show that between 1999 and 2001 Niger agreed to sell uranium to Iraq. In his January 28, 2003, State of the Union address, President Bush referred to this evidence: "The British government has learned that Saddam Hussein recently sought significant quantities of uranium from Africa." Secretary Powell turned these documents over to Mohamed ElBaradei, director-general of the International Atomic Energy Agency (IAEA), as proof of the Anglo-American charges that Iraq had revived its efforts to produce nuclear weapons after the U.N. inspections ended in 1998.

Allegations about Iraq's purchase of uranium actually first surfaced in a British government report published on September 24, 2002, which did not name Niger as the source. On December 19, 2002, the U.S. State Department elaborated on the British originals and for the first time said that Niger had supplied the fissionable material. According to the *Washington Post*, however, although U.S. intelligence officials had "extensively reviewed" the documents, they failed to notice the "relatively crude errors" in the letters, including names and titles that did not match up with the individuals who held office at the time the letters were purportedly written.[44]

On March 7, 2003, ElBaradei testified to the Security Council that "the

IAEA was able to review correspondence coming from various bodies of the government of Niger and to compare the form, format, contents, and signature[s] of that correspondence with those of the alleged procurement-related documentation. Based on thorough analysis, the IAEA has concluded, with the concurrence of outside experts, that these documents, which form the basis for the reports of recent uranium transaction[s] between Iraq and Niger, are in fact not authentic. We have therefore concluded that these specific allegations are unfounded."[45]

A final instance of the governmental manufacture of intelligence involves the question of ties between Iraq and al-Qaeda. On October 7, 2002, in testimony before the Senate Intelligence Committee, CIA director George Tenet said that the agency could find no ties between Baghdad and Osama bin Laden's network. Yet in a letter to the same committee on February 11, 2003, Tenet reversed himself. Two days later, Ray McGovern, an analyst for the CIA for twenty-seven years, denounced Tenet for having "caved in to political pressure."[46] McGovern noted that on February 5, as Tenet sat "like a potted plant" behind Powell at the Security Council, he "did not wince once" at what he heard. Instead, Tenet had ensured that statements based on America's vast, expensive intelligence apparatus would no longer be believed. It also seemed likely that Secretary Powell's integrity had been hopelessly compromised.

After the second Iraq war, no unconventional weapons of any kind were found that came even slightly close in terms of quantities or deadliness to the claims of the Bush administration. Postwar analysis strongly indicated that a small group of ideologues working for Deputy Secretary of Defense Paul Wolfowitz had manufactured the intelligence, sometimes based on reports of Iraqi exiles who had already been discredited by the CIA and the Defense Intelligence Agency, and then vigorously sold it to the secretary of defense, the secretary of state, and the president. An intelligence insider interviewed by *New Yorker* journalist Seymour Hersh said of this group, "They didn't like the intelligence they were getting [from the CIA and the DIA], and so they brought in people to write the stuff. They were so crazed and so far out and so difficult to reason with—to the point of being bizarre. Dogmatic, as if they were on a mission from God. If it doesn't fit their theory, they don't want to accept it."[47]

not usual for the aides and advisers of a president of the United
to allow him to deliver a fake intelligence report in a State of the
Union address. It is even more unusual that, such a blunder having
occurred, the director of central intelligence would keep his job. The only
logical explanation is that the director's political superiors instructed
him in what they wanted done. If so, then it seems that high government
officials falsified pretexts for the second Iraq war and committed a fraud
against the Congress and the American people. In a constitutional republic, these are impeachable offenses. The fact that such proceedings have
not even been mentioned is a further sign of the political decadence
brought about by militarism and imperialism.

The final sorrow of empire, financial ruin, is different from the other
three in that bankruptcy may not be as fatal to the Constitution as endless war, loss of liberty, or habitual official lying; but it is the only sorrow
that will certainly lead to a crisis, regardless of how cowed, deeply in
denial, or misinformed the public may be. During 2003, the United States
may have been ready *militarily* for a war in Iraq, even for wars in North
Korea and Iran, but it was unprepared economically for even one of
them, much less all three, or—equally important—their aftermaths.

Permanent military domination of the world is an expensive business.
For fiscal year 2003, our military appropriations bill, signed on October
23, 2002, came to $354.8 billion. For fiscal year 2004, the Department of
Defense asked Congress for and received an increase to $379.3 billion,
plus $15.6 billion for nuclear weapons programs administered by the
Department of Energy and $1.2 billion for the Coast Guard. The grand
total was $396.1 billion. These amounts included neither intelligence
budgets, most of which are controlled by the Pentagon, nor expenditures
for the second Iraq war itself, nor a Pentagon request for a special $10 bil-
lion account to combat terrorism. When this outsized budget was presented to the House, sycophantic members spent most of their time
asking the secretary of defense if he was sure he did not need yet more
money and suggesting weapons projects that might then be located in
their districts. The message they sent seemed to be: No matter how much
the United States spends on "defense," it will never be enough. The
budget of the next-largest military spender, Russia, is only 14 percent of

the U.S. total. The military budgets of the next twenty-seven highest spenders would have to be added together to equal our expenditures.[48]

The first Gulf War cost slightly over $61 billion. However, Saudi Arabia, Kuwait, the United Arab Emirates, Germany, Japan, South Korea, and other American allies chipped in $54.1 billion, about 80 percent of the total, leaving the U.S. financial contribution at a minuscule $7 billion.[49] Japan alone contributed $13 billion. Nothing like that will happen again soon. Virtually the entire world was agreed on the eve of the second Iraq war that if the lone superpower wanted to go off in personal pursuit of a "preventive" victory, it could pick up its own tab.

The problem with the Bush administration's unilateralist policies and their focus on military power is that the United States is actually quite short on cash. Forecasts based on the 2003 budget estimate a $480 billion federal deficit, excluding the costs of the Iraq war. Virtually every state in the country faces a severe fiscal shortage and is pleading with the federal government for a bailout, particularly to pay for congressionally mandated antiterrorism and civil defense programs. The Congressional Budget Office projects federal deficits over the next five years of a staggering $1.08 trillion, on top of an existing government debt in February 2003 of $6.4 trillion.[50]

Equally serious, as already mentioned, the country's trade deficits are increasingly difficult to finance. During 2002, the United States imported a record $435.2 billion more than it exported. At some 5 percent of gross domestic product (GDP), this deficit represents an unusual economic statistic for a country with imperial pretensions. In the nineteenth century, the British Empire ran huge current account surpluses, which allowed it to ignore the economic consequences of disastrous imperialist ventures like the Boer War. On the eve of the first World War, Britain had a surplus that was 7 percent of GDP.

Once the problem of oil is factored in, the future looks even more economically ominous. The United States imports about 3.8 billion barrels of oil a year, or about 10.6 million barrels a day. These imports are at the highest levels ever recorded and come increasingly from Persian Gulf countries. Bush administration projections show the country's import dependency growing substantially, particularly because the government is unwilling to enforce a serious program of auto fuel efficiency. Some Pentagon strategists seemed to think that by conquering Iraq, the United States could ensure its own future petroleum supplies and also dominate other industrialized regions by threatening their oil supplies. But Iraq's share of proven global oil reserves is only just over 10 percent, or about 112.5 billion barrels.[51] By contrast, Saudi Arabia possesses around 25 percent, or 262 billion barrels, and the other gulf states that often cooperate with Saudi Arabia control a further 20 percent. Saudi Arabia and its allies also possess another great advantage. They alone can produce profitably at very low prices.

One of the stated goals of the Bush administration in waging war against Iraq was to replace authoritarian rule there—and elsewhere in the Islamic Middle East—with "democracy." Instead, the Bush strategy may well generate intense opposition to Islamic governments that aided or tolerated the war, hastening the collapse of the Saudi government or of the smaller sheikhdoms around the gulf. It is more than possible that a truly popular government in Saudi Arabia would be hostile to the United States. A serious interruption of Saudi oil supplies would produce an economic catastrophe for the United States, even if it had exclusive control of Iraq's oil production.[52]

The economic consequences of imperialism and militarism are also transforming our value system by degrading "free enterprise," which many Americans cherish and identify with liberty. Our military is by far the largest bureaucracy in our government. Militarism removes capital and resources from the free market and allocates them arbitrarily, in accordance with bureaucratic decisions uninfluenced by market forces but often quite responsive to insider influence and crony capitalism. For example, on March 10, 2003, the government invited five engineering companies to submit bids for postwar reconstruction work in Iraq, including the Kellogg Brown & Root subsidiary of the Halliburton Company and the Bechtel Group. Brown & Root, as we noted earlier, is Vice President Dick Cheney's old company; Bechtel has half-century-old connections with the CIA and high-ranking Republican politicians.[53] Virtually all contracts coming from the military reflect insider trading. Robert Higgs, a senior fellow in political economy at the Independent Institute,

summarizes the military-industrial complex as follows: "a vas|
of mismanagement, waste, and transgressions not only borderi|
often entering deeply into criminal conduct. . . . The great ar
have managed to slough off much of the normal risks of doing _____
in a genuine market, passing on many of their excessive costs to the taxpayers while still realizing extraordinary rates of return on investment."[54]

Similarly, in allocating funds to the missile defense program, the Pentagon no longer specifies how the money is to be spent. Congress simply
gives public funds—$7.4 billion for missile defense research and devel-
opment in 2004—to the Pentagon's Missile Defense Agency. This agency
has invented something it calls the "national team" concept. The team
consists of uniformed officers from the Missile Defense Agency and executives of Lockheed Martin, Boeing, and TRW, the prime contractors,
who decide among themselves how the money is to be spent. As Fred
Kaplan, a reporter for *Slate*, notes, "The idea is that Congress gives us a
chunk of money; we'll figure out how to spend it once we have a better
idea what we're doing." This is increasingly the standard pattern throughout the United States's permanent war economy.[55]

None of this bears any relation to "free enterprise," whatever else it
might be called. Indifference to how public monies are spent ultimately
destroys those who tolerate it. Bankruptcy is one obvious possible outcome, but it is in some ways the least serious. More corrosive is contempt
for the government and its department entrusted with national defense.
Once the toothpaste is out of the tube, it is very hard to get it back in. The
most serious sorrow of empire is the irreversible damage we do to ourselves.

In 1952, the theologian and scholar of international relations Reinhold
Niebuhr predicted that the "winner" of the Cold War would inevitably
"face the imperial problem of using power in global terms but from one
particular center of authority, so preponderant and unchallenged that its
world rule would almost certainly violate basic standards of justice."[56]
Believing we had "won" the Cold War, we became even less able to recognize our injustices toward others and instead assumed that our "good
intentions" in world affairs were self-evident. The result of our hubris

was to transform our global reach into full-blown imperialism and our concern with national defense into full-blown militarism. In my judgment, both trends are so far advanced and obstacles to them so neutralized that our decline has already begun. Our refusal to dismantle our own empire of military bases when the menace of the USSR disappeared, and our inappropriate response to the blowback of September 11, 2001, makes this decline close to inevitable.

Empires do not last, and their ends are usually unpleasant. Americans like me, born before World War II, have personal knowledge—in some cases, personal experience—of the collapse of at least six empires: those of Nazi Germany, imperial Japan, Great Britain, France, the Netherlands, and the Soviet Union. If one includes all of the twentieth century, three more major empires came tumbling down—the Chinese, Austro-Hungarian, and Ottoman. A combination of imperial overstretch, rigid economic institutions, and an inability to reform weakened all these empires, leaving them fatally vulnerable in the face of disastrous wars, many of which the empires themselves invited. There is no reason to think that an American empire will not go the same way—and for the same reasons. If efforts at globalization delayed the beginnings of that collapse for a while, the shift to militarism and imperialism settles the issue.

At the same time, it must be recognized that any study of our empire is a work in progress. Although we may know the eventual outcome, it is not at all clear what comes next. Since the turn of the twenty-first century, only three years ago, the United States has fought two imperialist wars—in Afghanistan and Iraq—and is contemplating at least two more—in Iran and North Korea. For over eighteen months after the end of hostilities in Afghanistan it held 680 people from forty-three countries in a detention camp in Cuba without bringing any charges against them. The commandant has indicated that he plans to build a death row and an execution chamber. Law professor Jonathan Turley explains, "This camp was created to execute people. The administration has no interest in long-term prison sentences for people it regards as hard-core terrorists." It also has no interest in conforming to internationally recognized standards of justice—or in considering itself part of or in any way accountable to a community of nations, however defined.[57]

The United States is actively seeking more oil and more bases, particularly in West Africa, which appears likely to play a role in the future similar to that of Central Asia today, except that transportation costs from south Atlantic ports are much cheaper. Our military has announced plans to build a naval base on Sao Tomé, a small, desperately poor island in the Gulf of Guinea, which may be sitting on four billion barrels of high-quality crude oil. Exxon Mobil is expected to start drilling offshore by 2004. Sao Tomé's 160,000 inhabitants are descendants of Angolan slaves, Portuguese political exiles, and Jews who fled the Spanish Inquisition. Nigeria, Angola, and Equatorial Guinea already supply us with about 15 percent of our imported oil, nearly as much as Saudi Arabia; and that figure could grow to 25 percent by 2015. A similar picture emerges in Latin America, where one of the main purposes of our deployment of troops in Colombia is to protect Occidental Petroleum's oil and gas interests in Arauca province in the northeast.[58]

In a particularly audacious sign of our military unilateralism, the Air Force Space Command and the National Reconnaissance Office are now talking openly about denying the use of space for intelligence purposes to any other nation at any time—not just to adversaries but also to allies. In April 2003, at the National Space Symposium in Colorado Springs, air force secretary James Roche said, "If allies don't like the new paradigm of space dominance, they'll just have to learn to accept it." They will be given "no veto power."[59] This new policy, which is scheduled to be put into operation in 2004, implies that we will start destroying or jamming other nations' communications and intelligence satellites in order to make those countries dependent on us.

There is plenty in the world to occupy our military radicals and empire enthusiasts for the time being. But there can be no doubt that the course on which we are launched will lead us into new versions of the Bay of Pigs and updated, speeded-up replays of Vietnam War scenarios. When such disasters occur, as they—or as-yet-unknown versions of them—certainly will, a world disgusted by the betrayal of the idealism associated with the United States will welcome them, just as most people did when the former USSR came apart. Like other empires of the past century, the United States has chosen to live not prudently, in peace and

it as a massive military power athwart an angry, resistant

he development that could conceivably stop this process of
the people could retake control of Congress, reform it
along with the corrupted elections laws that have made it into a forum for
special interests, turn it into a genuine assembly of democratic representatives, and cut off the supply of money to the Pentagon and the secret
intelligence agencies. We have a strong civil society that could, in theory,
overcome the entrenched interests of the armed forces and the military-
industrial complex. At this late date, however, it is difficult to imagine
how Congress, much like the Roman senate in the last days of the republic, could be brought back to life and cleansed of its endemic corruption.
Failing such a reform, Nemesis, the goddess of retribution and vengeance,
the punisher of pride and hubris, waits impatiently for her meeting with us.

NOTES

PROLOGUE: THE UNVEILING OF THE AMERICAN EMPIRE

1. Paul Sperry, "Defense Department Orders 273,000 Bottles of Sunblock," *WorldNetDaily,* October 9, 2002, <http://www.worldnetdaily.com/news/article.asp?ARTICLE_ID=29225>.
2. Arthur Schlesinger Jr., "The Immorality of Preventive War," History News Network, August 26, 2002. Also see Jimmy Carter, "The Troubling New Face of America," *Washington Post,* September 5, 2002.
3. "U.S. Soldiers in Prison Handled Well Thanks to SOFA; Even Beefsteak Served; 40 Percent More in Calories Taken by Them than Japanese, with Even Desserts Served at Every Supper," *Asahi Shimbun* (Tokyo), October 11, 2002, p. 39.
4. See, e.g., "The Pentagon's Colonial Pretensions Thrive in Asia," *Los Angeles Times,* November 2, 1995; "Fort Okinawa: *Go-banken-sama,* Go Home!" *Bulletin of the Atomic Scientists* 52:4 (July/August 1996), pp. 22–29; "The Okinawan Rape Incident and the End of the Cold War in East Asia," *California Western International Law Journal* 27:2 (Spring 1997), pp. 389–97; *Okinawa: Cold War Island* (Cardiff, Calif.: Japan Policy Research Institute, 1999) (editor and contributor); "Time to Bring the Troops Home: America's Provocative Military Posture in Asia Makes War with China More Likely," *Nation,* May 14, 2001, pp. 20–22; and "Okinawa between the United States and Japan," in Josef Kreiner, ed., *Ryukyu in World History, JapanArchiv 2* (Bonn: Bier'sche Verlagsanstalt, 2001), pp. 365–94.

5. See Chalmers Johnson, "The CIA and Me," *Bulletin of Concerned Asian Scholars* 29:1 (Jan.–Mar. 1997), pp. 34–37. Also see Willard C. Matthias, *America's Strategic Blunders: Intelligence Analysis and National Security Policy, 1936–1991* (University Park: Pennsylvania State University Press, 2001), pp. 297–98.

6. Tim Weiner, *Blank Check: The Pentagon's Black Budget* (New York: Warner Books, 1990), p. 114.

7. Eric Schmitt and Alison Mitchell, "U.S. Lacks Up-to-Date Review of Iraqi Arms," *New York Times,* September 11, 2002.

8. Tom Bowman, "Special Forces' Role May Expand," *Baltimore Sun,* August 3, 2002; Lawrence J. Korb and Jonathan D. Tepperman, "Soldiers Should Not Be Spying," *New York Times,* August 21, 2002; Rowan Scarborough, "Study Urges Wider Authority for Covert Troops vs. Terror," *Washington Times,* December 12, 2002; Scarborough, "Rumsfeld Bolsters Special Force," *Washington Times,* January 6, 2003; and Douglas Waller, "The CIA's Secret Army," *Time,* January 26, 2003. For an excellent summary of the CIA's record in running "secret wars," see "America's Shadow Warriors," *New York Times,* March 3, 2003.

9. Max Weber, *Economy and Society* (1922), in H. H. Gerth and C. Wright Mills, eds. and trans., *From Max Weber: Essays in Sociology* (New York: Oxford University Press, 1958), pp. 233–34. Also see William Pfaff, "Governments Don't Like to Be Accountable," *International Herald Tribune,* September 2, 2002; and Daniel P. Moynihan, *Secrecy: The American Experience* (New Haven: Yale University Press, 1999).

1: IMPERIALISMS, OLD AND NEW

1. Manuel Miles, "The USA Is Not an Empire," <http://www.strike-the-root.com/miles14.html>.

2. Robert M. Gates, *From the Shadows: The Ultimate Insider's Story of Five Presidents and How They Won the Cold War* (New York: Touchstone Books, 1996), p. 266. Also see John Tirman, "How the Cold War Ended," *Global Dialogue* 3:4 (Autumn 2001), pp. 80–90. For the White House's version, see George Bush and Brent Scowcroft, *A World Transformed* (New York: Vintage, 1998).

3. Anatoly Dobrynin, *In Confidence: Moscow's Ambassador to America's Six Cold War Presidents (1962–1986)* (New York: Times Books, 1995), p. 620.

4. Quoted by Frances Fitzgerald, *Way Out There in the Blue: Reagan, Star Wars and the End of the Cold War* (New York: Touchstone Books, 2000), p. 410.

5. Ibid., p. 331.

6. Hans-Hermann Hertle, "The Fall of the Wall: The Unintended Self-Dissolution of East Germany's Ruling Regime," in "The End of the Cold War," Cold War International History Project, Woodrow Wilson International Center for Scholars, *Bulletin,* no. 12/13 (Fall/Winter 2001), pp. 133–34.

7. Vladislav M. Zubok, "New Evidence on the 'Soviet Factor' in the Peaceful Revolutions of 1989," in "The End of the Cold War," p. 6.

8. Thomas Blanton, "When Did the Cold War End?" Cold War International History Project, Woodrow Wilson International Center for Scholars, *Bulletin,* no. 10 (March 1998), pp. 185, 191.

9. See Chalmers Johnson, "The Three Cold Wars," in Ellen Schrecker and Maurice Isserman, eds., *Cold War Triumphalism* (New York: New Press, 2004).

10. See Ed A. Hewitt [NSC staff official], "An Idle U.S. Debate about Gorbachev," *New York Times,* March 30, 1989; Michael Wines, "CIA Accused of Overestimating Soviet Economy," *New York Times,* July 23, 1990; and Colin Hughes, "CIA Is Accused of Crying Wolf on Soviet Economy," *Independent,* July 25, 1990. Michael R. Gordon, *New York Times,* January 31, 1990; and *National Security Strategy of the United States,* March 1990, both quoted by Noam Chomsky, *Deterring Democracy* (New York: Hill and Wang, 1992), pp. 29–30. My thanks to Professor Chomsky for drawing my attention to these important sources.

11. William A. Galston, "Why a First Strike Will Surely Backfire," *Washington Post,* June 16, 2002.

12. Alfred Vagts, *A History of Militarism* (New York: Meridian, 1959), pp. 14–15, 41.

13. "Battle of the Boffins," *Sydney Morning Herald,* January 4, 2003; and James Dao and Andrew C. Revkin, "Machines Are Filling In for Troops,"

New York Times, April 16, 2002. Also see Neil King Jr., "CIA Drones Spotted bin Laden but Couldn't Shoot," *Wall Street Journal,* November 23, 2001; and Eric Schmitt, "Improved U.S. Accuracy Claimed in Afghan Air War," *New York Times,* April 9, 2002. On the excessive complexity and numerous errors of the "precision warfare" aerial guidance systems, see David Wood, "Grisly Accidents Call 'Precision Warfare' into Question," Newhouse News Service, February 7, 2003, <http://www.newhouse.com//wood020703.html>.

14. Jonathan S. Landay, "Missile Kills Top bin Laden Associate: Unmanned CIA Plane Hits al-Qaeda Target in Yemen," *San Diego Union-Tribune,* November 5, 2002; Esther Schrader and Henry Weinstein, "U.S. Enters a Legal Gray Zone: Strike in Yemen Raises Thorny Questions of Assassination and the Definition of War," *Los Angeles Times,* November 5, 2002; Robert Schroeder, "Tell the Truth about U.S. Assassination Policy," *Baltimore Sun,* November 14, 2002; Associated Press, "American al-Qaeda Operatives Can Be Killed: Secret Finding by Bush Gives CIA Authority," *Houston Chronicle,* December 3, 2002; Tony Geraghty and David Leigh, "The Name of the Game Is Assassination," *Guardian,* December 19, 2002; Seymour M. Hersh, "Manhunt," *New Yorker,* December 30, 2002, pp. 66–74; and Doyle McManus, "A U.S. License to Kill," *Los Angeles Times,* January 11, 2003.

15. Sven Lindquist, *A History of Bombing* (New York: New Press, 2001), s.v. pars. 5, 26.

16. John A. Hobson, *Imperialism: A Study* (New York: Pott, 1902); quoted by Hannah Arendt, *The Origins of Totalitarianism* (New York: Meridian Books, 1958), p. 152. Also see W. G. Beasley, *Japanese Imperialism, 1894–1945* (Oxford: Clarendon Press, 1987), p. 2.

17. David B. Abernethy, *The Dynamics of Global Dominance: European Overseas Empires, 1415–1980* (New Haven: Yale University Press, 2000), p. 382.

18. Cited in "History of U.S. Territorial Acquisitions," <http://www.phil-am-war.org/territorial.htm>.

19. Abernethy, *Dynamics,* p. 22.

20. Vagts, *History of Militarism,* pp. 14–15.

21. Quoted by John Gerassi, *Los Angeles Times Book Review,* December 16, 2001, p. 7.

22. John M. Collins, "Military Bases," *Military Geography for Professionals and the Public* (Washington: U.S. National Defense University, Institute for National Strategic Studies, March 1998), <http://www.ndu.edu/inss/books/milgeo/milgeoch12.html>; The Editors, "U.S. Military Bases and Empire," *Monthly Review* 53:10 (March 2002); and Diana Johnstone and Ben Cramer, "The Burdens and the Glory: U.S. Bases in Europe," in Joseph Gerson and Bruce Birchard, eds., *The Sun Never Sets: Confronting the Network of Foreign U.S. Military Bases* (Boston: South End Press for the American Friends Service Committee, 1991), p. 199.

23. Johnstone and Cramer, "Burdens," p. 219.

24. Ibid., p. 200. Also see Andrew Alexander, "The Soviet Threat Was Bogus," *Spectator,* April 20, 2002.

25. DeNeen L. Brown, "Trail of Frozen Tears: The Cold War Is Over but to Native Greenlanders Displaced by It, There's Still No Peace," *Washington Post,* October 22, 2002; and Mike Davis, "Bush's Ultimate Thule," March 14, 2003, <http://www.nationinstitute.org/tomdispatch/index.mhtml?mm=3&yr=2003>.

26. Patrick Lloyd Hatcher, "'Base-mania' in Central Asia," *JPRI Critique* 9:3 (April 2002).

27. Rachel Cornwell and Andrew Wells, "Deploying Insecurity," *Peace Review* 11:3 (1999), p. 410.

28. William Arkin, "U.S. Air Bases Forge Double-Edged Sword," *Los Angeles Times,* January 6, 2002.

29. See, e.g., "Bush Plays Caligula while Blair Strews His Path with Rose Petals," *Scotsman,* September 16, 2002.

2: THE ROOTS OF AMERICAN MILITARISM

1. Hyman G. Rickover, *How the Battleship* Maine *Was Destroyed* (Washington: Government Printing Office, 1976).

2. Stuart Creighton Miller, *"Benevolent Assimilation": The American Conquest of the Philippines, 1899–1903* (New Haven: Yale University Press, 1982), p. 11.

3. "The Spanish American War," <http://www.smplanet.com/imperialism/splendid.html>.

4. "A Gift from the Gods," <http:/www.smplanet.com /imperialism/gift.html>.

5. Amy Forliti, "Camp Commander Relieved of Duties," Associated Press, October 14, 2002; and "'Too Nice' Jail Commander Is Fired," *Sydney Morning Herald,* October 17, 2002.

6. Miller, *"Benevolent Assimilation,"* p. 1.

7. Cited in Howard Zinn, *A People's History of the United States* (New York: Harper & Row, 1980), p. 306.

8. Quoted by Miller, *"Benevolent Assimilation,"* p. 26.

9. Joseph Lepgold and Timothy McKeown, "Is American Foreign Policy Exceptional? An Empirical Analysis," *Political Science Quarterly,* Fall 1995, <http://www.mtholyoke.edu/tag/intrel/lepgold.htm>.

10. For the fullest details on the "Farewell Address, Washington's Final Manuscript," see <http://www.virginia.edu/gwpapers/farewell/>.

11. Quoted by Ralph Raico, "American Foreign Policy—The Turning Point, 1898–1919: Part I," <http://www.fff.org/freedom/0495c.asp>.

12. Elihu Root, *The Military and Colonial Policy of the United States: Addresses and Reports* (Cambridge: Harvard University Press, 1916), pp. 417–40, <http://www.google.com/search?q=cache:aF2E4_ mZg 9YC:www.shsu.edu/~his_ncp/RootGS.html+Elihu+Root&hl=en>.

13. *Parameters* (U.S. Army War College Quarterly) 31:1 (Spring 2001), inside back cover.

14. Arthur S. Link, "Woodrow Wilson Biography," <http://www.gi.grolier.com/presidents/ea/bios/28pwils.html>.

15. See Peter van den Maas, "The American Tradition in Diplomacy," <http://odur.let.rug.nl/~usa/E/kissinger/kiss03.htm>.

16. "President Woodrow Wilson's War Message, April 2, 1917," <http://www.lib.byu.edu/~rdh/wwi/1917/wilswarm.html>.

17. Alistair Cooke, "Letter from America: The Pursuit of Self-Determina-

tion," <http://news.bbc.co.uk/hi/english/world/letter_from_america/
newsid_288000/2882_50.stm>.

18. Ibid.

19. William Pfaff, *Barbarian Sentiments: America in the New Century,* rev. ed. (New York: Hill and Wang, 2000), p. 275.

20. James A. Donovan, *Militarism U.S.A.* (New York: Charles Scribner's Sons, 1970), p. 10.

21. James Dunnigan, "A Long American Tradition," *Strategy Page,* August 20, 2001.

22. United States Civil War Center, "Statistical Summary of America's Major Wars," June 13, 2001, <http://www.cwc.lsu.edu/cwc/other/ stats/warcost.htm>.

23. Cordell Hull, *The Memoirs of Cordell Hull,* (New York: Macmillan, 1948), p. 1111; cited by Alfred Vagts, *A History of Militarism* (New York: Meridian, 1959), p. 474.

24. Donovan, *Militarism U.S.A.,* pp. 114–15.

25. Quoted by Telford Taylor, *Sword and Swastika: Generals and Nazis in the Third Reich* (New York: Simon and Schuster, 1952), p. 368.

26. United States Civil War Center, "Statistical Summary." Also see U.S. Department of Veterans Affairs, Office of Public Affairs, *America's Wars* (Washington, May 2001), <http://www.va.gov/pressrel/amwars01. htm>, which gives slightly different totals but offers no figures at all on the Confederate side in the Civil War.

27. See, in particular, Robert Higgs, "The Cold War: Too Good a Deal to Give Up," *Intervention Magazine Online,* March 2002; and Robert Higgs, "The Cold War Is Over, but U.S. Preparation for It Continues," *Independent Review* 6:2 (Fall 2001). The totals used here are based on the purchasing power of 2002 dollars. For actual amounts in billions of 1996 dollars, compare Martin Calhoun, Senior Research Analyst, Center for Defense Information, *U.S. Military Spending, 1945–1996,* <http://www.cdi.org/issues/milspend.html>. Calhoun places military spending for 1950 at $133.0 billion; for 1953 at $437.0 billion; for 1968 at $388.9 billion; and for 1989 at $376.2 billion.

28. Peter Pae, "Southland Defense Industry Quietly Heeds War's Drumbeat," *Los Angeles Times,* September 27, 2002. Also see Patrick Lloyd

Hatcher, *Economic Earthquakes: Converting Defense Cuts to Economic Opportunities* (Berkeley: Institute of Governmental Studies, University of California, 1994).

29. Jonathan Reingold, "Attack of the Pork Barrel Posse," *AlterNet,* April 23, 2002. Also see Julian E. Barnes, Peter Cary, and Christopher H. Schmitt, "Special Investigative Report: War Profiteering," *U.S. News & World Report,* May 13, 2002, pp. 20–34; Gopal Ratnam and Gail Kaufman, "A New Way to Pay for Weapons? Boeing, U.S. Air Force Eye Third-Party Financing for B-52 Work," *DefenseNews.com,* March 31, 2003; Michelle Ciarrocca, "Boeing: 'Forever New Frontiers' or 'The Purse Is Now Open,'" Arms Trade Resource Center, April 4, 2003; and Leslie Wayne, "Creative Deal or Highflying Pork?" *New York Times,* April 20, 2003.

30. Kelly Patricia O'Meara, "Rumsfeld Inherits Financial Mess," *Insight-Mag.com,* August 2001.

31. See John Dower, *War without Mercy* (New York: Pantheon, 1987); and Sheila K. Johnson, *The Japanese through American Eyes* (Stanford: Stanford University Press, 1991).

32. William Manchester, "The Bloodiest Battle of All," *New York Times Magazine,* June 14, 1987.

33. See William Rivers Pitt, "Think the Days of the Draft Are Gone? Think Again," *Truthout/Perspective,* September 11, 2002, <http://www.truthout.com/docs_02/09.12A.wrp.draft.htm>.

34. See Tom Engelhardt, *The End of Victory Culture: Cold War America and the Disillusioning of a Generation* (New York: Basic Books, 1995), particularly part 3: "The Era of Reversals (1962–1975)."

35. Christian G. Appy, *Working-Class War: American Combat Soldiers and Vietnam* (Chapel Hill: University of North Carolina Press, 1993), p. 5.

36. Vagts, *History of Militarism,* p. 463.

37. See, e.g., Walter V. Robinson, "One-Year Gap in Bush's National Guard Duty," *Boston Globe,* May 23, 2000; Wayne Slater, "Records of Bush's Alabama Military Duty Can't Be Found," *Dallas Morning News,* June 26, 2000; "G. W. Bush Went AWOL," *New Republic,* November 13, 2000; Richard Sisk, "General Raps Plans for Invasion," *New York Daily News,* August 27, 2002; James Bamford, "Untested Administration

Hawks Clamor for War," *USA Today,* September 17, 2002; Eric Margolis, "Bush Looks for Buddies in Bad Times," *Toronto Sun,* September 29, 2002; George Johnson, "The Chicken Hawks' War," *TomPaine.com,* November 14, 2002; and Linda McQuaig, "What Did Dubya Do in the War, Daddy?" *Toronto Star,* November 17, 2002.

38. H. R. McMaster, *Dereliction of Duty: Lyndon Johnson, Robert McNamara, the Joint Chiefs of Staff, and the Lies That Led to Vietnam* (New York: Harper Perennial, 1997), p. 329.

39. See Frances Fitzgerald, *Way Out There in the Blue: Reagan, Star Wars, and the End of the Cold War* (New York: Touchstone, 2000).

40. See Chalmers Johnson, "In Search of a New Cold War," *Bulletin of the Atomic Scientists,* September/October 1999, pp. 44–51; and editorial, "China Viewed Narrowly," *New York Times,* June 10, 2001.

41. Kurt M. Campbell, "China Watchers Fighting a Turf War of Their Own," *New York Times,* May 20, 2000. The *Times* failed to identify Campbell as a former member of the Pentagon establishment.

42. "Pentagon Lines Up Industry Chiefs for Top Jobs," *Newsday,* June 1, 2001.

43. Richard Gardner, "Foreign Policy on the Cheap," *Financial Times,* June 8, 2001.

44. *Newsweek,* June 25, 2001.

45. Ronald Steel, *Pax Americana* (New York: Viking, 1967), pp. 17–18.

3: TOWARD THE NEW ROME

1. Andrew J. Bacevich, "Different Drummers, Same Drum," *National Interest,* Summer 2001, pp. 74–75.

2. Quoted by Matthew Engel, "Iraqmania Grips the U.S.," *Guardian,* December 5, 2001.

3. Charles Krauthammer, "The Bush Doctrine," *Time,* March 5, 2001. Also see Max Boot, "The Case for American Empire," *Weekly Standard,* October 15, 2001; Richard Gwyn, "Imperial Rome Lives in the U.S.," *Toronto Star,* December 9, 2001.

4. Robert D. Kaplan, "Supremacy By Stealth," *Atlantic Monthly,* July/August 2003, pp. 67–83.

5. See Walter Russell Mead, *Special Providence: American Foreign Policy and How It Changed the World* (New York: Knopf, 2001). Cf. Christopher Layne, "Masters of the Universe," *Washington Post,* December 23, 2001.

6. National Security Archive, "State Historians Conclude U.S. Passed Names of Communists to Indonesian Army, Which Killed at Least 105,000 in 1965–66," July 27, 2001, <http://www.gwu.edu/~nsarchiv/NSAEBB/NSAEBB52/>; BBC News, "U.S. Blocks Indonesia History Revelations," July 28, 2001; George Lardner Jr., "Papers Show U.S. Role in Indonesian Purge," *Washington Post,* July 28, 2001; Isabel Hilton, "Our Bloody Coup in Indonesia," *Guardian,* August 1, 2001; and Jaechun Kim, "U.S. Covert Action in Indonesia in the 1960s," *Journal of International and Area Studies* 9:2 (December 2002), pp. 63–85.

7. See Thomas Blanton, "When Did the Cold War End?" and attached documents, in Cold War International History Project, Woodrow Wilson International Center for Scholars, *Bulletin,* no. 10 (March 1998), pp. 184–91.

8. Quoted by Emily Eakin, "'It Takes an Empire,' Say Several U.S. Thinkers," *New York Times,* April 2, 2002.

9. A good analysis of the backgrounds of the neocon defense intellectuals is Michael Lind, "How Neoconservatives Conquered Washington—and Launched a War," *New Statesman,* April 7, 2003, <http://www.antiwar.com/orig/lind1.html>. Also see Philip Gold, "There Are Some Unflattering Truths to 'Neocons,'" *Seattle Post-Intelligencer,* May 11, 2003.

10. Paul Kennedy, "The Perils of Empire," *Washington Post,* April 20, 2003.

11. See, e.g., Lewis H. Lapham, "The American Rome: On the Theory of Virtuous Empire," *Harper's,* August 2001, pp. 31–38; Richard Gwyn, "Imperial Rome Lives in the U.S.," *Toronto Star,* December 9, 2001; David Chandler, "Imperialism May Be Out, but Aggressive Wars and Colonial Protectorates Are Back," *Observer,* April 14, 2002; Samuel Brittan, "Liberal Imperialism Is a Dangerous Temptation," *Financial Times,* April 11, 2002; "Building 'Empire' Shouldn't Be Goal," *Jacksonville Daily News,* October 15, 2001; Mark Weisbrot, "Should We

Police World?" *Philadelphia Inquirer,* April 13, 2001; William Pfaff, "America's Imperial Instinct," *International Herald Tribune,* April 8, 2002; John Pilger, "Behind the Jargon about Failed States and Humanitarian Interventions Lie Thousands of Dead," November 23, 2001, <http://pilger.carlton.com/print/88462>; and Hugo Young, "A New Imperialism Cooked Up over a Texan Barbecue," *Guardian,* April 2, 2002.

12. Sebastian Mallaby, "The Reluctant Imperialist: Terrorism, Failed States, and the Case for American Empire," *Foreign Affairs* 81:2 (March/April 2002), pp. 2–7.

13. See the Report of the International Commission on Intervention and State Sovereignty, *The Responsibility to Protect* (Ottawa: International Development Research Centre, 2001). Also see Ernst B. Haas, *Beware the Slippery Slope: Notes toward the Definition of Justifiable Intervention,* Policy Papers in International Affairs no. 42 (Berkeley: Institute of International Studies, University of California, 1993); Stanley Hoffmann, *The Ethics and Politics of Humanitarian Intervention* (Notre Dame: University of Notre Dame Press, 1996); and Samantha Power, *A Problem from Hell: America and the Age of Genocide* (New York: Basic Books, 2002).

14. "U.S. Said Violating International Treaties," Reuters, Washington, April 4, 2002.

15. David Moberg, "Courting Disaster," *In These Times,* June 10, 2002.

16. Carola Hoyos, "Milosevic War Crimes Trial Threatened by U.S. Demand," *Financial Times,* June 12, 2002. See also David Teather, "U.S. Threat to Wreck Treaty System," *Guardian,* May 6, 2002; Neal A. Lewis, "U.S. to Renounce Its Role in Pact for World Tribunal," *New York Times,* May 5, 2002; and Lewis, "U.S. Rejects All Support for New Court on Atrocities," *New York Times,* May 7, 2002.

17. The legislation is H.R. 4775, 107th Cong., 2nd sess.: "A bill making supplemental appropriations for further recovery from and response to terrorist attacks on the United States for the fiscal year ending September 30, 2002, and for other purposes." Also see Expatica News, The Hague, "U.S. Invasion Proposal Shocks MPs," June 10, 2002, <http://www.expatica.com/block.gif>; "Dutch Citizens Up in Arms

over U.S. Congressional Act That Would Protect U.S. Officials or Service Personnel from War Crimes Convictions in The Hague," National Public Radio, *Morning Edition,* June 14, 2002.

18. Elizabeth Becker, "On World Court, U.S. Focus Shifts to Shielding Officials," *New York Times,* September 7, 2002; "U.S. Fears Prosecution of President in World Court," Reuters, November 15, 2002.

19. See, e.g., Conn Hallinan, "America's War Criminals," *San Francisco Examiner,* July 10, 2001; Marcus Gee, "Is Henry Kissinger a War Criminal?" *Toronto Globe & Mail,* June 11, 2002.

20. William Burr and Michael L. Evans, eds., "East Timor Revisited: Ford, Kissinger, and the Indonesian Invasion, 1975–1976," National Security Archive, December 6, 2001, <http://www.gwu.edu/~nsarchiv NSAEBB/NSAEBB62/>. Also see Agence France-Presse, "U.S. Endorsed Indonesia's East Timor Invasion: Secret Documents," December 7, 2001; Jim Wolf, Reuters, "U.S. Agreed to Indonesia's Invasion of E. Timor, Documents Reveal," *San Diego Union-Tribune,* December 20, 2001.

21. See, e.g., Jim Mann, "Unilateralism Dead? That's a Myth Perception," *Los Angeles Times,* October 24, 2001; and Michael Byers, "The World according to Cheney, Rice, and Rumsfeld," *London Review of Books,* February 21, 2002.

22. Nicholas Watt, Richard Norton-Taylor, and Oliver Burkeman, "Camp X-Ray Row Threatens First British Split with U.S.," *Guardian,* January 21, 2002; Caroline Daniel, "Legitimacy of U.S. Detentions Challenged," *Financial Times,* December 3, 2002; Neil A. Lewis, "Guantánamo Prisoners Ask for Rights," *New York Times,* December 3, 2002; Jane Sutton, "A Year Later, Guantánamo Prisoners Still in Limbo," Reuters, January 10, 2003.

23. William D. Hartung, "Making the World Safe for Nuclear Weapons," May 14, 2002, <www.CommonDreams.org>; Richard Butler, "Nuclear Testing and National Honor," *New York Times,* July 13, 2001; and Rebeca E. Johnson, "Who's for a Nuclear Free-For-All?" *Disarmament Diplomacy,* no. 58 (June 2001).

24. *International Herald Tribune,* July 14, 2001.

25. Michael J. Glennon, "How War Left the Law Behind," *New York Times*, November 21, 2002.

26. "America as Sparta," *Boston Globe Online*, March 12, 2002.

27. Alan W. Bock, "War and Peace and Liberty," *Orange County Register*, September 16, 2002.

28. Edward Alden, "A Spaceman in the Pentagon," *Financial Times*, August 25–26, 2001; and James Dao, "A Low-Key Space Buff," *New York Times*, August 25, 2001.

29. See Seumas Milne, "The Innocent Dead in a Coward's War," *Guardian*, December 20, 2001; Roberto J. Gonzales, "Ignorance of Casualties Isn't Bliss," *San Diego Union-Tribune*, January 4, 2002; Fairness and Accuracy in Reporting, "*NYT* Buries Story of Airstrikes on Afghan Civilians," January 9, 2002, <http://www.fair.org/activism/nyt-niazi-kala.html>; and Marc Herold, "Counting the Dead," *Guardian*, August 8, 2002. Also see Herold's Web sites for the raw data and further analysis: (1) "Dead Afghan Civilians: Disrobing the Non-Counters," <http://www.cursor.org/stories/noncounters.htm>; and (2) "Herold's Research," <http://pubpages.unh.edu/~mwherold/>. The United Nations estimates that American bombing killed about 5,000 civilians directly and that up to 20,000 other Afghans died through the disruption of drought relief and the bombing's other indirect effects. See Jonathan Steele, "Counting the Dead," *Guardian*, January 29, 2003. The leaked U.N. report is available online at <http://www.casi.org.uk>.

30. Loring Wirbel, "NRO, Space Command, NASA Tout Common Language of 'Space Supremacy' at Conference," *Global Network against Weapons and Nuclear Power in Space*, April 11, 2002.

31. Ibid.

32. On the so-called fourth generation of warfare, i.e., one dominated by space-based warfare and "asymmetric" threats such as terrorism, see Peter J. Boyer, "A Different War: Is the Army Becoming Irrelevant?" *New Yorker*, July 1, 2002, pp. 54–67.

33. See Joseph Kay, "Bush Administration Renews U.S. Drive to Militarize Space," July 25, 2001, <http://www.wsws.org/articles/2001/jul2001/spac-j25_prn.shtml>; Rob Larson, "Space for Rent: A Free Society

Militarizes Space," August 23, 2001, <http://www.indepen.com/ 2001/Aug09.01/profit.html>; "The Final Frontier: The U.S. Military's Drive to Dominate Space," *Colorado Springs Independent,* December 13, 2001, <http://www.csindy.com/csindy/2001–12–13/cover.html>; and Theresa Hitchens, "U.S. Space Policy: Time to Stop and Think," *Disarmament Diplomacy,* no. 67 (October-November 2002). Also relevant are: Carlton Meyer, "Preparing for War in Space," *G2mil: The Magazine of Future Warfare,* June 2001, <http://www.g2mil.com/ June2001.htm>; Charles Aldinger, "U.S. Likely to Put Arms in Space— Air Force Chief," Reuters, August 1, 2001; Hu Xiaoming, "U.S. Will Probably Deploy Weapons in Outer Space," *People's Daily* (Beijing), August 3, 2001; Steve Boggin, "Space—The Final Frontier in a New and Terrifying Arms Race," *Independent* (London), August 8, 2001; Bill McAllister, "AFA Grad May Lead Era of Space Warriors," *Denver Post,* August 12, 2001; "U.S. Missile Experts Meet to Save the Nation— and Make a Few Bucks," *Space Daily,* August 26, 2001, <http://www. spacedaily.com/news/010826123032.51ofx47q.html>.

34. For details on the British death camps and statistics on the number who died, see Paul Harris, "'Spin' on Boer Atrocities," *Observer,* December 9, 2001. Also see BBC News, "Imperialism in the Dock— The Boer War," November 10, 1999.

35. Quoted by Kay, "Bush Administration."

36. See Jason Vest, "The Dubious Genius of Andrew Marshall," *American Prospect,* February 15, 2001; and Nicholas Lemann, "Dreaming about War," *New Yorker,* July 16, 2001, pp. 32–38.

37. Nora K. Wallace, "Without Space, We're Back to World War II," *Santa Barbara News-Press,* April 23, 2003, <http://globalsecurity.org/org/ news/2003/030423-space-war01.htm>.

38. Gail Kaufman and Gopal Ratnam, *Space News,* June 13, 2001. For other reports on attempts to cover up the BMD's failings, see William J. Broad, "Missile Contractor Doctored Tests, Ex-Employee Charges," *New York Times,* March 7, 2000; Broad, "Pentagon Classifies a Letter Critical of Antimissile Plan," *New York Times,* May 20, 2000; Broad, "M.I.T. Studies Accusations of Lies and Cover-Up of Serious Flaws in

Antimissile System," *New York Times,* January 2, 2003; Broad, "U.S. Seeks Dismissal of Suit by Critic of Missile Defense," *New York Times,* February 3, 2003; Arianna Huffington, "Blowing the Whistle on Bad Science," *AlterNet.org,* March 14, 2002; Bradley Graham, "Secrecy on Missile Defense Grows," *Washington Post,* June 12, 2002; and Graham, *Hit to Kill: The New Battle over Shielding America from Missile Attack* (New York: Public Affairs, 2001).

39. Lawrence F. Kaplan, *New Republic,* March 12, 2001. Kaplan is a senior editor at the *New Republic.* He is coauthor with William Kristol of the neoconservative book *The War over Iraq* (San Francisco: Encounter Books, 2003).

40. Jim Walsh, "The Two Faces of Bush on Defense," *Los Angeles Times,* May 1, 2001.

41. Bill Keller, "Missile Defense: The Untold Story," *New York Times,* December 29, 2001.

42. U.S. Department of Defense, *Report of the Commission to Assess the Ballistic Missile Threat to the United States,* July 15, 1998. For implementation of this report, see Donald H. Rumsfeld, *2001 Quadrennial Defense Review,* June 22, 2001, "classified contents removed," p. 13.

43. Paul Wolfowitz, "Remembering the Future," *National Interest,* Spring 2000, p. 36. For the 1992 background, see David Armstrong, "Dick Cheney's Song of America: Drafting a Plan for Global Dominance," *Harper's,* October 2002, pp. 76–83; and Tom Berry and Jim Lobe, "The Men Who Stole the Show," *Foreign Policy in Focus,* Special Report, October 2002.

44. Quoted by Quentin Peel, "Face It, The Cold War Is Over," *Financial Times,* August 20, 2001.

45. See Wen-ho Lee (with Helen Zia), *My Country versus Me* (New York: Hyperion, 2001); and Dan Stober and Ian Hoffman, *A Convenient Spy: Wen-ho Lee and the Politics of Nuclear Espionage* (New York: Simon and Schuster, 2001).

46. William Arkin and Robert Windrem, "The U.S.-China Information War," August 20, 2001, <http://www.msnbc.com/news/607031.asp?cp1=1>.

47. *Asahi Shimbun* (Tokyo), April 25, 2003 (in Japanese).

48. Office of the Deputy Under Secretary of Defense (Installations and Environment), *Base Structure Report (A Summary of DoD's Real Property Inventory)* (Washington: Department of Defense, 2002), s.v. "South Korea."

49. Bruce Cumings, *Korea's Place in the Sun: A Modern History* (New York: Norton, 1997), p. 153. Also see Doug Bandow, *Tripwire: Korea and U.S. Foreign Policy in a Changed World* (Washington, DC: Cato Institute, 1996).

50. Jim Lea, "S. Korean Protesters Hurl Rocks, Eggs at Camp Casey," *Stars & Stripes*, July 21, 2002; K. T. Kim, "Trial of U.S. Soldiers to Open to Media Only," *Korea Times*, November 8, 2002; James Brooke, "First of 2 G.I.'s on Trial in Deaths of 2 Korean Girls Is Acquitted," *New York Times*, November 21, 2002; Don Kirk, "2nd U.S. Sergeant Is Cleared in the Death of 2 Korean Girls," *New York Times*, November 23, 2002; BBC News, "S. Koreans Stage Huge Anti-U.S. Rally," December 14, 2002; Robert Fouser, "Putting Alliance to a 'Democracy Test,'" *Korea Now*, December 14, 2002; Tim Shorrock, "Roh's Election Victory and the Widening Gap between the U.S. and South Korea," *Foreign Policy in Focus*, January 7, 2003; Jaewoo Choo, "Vigils in Korea: U.S. Alliances on Trial," *Asia Times*, January 7, 2003; and Peter S. Goodman and Joohee Cho, "Anti-U.S. Sentiment Deepens in S. Korea," *Washington Post*, January 9, 2003.

51. Barbara Demick, "A Less Intrusive Presence for Troops in South Korea," *Los Angeles Times*, April 2, 2003.

52. Walter Pincus, "CIA Head Predicts Nuclear Race: Small Nations Pursuing Arms," *Washington Post*, February 12, 2003.

4: THE INSTITUTIONS OF AMERICAN MILITARISM

1. Brian Kennedy, "Uncle Sam Wants You to Play This Game," *New York Times*, July 11, 2002; Steve Osunsami, "Simulated Sniping: U.S. Army Recruits Teens with Internet Game," ABC News, October 31, 2002; and Steve Rubenstein, "Military Recruits Motivated by Promises of Perks, Not Patriotism," *San Francisco Chronicle*, December 13, 2002.

2. See the following official Web sites: <www.nhra.com> and <www.goarmy.com>. Also see Chris Grenz, "Dragster an Army of One," *Topeka Capital-Journal*, May 24, 2001; Jeff Wolf, "Army Mixes Recruiting, Racing," *Las Vegas Review-Journal*, April 8, 2002. For a photograph of "The Sarge," see *Popular Mechanics*, 2002, <http:/popularmechanics.com/automotive/motor_sports/2002/2/go_army/index.p-html>.

3. David Wood, "Shaky Economy Alters Equations of Risk in Today's Military," *San Diego Union-Tribune*, April 27, 2003.

4. Doug Rokke, "Gulf War Casualties," September 30, 2002, <http://www.traprockpeace.org>; Karsten Strauss, "When the Dust Settles," ABC News, May 5, 2003; Scott Peterson, "A Rare Visit to Iraq's Radioactive Battlefield," *Christian Science Monitor*, April 29, 1999; and Peterson, "Remains of Toxic Bullets Litter Iraq," *Christian Science Monitor*, May 15, 2003.

5. Susanna Hecht, "Uranium Warheads May Leave Both Sides a Legacy of Death for Decades," *Los Angeles Times*, March 30, 2003; Neil Mackay, "U.S. Forces' Use of Depleted Uranium Is 'Illegal,'" *Glasgow Sunday Herald*, March 30, 2003; Steven Rosenfeld, "Gulf War Syndrome, the Sequel," *TomPaine.com*, April 8, 2003; "UK to Aid DU Removal," BBC News, April 23, 2003; Frances Williams, "Clean-Up of Pollution Urged to Reduce Health Risks," and Vanessa Houlder, "Allied Troops Risk Uranium Exposure,'" *Financial Times*, April 25, 2003; Jonathan Duffy, "Iraq's Cancer Children Overlooked in War," BBC News, April 29, 2003.

6. Office of the Assistant Secretary of Defense for Force Management Policy, *Population Representation in the Military Services* (Washington: Department of Defense, November 2000), <http://dticaw.dtic.mil/prhome/poprep99/>.

7. Leonel Sanchez, "Hispanics Overrepresented in Combat Roles, Report Says," *San Diego Union-Tribune*, March 28, 2003; "Baja Upset at U.S. Army Bid to Recruit in Tijuana," *San Diego Union-Tribune*, May 9, 2003; Mark Stevenson, "U.S. Army Recruiter Crosses Mexico Border," Associated Press, May 9, 2003; "Green Card Marines," *Los Angeles Times*, May 25, 2003.

8. Adam Clymer, "Service Academies Defend Use of Race in Their Admissions Policies," *New York Times*, January 28, 2003.

9. U.S. Department of Defense, "News Transcript: Background Briefing on the All Volunteer Force," January 13, 2003, <http://www.defenselink.mil/news/Jan2003/t01132003_t113bkgd.html>; Earl Ofari Hutchinson, "Echoes of 'Fragging,'" *San Francisco Chronicle*, March 27, 2003; and Kimberly Hefling, "Military Trial Urged in Kuwait Fragging," *Washington Times*, June 21, 2003.

10. Marie Tessier, *Women's ENews*, posted on *AlterNet.org*, April 8, 2003.

11. Michael Janofsky, "Top Air Force Officer, at Academy, Issues Warning," *New York Times*, March 8, 2003.

12. Roland Watson and Glen Owen, "*Kitty Hawk* Captain Loses Control," *Times Online*, "World News," September 4, 2002.

13. Norman Soloman, "Media Sizzle for an Army of Fun," *Media Monitors*, July 8, 2002, <http://www.mediamonitors.net/solomon 85.html>.

14. Kevin Heldman, "On the Town with the U.S. Military in Korea," *Z Magazine*, February 1997, <http://www.zmag.org/zmag/articles/feb97 army.html>.

15. Ibid.

16. Marianne Szegedy-Maszak, "Death at Fort Bragg," *U.S. News & World Report*, August 12, 2002, p. 44.

17. Bill Vann, "The Fort Bragg Murders: A Grim Warning on the Use of the Military," *World Socialist Web Site*, August 2, 2002.

18. Colin Soloway, "'I Yelled at Them to Stop,'" *Newsweek*, October 7, 2002, <http://www.msnbc.com/news/814576.asp>; and Dan Plesch, "Failure of the 82nd Airborne," *Guardian*, December 19, 2002. Also see Marc W. Herold, "Vietnam Redux," October 31, 2002, <http://www.cursor.org/stories/vietnam_redux.htm>, where full citations to Afghan incidents are given.

19. Associated Press, "Marine Corps Cancels Annual Sniper Meet," October 23, 2002.

20. John M. Broder, "Arizona Gunman Chose Victims in Advance," *New York Times*, October 30, 2002.

21. Roland Watson and Glen Owen, "*Kitty Hawk* Captain"; and "*Kitty Hawk* Captain Dismissed Over Crewmen's Incidents," *Yomiuri Shimbun* (Tokyo), September 4, 2002.

22. Heldman, "On the Town."

23. Ibid. Also see Associated Press, "Uncle Sam Wants Your Kid," December 3, 2002; and Suzanne Goldenberg, "Parents Furious as Pentagon Slides Recruiting Officers into Classrooms," *Guardian,* December 5, 2002.

24. See "Military Escalates Assault on Civilian Schools," Committee Opposed to Militarism and the Draft, *Draft Notices,* May–July 2001, <www.comdsd.org>; Carl Campanile, "New Law Lets Army Get Info on High School Kids," *New York Post,* July 17, 2002; David Goodman, "No Child Unrecruited: Should the Military Be Given the Names of Every High School Student in America?" *Mother Jones,* November–December 2002; Helen Thomas, "Military Recruitment: An Invasion of Privacy," *TheJacksonChannel.com,* November 18, 2002.

25. George Fisher, "Power over Principle," *New York Times,* September 7, 2002. Also see Rebecca Trounson, "Law Schools Bow to Pentagon on Recruiters," *Los Angeles Times,* October 12, 2002.

26. Lawrence H. Suid, *Guts and Glory: The Making of the American Military Image in Film* (Lexington: University Press of Kentucky, 2002), p. 8.

27. Nancy Benac, "More Movies with Pentagon Help," Associated Press, May 16, 2001.

28. V. Dion Haynes, "Hollywood Boosts the Military," *Chicago Tribune,* May 27, 2001.

29. Claudia Eller and Richard Natale, "Hit Status Elusive Target for 'Pearl Harbor,'" *Los Angeles Times,* June 17, 2001. Also see Simon Davis, "U.S. Critics Attack 'Pearl Harbor' as Ultimate Hollywood Bilge," *London Telegraph,* May 26, 2001; and Todd McCarthy, "'Pearl Harbor,' a Film That Will Live in Infamy," Reuters, May 25, 2001.

30. Dana Calvo, "Military Using Its Promotional Arms in Theaters," *Los Angeles Times,* October 15, 2002.

31. Rupert Wingfield Hayes, "Doubts Set In on Afghan Mission," BBC News, September 28, 2002. Also see James W. Crawley, "The War News—With No Last Names Allowed," *San Diego Union-Tribune,* October 21, 2001.

32. See Carol Brightman, "U.S. Military Plans the War of Words," *Los Angeles Times,* February 16, 2003; and Ralph Blumenthal and Jim Rutenberg, "Journalists Are Assigned to Accompany U.S. Troops," *New York Times,* February 18, 2003.

33. *Time*, April 16, 2001; *Honolulu Advertiser*, April 16, 2001; as cited by John Kifner, "Despite Sub Inquiry, Navy Still Sees Need for Guests on Ships," *New York Times*, April 23, 2001. Also see Tony Perry, "Sub Skipper Is Forced into Retirement," *Los Angeles Times*, April 24, 2001.

34. Tony Perry, "Morale Likely a Factor in Decision on Sub Crew," *Los Angeles Times*, April 4, 2001.

35. Phil Patton, "Exposing the Black Budget," *Wired*, November 1995, <http:www.wired.com/wired/archive/3.11/patton_pr.html>.

36. George Caldwell, "U.S. Defense Budgets and Military Spending," Library of Congress, March 1992, <http://www.loc.gov/rr/news/militaryspending.html>; Bill Sweetman, "In Search of the Pentagon's Billion Dollar Hidden Budgets," <http://www.geocities.com/Athens/Crete/2546/black.html>; and Dan Morgan, "Classified Spending on the Rise; Report: Defense to Get $23.2 Billion," *Washington Post*, August 27, 2003.

37. Sweetman, "In Search."

38. Ibid.

39. John Kelly, Chris Kridler, and Kelly Young, "Billion Dollar Question: Where Has All the Air Force's EELV Money Gone?" *Florida Today*, August 25, 2002.

40. Robert Windrem, NBC News, "Military Role Grows on Home Front," April 18, 2001, <www.msnbc.com/news/546844.asp?Osp=n5b5z1>. Also see editorial, "Domestic Law Enforcement Is Not a Job for the Military," *Atlanta Journal-Constitution*, July 19, 2002.

41. See, in particular, Alan W. Bock, *Ambush at Ruby Ridge: How Government Agents Set Randy Weaver Up and Took His Family Down* (Irvine, Calif.: Dickens Press, 1995).

42. *Boston Globe* and Associated Press, "New Command Being Set Up to Defend North America," *San Diego Union-Tribune*, April 18, 2002; Eric Schmitt, "General Backs More Policing Power for Military," *San Diego Union-Tribune*, July 21, 2002; David Johnston et al., "Administration Begins to Rewrite Decades-Old Spying Restrictions," *New York Times*, November 30, 2002; Robert Dreyfuss, "Bringing the War Home," *Nation*, May 26, 2003.

43. U.S. Department of Defense, "Homeland Security," *Defense Link*, February 6, 2003, <http://www.defenselink.mil/specials/homeland/>.

44. "Defense Takeover," *Financial Times*, April 8, 2002.

45. Eric Lichtblau and James Risen, "Broad Domestic Role Asked for CIA and the Pentagon," *New York Times*, May 2, 2003.

46. Jeanette Steele, "Corps' War with Law: Marines Say Protection of Species Hurts Combat Training," *San Diego Union-Tribune*, September 26, 2002; and Esther Schrader, "Defense Seeking Greater Latitude," *Los Angeles Times*, July 15, 2002. Also see Katharine Q. Seelye, "Defense Dept. Forum Focuses on Environment," *New York Times*, February 6, 2003; Jennifer Lee, "Military Seeks Exemptions on Harming Environment," *New York Times*, March 6, 2003; Andrew Gumbel, "Pentagon Seeks Freedom to Pollute Land, Air and Sea," *Independent*, March 13, 2003.

47. Charlie A. Beckwith, *Delta Force* (New York: Dell Books, 1985), p. 268.

48. Stratfor Global Intelligence Update, "Foreign Policy and the U.S. Military," July 9, 2001 <http://www.worldnetdaily.com/news/article.asp?ARTICLE_ID=23554>.

49. Dana Priest, "A Four-Star Foreign Policy: U.S. Commanders Wield Rising Clout, Autonomy," *Washington Post*, September 28, 2000. Also see Dana Priest, *The Mission: Waging War and Keeping Peace with America's Military* (New York: Norton, 2003).

50. Dana Priest, "Standing Up to State and Congress," *Washington Post*, September 30, 2000; Karen DeYoung, "Powell Says U.S. to Resume Training Indonesia's Forces: Terrorism Fears Overtake Concerns about Army Abuses," *Washington Post*, August 3, 2002.

51. Daniel Siegel and Joy Hackel, "El Salvador: Counterinsurgency Revisited," in Michael T. Klare and Peter Kornbluh, eds., *Low-Intensity Warfare* (New York: Pantheon, 1988), pp. 112–35. Also see Cynthia J. Arnson, "Window on the Past: A Declassified History of Death Squads in El Salvador," in Bruce B. Campbell and Arthur D. Brenner, eds., *Death Squads in Global Perspective: Murder with Deniability* (New York: St. Martin's Press, 2000), pp. 85–124.

52. Priest, "Standing Up."

53. Eric Schmitt and Thom Shanker, "Pentagon Sets Up Intelligence Unit," *New York Times*, October 24, 2002.

54. Canadian Broadcasting Corp., "Experts Doubt Iraq, al-Qaeda Terror Link," November 1, 2002.

55. Linda Robinson, "Moves That Matter: In the Intelligence Wars, a Preemptive Strike by the Pentagon Surprises Many in Congress," *U.S. News & World Report*, August 12, 2002, p. 18. Also see Leona C. Bull, "Rivalry between Defense Department, CIA Reportedly Growing," *Journal of Aerospace and Defense Industry News*, November 1, 2002, p. A6; Pat M. Holt, "U.S. Intelligence: Seeing What It Wants to See in Iraq," *Christian Science Monitor*, November 7, 2002; Robert Dreyfuss, "The Pentagon Muzzles the CIA," *American Prospect* 13:22 (December 16, 2002); and Eric Schmitt, "Pentagon Draws Up a 20-to-30-Year Antiterror Plan," *New York Times*, January 17, 2003.

56. Robert Schlesinger, "Expanding Role of Defense Department Spurs Concerns; Some Say Officials Overstep Bounds, Limit other Agencies," *Boston Globe*, June 8, 2003; Schmitt and Shanker, "Pentagon Sets Up Intelligence Unit."

57. Greg Miller, "Wider Pentagon Spy Role Is Urged," *Los Angeles Times*, October 26, 2002.

58. Patrick Martin, "Billions for War and Repression: Bush Budget for a Garrison State," *World Socialist Web Site*, February 6, 2002.

59. Tim Weiner, *Blank Check* (New York: Warner Books, 1990), p. 178.

60. Ibid., pp. 172–98; and Stephen D. Goose, "Low-Intensity Warfare: The Warriors and Their Weapons," in Klare and Kornbluh, *Low-Intensity Warfare*, p. 87.

61. Martin, "Billions for War"; and Rowan Scarborough, "Commandos Resist Loss of Purchasing Authority," *Washington Times*, October 17, 2002.

62. Tom Bowman, "Special Forces' Role May Expand," *Baltimore Sun*, August 3, 2002; Pamela Hess, "Panel Wants $7 Billion Elite Counter-Terror Units," United Press International, September 26, 2002; and William M. Arkin, "The Secret War: Frustrated by Intelligence Failures, the Defense Department Is Dramatically Expanding Its 'Black World' of Covert Operations," *Los Angeles Times*, October 27, 2002.

63. *New York Times*, op-ed, August 21, 2002.

64. Greg Miller, "Military Wants Its Own Spies," *Los Angeles Times,* March 4, 2003.

1. See A. J. Langguth, *Our Vietnam: The War, 1954–1975* (New York: Simon and Schuster, 2000), pp. 184–85. Peter Schweizer, a research fellow at the right-wing think tank, the Hoover Institution, located on the campus of Stanford University, advocates that the United States solve its military manpower needs by creating an American version of the French foreign legion. See his "All They Can Be, except American," *New York Times,* February 18, 2003.
2. See Tamar Gabelnick, "Security Assistance after September 11," *Foreign Policy in Focus* 7:4 (May 2002); and North American Congress on Latin America, "15,000 Latin Americans Trained by the U.S. Military Last Year," June 27, 2002, <http://www.nacla.org/bodies/body29.php>.
3 Lora Lumpe, "U.S. Foreign Military Training: Global Reach, Global Power, and Oversight Issues," *Foreign Policy in Focus,* Special Report, May 2002.
4. See, for example, reports of the U.S. Special Forces attack of January 24, 2002, on the Afghan village of Uruzgan. After killing at least nineteen villagers, the Americans, wearing masks, took twenty-seven men prisoner. They bound and tortured them for several days and then shot some of the bound prisoners in the back. It turned out that none of them were members of the Taliban or al-Qaeda. One officer said, "We are sorry. We committed a mistake bombing this place." The CIA distributed reparations money to the families of those killed (Molly Moore, "Villagers Released by American Troops Say They Were Beaten, Kept in 'Cage,'" *Washington Post,* February 11, 2002).
5. Quoted in Victoria Garcia, "U.S. Foreign Military Training: A Shift in Focus," Center for Defense Information, "Terrorism Project," April 8, 2002.
6. On the roles of the CIA and the Pentagon in the overthrow of democracy

in Brazil and the fostering of military takeovers in Uruguay, Chile, and Argentina, see A. J. Langguth, *Hidden Terrors* (New York: Pantheon, 1978).

7. Alfred W. McCoy, *The Politics of Heroin: CIA Complicity in the Global Drug Trade* (Chicago: Lawrence Hill Books, 1991), p. 306.

8. Linda Robinson, "America's Secret Armies: A Swarm of Private Contractors Bedevils the U.S. Military," *U.S. News & World Report,* November 4, 2002; James Gerstenzang, "Vinnell Corp., Targeted in Riyadh Before, Loses 9 More Workers," *Los Angeles Times,* May 14, 2003.

9. Dana Priest, "U.S. Instructed Latins on Executions, Torture," *Washington Post,* September 21, 1996. Also see Raymond Ker, "CIA and School of the Americas," *MediaMonitors,* November 26, 2001, <http://www.mediamonitors.net/raymondker3.html>.

10. The Athenaeum, "The Sepoy Mutiny—India, 1857," <http://www.lexicorps.com/sepoy.htm>.

11. George Crile, *Charlie Wilson's War: The Extraordinary Story of the Largest Covert Operation in History—the Arming of the Mujahideen* (New York: Atlantic Monthly Press, 2003).

12. See International Consortium of Investigative Journalists, "Making a Killing: The Business of War," October 28, 2002, a segment of a Center for Public Integrity eleven-part series, <http://www.public-i.org>; Deborah Avant, "Private Military Companies Part of U.S. Global Reach," *Progressive Response* 6:17 (June 7, 2002); Robinson, "America's Secret Armies"; Esther Schrader, "U.S. Companies Hired to Train Foreign Armies," *Los Angeles Times,* April 14, 2002; James Dao, "U.S. Company to Take Over Karzai Safety," *New York Times,* September 19, 2002; Leslie Wayne, "America's For-Profit Secret Army," *New York Times,* October 13, 2002; David Isenberg, "Security for Sale in Afghanistan," *Asia Times,* January 6, 2003; and Isenberg, "There's No Business like Security Business," *Asia Times,* April 30, 2003.

13. Quoted in Lumpe, "U.S. Foreign Military Training."

14. Robinson, "America's Secret Armies"; and John J. Lumpkin, "Spy Plane Too Costly for Operations," Associated Press, August 28, 2002.

15. Halliburton Company Web Site, "Halliburton Awarded Services Con-

tract to Support Troops in Balkans," February 18, 1999, <http://www.
freerepublic.com/forum/a371d59862125.htm>.

16. Kathleen Hennessey, "A Contract to Spend," *Mother Jones,* May 23,
2002; "The Biggest Camp There Is: Houses Being Built for 5,000
Personnel at Camp Bondsteel," September 27, 1999, <http://www.
freerepublic.com/forum/a38deddd77282.htm>; Global Security Organization, "Camp Bondsteel," <www.globalsecurity.org/military/facility/
camp-bondsteel.htm>. Also see Ivana Avramovic, "Civilians Take Over
Security at Bosnia's Task Force Eagle Base Camps," *Stars & Stripes,*
August 17, 2002.

17. Robert Bryce, "The Candidate from Brown & Root," *Austin Chronicle,*
August 28, 2000.

18. Lee Drutman and Charlie Gray, "Cheney, Halliburton and the Spoils
of War," *Citizen Works,* April 4, 2003, <http://www.corpwatch.org/
issues/PID.jsp?articleid=6288>.

19. See, inter alia, Robert Caro, *LBJ: Master of the Senate* (New York:
Knopf, 2002); Knut Royce and Nathaniel Heller, "Cheney Led Halliburton to Feast at Federal Trough," Investigative Report, Center for
Public Integrity, <http://www.public-i.org/story_01_080200_txt.htm>;
Martin A. Lee, "Reality Bites," *San Francisco Bay Guardian,* November
13, 2000; Jeff Gerth and Don Van Natta Jr., "In Tough Times, a Company Finds Profits in Terror War," *New York Times,* July 13, 2002;
Frank Rich, "The Road to Perdition," *New York Times,* July 20, 2002;
and Molly Ivins, "Dirtied by Iraqi Oil," Creators Syndicate, September
5, 2002.

20. Paul Stuart, "Camp Bondsteel and America's Plans to Control
Caspian Oil," *World Socialist Web Site,* April 29, 2002.

21. James K. Galbraith, "The Unbearable Costs of Empire," *American
Prospect* 13:21 (November 18, 2002).

22. Tech. Sgt. Theresa McCullough, "U.S. Tankers Deploy to Bulgaria," *Air
Force Link,* November 21, 2001; Ian Traynor, "Payback Time for America's Allies as GIs Set Up Camp in the New Europe," *Guardian,* March
4, 2003; Doug Sanders, "Ex-Enemy Helping U.S. Fight in Iraq," *Globe
and Mail,* March 20, 2003; Global Security Organization, "Burgas

Airport," <http://www.globalsecurity.org/military/facility/burgas-ap. htm>.

23. Global Security Organization, "Camp Doha," <http://www.global-security.org/military/facility/camp-doha.htm>.

24. "Top 200 Contractors 2000," *Government Executive Magazine,* August 1, 2000.

25. Global Security Organization, "Camp Doha."

26. Patrick E. Tyler, "Two U.S. Computer Workers Are Shot, One Fatally, Near Army Base in Kuwait," *New York Times,* January 22, 2003; Craig D. Rose and Penni Crabtree, "Tapestry Solutions Is a Software Supplier," *San Diego Union-Tribune,* January 22, 2003; Kenneth Brede-meier, "Thousands of Private Contractors Support U.S. Forces in Persian Gulf," *Washington Post,* March 3, 2003.

6: THE EMPIRE OF BASES

1. Center for Defense Information, "The Global Network of United States Military Bases," *Defense Monitor* 18:2 (1989).

2. U.S. Senate Subcommittee on Security Agreements and Commitments Abroad, Committee on Foreign Relations, December 21, 1970; quoted in *Monthly Review* 53:10 (March 2002).

3. Office of the Deputy Undersecretary of Defense (Installations and Environment), *Base Structure Report (A Summary of DoD's Real Property Inventory)* (Washington: Department of Defense, 2002); and U.S. Department of Defense, Washington Headquarters Services, Direc-torate for Information, Operations, and Reports, *Worldwide Manpower Distribution by Geographical Area,* September 30, 2001, <http://web1.whs.osd.mil/DIORCAT.HTM#M05>. The best unofficial sources on the American empire of bases are William R. Evinger, ed., *Directory of U.S. Military Bases Worldwide,* 3rd ed. (Phoenix: Oryx Press, 1998); and the database of the Global Security Organization, <www.global-security.org>.

4. Charles Glass, "Diary," *London Review of Books,* February 21, 2002, p. 37.

5. William M. Arkin, "The Underground Military; Israel: Capital of

Classified Bases," *Washington Post,* May 7, 2001. Also see Agence France-Presse, "U.S. May Use Israeli Army Bases against Iraq," September 9, 2002.

6. Michael Moran, "G. I. Joe as Big Brother," MSNBC, April 6, 2001, <http://www.msnbc.com/news/546845.asp?Osp=n5b4b4>.

7. Statement for the Record of Lt. Gen. Michael V. Hayden, USAF, Director, National Security Agency, and Chief, Central Security Service, before the Joint Inquiry of the Senate Select Committee on Intelligence and the House Permanent Select Committee on Intelligence, October 17, 2002. On Intelsat, see Renae Merle, "U.S. Probes Military Use of Commercial Satellites," *Washington Post,* December 6, 2002.

8. The main sources are Patrick S. Poole, *Echelon: America's Secret Global Surveillance Network,* <http://fly.hiwaay.net/~pspoole/echelon.html>; Duncan Campbell, *Development of Surveillance Technology and Risk of Abuse of Economic Information,* Working Document for the Scientific and Technical Options Assessment (STOA) Program of the European Parliament (Luxemburg: European Parliament, October 1999); Niall McKay, "Lawmakers Raise Questions about International Spy Network," *New York Times,* May 27, 1999; Associated Press, "U.S.-Led Spy Net in Japan," *Washington Post,* June 27, 2001; Duncan Campbell, Richard Norton-Taylor, David Pallister, and Jamie Wilson, "The Lessons for the U.S.: Money Can't Buy Safety from Terrorism," *Guardian,* September 15, 2001; Tatsushi Doi, "In-depth Study of Echelon," *Sankei Shimbun* (Tokyo), May 16, 2001; Doi, "Intelligence Activities in Taiwan," *Sankei Shimbun,* May 30, 2001; Hiroaki Horiuchi, "Echelon Has Been Intercepting Japanese Diplomatic Telegrams since 1981," *Mainichi Shimbun* (Tokyo), June 27, 2001; and "Echelon," *Tokyo Shimbun,* August 26, 2001. (The last four articles are in Japanese.)

9. Joseph Gerson and Bruce Birchard, eds., *The Sun Never Sets: Confronting the Network of Foreign U.S. Military Bases* (Boston: South End Press, 1991), p. 16; Public Radio News Services, Melbourne, Australia, Transcript, "The CIA in Australia, Part 3," October-November 1986, <http://serendipity.magnet.ch/cia/cia_oz/cia_oz3.htm>; and Andrew Clark, "Kerr Briefed on CIA Threat to Whitlam," *Sunday Age,* October 15, 2000, <http://www.ozpeace.net/pinegap/kerrsbriefing.htm>.

10. "Spy Agency Taps into Undersea Cable," *Wall Street Journal Online,* May 22, 2001. The USS *Jimmy Carter* is scheduled to go into service tapping underseas optical fiber cables in 2004.

11. Campbell, *Development of Surveillance Technology,* pp. 48–50; Evinger, *Directory of U.S. Military Bases Worldwide;* and Vernon Loeb, "Espionage Demands Prod Navy on Sub Construction," *Washington Post,* July 5, 2002.

12. Mark Thomas, "If the French Had Asked for Military Bases in Britain, We'd Be Torching Citroens and Picketing Patisseries," *New Statesman,* April 9, 2001; and Diana Johnstone and Ben Cramer, "The Burdens and the Glory: U.S. Bases in Europe," in Gerson and Birchard, *The Sun Never Sets,* p. 210.

13. Gerson and Birchard, eds., *The Sun Never Sets,* p. 16. In January 2003, the British defense secretary made the decision, without a vote of Parliament, to allow the United States to upgrade and use its secret base at Fylingdales in northern Yorkshire as part of its proposed missile defense network (Associated Press, *New York Times,* January 16, 2003).

14. Evinger, *Directory of U.S. Military Bases Worldwide,* p. 291.

15. Richard Norton-Taylor, "Embarrassed U.S. Blocks Case against Peace Fighter," *Guardian,* June 29, 2002.

16. Poole, *Echelon,* p. 13; Interview with James Bamford, author of *Body of Secrets,* in *WorldNetDaily,* June 24, 2001, <http://www.worldnetdaily. com/news/article.asp?ARTICLE_ID=23342>; and CBS News, *60 Minutes,* "Ex-Snoop Confirms Echelon Network," New York, February 27, 2000 (transcript posted March 1, 2000).

17. See Yorkshire Campaign for Nuclear Disarmament, "Menwith Hill, Commercial Espionage," <http://cndyorks.gn.apc.org/mhs/index.htm>. Also see Jeffrey Richelson, "Desperately Seeking Signals," *Bulletin of the Atomic Scientists* 56:2 (March-April 2000), pp. 47–51; American Civil Liberties Union's special Web site <www.echelonwatch.org>; Stuart Miller, Richard Norton-Taylor, and Ian Black, "Worldwide Spying Network Is Revealed," *Guardian,* May 26, 2001; Rupert Goodwins, "Echelon: How It Works," *ZDNet UK,* <http://news.zdnet. co.uk/story/0,,t269–s2079849,00.html>; and ZDNet's "Echelon Bibliography," <http://www.zdnet.co.uk/news/specials/2000/06/echelon/>.

18. For the simplest explanation of one-time pads, see Francis Litterio, "Why Are One-Time Pads Perfectly Secure?" <http://world.std.com/~franl/crypto/one-time-pad.html>.

19. *60 Minutes,* "Ex-Snoop Confirms Echelon Network."

20. Derrick Z. Jackson, "A Nation Changed—and Unchanged," *Boston Globe,* September 11, 2002; Dara Colwell, "The SUV-Terrorism Connection," *AlterNet.org,* October 15, 2001; Terry Golway, "Time to Junk Gas-Guzzling SUV's," *New York Observer,* November 12, 2001, p. 5; Ian Roberts, "Car Wars," *Guardian,* January 18, 2003; Jeff Plungis, "SUV Tax Break May Reach $75,000," *Detroit News,* January 20, 2003; and Keith Bradsher, *High and Mighty: SUV's—The World's Most Dangerous Vehicles and How They Got That Way* (New York: Public Affairs, 2002).

21. Federation of American Scientists, "Smedley Butler on Interventionism," <http://www.fas.org/man/smedley.htm>; and Hans Schmidt, *Maverick Marine: Gen. Smedley D. Butler and the Contradictions of American Military History* (Lexington: University Press of Kentucky, 1987), p. 2 et passim.

22. Energy Information Administration, U.S. Department of Energy, *Caspian Sea Region: Reserves and Pipelines Tables,* June 2002. Also see Dale Allen Pfeiffer, "The Forging of 'Pipelineistan': Oil, Gas Pipelines High Priority for U.S. in Central Asian Military Campaigns," *From theWilderness.com,* July 11, 2002.

23. Michael T. Klare, "Oil Moves the War Machine," *Progressive,* June 2002; and Klare, "Oiling the Wheels of War," *Nation,* October 7, 2002, pp. 6–7. For other estimates of Caspian Sea oil and gas reserves, see Ahmed Rashid, *Taliban: Militant Islam, Oil, and Fundamentalism in Central Asia* (New Haven: Yale University Press, 2000), pp. 144–45; Stephen Kinzer, "A Perilous New Contest for the Next Oil Prize," *New York Times,* September 21, 1997; and "Russia Appears to Be Leading in Caspian Sea Resources Export Race," *Alexander's Gas & Oil Connections* 6:18 (September 25, 2001).

24. "How Oil Interests Play Out in U.S. Bombing of Afghanistan," *Drillbits & Tailings* 6:8 (October 31, 2001); Pratap Chatterjee, "Afghan Pipe Dream: Is the U.S. War on Terrorism Really a War for a Caspian

Natural Gas Pipeline? Maybe Yes, and Maybe No," *CorpWatch*, June 28, 2002.

25. The Editors, "U.S. Military Bases and Empire," *Monthly Review* 53:10 (March 2002), quoting the U.S. State Department from the *New York Times*, December 15, 2001.

26. Phar Kim Beng, "Oil Needs Drive China West," *Asia Times*, November 20, 2002; Sabrina Tavernise, "Putin Will Focus on Energy in Visit to China This Week," *New York Times*, December 2, 2002. Also see Kang Wu and Fereidun Fesharaki, "Managing Asia Pacific's Energy Dependence on the Middle East: Is There a Role for Central Asia?" *Analysis from the East-West Center*, no. 60 (June 2002).

27. J. Eric Duskin, "Permanent Installation: Thousands of U.S. Troops Are Headed to Central Asia, and They're Not Leaving Anytime Soon," *In These Times*, March 29, 2002; Robert G. Kaiser, "U.S. Plants Footprint in Shaky Central Asia," *Washington Post*, August 27, 2002.

28. Chatterjee, "Afghan Pipe Dream." Also see Jeff Gerth, "Bribery Inquiry Involves Kazakh Chief, and He's Unhappy," *New York Times*, December 11, 2002; and Joshua Chaffin, "The Kazakh Connection: How Money Buys Access to the Politicians and Power-brokers in Washington," *Financial Times*, June 26, 2003.

29. Bob Woodward, *Bush at War* (New York: Simon & Schuster, 2002), p. 340; and Mike Allen, "CIA's Cash Toppled Taliban," *Washington Post*, November 16, 2002.

30. Colonel Stanislav Lunev, "Welcoming Our New Ally, Uzbek President Karimov," *NewsMax.com*, March 11, 2002; Robert Burns, "Rumsfeld Meets C. Asian Leaders," *Washington Post*, April 28, 2002; Ahmed Rashid, "Central Asia Trouble Ahead," *Far Eastern Economic Review*, May 9, 2002; Duskin, "Permanent Installation"; Kari Huus, "Critical Ally Calling, with Baggage," *MSNBC.com*, September 24, 2002; Yonatan Pomrenze, "Uzbekistan Basks in U.S. Spotlight," *MSNBC.com*, September 24, 2002.

31. See Kinzer, "Perilous New Contest."

32. Sabrina Tavernise, "Kazakhstan Reaches Oil Accord with Foreign Group," *New York Times*, January 28, 2003.

33. Carla Marinucci, "Chevron Redubs Ship Named for Bush Aide; Condoleezza Rice Drew Too Much Attention," *San Francisco Chronicle*, May 5, 2001.

34. Andrew Jack and David Stern, "Pipeline Plan for Borjomi Valley Is Approved," *Financial Times*, December 3, 2002. Also see Jay Hancock, "Is Bush Pro-Azeri or Just Pro-Oil?" *Baltimore Sun*, April 2, 2001; Armen Georgian (Agence France-Presse), "U.S. Eyes Caspian Oil in 'War on Terror,'" *ZNet*, May 1, 2002; Georgian, "Guzzling the Caspian," *Christian Science Monitor*, September 27, 2002.

35. See Kaiser, "U.S. Plants Footprint."

36. Georgian, "U.S. Eyes Caspian Oil." Also see Misha Dzhindzhikhashvili (Associated Press), "Plan for U.S. Troops in Georgia Irks Russia," *San Diego Union-Tribune*, February 28, 2002; and Patrick Martin, "U.S. Troops Deployed to Former Soviet Republic of Georgia," *World Socialist Web Site*, March 1, 2002.

37. Patrick Martin, "U.S. Planned War in Afghanistan Long before September 11," *World Socialist Web Site*, November 20, 2001. Also see James Risen, "New Breed of Roughnecks Battles over Caspian Oil Fields," *Los Angeles Times*, May 24, 1998; and Pierre Abramovici, "Background to Washington's War on Terror," *Le Monde Diplomatique*, January 2002.

38. Steven Levine, "UNOCAL Quits Afghanistan Pipeline Project," *New York Times*, December 5, 1998; Rashid, *Taliban*, p. 160; Jennifer Van Bergen, "Zalmay Khalilzad and the Bush Agenda," *Truthout*, January 13, 2001, <http://www.truthout.org/docs_01/01.14A.Zalmay.Oil.htm>; "Vital Statistics: Greasing the Machine—Bush, His Cabinet, and Their Oil Connections," *Drillbits & Tailings* 6:5 (June 30, 2001); Daniel Fisher, "Afghanistan: Oil Execs Revive Pipeline from Hell," *Forbes*, February 4, 2002; Larry Chin, "Players on a Rigged Grand Chessboard: Bridas, UNOCAL, and the Afghanistan Pipeline," *Online Journal*, March 6, 2002; Halima Kazem, "Afghanistan Eyes a Pipeline, but Prospects Look Dim," *Eurasianet*, June 6, 2002; and "Joe Conason's Journal," *Salon.com*, December 3, 2002, <http://www.salon.com/poitics/conason/2002/12/03/bush/print.html>.

39. Jacob Weisberg, "Bush's Favorite Afghan," *Slate*, October 5, 2001,

<http://www.slate.msn.com/?id=1008402>; and Wayne Madsen, "Afghanistan, the Taliban, and the Bush Oil Team," January 10, 2002, <http://www.democrats.com/view2.cfm?id=5496>.

40. Rashid, *Taliban,* p. 163.

41. Levine, "UNOCAL Quits." Also see Mary Pat Flaherty, David B. Ottaway, and James V. Grimaldi, "How Afghanistan Went Unlisted as Terrorist Sponsor," *Washington Post,* November 5, 2001.

42. "Pipelineistan: The Rules of the Game," *Alexander's Gas & Oil Connections* 7:4 (February 21, 2002).

43. Allen, "CIA's Cash."

44. Kaiser, "U.S. Plants Footprint."

45. Martin Walker, "Bases, Bases Everywhere," United Press International, December 23, 2001; Kamran Khan, "Pakistan Wants Its Airbases Back," *News,* Pakistan, January 11, 2002; and Anwar Iqbal, "U.S. Flew 57,800 Sorties from Pakistan," United Press International, May 19, 2003.

46. Duskin, "Permanent Installation."

47. Eric Schmitt and James Dao, "U.S. Is Building Up Its Military Bases in Afghan Region," *New York Times,* January 9, 2002.

48. Edmund L. Andrews, "A Bustling U.S. Air Base Materializes in the Mud," *New York Times,* April 27, 2002. Also see Global Security Organization, "Manas International Airport, Ganci Air Base, Bishkek, Kyrgyzstan," <http://www.globalsecurity.org/military/facility/manas.htm>; Burns, "Rumsfeld Meets"; Patrick Martin, "U.S. Bases Pave the Way for Long-Term Intervention in Central Asia," *World Socialist Web Site,* January 11, 2002; Duskin, "Permanent Installation"; and Steven Lee Myers, "Russia to Deploy Air Squadron in Kyrgyzstan, Where U.S. Has Base," *New York Times,* December 4, 2002.

49. Ahmed Rashid, "New Wars to Fight," *Far Eastern Economic Review,* September 12, 2002. Also see Global Security Organization, "Khanabad, Uzbekistan," <http://www.globalsecurity.org/military/facility/khanabad.htm>; "U.S. Indicates New Military Partnership with Uzbekistan," *Wall Street Journal,* October 15, 2001; Schmitt and Dao, "U.S. Is Building Up"; Martin, "U.S. Bases Pave the Way"; Duskin, "Permanent Installation"; Andrews, "Bustling U.S. Air Base"; Baglia Bukharbaeva (Associated Press), "U.S. Still Digging In at Secret Forward

Base," *San Diego Union-Tribune,* May 29, 2002; and Sean Gonsalves, "War on Terrorism Has Oily Undercurrent," *Seattle Post-Intelligencer,* September 3, 2002.

50. Chatterjee, "Afghan Pipe Dreams"; "USA Pledges Not to Abandon Central Asia after Afghan War," BBC, from Interfax-Kazakhstan News Agency, December 19, 2001; and George Monbiot, "America's Imperial War," *Guardian,* February 12, 2002.

7: THE SPOILS OF WAR

1. The number of domestic bases is taken from William R. Evinger, ed., *Directory of U.S. Military Bases Worldwide,* 3rd ed. (Phoenix: Oryx Press, 1998).
2. "The Monroe Doctrine Declared, 1823," <http://campus.northpark. edu/history/WebChron/USA/MonDoc.html>; and "Monroe Doctrine," <http://gi.grolier.com/presidents/ea/side/mondoc.html>.
3. Harry Magdoff, introduction to *Remaking Asia: Essays on the American Uses of Power,* ed. Mark Selden (New York: Pantheon, 1974), p. 4.
4. Ronald Steel, *Pax Americana* (New York: Viking, 1968), p. 10.
5. Garrett Moritz, "Explaining 1898: Conquest of Empire in the Gilded Age," <http://www.gtexts.com/college/papers/s4.html>; and Stuart Creighton Miller, *"Benevolent Assimilation": The American Conquest of the Philippines, 1899–1903* (New Haven: Yale University Press, 1982), p. 3. A thought-provoking book that throws doubt on Turner's frontier thesis is Andro Linklater, *Measuring America: How An Untamed Wilderness Shaped the United States and Fulfilled the Promise of Democracy* (New York: Walker & Co., 2002).
6. "U.S. Intervention in Latin America," <http://www.smplanet.com/ imperialism/teddy.html>; and "The Roosevelt Corollary to the Monroe Doctrine," <http://www.uiowa.edu/~c030162/Common/Handouts/ POTUS/TRoos.html>.
7. Zoltan Grossman, comp., "A Century of U.S. Military Interventions," <http://zmag.org/CrisesCurEvts/interventions.htm>.
8. David B. Abernethy, *The Dynamics of Global Dominance: European Overseas Empires, 1415–1980* (New Haven: Yale University Press, 2000), p. 86.

9. John M. Collins, "Military Bases," *Military Geography for Professionals and the Public* (Washington: U.S. National Defense University, Institute for National Strategic Studies, March 1998), <http://www.ndu.edu/inss/books/milgeo/milgeoch12.html>; and Kenneth Hunt, *NATO without France: The Military Implications*, Adelphi Paper no. 32 (London: Institute for Strategic Studies, December 1966).

10. Keith B. Cunningham and Andreas Klemmer, *Restructuring the U.S. Military Bases in Germany: Scope, Impacts, and Opportunities. Report 4* (Bonn: Bonn International Center for Conversion, 1995), p. 6.

11. Ibid., p. 10.

12. Ibid., p. 14.

13. Michael Goldfarb, "Origins of Pax Americana," <http://www.insideout.org/documentaries/pax/notebook.asp>. Also see Mark Landler, "Germans Near Bases Don't Hate U.S., Just the Noise," *New York Times*, February 17, 2003.

14. Evinger, *Directory of U.S. Military Bases Worldwide*, p. 255.

15. See Ken Silverstein, "Police Academy in the Alps: The Tax-Supported Marshall Center Offers More Fun and Games Than War Games," *Nation*, October 7, 2002, pp. 17–22; Rick Emert, "Army Cranking Out New Facilities," *Stars & Stripes*, December 14, 2002; David Rennie, "Pentagon Plans NATO Blitz on Germany by Pulling Out," *Sydney Morning Herald*, February 12, 2003.

16. Cunningham and Klemmer, *Restructuring the U.S. Military Bases*, p. 23.

17. Kozy K. Amemiya, "The Bolivian Connection: U.S. Bases and Okinawan Emigration," in Chalmers Johnson, ed., *Okinawa: Cold War Island* (Cardiff, Calif.: Japan Policy Research Institute, 1999), pp. 53–69.

18. See, in particular, Ichiro Tomiyama, "The 'Japanese' of Micronesia," in Ronald Y. Nakasone, ed., *Okinawan Diaspora* (Honolulu: University of Hawaii Press, 2002), pp. 64–68 et passim; Koji Taira, "Okinawa's Choice: Independence or Subordination," in Johnson, ed., *Okinawa: Cold War Island*, pp. 171–85; and Steve Rabson, introduction to *Okinawa: Two Postwar Novellas By Oshiro Tatsuhiro and Higashi Mineo* (Berkeley: Institute of East Asian Studies, University of California, 1989), pp. 1–30.

19. See Kensei Yoshida, *Democracy Betrayed: Okinawa under U.S. Occupation* (Bellingham: Center for East Asian Studies, Western Washington University, 2001), p. 17.

20. Ibid., p. 54.

21. Morton Mintz, "U.S. Stationed A-Bomb Ship 200 Yards off Japan's Coast," *Washington Post,* May 22, 1981; Edwin O. Reischauer, "Japan: The Meaning of the Flap," *Washington Post,* June 5, 1981; and Hans M. Kristensen, *Japan under the U.S. Nuclear Umbrella* (Berkeley: Nautilus Institute, July 1999).

22. Chii Kyotei Kenkyukai (Status of Forces Agreement Research Association), *Nichi-Bei chii kyotei chikujo hihan* (Point-by-point criticism of the Japanese-American status of forces agreement) (Tokyo: Shin Nihon Shuppansha, 1997), pp. 253–56. In Japanese.

23. See, e.g., Takis Michas, "America the Despised," *National Interest,* Spring 2002, pp. 94–102; Anthee Carassava, "Anti-Americanism in Greece Is Reinvigorated by War," *New York Times,* April 7, 2003; and John Brady Kiesling, "Diplomatic Breakdown," *Boston Globe,* April 27, 2003.

24. Quoted by Jim Huck, "1947–1970s, Greece: Helping Fascists in Civil War & Coup," <http://www.ncf.carleton.ca/coat/our_magazine/links/issue43/articles/1947_1970s_greece.htm>.

25. Quoted by William Blum, *Killing Hope: U.S. Military and CIA Interventions since World War II* (Monroe, Maine: Common Courage Press, 1995), p. 216.

26. Seymour M. Hersh, *Kissinger: The Price of Power* (1983); quoted in Blum, *Killing Hope,* p. 220.

27. Helena Smith, "The CIA Claims to Have Changed," *Guardian,* August 28, 2001; "A U.S. History of Greece Is Kept Secret," *Kathimerini* (English ed.), Athens, July 30, 2001.

28. Thomas Patrick Carroll, "Last Tango in Nicosia," *Middle East Intelligence Bulletin* 3:12 (December 2001).

29. William J. Pomeroy, "The Philippines: A Case History of Neocolonialism," in Mark Selden, ed., *Remaking Asia: Essays on the American Uses of Power* (New York: Pantheon, 1974), p. 162.

30. Alva M. Bowen Jr., "The Historical Setting: 1947–1975," in John W. McDonald Jr. and Diane B. Bendahmane, eds., *U.S. Bases Overseas: Negotiations with Spain, Greece, and the Philippines* (Boulder, Colo.: Westview, 1990), p. 74.

31. See Bryan Johnson, *The Four Days of Courage: The Untold Story of the People Who Brought Marcos Down* (New York: Free Press, 1987).

32. Roland G. Simbulan, "How 'The Battle of the Bases' Was Won," <http://www.boondocksnet.com/centennial/sctexts/simbulan.html>.

33. Michael Satchell, "Toxic Legacy: What the Military Left Behind," *U.S. News & World Report*, January 24, 2000, pp. 30–31; and Benjamin Pimentel, "Deadly Legacy: Leftover Bombs, Chemicals Wreak Havoc at Former U.S. Bases in Philippines," *San Francisco Chronicle*, July 5, 2001.

34. Dan Murphy, "Long-Term U.S. Strategy Emerges out of Philippines," *Christian Science Monitor*, July 3, 2002; Michael Satchell, "Back to the Philippines: Eight Years after Base Closings, the U.S. Is Rebuilding a Military Relationship," *U.S. News & World Report*, January 24, 2000, pp. 30–31; Doug Bandow, "Instability in the Philippines: A Case Study for U.S. Disengagement," CATO Institute *Foreign Policy Briefing*, no. 64, March 21, 2001; Oliver Teves, "Philippine Base Ready for U.S.-Led Training," Associated Press, *San Diego Union-Tribune*, January 20, 2002; Luis H. Francia, "U.S. Troops in the Philippines," *Village Voice*, February 20–26, 2002; Jane Perlez, "U.S. Troops Likely to Remain in Philippines Longer Than Planned," *New York Times* Service, *San Diego Union-Tribune*, March 31, 2002; and Tyler Marshall and John Hendren, "U.S. to Leave Philippines Despite Hostage Situation," *Los Angeles Times*, May 27, 2002.

35. Kari Huus, "In Philippines, G.I. Joe Is Back," MSNBC, August 2, 2002, <http://www.msnbc.com/news/787670.asp>; BBC News, "U.S. Unwelcome in Southern Philippines," March 17, 2003; Karen DeYoung, "Powell Says U.S. to Resume Training Indonesia's Forces," *Washington Post*, August 3, 2002.

36. Eric Schmitt, "U.S. to Send Nearly 2,000 Troops to Fight Militants in Philippines," *New York Times*, February 20, 2003; and Jim Gomez

(Associated Press), "Philippines Says U.S. Troops Not Welcome in Combat Patrols," *San Diego Union-Tribune,* April 22, 2003.

37. William Greider, *Fortress America: The American Military and the Consequences of Peace* (New York: Public Affairs, 1998), p. 101.

38. Haroon Siddiqui, "Real American Agenda Now Becoming Clear," *Toronto Star,* May 4, 2003. Also see Peter Grier, "A Reluctant Empire Stretches More," *Christian Science Monitor,* January 17, 2002; Thom Shanker and Eric Schmitt, "Pentagon Expects Long-Term Access to Four Key Bases in Iraq," *New York Times,* April 20, 2003; Michael R. Gordon and Eric Schmitt, "U.S. Will Move Air Operations to Qatar Base," *New York Times,* April 28, 2003; Eric Schmitt, "U.S. to Withdraw All Combat Units from Saudi Arabia," *New York Times,* April 30, 2003; Esther Schrader, "U.S. Expedites Reshuffling of Europe Troops," *Los Angeles Times,* May 1, 2003; Seth Stern, "New Map for U.S. Outposts," *Christian Science Monitor,* May 1, 2003.

8: IRAQ WARS

1. See Anthony Cave Brown, *Oil, God, and Gold: The Story of Aramco and the Saudi Kings* (Boston: Houghton Mifflin, 1999).

2. On the origins of American oil diplomacy in the Middle East, see Douglas Little, "Opening the Door: Business, Diplomacy, and America's Stake in Middle East Oil," in *American Orientalism: The United States and the Middle East since 1945* (Chapel Hill: University of North Carolina Press, 2002), pp. 43–75.

3. See Robert Fisk, "New Crisis, Old Lessons: The Suez Crisis Has Haunted British Government for Almost 50 Years," *Independent,* January 15, 2003.

4. Global Security Organization, "King Abdul Aziz Air Base, Dhahran, Saudi Arabia," <http://www.globalsecurity.org/military/facility/dhahran. htm>; and Patrick E. Tyler, "Saudis Plan to End U.S. Presence," *New York Times,* February 9, 2003.

5. The indispensable source is Ervand Abrahamian, "The 1953 Coup in Iran," *Science & Society* 65:2 (Summer 2001), pp. 182–215. Also see

Phillip Knightley, "Iraq Chose Saddam for Good Reason: The West Needs a History Lesson," *Independent*, August 4, 2002; and the important book by Stephen Kinzer, *All the Shah's Men: An American Coup and the Roots of Middle East Terror* (New York: John Wiley & Sons, 2003).

6. C. T. Sandars, *America's Overseas Garrisons: The Leasehold Empire* (Oxford: Oxford University Press, 2000), pp. 287, 293, 299; Robert Burns, "U.S. Building Up Forces at Obscure but Important Air Base in Qatari Desert," Associated Press, June 30, 2002.

7. Denis F. Doyon, "Middle East Bases," in Joseph Gerson and Bruce Birchard, eds., *The Sun Never Sets: Confronting the Network of Foreign U.S. Military Bases* (Boston: South End Press for the American Friends Service Committee, 1991), pp. 15, 275–307; Sandars, *America's Overseas Garrisons*, pp. 55–59; and BBC News, "Diego Garcia Islanders Battle to Return," October 31, 2002. For a few details on Diego Garcia in 2002, see Office of the Deputy Undersecretary of Defense (Installations and Environment), *Base Structure Report (A Summary of DoD's Real Property Inventory)* (Washington: Department of Defense, 2002), s.v. "British Indian Ocean Territory."

8. David Morgan, "Ex-U.S. Official Says CIA Aided Ba'athists," Reuters, April 20, 2003, posted on *CommonDreams.org*, May 19, 2003; CBS News, "Profile: Saddam Hussein," April 8, 2003; Richard Sale, "Saddam Key in Early CIA Plot," United Press International, April 10, 2003; "Bush Topples an Old U.S. Ally," *SocialistWorkerOnline*, April 18, 2003.

9. Michael Dobbs, "U.S. Had Key Role in Iraq Buildup; Trade in Chemical Arms Allowed Despite Their Use on Iranians, Kurds," *Washington Post*, December 30, 2002; and "Arming Iraq: A Chronology of U.S. Involvement," March 17, 2003, <http://www.rehberg.net/arming-iraq.html>.

10. Tony Paterson, "Leaked Report Says German and U.S. Firms Supplied Arms to Saddam," *Independent*, December 18, 2002; *Die Tageszeitung* (Berlin), December 20, 2002; and James Cusick and Felicity Arbuthnot, "America Tore Out 8,000 Pages of Iraq Dossier," *Sunday Herald* (Scotland), December 22, 2002. Also see Russ W. Baker, "Iraqgate," *Columbia Journalism Review*, March/April 1993; Christian Dewar, "Arming Iraq: How George H. W. Bush and Ronald Reagan Helped Iraq Develop Weapons of Mass Destruction," *Democratic Underground*, December

13, 2002; Stephen Green, "Rumsfeld's Account Book: Who Armed Saddam?" *CounterPunch,* February 24, 2003; Paul Rockwell, "Who Armed Iraq?" *San Francisco Chronicle,* March 2, 2003; and "Yes, U.S. Helped Iraq Get Chemical, Biological Weapons," *Belleville News-Democrat* (Southern Illinois and St. Louis metropolitan area), April 20, 2003, <http://www.belleville.com/mld/newsdemocrat/5674107.htm>.

11. Jeremy Scahill, "What about Those Chemical Weapons? The Saddam in Rummy's Closet," *CounterPunch,* August 2, 2002. For other discussions of the United States' supply of poison gas and germ warfare feeder stocks to Iraq during its 1980s war with Iran, see Eric Margolis, "Old Dreams of Empire Dance in Blair's Head," *Toronto Sun,* March 31, 2002; Patrick E. Tyler, "Iraqi Gas Use Didn't Stop U.S. Aid in '88," (*New York Times* News Service), *San Diego Union-Tribune,* August 18, 2002; Neil Mackay and Felicity Arbuthnot, "How Did Iraq Get Its Weapons? We Sold Them," *Sunday Herald* (Scotland), September 8, 2002; Robert Novak, "Following Iraq's Bioweapons Trail," *Chicago Sun-Times,* September 26, 2002; Matt Kellcy, "U.S. Supplied Germs to Iraq in '80s," Associated Press, September 30, 2002; Elson E. Boles, "Helping Iraq Kill with Chemical Weapons," *CounterPunch,* October 10, 2002; Jost R. Hiltermann, "America Didn't Seem to Mind Poison Gas," *International Herald Tribune,* January 17, 2003; Stephen C. Pelletiere, "A War Crime or an Act of War?" *New York Times,* January 31, 2003; and Philip Shenon, "Iraq Links Germs for Weapons to U.S. and France," *New York Times,* March 16, 2003.

12. Ritt Goldstein, "Oil Wars Pentagon's Policy since 1999," *Sydney Morning Herald,* May 20, 2003.

13. CBS News, as reported in *New York Times,* September 5, 2002, p. A10; Bob Woodward, *Bush at War* (New York: Simon and Schuster, 2002), pp. 49, 60–61; Chris Bury, "A Tortured Relationship: U.S.-Iraq Relations. Part 2: War," ABC News, September 18, 2002; Michael T. Klare, "Scheduling War," February 12, 2003, <http://www.nationinstitute. org/tomdispatch/index.mhtml?pid=391>; and Stephen Fidler, "Just When *Did* the President Decide to Go to War?" *Financial Times,* March 27, 2003.

14. Robert Kagan and William Kristol, eds., *Present Dangers: Crisis and*

Opportunity in American Foreign and Defense Policy (San Francisco: En-
counter Books, 2000); and *Rebuilding America's Defenses,* <http://www.
newamericancentury.org/>,s.v.RebuildingAmericanDefensespdf>.
On PNAC and the backgrounds of the neoconservatives in the second
Bush administration, see Elisabeth Bumiller and Eric Schmitt, "On
the Job and at Home, Influential Hawks' 30-Year Friendship Evolves,"
New York Times, September 11, 2002; Tom Barry and Jim Lobe, "The
Men Who Stole the Show," *Foreign Policy in Focus,* October 2002;
Steven R. Weisman, "Abrams Back in Capital Fray at Center of Mid-
east Battle," *New York Times,* December 7, 2002; Glenn Kessler, "U.S.
Decision on Iraq Has Puzzling Past," *Washington Post,* January 12,
2003; ABC News, "The Plan: Were Neo-Conservatives' 1998 Memos a
Blueprint for Iraq War?" March 10, 2003; and William O. Beeman,
"Military Might: The Man behind 'Total War' in the Mideast," *San
Francisco Chronicle,* May 14, 2003.

15. PNAC, *Rebuilding America's Defenses,* p. 51; and Nicholas Lemann,
    "The Next World Order," *New Yorker,* April 1, 2002, p. 44. I am
    indebted to John Pilger for drawing my attention to PNAC's activi-
    ties. See his article in the *New Statesman,* December 16, 2002.

16. Scott Ritter, "Is Iraq a True Threat to the U.S.?" *Boston Globe,* July 20,
    2002. On April 5, 2003, British Home Secretary David Blunkett admit-
    ted that no weapons of mass destruction were likely to be found in
    Iraq because they did not exist. See al-Jazerra (English), April 6, 2003.

17. PNAC, *Rebuilding America's Defenses,* p. 14.

18. See Tom Regan, "When Contemplating War, Beware of Babies in
    Incubators," *Christian Science Monitor,* September 6, 2002; Associated
    Press, "Not All Iraq Claims Backed by Evidence," December 22, 2002;
    and Mitchell Cohen, "How Bush Sr. Sold the Bombing of Iraq," *Coun-
    terPunch,* December 28, 2002.

19. See Victoria Samson, "Unmanned Aerial Vehicles: Iraq's 'Secret'
    Weapon?" Center for Defense Information, Terrorism Project, Octo-
    ber 10, 2002.

20. The most important source on this subject is Seymour Hersh, "A Case
    Not Closed," *New Yorker,* November 1, 1993.

21. Stephen Zunes, *Tinderbox: U.S. Foreign Policy and the Roots of Terror-*

ism (Monroe, Maine: Common Courage Press, 2003), p. 86; Robert Dreyfuss, "Persian Gulf—or Tonkin Gulf?" *American Prospect* 13:23 (December 2002); and Eric Schmitt, "Pentagon Shows Videos of Iraq Firing at Allied Jets," *New York Times*, October 1, 2002.

22. James Harding, Richard Wolffe, and James Blitz, "U.S. Will Rebuild Iraq as Democracy, Says Rice," *Financial Times*, September 22, 2002.

23. Anthony Sampson, "West's Greed for Oil Fuels Saddam Fever," *Observer*, August 11, 2002. On the younger Bush's dubious past as a member of the board of Harken Energy Corporation of Houston, see "Bush Was Told of Risks before Stock Sale: Harken Memo Went to SEC after Probe," *Boston Globe*, October 30, 2002; and Michael Lind, *Made in Texas* (New York: Basic Books, 2003), pp. 102–3. For a summary of American oil machinations in the Persian Gulf over the past fifty years, see Robert Dreyfuss, "The Thirty-Year Itch," *Mother Jones*, March 1, 2003.

24. Ed Vulliamy, "Troops 'Vandalize' Ancient City of Ur," *Observer*, May 18, 2003.

25. Julian Borger, "Anger at Peace Talks 'Meddling,'" *Guardian*, July 13, 2000; Brian Whitaker, "U.S. Thinktanks Give Lessons in Foreign Policy," *Guardian*, August 19, 2002; Jill Junnola, "Perspective: Who Funds Whom?" *Energy Compass*, October 4, 2002; Eric Margolis, "After Iraq, Bush Will Attack His Real Target," *Toronto Sun*, November 10, 2002; Margolis, "Bush's Mideast Plan: Conquer and Divide," *Toronto Sun*, December 8, 2002; Sandy Tolan, "Beyond Regime Change," *Los Angeles Times*, December 1, 2002; Jim Lobe, "Neoconservatives Consolidate Control over U.S. Mideast Policy," *Foreign Policy in Focus*, December 6, 2002; Bill Christison and Kathleen Christison, "Too Many Smoking Guns to Ignore: Israel, American Jews, and the War on Iraq," *CounterPunch*, January 25, 2003; and Michael Lind, "The Weird Men behind George W. Bush's War," *New Statesman*, April 7, 2003, <http://www.newamerica.net/index.cfm?sec=programs&pg=article&pubID=1189&T2=Article>.

26. Dan Plesch, "Weapons of Mass Distraction," *Observer*, September 29, 2002; and Brian J. Foley, "War Cries: Weapons of Mass Distraction," *CounterPunch*, November 8, 2002.

27. On presidential decision making during the Vietnam War, see Daniel Ellsberg, *Secrets: A Memoir of Vietnam and the Pentagon Papers* (New York: Viking, 2002). On Ellsberg's analysis, see Chalmers Johnson, "The Addiction to Secrecy," *London Review of Books*, February 6, 2003. On Karl Rove, see James C. Moore and Wayne Slater, *Bush's Brain: How Karl Rove Made Bush Presidential* (New York: Wiley, 2003).

28. Jay Bookman, "The President's Real Goal in Iraq," *Atlanta Journal-Constitution*, September 29, 2002.

29. Carol Morello, "Saudi Officials Shield U.S. Troop Presence from Public," *Washington Post*, March 22, 2003; and Robin Allen, "Gulf States Keep Lid on Extent of Defense Ties," *Financial Times*, February 18, 2003.

30. Global Security Organization, "Eskan Village," <http://www.global-security.org/military/facility/eskan-village. htm>. The Global Security Organization's collection of reports on CENTCOM bases is an invaluable source.

31. Catherine Taylor, "U.S. Air Base Ready for War after Millions in Upgrades," *Christian Science Monitor*, December 31, 2002. Also see Vernon Loeb and Dana Priest, "Saudis Balk at U.S. Use of Key Facility," *Washington Post*, September 22, 2001; Julian Borger, "U.S. Paves Way for War on Iraq; Attack Base to Be Moved into Qatar to Bypass Saudi Objections," *Guardian*, March 27, 2002; Kim Sengupta and Andrew Buncombe, "Saudi Bans Use of Its Air Bases to Attack Iraq," *Independent*, August 8, 2002; and Reuters, "Saudi Says Will Not Help Any U.S. Strike on Iraq," November 3, 2002.

32. "U.S. Military Women Cast Off Abayas," CBS News, January 22, 2002.

33. Eric Schmitt, "U.S. to Withdraw All Combat Units from Saudi Arabia," *New York Times*, April 30, 2003; and Maureen Dowd, "Hypocrisy and Apple Pie," *New York Times*, April 30, 2003.

34. Global Security Organization, "Ahmed al Jaber Air Base," <http://www.globalsecurity.org/military/facility/ahmed-al-jaber.htm>.

35. Global Security Organization, "Ali al Salem Air Base," <http://www.globalsecurity.org/military/facility/ali-al-salem.htm>.

36. Global Security Organization, "Manama, Bahrain," <http://www.globalsecurity.org/military/facility/manama.htm>.

37. Ali Akbar Dareini, "Bahrain Joins Iran in Opposing U.S. Attack on Iraq," Associated Press, August 18, 2002.

38. Gary C. Gambill, "Qatar's al-Jazeera TV: The Power of Free Speech," *Middle East Intelligence Bulletin* 2:5 (June 1, 2000); Andrea Koppel and Elise Labott, "U.S. Pressures Qatar to Restrain TV Outlet," CNN.com, October 3, 2001; Tariq Ali, "Diary," *London Review of Books,* August 22, 2002; and Robin Shulman, "From Ramallah to Oakland: Al-Jazeera Is a Rising Star in the New Information Age," *San Francisco Chronicle,* August 18, 2002. During the second Iraq war, the United States kept up a drumbeat of criticism against al-Jazeera's reporting. See Elizabeth Ptacek, "Backlash against al-Jazeera," *In These Times,* April 4, 2003.

39. 1st Lt. Johnny Rea, 379th Air Expeditionary Wing Public Affairs Officer, <http://198.65.138.161/military/library/news/2002/06/mil-020611–usaf01.htm>.

40. Associated Press, "U.S. to Close One Air Base, Upgrade Another," *Washington Times,* May 12, 2003; Global Security Organization, "Al-Udeid Air Base, Qatar," <http://www.globalsecurity.org/military/facility/udeid.htm>.

41. Michael Wolff, "Live from Doha," *New York Magazine,* April 7, 2003; Verne Gay, "Brig. Gen. Vincent Brooks, the Face of the War Effort," *Chicago Tribune,* April 10, 2003.

42. BBC News, "U.S. to Expand Abu Dhabi Air Base," May 14, 2003.

43. See "Oman Open to Closer U.S. Military Ties," *WorldNetDaily.com,* January 14, 2002; Ian Bruce, "U.S. to Spend £90m on Air Base in Oman," *Herald,* April 19, 2002; and "Oman Allocates Land for New Base," *World Tribune.com,* April 25, 2002.

9: WHATEVER HAPPENED TO GLOBALIZATION?

1. Hannah Arendt, *The Origins of Totalitarianism* (New York: Meridian Books, 1958), p. 125.

2. World Trade Organization, *Annual Report 1998: International Trade Statistics* (Geneva: WTO, 1998), p. 12. Quoted in Walden Bello, *The Future in the Balance* (Oakland, Calif.: Food First Books, 2001), p. 36.

3. Bruce R. Scott, "The Great Divide in the Global Village," *Foreign Affairs* 80:1 (January/February 2001), p. 160.

4. Manfred B. Steger, *Globalism: The New Market Ideology* (Lanham, Md.: Rowman & Littlefield, 2002), pp. 12–13.

5. For a sunny argument that globalization will undercut the state and usher in a period of lasting peace, see Richard N. Rosecrance, *The Rise of the Virtual State: Wealth and Power in the Coming Century* (New York: Basic Books, 2000).

6. Steger, *Globalism,* p. 54.

7. Bill Clinton, "Remarks by the President on Foreign Policy," invitation-only address in San Francisco, February 26, 1999; and Sonya Ross, "Clinton Talks of Better Living," Associated Press, October 15, 1997. Quoted in Steger, *Globalism,* p. 55.

8. See Bush's press conference after the April 22, 2001, Summit of the Americas in Quebec. Also see Maude Barlow, *The Free Trade Area of the Americas: The Threat to Social Programs, Environmental Sustainability and Social Justice* (San Francisco: International Forum on Globalization, 2001).

9. Oswaldo de Rivero, *The Myth of Development* (London: Zed Books, 2001), p. 138.

10. Ibid., p. 22.

11. Harvey Cox, "The Market as God: Living in the New Dispensation," *Atlantic Monthly,* March 1999, pp. 18–23.

12. Arendt, *Origins of Totalitarianism,* p. 209. On the racism and genocide of the British Empire, see Sven Lindquist, *Exterminate All the Brutes* (New York: New Press, 1996).

13. Joseph E. Stiglitz, "A Fair Deal for the World," *New York Review of Books,* May 23, 2002, p. 24. Also see Stiglitz, *Globalization and Its Discontents* (New York: W. W. Norton, 2002).

14. De Rivero, *Myth of Development,* pp. 3, 9, 24.

15. Quoted in Ha-Joon Chang, *Kicking Away the Ladder: Development Strategy in Historical Perspective* (London: Anthem Press, 2002). Chang is a professor of economics at Cambridge University.

16. On how Japan became the world's second most productive economy, see Chalmers Johnson, *MITI and the Japanese Miracle: The Growth of*

Industrial Policy, 1925–1975 (Stanford: Stanford University Press, 1982); Linda Weiss, *The Myth of the Powerless State* (Ithaca: Cornell University Press, 1998); and Meredith Woo-Cumings, ed., *The Developmental State* (Ithaca: Cornell University Press, 1999).

17. De Rivero, *Myth of Development,* p. 109; Ted C. Fishman, "Making a Killing: The Myth of Capital's Good Intentions," *Harper's,* August 2002, p. 34.

18. Thomas Ferguson, "Blowing Smoke: Impeachment, the Clinton Presidency, and the Political Economy," in William J. Crotty, ed., *The State of Democracy in America* (Washington: Georgetown University Press, 2001), p. 233. On the workings of the IMF and the World Bank, see William Finnegan, "The Economics of Empire: Notes on the Washington Consensus," *Harper's,* May 2003, pp. 41–54.

19. Nicholas Guyatt, *Another American Century? The United States and the World after 2000* (London: Zed Books, 2000), p. 8.

20. Bello, *Future in the Balance,* p. 49.

21. John Madeley, *Hungry for Trade: How the Poor Pay for Free Trade* (London: Zed Books, 2000), p. 58; Guyatt, *Another American Century?,* pp. 12, 37.

22. Lawrence Summers, "The Memo," <http://www.whirledbank.org/ourwords/summers.html>. Also see Jonathan R. Pincus and Jeffrey A. Winters, eds., *Reinventing the World Bank* (Ithaca: Cornell University Press, 2002), pp. 13–14.

23. Jeffrey E. Garten, "The Root of the Problem," *Newsweek,* March 31, 1997. Quoted by Guyatt, *Another American Century?,* p. 185. Also see Garten, "Business and Foreign Policy," *Foreign Affairs* 76:5 (1997), pp. 67–79.

24. Bello, *Future in the Balance,* p. 52.

25. Ibid., p. 51.

26. Ibid., p. xiv.

27. Ibid., pp. 45, 69; Steve Schifferes, "Doha Trade Deal Unraveling," BBC News, November 10, 2002.

28. Stiglitz, "Fair Deal for the World," p. 28.

29. See "WTO Pact on Generic Drugs Blocked by U.S.," *Financial Times,* December 21–22, 2002; and Nicola Bullard, "Is the WTO Collapsing

under Its Own Ambitions?" *Focus on Trade*, no. 82 (December 2002). For the WTO agreement weakening patent protection on drugs, see World Trade Organization, Doha, Qatar, WTO Ministerial, 2001, "Declaration on the TRIPS Agreement and Public Health," November 14, 2001.

30. Andrew Pollack, "Widely Used Crop Herbicide Is Losing Weed Resistance," *New York Times*, January 14, 2003.

31. Madeley, *Hungry for Trade*, pp. 100–03.

32. The most comprehensive treatment of these complex issues is Edith Terry, *How Asia Got Rich* (Armonk, N.Y.: M. E. Sharpe, 2002).

33. Thomas L. Friedman, *The Lexus and the Olive Tree* (New York: Farrar, Straus & Giroux, 1999), pp. 112–13.

34. Fishman, "Making a Killing," p. 41, n. 10; David Hale, "Will Argentina Recover without the IMF?" Zurich Financial Services, December 20, 2002. Hale is chief economist for Zurich Financial Services.

35. De Rivero, *Myth of Development*, p. 17.

36. Robert Naiman (Center for Economic and Policy Research), "Secrecy at the IFIs [international financial institutions]," *Progressive Response* 5:38 (November 13, 2001); and Bello, *Future in the Balance*, pp. 28–29.

37. *Focus on Trade*, January 2002; and James Harding, "Globalization's Children Strike Back," *Financial Times*, September 11, 2001.

38. Robert B. Zoellick, "American Trade Leadership: What Is at Stake?" Institute for International Economics, Washington, DC, September 24, 2001.

39. Thomas Friedman, "Senseless in Seattle," *New York Times*, December 1, 1999; and Peter Wahl, "European Social Forum," *Focus on Trade*, no. 83 (December 2002).

40. See J. Bradford DeLong, "The Meltzer Report," <http://www.j-bradford-delong.net/TotW/meltzer.html>; Christian Weller, "Meltzer Report Misses the Mark: Commission's Recommendations for World Bank, IMF Need Further Consideration," Economic Policy Institute, Issue Brief 141, April 13, 2000 ; and Bello, *Future in the Balance*, pp. xiv, 60.

41. Shihoko Goto, "Argentina's Menem Says Woes Not His Fault," *Washington Times*, June 12, 2002.

42. See the important analysis of John Feffer, "Militarization in the Age of Globalization," *Foreign Policy in Focus*, November 6, 2001. Also see William Pfaff, "Bush Team's Military Focus Is Skewing U.S. Foreign Policy," *International Herald Tribune*, June 30, 2001.

43. David Lague, "Gripes over U.S. Grip on Arms Trade," *Far Eastern Economic Review*, September 26, 2002; Kim Kwang-tae, "U.S. to Ditch Korea's Weapons Integration if It Buys Non-U.S. Aircraft in F-X Plan," *Korea Times*, July 22, 2001; Hwang Jang-jin, "Boeing F-15K, with GE Engine, Wins Deal Worth $4.46 Billion," *Korea Now*, May 4, 2002, p. 24.

44. Larry Rohter, "Jet Purchase Splits Brazil: New Leader Wants Voice," *New York Times*, November 29, 2002.

45. Larry Rohter, "Brazil: U.S. Offers Missiles," *New York Times*, May 24, 2002; Raymond Colitt, "Lula to Use Defense Funds in Famine Fight," *Financial Times*, January 4–5, 2003.

46. Michelle Ciarrocca, "Post 9/11 Economic Windfalls for Arms Manufacturers," *Foreign Policy in Focus* 7:10 (September 2002).

47. Gwyn Kirk and Margo Okazawa-Rey, "Neoliberalism, Militarism, and Armed Conflict," *Social Justice* 27:4 (Winter 2000), p. 9; Charles M. Sennott, "Arms Deal Criticized as Corporate U.S. Welfare," *Boston Globe*, January 14, 2003.

48. Karen Talbot, "The Real Reasons for War in Yugoslavia: Backing Up Globalization with Military Might," *Social Justice* 27:4 (Winter 2000), p. 100.

49. William Greider, "The End of Empire," *Nation*, September 23, 2002.

10: THE SORROWS OF EMPIRE

1. Madeleine Bunting, "Beginning of the End: The U.S. Is Ignoring an Important Lesson from History—That an Empire Cannot Survive on Brute Force Alone," *Guardian*, February 3, 2003.

2. "Bush's United States Military Academy Graduation Speech," *Washington Post*, June 2, 2002; and "Full Text: Bush's National Security Strategy," *New York Times*, September 20, 2002.

3. Ewen MacAskill, "Up to 50 States Are on Blacklist, Says Cheney,"

Guardian, November 17, 2001; James Doran, "Terror War Must Target 60 Nations, Says Bush," *Times* (London), June 3, 2002.

4. Arthur Schlesinger Jr., "Good Foreign Policy a Casualty of War," *Los Angeles Times,* March 23, 2003.

5. Cf. William Pfaff, "Al Qaeda vs. the White House," *International Herald Tribune,* December 28, 2002; Pfaff, "Religiosity and Foreign Policy: When Power Disdains Realism," *International Herald Tribune,* February 3, 2003; Anatol Lieven, "The Push for War," *London Review of Books,* October 3, 2002; and Jack Beatty, "In the Name of God," *Atlantic Monthly,* March 5, 2003.

6. Stanley Hoffmann, "The High and the Mighty," *American Prospect* 13:24 (January 13, 2003).

7. Immanuel Wallerstein, "The Righteous War," Commentary no. 107, University of Binghamton, February 15, 2003.

8. Letter of John Brady Kiesling, *New York Times,* February 27, 2003.

9. Tom Barry, "The U.S. Power Complex: What's New?" *Foreign Policy in Focus,* Special Report, November 2002, n. 11.

10. See chapter 6 above; and Madhavee Inamdar, "Global Vigilance in a Global Village: U.S. Expands Its Military Bases," *Progressive Response* 6:41 (December 31, 2002).

11. William M. Arkin, "The Best Defense," *Los Angeles Times,* July 14, 2002; "War Designed to Test New Weapons: Interview with Vladimir Slipchenko," *Rossiyskaya Gazeta,* February 22, 2003, <http://global-research.ca/articles/SLI303A.html>.

12. John A. Gentry, "Doomed to Fail: America's Blind Faith in Military Technology," *Parameters,* Winter 2002–03, pp. 88–103. Also see Mike Davis, "Slouching toward Baghdad," *Tomdispatch.com,* February 26, 2003. For the computer crash of January 2000, see James Bamford, *Body of Secrets: Anatomy of the Ultra-Secret National Security Agency* (New York: Anchor Books, 2002), pp. 451–53.

13. Gentry, "Doomed to Fail," p. 99.

14. Jason Vest, "The Army's Empire Skeptics," *Nation,* March 3, 2003, pp. 27–30. Also see Thomas E. Ricks and Vernon Loeb, "Unrivaled Military Feels Strains of Unending War," *Washington Post,* February 16, 2003.

15. See Ira Chernus, "Shock & Awe: Is Baghdad the Next Hiroshima?" *CommonDreams.org,* January 27, 2003. On the proposed Anglo-American use of such weapons as lasers that can blind and stun and microwave beams that can heat the water in human skin to the boiling point, see Antony Barnett, "Army's Secret 'People Zapper' Plans," *Observer,* November 3, 2002. The United States is sponsoring research on chemical and biological weapons that violates the 1972 Biological Weapons Convention and other international treaties. One of the projects is to produce antibiotic-resistant anthrax (Julian Borger, "U.S. Weapons Secrets Exposed," *Guardian,* October 29, 2002; and Thomas Fuller, "Microwave Weapons: The Dangers of First Use," *International Herald Tribune,* March 17, 2003).

16. Julian Borger, "U.S. Plan for New Nuclear Arsenal," *Guardian,* February 19, 2003. Also see Ellen Goodman, "War Is Now the Cover Story for Making More Terror," *Newsday,* March 14, 2002; Tad Daley, "America's Nuclear Hypocrisy," *International Herald Tribune,* October 21, 2002; Jonathan Schell, "The Bomb Is Back," *Sojourners Magazine,* November-December 2002, pp. 20–25, 58–59; Ira Chernus, "Brandishing Nukes—A Self-Defeating Policy," *CommonDreams.org,* February 4, 2003; Dan Stober, "Administration Moves Ahead on Nuclear 'Bunker Busters,'" *San Jose Mercury News,* April 23, 2003; and Noah Shachtman, "Embattled Lab Unveils New Nukes," *Wired,* April 23, 2003.

17. Elaine Scarry, "A Nuclear Double Standard," *Boston Globe,* November 3, 2002.

18. See Marilyn W. Thompson, *The Killer Strain: Anthrax and a Government Exposed* (New York: HarperCollins, 2003); and Chuck Murphy, "Not Iraq, but Anniston, Ala.," *St. Petersburg Times,* March 16, 2003. According to Murphy, the U.S. Army is currently storing in the United States 873,020 pounds of sarin, 1,657,480 pounds of VX nerve agent, and 1,976,760 pounds of mustard gas.

19. "Complete Text of President Bush's State of the Union Address," *Los Angeles Times,* January 28, 2003. Also see Ian Urbina, "On the Road with Murder, Inc.," *Asia Times,* January 24, 2003; Ori Nir, "Bush Seeks Israeli Advice on 'Targeted Killings,'" *Forward,* February 7, 2003.

20. Bob Woodward, *Bush at War* (New York: Simon and Schuster, 2002), pp. 145–46.

21. James Madison, as quoted by Senator Robert C. Byrd (D-West Virginia), October 3, 2002, speaking in opposition to a resolution granting the president open-ended authority to go to war whenever he chooses. See John C. Bonifaz, "War Powers: The White House Continues to Defy the Constitution," *TomPaine.com*, February 4, 2003.

22. Doug Thompson, "Role Reversal: Bush Wants a War, Pentagon Urges Caution," *Capitol Hill Blue*, January 22, 2002; quoted by Winslow T. Wheeler, "The Week of Shame: Congress Wilts as the President Demands an Unclogged Road to War" (Washington: Center for Defense Information, January 2003), p. 17.

23. Wheeler, "Week of Shame," p. 17. Also see Steve Lopez, "Hindsight Casts Harsh Light on Use-of-Force Resolution," *Los Angeles Times*, March 5, 2003.

24. I am indebted to William Norman Grigg's analysis in his "Suspending Habeas Corpus," *New American* 18:14 (July 15, 2002). Also see "Detaining Americans," *Washington Post*, June 13, 2002; and Nat Hentoff, "George W. Bush's Constitution," *Village Voice*, January 3, 2003.

25. Benjamin Weiser, "U.S. to Appeal Order Giving Lawyers Access to Detainee," *New York Times*, March 26, 2003.

26. Dick Meyer, "John Ashcroft: Minister of Fear," *CBSNews.com*, June 12, 2002. Also see Geov Parrish, "Hello? Is Anybody Getting This Down?" *WorkingForChange.com*, June 11, 2002; and Edward Alden and Caroline Daniel, "Battle Lines Blurred as U.S. Searches for Enemies in the War on Terrorism," *Financial Times*, January 2, 2003.

27. For details, see Paul Brodeur, *Secrets: A Writer in the Cold War* (Boston: Faber and Faber, 1997), pp. 159–65. On the CIA's illegal domestic spying, see Angus Mackenzie, *Secrets: The CIA's War at Home* (Berkeley: University of California Press, 1997). There is direct continuity between these thirty-year-old assaults on civil liberties and the Bush administration's 2003 proposal to give the Pentagon and the CIA subpoena powers, which would allow them to demand personal and financial records on people in the United States as part of alleged

counterterrorism operations. See Eric Lichtblau and James Risen, "Broad Domestic Role Asked for CIA and the Pentagon," *New York Times,* May 2, 2003.

28. James Bamford, "Washington Bends the Rules," *New York Times,* August 27, 2002.

29. Patrick S. Poole, "Inside America's Secret Court: The Foreign Intelligence Surveillance Court," <http://fly.hiwaay.net/~pspoole/fiscshort.html>.

30. Anita Ramasastry, "Why the Foreign Intelligence Surveillance Act Court Was Right to Rebuke the Justice Department," September 4, 2002, <http://writ.news.findlaw.com/ramasastry/20020904.html>. Ramasastry is a professor of law at the University of Washington School of Law in Seattle.

31. Richard B. Schmitt, "U.S. Expands Clandestine Surveillance Operations," *Los Angeles Times,* March 5, 2003.

32. Bob Egelko, "Spy Court to Review Prosecutors' Powers," *San Francisco Chronicle,* September 1, 2002; and Anita Ramasastry, "The Foreign Intelligence Surveillance Court of Review Creates a Potential End Run around Traditional Fourth Amendment Protections for Certain Criminal Law Enforcement Wiretaps," November 26, 2002, <http://writ.news.findlaw.com/ramasastry/20021126.html >.

33. "U.S. Considers New Anti-Terrorism Legislation," Reuters, February 7, 2003.

34. William M. Arkin, "The Military's New War of Words," *Los Angeles Times,* November 24, 2002.

35. Bob Kemper, "Team Makes Sure War Message Is Unified, Positive," *Chicago Tribune,* April 7, 2003.

36. "U.S. Lobbyist Helped Draft Eastern Europeans' Iraq Statement," Yahoo News, February 20, 2003.

37. Pervez Hoodbhoy, "America's Dreams of Empire," *Los Angeles Times,* January 26, 2003; Chris Floyd, "Bush Uses War to Bury Probe of 9/11," *CounterPunch,* March 22, 2003.

38. James Bamford, *Body of Secrets: Anatomy of the Ultra-secret National Security Agency* (New York: Anchor Books, 2002), pp. 78–91. Also see Bamford, "Bush Wrong to Use Pretext as Excuse to Invade Iraq," *USA*

Today, August 29, 2002; Adam Hochschild, "War or Peace? The U.S. Is Looking for an Excuse to Fight," *San Francisco Chronicle,* January 19, 2003; and Jennifer A. Gritt, "Weapons of Mass Delusion," April 30, 2003, <http://www.antiwar.com/orig/gritt2.html>.

39. "Weighing the Evidence," *New York Times,* February 15, 2003.

40. The transcript is online at <http://www.fair.org/press-releases/kamel. pdf>. Also see "Star Witness on Iraq Said Weapons Were Destroyed," Fairness and Accuracy in Reporting, *Media Advisory,* February 27, 2003; John Barry, "The Defector's Secrets," *Newsweek,* March 3, 2003; Andrew Gumbel, "Anthrax, Chemicals, and Nerve Gas: Who Is Lying?" *Independent,* April 20, 2003; and "So Where Are They, Mr. Blair?" *Independent,* April 20, 2003.

41. The most useful statement from Ritter is his interview with the PBS television program *Frontline* in 1999, <http://www.pbs.org/wgbh/ pages/frontline/shows/unscom/interviews/ritter.html>.

42. Jonathan Rugman, "Downing Street Dossier Plagiarized," Channel 4 News, February 6, 2003, <http://www.channel4.com/news/2003/02/ week_1/06_dossier.html>; and Alexander Cockburn, "The Great 'Intelligence Fraud,'" *CounterPunch,* February 15, 2003.

43. "U.N. Inspectors: U.S. Used Forged Reports," *Guardian,* March 8, 2003.

44. Joby Warrick, "Some Evidence on Iraq Called Fake," *Washington Post,* March 8, 2003; Stephen Fidler, "Niger Documents Fake, Says ElBaradei," *Financial Times,* March 8–9, 2003; Louis Charbonneau, "'Proof' That Iraq Sought Uranium Was Fake," Reuters, March 7, 2003; Bob Drogin and Greg Miller, "Intelligence Value in Iraq Questioned," *Los Angeles Times,* March 8, 2003; Mark Phillips, "Inspectors Call U.S. Tips 'Garbage,'" *CBSNews.com,* February 20, 2003; Congressman Henry A. Waxman to President George W. Bush, March 17, 2003, <http://www.house.gov/waxman/text/admin_iraq_march_17_ let.htm>; Dana Priest and Karen De Young, "CIA Questioned Documents Linking Iraq, Uranium Ore," *Washington Post,* March 22, 2003; and Seymour M. Hersh, "Who Lied to Whom?" *New Yorker,* March 31, 2003, pp. 41–43.

45. Quoted by Ray Close, "A CIA Analyst on Forging Intelligence," *CounterPunch,* March 10, 2003.

46. Ray McGovern, "CIA Director Caves In," *CommonDreams.org,* February 13, 2003.

47. Seymour M. Hersh, "Selective Intelligence," *New Yorker,* May 12, 2003, pp. 44–51. Also see Paul Harris, Martin Bright, Taji Helmore, and Ed Helmore, "U.S. Rivals Turn On Each Other as Weapons Search Draws a Blank," *Observer,* May 11, 2003; Barton Gellman, "Frustrated, U.S. Arms Team to Leave Iraq; Task Force Unable to Find Any Weapons," *Washington Post,* May 11, 2003; and Harold Meyerson, "Enron-like Unreality," *Washington Post,* May 13, 2003.

48. Thom Shanker and Richard W. Stevenson, "Pentagon Wants $10 Billion a Year for Antiterror Fund," *New York Times,* November 27, 2002; Leslie Wayne, "Rumsfeld Warns He Will Ask Congress for More Billions," *New York Times,* February 6, 2003. Llewellyn H. Rockwell Jr., "War and the Economy," *Mises.org,* March 10, 2003.

49. David R. Sands, "Allies Unlikely to Help Pay for Second Iraq Invasion," *Washington Times,* March 10, 2003.

50. Edmund L. Andrews, "Federal Debt Near Ceiling; Second Time in 9 Months," *New York Times,* February 20, 2003.

51. David Hale, "Are the Financial Markets Ready for One War or Two?" Zurich Financial Services, March 12, 2003.

52. Vincent Cable, "The Economic Consequences of War," *Observer,* February 2, 2003.

53. Laton McCartney, *Friends in High Places. The Bechtel Story: The Most Secret Corporation and How It Engineered the World* (New York: Ballantine, 1989); "U.S. Invites Bids for Iraq Reconstruction Work," Reuters, March 10, 2003; Joshua Chaffin, "Halliburton's Links Sharpen Bids Dispute," *Financial Times,* March 27, 2003; Oliver Morgan and Ed Vulliamy, "Cronies Set to Make a Killing," *Observer,* April 6, 2003; Stephen Glain, "Halliburton Unit Could Make $7 Billion," *Boston Globe,* April 11, 2003; and David Ivanovich, "Pentagon Defends Halliburton Job," *Houston Chronicle,* April 10, 2003.

54. Robert Higgs, "Free Enterprise and War, a Dangerous Liaison," Independent Institute, January 22, 2003, <http://www.independent.org/tii/news/030122Higgs.html>.

55. Fred Kaplan, "Star Wars Spending Spree," *Slate,* November 7, 2002;

and Seymour Melman, "In the Grip of a Permanent War Economy," *Bear Left!*, March 9, 2003, <http://www.bear-left.com/original/2003/0309permanent.html>.

56. Reinhold Niebuhr, *The Irony of American History* (New York: Scribner, 1952); quoted by Joseph C. Hough Jr., "President's Newsletter," Union Theological Seminary in the City of New York, March 2003.

57. "U.S. Plans Death Camp," *Herald Sun* (Australia), May 26, 2003, <news.com.au>; "Guantánamo Courtrooms Being Prepared," *Los Angeles Times*, June 2, 2003.

58. Michael Klare, *Resource Wars: The New Landscape of Global Conflict* (New York: Owl Books, 2002); Ken Silverstein, "The Crude Politics of Trading Oil," *Los Angeles Times*, December 6, 2002.

59. Loring Wirbel, "U.S. 'Negation' Policy in Space Raises Concerns Abroad," *EETimes*, May 22, 2003.

ACKNOWLEDGMENTS

This book was not easy to write. I do not like what it has to say about my country. But I am convinced by the course of events leading up to and the developments following the terrorist attacks of September 11, 2001, that this analysis is fundamentally correct. It is because I do not like stating that the United States is probably lost to militarism that this book is so heavily documented. I want to ensure that readers know how I claim to know something. Of course, I leave it to others to decide whether I have been convincing and whether my alarm about the course our country is taking is well-founded. I do not think we shall have to wait long to find out.

In the course of writing, I received much editorial help and many useful comments from Sheila K. Johnson, my companion for forty-six years and herself a gifted writer and intellectual. I owe a great debt to Tom Engelhardt, my editor, who has himself been deeply involved in trying to find the analogies and precedents that might throw light on the suicide of the United States as a democracy. Sandra Dijkstra, my agent, and her associate, Babette Sparr, worked tirelessly to see that my ideas got a public hearing. Others who have drawn my attention to aspects of imperialism and militarism I did not know about or might have overlooked include Kozy Amemiya, Maricler and Alfredo Antognini, Walden Bello, Steve Clemons, Patrick Hatcher, Barry Keehn, Brian Loveman, Thomas Royden, Odete Sousa, Yoshihiko Nakamoto, and the editors of antiwar.com.

INDEX

ABOUT THE AUTHOR

CHALMERS JOHNSON is the author of the acclaimed *Blowback* and president of the Japan Policy Research Institute, as well as professor emeritus at the University of California, San Diego. A frequent contributor to the *Los Angeles Times* and *The Nation,* among other periodicals, he has also written numerous books on Japan and Asia, including *MITI and the Japanese Miracle* and *Japan: Who Governs?* He lives near San Diego.